The series Lecture Notes in Computer Science (LNCS), including its subseries Lecture Notes in Artificial Intelligence (LNAI) and Lecture Notes in Bioinformatics (LNBI), has established itself as a medium for the publication of new developments in computer science and information technology research, teaching, and education.

LNCS enjoys close cooperation with the computer science R & D community, the series counts many renowned academics among its volume editors and paper authors, and collaborates with prestigious societies. Its mission is to serve this international community by providing an invaluable service, mainly focused on the publication of conference and workshop proceedings and postproceedings. LNCS commenced publication in 1973.

Luciana Zaina · José Creissac Campos ·
Davide Spano · Kris Luyten · Philippe Palanque ·
Gerrit van der Veer · Achim Ebert ·
Shah Rukh Humayoun · Vera Memmesheimer
Editors

Engineering Interactive Computer Systems

EICS 2024 International Workshops

Cagliari, Sardinia, Italy, June 24–26, 2024
Revised Selected Papers

Springer

Editors
Luciana Zaina
Federal University of São Carlos
São Paulo, Brazil

José Creissac Campos
Universidade do Minho
Braga, Portugal

Davide Spano
University of Cagliari
Cagliari, Italy

Kris Luyten
Hasselt University
Hasselt, Belgium

Philippe Palanque
Université Paul Sabatier
Toulouse, France

Gerrit van der Veer
Vrije Universiteit Amsterdam
Amsterdam, The Netherlands

Achim Ebert
University of Kaiserslautern-Landau
Kaiserslautern, Germany

Shah Rukh Humayoun
San Francisco State University
San Francisco, CA, USA

Vera Memmesheimer
University of Kaiserslautern-Landau
Kaiserslautern, Germany

ISSN 0302-9743 ISSN 1611-3349 (electronic)
Lecture Notes in Computer Science
ISBN 978-3-031-91759-2 ISBN 978-3-031-91760-8 (eBook)
https://doi.org/10.1007/978-3-031-91760-8

This Springer imprint is published by the registered company Springer Nature Switzerland AG
The registered company address is: Gewerbestrasse 11, 6330 Cham, Switzerland

Foreword

This book presents a series of revised papers selected from the Workshops organized in conjunction with the 16th ACM SIGCHI Symposium on Engineering Interactive Computing Systems (EICS 2024), which was held in Cagliari, Italy, in June 2024. Even though EICS itself has a long track record, this is the second time that papers submitted to workshops at EICS have been compiled in a single volume.

The Symposium on Engineering Interactive Computing Systems (EICS) is the primary venue for research contributions at the intersection of Human-Computer Interaction (HCI) and Software Engineering. EICS is organized by the Special Interest Group on Human-Computer Interaction of the Association for Computing Machinery (ACM SIGCHI) and the Working Group on User Interface Engineering (WG 2.7/13.4) of the International Federation for Information Processing (IFIP). EICS 2024 was the sixteenth edition of a series of conferences devoted to engineering interactive computing systems and their user interfaces. The conference is best known for rigorously contributing and disseminating research results that fall in the area in between user interface design, software engineering, and computational interaction. EICS focuses on models, languages, notations, methods, techniques, and tools that support designing, developing, validating, and verifying interactive systems. Whilst this focus concerns a large spectrum of traditional application domains (e.g. aviation, command and control systems), EICS also encourages and promotes by the means of specialized workshops research on emerging topics related to engineering interactive systems.

Workshop proposals submitted to EICS are juried. Criteria selections include the relevance of the workshop topics and goals to EICS, scientific background and experience of the workshop's organizers in organizing events, advertising, and dissemination plan. For EICS 2024, Luciana Zaina (Federal University of São Carlos, Brazil), Emanuele Panizzi (University of Rome La Sapienza, Italy) and Klen Čopič Pucihar (University of Primorska, Slovenia) were responsible for the selection process, which ended up with three full-day workshops held in parallel on June 25th, 2024. In this volume, 18 papers from the two workshops described below were selected based on workshop organizers' selection; these represent extended versions of the initial submissions prior to the workshops.

The main goal of the **Second Workshop on Engineering Interactive Systems Embedding AI Technologies (EISEAIT 2024), organized by IFIP Working Group on User Interface Engineering WG 2.7/13.4,** was to offer a platform for scientists who are interested in the design, development, evaluation, and use of interactive systems embedding AI technologies. Four objectives were settled: to identify and gather information about knowledge and practice in the workshop's domain; to elicit the main gaps in AI technologies which hinder their exploitation in the design and development of interactive systems, especially if a user-centered design process is followed; and to focus on exploring the specific issue of engineering interaction-driven AI; and to propose the design and use of AI technologies in methods, processes, and tools for building interactive systems in all stages of the engineering lifecycle.

The papers from this workshop present a range of contributions exploring the integration of AI technologies into interactive systems. Ziegler addresses the challenges of integrating conversational AI with interactive systems. Griot et al. and Bisante et al. explore the collaboration between technical and non-technical stakeholders, with Griot et al. bridging the gap between computer scientists and medical doctors, and Bisante et al. leveraging LLMs in early design stages. Menten et al. explore the use of a Wizard of Oz approach for incremental AI integration in interactive systems. Mereu et al. and Aziz et al. focus on user-centered design, with Mereu et al. empowering end-user developers in XR environments and Aziz et al. tailoring music chatbots for older adults. Eerlings et al. and Coppens and Maquil discuss AI's role in enhancing system transparency and behavior analysis, while Bachert and Hesenius analyze gesture synthesis using generative AI algorithms. Veloso and Campos, along with Carayon et al., examine the role of formal verification and dependable AI components in critical systems, highlighting the potential of LLMs to bridge gaps in understanding.

As for the other workshop in this volume, augmented and mixed reality (AR/MR) are applied in a growing variety of applications: handheld displays, head-mounted displays like Apple's Vision Pro, smart tattoos, interactive clothing, and wearables propose an even higher immersion and are opening totally new exciting worlds for researchers, developers, and users. At the same time, research in this area faces many challenges, e.g., suitable interaction techniques, better user experience, navigation in MR environments, high cross-device UX, etc. Targeting these challenges, the workshop **Experience 2.0 and Beyond on Engineering Cross Devices and Multiple Realities, organized by IFIP Working Group on Visualization WG 13.7,** discussed two aspects: conceptual analysis and frameworks, and experience and applicability in practice.

In the aspect of conceptual analysis and frameworks, Rosa discusses the literature on semantic coupling, place, and aura, and describes which types of places future AR studies studying or applying semantic coupling should consider, how to create semantic coupling without the need for a complex narrative, and how to ensure and verify a degree of connection in semantic coupling experiments. Li and van der Veer explore the integration of visual and auditory perception in real and virtual contexts, emphasizing the need for synchronized soundscapes in artistic experiences. The study shows the impact of AR and MR on sensory experiences in dynamic visual arts. The contribution by MacKenzie examines a rich variety of current mixedreality (MR) studies that include novel devices triggering multiple human senses, in different contexts, looking at what they are, what can and cannot be done, and the challenges and possibilities looking forward. These challenges are presented in a series of community challenges. Considering experience and applicability in practice, the study by Khan et al. provides an analysis of future use of AR for remote collaborative systems to enable telework in industrial productions (part manufacturing), aiming at evaluation models that include economic, technical, and user-experience values. The paper by Weerasinghe et al. presents a mixed reality study on usability and experience in vocabulary learning, supported by a combination of two devices, smartphone and head-mounted display. The phone supports text input, and the display provides contextually relevant information; the system enables users to visually annotate objects with personalized keyword associations.

Each workshop had its own program committee that oversaw the selection process of contributions to be presented in Cagliari. Following the discussions during the workshops, authors were then invited to revise their work and submitted the contribution for a second round of reviews. In the end, twenty-one papers were selected for inclusion in this book featuring the post-proceedings of the EICS 2024 workshops.

Altogether, the work is promising and encouraging, and we look forward to seeing further developments from the authors.

Luciana Zaina
José Creissac Campos
Davide Spano
Kris Luyten
Philippe Palanque
Gerrit van der Veer
Achim Ebert
Shah Rukh Humayoun
Vera Memmesheimer

Organization

EICS 2024 Committee

General Chairs

Davide Spano	University of Cagliari, Italy
Michael Nebeling	University of Michigan, USA

Technical Program Chair

José Creissac Campos	University of Minho & INESC TEC, Portugal

Full Paper and Technical Notes Chairs

Anke Dittmar	University of Rostock, Germany
Carmen Santoro	ISTI-CNR, Pisa, Italy

Late-Breaking Results Chairs

Marco Manca	ISTI-CNR Pisa, Italy
Sophie Dupuy Chessa	Université Grenoble Alpes, France
Teresa Hirzle	University of Copenhagen, Denmark

Workshops Chairs

Luciana Zaina	Federal University of São Carlos, Brazil
Emanuele Panizzi	University of Rome La Sapienza, Italy
Klen Čopič Pucihar	University of Primorska, Slovenia

Doctoral Consortium Chairs

Fabio Paternò	ISTI-CNR, Italy
Laurence Nigay	Université Grenoble Alpes, France
Germán Leiva	Aarhus University, Denmark

Tutorials Chairs

Enes Yigitbas	Paderborn University, Germany
Célia Martinie	Université Toulouse III, France

Demo and Posters Chairs

Marc Hesenius	University of Duisburg-Essen, Germany
Vivian Genaro Motti	George Mason University, USA

Local Organization Chair

Ivan Blečić	University of Cagliari, Italy

Proceedings Chairs

Valentino Artizzu	University of Cagliari, Italy
Alpay Sabancuoglu	Alan Turing Institute, UK
Mina Alipour	University of Southern Denmark, Denmark

Accessibility Chair

Gianmarco Cherchi	University of Cagliari, Italy

Web Chair

Vittoria Frau	University of Cagliari, Italy

Publicity Chairs

Tommaso Calò	Politecnico di Torino, Italy
Mahyar Tourchi Moghaddam	University of Southern Denmark, Denmark

SIGCHI/ACM Liaison

Giuliana Vitiello	University of Salerno, Italy

Steering Committee Chair

Davide Spano	University of Cagliari, Italy

Steering Committee Members

Aaron Quigley	University of New South Wales, Australia
Alan Dix	Swansea University, UK
Anke Dittmar	University of Rostock, Germany
Carmen Santoro	CNR-ISTI, Italy
Jeffrey Nichols	Apple, USA
José C. Campos	Universidade do Minho, Portugal
Kris Luyten	Hasselt University, Belgium
Marco Winckler	Université Côte d'Azur, France
Philippe Palanque	Université Toulouse III, France

EICS 2024 Associated Chairs

Aaron Quigley	UNSW, Australia
Albrecht Schmidt	LMU Munich, Germany
Anke Dittmar	University of Rostock, Germany
Carmen Santoro	CNR-ISTI, Italy
Christian Kray	University of Münster, Germany
Célia Martinie	Paul Sabatier University Toulouse III, France
Lucio Davide Spano	University of Cagliari, Italy
Davy Vanacken	Hasselt University - tUL - Flanders Make, Belgium
Fabio Paternò	CNR-ISTI, Italy
Gustavo Rovelo Ruiz	Hasselt University, Belgium
Jean Vanderdonckt	Université catholique de Louvain, Belgium
Jeffrey Nichols	Google, USA
José Creissac Campos	Universidade do Minho & INESC TEC, Portugal
Judy Bowen	University of Waikato, New Zealand
Jürgen Ziegler	University of Duisburg-Essen, Germany
Kris Luyten	Hasselt University - tUL - Flanders Make, Belgium
Laurence Nigay	Université Grenoble Alpes, France
Marco Winckler	Université Côte d'Azur, France
Mathias Funk	Eindhoven University of Technology, Netherlands
Michael Harrison	Newcastle University, UK
Peter Forbrig	University of Rostock, Germany
Philippe Palanque	Université Toulouse III, France
Sophie Dupuy-Chessa	Université Grenoble Alpes, France
Stéphane Huot	Inria, Lille, France

EICS 2024 - EXDMR Workshop Chairs

Gerrit van der Veer	Vrije Universiteit Amsterdam, Netherlands
Achim Ebert	University of Kaiserslautern-Landau, Germany
Shah Rukh	San Francisco State University, USA
Vera Memmesheimer	University of Kaiserslautern-Landau, Germany

EICS 2024 - EISEAIT Workshop Chairs

Alan Dix	Swansea University, UK
Kris Luyten	Hasselt University, Belgium
Sven Mayer	LMU Munich, Germany
Philippe Palanque	Université Toulouse III, France
Emanuele Panizzi	University of Rome La Sapienza, Italy
Lucio Davide Spano	University of Cagliari, Italy
Jürgen Ziegler	University of Duisburg-Essen, Germany

Sponsors

Association for Computing Machinery

SIGCHI

UNIVERSITÀ DEGLI STUDI DI CAGLIARI

Università degli Studi di Cagliari
Centro Interdipartimentale
Glab

ifip
IFIP WG 2.7/13.4

Contents

Engineering Interactive Systems Embedding AI Technologies (EISEAIT)

Synthesizing 2D vs. 3D Gestures

Marvin Bachert(✉) and Marc Hesenius

University of Duisburg-Essen, Institute for Software Engineering, Schützenbahn 70, 45127 Essen, Germany
{marvin.bachert,marc.hesenius}@uni-due.de

Abstract. Synthetic gestures are necessary for automating User Interface tests in applications using gestures, which often embed techniques from Artificial Intelligence and Machine Learning for gesture recognition. However, synthetic gestures must closely mimic the variances in human gestures. Therefore, algorithms capable of generating human-like fuzzy gestures depending on the configuration of user groups are necessary. In this paper, we analyze the differences between 2D and 3D gestures and correlate them with algorithms from Generative Artificial Intelligence designed for synthesizing gestures. Our findings support researchers and developers when developing components for gesture synthesis.

Keywords: Artificial Intelligence · Human-Computer Interaction · Synthetic Gestures · Testing · Test Automation

1 Introduction

Gestures are a type of interaction modality in which the user's movement itself is interpreted as input to the machine. Hands are commonly used for gesture-based Human-Computer Interaction (HCI), but any body part is possible (e.g., feet [31]). Today, touch gestures (also 2D gestures) are common for interacting with mobile and other devices, but the advances in Augmented and Virtual Reality (AR/VR) make mid-air gestures (3D gestures, sometimes also referred to as spatial gestures) available for mainstream HCI, although these require additional engineering research [4]. 3D gestures also offer interesting use cases beyond AR/VR, but especially scenarios for specific user groups, e.g., police officers commandeering drones during operations [14], require dedicated design and engineering of the used gestures and intensive testing of the resulting User Interface (UI). Isolated tests of technical components, such as the accuracy of gesture recognizers, are insufficient: gesture recognizers have been reported to suffer from performance decreases when applications are operated by children [28] or the elderly [3], because they are typically trained with data from healthy adults. Instead, dedicated application scenarios consisting of multiple interactions and additional user behavior (e.g., normal movement with no meaning for the application) must be tested. As manual tests are error-prone and time-consuming, test automation is desirable, but requires to simulate users performing gestures in virtual scenarios, i.e., components that generate synthetic gestures.

L. Zaina et al. (Eds.): EICS 2024, LNCS 15518, pp. 3–15, 2025.
https://doi.org/10.1007/978-3-031-91760-8_1

Gestures, however, are fuzzy, i.e., their performance depends on several factors, most notably the users themselves (gestures are a biometric marker suitable for user authentication [2]), but also contextual factors such as current task, device, or tool used can influence gesture performances. Suitable gesture generators for test automation must take these into account to incorporate variances representing different users and user groups [15]. With the advances in Generative AI (GenAI), we have various algorithms at our disposal that offer the necessary capabilities, but still need to decide on concrete implementations.

In this paper, we discuss the differences between 2D and 3D gestures with regard to gesture synthesis. We argue that 2D gestures are not merely a subset of 3D gestures and that the substantial differences between them justify to use different approaches and models. We aim to identify arguments supporting this hypothesis. Our contribution to the engineering of HCI in general and the development of gesture-based applications in particular is thus two-fold: we discuss the differences between surface (2D) and mid-air (3D) gestures with regard to test automation and derive necessary foundations for choosing suitable generation algorithms. In this position paper, we will focus on Generative Adversarial Networks (GANs) and Reinforcement Learnin, as these are common in related approaches (see Sect. 2), but findings may also be applied to other algorithms capable of generating new data (e.g., Gaussian Mixture Models). Our findings indicate that GANs are more suited for 2D gestures and Reinforcement Learning for 3D gestures, which can support researchers and developers to identify suitable algorithms for approaching gesture synthesis.

We will first review Related Work (Sect. 2) and discuss existing synthesis approaches. We will then focus on the characteristics of and differences between surface and mid-air gestures (Sect. 3) and then discuss our findings (Sect. 4). In (Sect. 5) we discuss different implementation details. We will conclude the paper with an outlook for future work (Sect. 6).

2 Related Work

We focus on two different families of algorithms for gesture synthesis: GANs and Reinforcement Learning. We will first briefly introduce the their foundations and then review some state of the art approaches to gesture synthesis.

GANs consist of two neural networks, namely a generator and a discriminator. During a training process, the generator learns to replicate data from a training dataset, while the discriminator distinguishes between real and generated data and provides feedback to the generator. However, the generator does not memorize the training data, but learns a mapping from a latent input space to the training space, allowing it to generate new, realistically looking data corresponding to the training distribution [11]. Mirza and Osindero [24] use conditions provided as additional input to influence the output of the generator and generate desired classes, which could be an interesting option to influence the GAN to generate gestures with specific characteristics, e.g., mobility differences between user groups.

Reinforcement Learning refers to an Artificial Intelligence (AI) model, now called an *agent*, that learns to interact with its environment using a reward system. In this process, the agent receives the current state of the environment as a mathematical representation and learns to make correct decisions, or actions, that lead to a goal. The actions of the agent modify the current state of the environment. During the training process, a reward system is implemented, which distributes negative or positive rewards depending on the chosen action and the change in state. The agent learns during the training process to choose actions based on the current state that maximize the received cumulative reward [20].

Buriro et al. [5] trained a GAN to generate synthetic touchscreen gesture swipes. The executions are enriched with biometrical information which makes them characteristic for a specific user. Chu et al. [6] trained a GAN to generate conditioned touchscreen gestures which representate a word on a touchscreen keyboard. The desired word can be passed as input to the generator to condition the output by the word itself.

Tang et al. [30] use a GAN to translate images of specific hand poses to similar images with different hand poses. The generator receives the original image and an image of a hand skeleton performing the new pose as the input and learns to generate a new image maintaining the context information while changing the pose of the hand. Sun et al. [29] use Reinforcement Learning to synthesize 3D gestures matching the semantics of simultaneous speech. They use an embedding space with generated representations of gestures from which a Variational AutoEncoder [8] reconstructs the gestures themselves. The reward for the chosen actions is calculated using a reward model which does not evaluate just one target gesture but acknowledges the possibility of different matching gestures for given speech. Wu et al. [34] train a GAN to generate 3D gestures. The generator learns to produce rotation angles for the upper body joint of an avatar, conditioned by a speech signal. The presented approaches for 3D gesture generation have in common that only gestures themselves are generated. Noise between gesture executions and context information are neglected, except for GestureGan [30], which maintains context information without new generation.

3 Characteristics of 2D and 3D Gestures

In this chapter, characteristics of 2D and 3D gestures are presented. Xia et al. [35] introduce 13 different requirements for gestures that must be considered in gesture design. These are divided into situational factors (context, modality, social acceptability), cognitive factors (discoverability, intuitiveness, learnability, transferability), physical factors (efficiency, complexity, ergonomics, occlusion), and system factors (feedback, recognition). We argue that differences in requirements for gestures indicate differences in the characteristics of the gestures. In this regard, we disregard factors such as social acceptability, discoverability, intuitiveness, efficiency, occlusion and feedback, as they are irrelevant for the generation of synthetic gesture data.

For touchscreen gestures, the context is highly constrained. Not only is the action space for gestures strictly limited by the input touchscreen, but the gestures also have clear starting and ending points due to touching and lifting off the touchscreen [17]. Additionally, there are no relevant environmental cues. In contrast, the context for mid-air gestures is arbitrarily complex. Gestures can be performed in any environment, and gesture executions are not clearly delineated from non-gestures [17]. Thus, it is often unclear when a gesture begins and when execution stops, which is why many applications using 3D gestures require users to perform a *clutch*, i.e., a gesture specifically designed to start and end another gesture [32]. Furthermore, Grandhi et al. [12] demonstrated that the execution of gestures varies depending on machines or humans on the receiving end. Since people are accustomed to using 3D gestures to support communication with others, this results in another difference between 2D and 3D gestures. 2D gestures are used solely for communication with a machine. Therefore, the different manner of gesture execution for 3D gestures in interaction with a machine must be considered, whereas this is not necessary for 2D gestures.

2D gestures are typically performed with fingers or a stylus, but alternative tools that can touch a surface are possible (e.g., feet [31]). This results in a maximum of 10 different tools if all fingers of both hands touch the surface that can execute a gesture simultaneously, but in most cases, there are fewer (besides from special cases such as cooperative gestures with multiple users [25]). In contrast, mid-air gestures often use the hands as a tool, although again alternatives are possible. Consequently, the positions and rotations of all fingers, the hand, and also the arms can be relevant. The inputs can be purely visual, as summarized by Xia et al. [36], but they can also be made using sensors such as sEMG [19] or gloves [27].

The learnability of the gestures themselves is not relevant for the synthesis of gestures, but generally, conclusions can be drawn about details relevant for generation. Research on mid-air gestures is based on inter-personal communication in everyday life, for example, as support during speech, but also generally in non-verbal communication [22]. In contrast to the use of touchscreen gestures, people are thus accustomed to using mid-air gestures independently of technology. Therefore, the level of experience of users must be taken into account for touchscreen gestures. Supporting this, Kopinski et al. [18] show that the driving performance of participants in their study is equally restricted by both using touchscreen and mid-air gestures, even though the participants had no experience with mid-air gestures, but were very familiar with touchscreen gestures for machine interaction.

The complexity of touchscreen gestures is limited on the one hand by the maximum number of tools, as well as by the number of degrees of freedom in 2-dimensional movements, namely 3 per tool (translation in x and y, as well as rotation around z). In contrast, hands in 3-dimensional space use 27 degrees of freedom [9]. Moreover, any number of additional tools can be used, which can have up to 6 degrees of freedom (translation in x, y, and z, as well as rotation around x, y and z).

In a similar vein, gestures are also limited by physically possible movements - not every joint can be moved arbitrarily in all degrees of freedom, resulting in the 27 degrees of freedom of the hand. Additionally, some joints are dependent on each other. For example, it is difficult to bend individual fingers of the hand when all others are extended [26]. These limitations have a greater impact on 3D than on 2D gestures, as the touchscreen does not differentiate between the inputting tools. Thus, equivalent gestures can be entered with different tools in touchscreen gestures, and a different finger can be used if one is unable to do so.

Gesture recognition in the 2D and 3D domains is commonly performed using classifiers with AI/Machine Learning (ML) techniques. The areas differ primarily in pre-processing and feature extraction steps, as well as in the choice of classifiers. A popular approach for 2D gestures is template matching [23]. However, characteristic information such as execution speed are often removed by these methods as gestures are normalized to make comparison with templates easier. Furthermore, such methods heavily focus on the shape is the determining factor, but gestures allow for more characteristics [16]. While 3D gestures can also be recognized using template matching, hidden Markov models and deep learning approaches are often used [21].

4 Discussion

Generating 2D gesture data does not need to consider contextual information, as it does not exist in the context of gesture execution. However, when generating 3D gesture data, the question arises of which environmental information needs to be generated along with it. This strongly depends on the representation in which gesture data is generated. Just as there are different forms of input for the recognition of 3D gestures (visual-, sensor-based), the representation of gestures can also vary. If it is visual, for example, the background and environment would need to be realistically generated. However, since this is not feasible for arbitrary environments, a representation in the form of spatial coordinates of relevant tools makes much more sense.

Regardless of the modality, the lack of distinction between gesture and non-gesture means that non-gesture movements must also be generated. This can be seen as a kind of noise between gesture executions. However, a consequence of the different modalities for 3D gestures arises in ergonomics. Generated executions must be realistic, meaning that no physically impossible movements are generated. This can be implemented, for example, by setting constraints for each joint, but it must be considered much more than in the 2D domain. While there are also certain physical execution limits for 2D gestures, as described in the previous chapter, these are less rigid because gesture executions are tool-independent and users prefer to input single-point gestures with few tools (usually 1–3) [33]. The use of a hand or human model in gesture generation allows for an inherent limitation of mobility, but for 2D gestures, it represents a significant overhead between the resulting gesture and the information used for generation. Learning these limitations during generation based on existing, real gesture executions seems much more sensible in this context, with a focus on training and inference time.

The factors of learnability and transferability result in certain additional conditions for the generated gestures. For example, gesture executions must be generated differently when considering different performing users with different levels of experience. However, these additional conditions in the generation are independent of 2D or 3D data and go beyond different levels of experience. Therefore, they represent a general limitation in the choice of generation methods regardless of dimensionality.

The complexity of the gestures to be generated must definitely be considered when choosing the generation method. For example, if using deep learning methods, a greater complexity in the output often also requires a greater complexity within the neural networks, which directly affects the number of required training data and training time. Therefore, a significantly greater complexity may render a method that works well for 2D unusable for 3D, as the training process cannot be carried out sensibly and within an acceptable time frame. However, this varies from case to case, making it difficult to make a general statement about the consequences of different complexities.

The omission of specific information in 2D gesture recognition, such as kinetic data, raises the question of whether gesture generation methods even need to accurately represent this information. We argue that generation methods should not be chosen solely for specific gesture recognizers but should aim to produce generally realistic gesture executions. Furthermore, it is to be expected that ignoring this information during generation will not result in realistic gesture executions.

From these discussed differences between 2D and 3D gestures, consequences for the use of different generation algorithms can be inferred. As presented in Sect. 2, there are already works that have successfully generated touchscreen gestures using GANs. GANs offer the possibility to generate gestures in a time series representation and to add additional information (e.g., experience) during generation by means of conditions. Human performance limits could be implicitly learned through a not too divergent execution from the target gesture. This also applies to different gesture executions originating from different tools. In general, this demonstrates that, for 2D gesture generation, the construction of the dataset plays a major role in the success of the training, in addition to the choice of generation method. Inherent differences in gesture executions due to modalities and the space of ergonomic possibilities must be represented in the dataset, as modeling these within the generation process itself is not feasible.

In contrast, with Reinforcement Learning, the question arises about how the current state can accurately be represented. For example, the current position of each tool would have to represent the current state and the target gesture would have to be passed as an additional state variable at all times. This not only entails significantly more effort in gesture generation but also raises the question of whether a frame-by-frame generation corresponds to a human execution of a gesture. Further research would be needed to determine how these characteristics of gesture execution could be optimally transferred into the settings of Reinforcement Learning. Reinforcement Learning offers the ability to learn the manipulation of human models in order to generate gestures. This allows any potential limitations to be directly defined within the model, rather than needing to be represented by the dataset itself.

Unlike the 2D approach, we speculate that Reinforcement Learning is better suited for the generation of 3D gesture data than GANs. We attribute this not only to a significantly increased complexity of the gestures but also to a significantly greater and more complicated amount of contextual information, which Reinforcement Learning is explicitly designed to solve. Although the question of observation states and rewards remains open, we claim that the problems encountered in this regard are much easier to solve than the problem of training a GAN on arbitrarily complex contextual information and noise between gesture executions. However for contextless physical representations of 3D gestures, such as joint positions/rotations, we speculate that GANs would still be a well-suited approach to solving the problem, as previous work has already shown [34].

5 Engineering Details

This chapter discusses the implementation of a GAN for generating 2D gesture data, as well as the implementation of Reinforcement Learning with and without models.

5.1 Data Collection

The most critical factor for successful training of GenAI is the data foundation. Ideally, this data should contain as much variation as possible and be capable of covering the entire problem space. Only in this way can a robust model be trained that can generate diverse data in all realistic variations. For gesture data, various types of variance within the data must be considered: natural execution variance (intra-user variance), performer variance (inter-user variance), and gesture definition variance. Execution variance describes the natural fuzziness of gestures - each new gesture performed by the same user varies slightly and deviates from previous executions. Performer variance refers to differences in gesture executions among different user groups. Various studies (e.g., [7,10,13]) have shown that gesture executions carry different biometric and demographic information, which allows for inferences about the executing user group. Therefore, different user groups can be identified by biometrical and demographic data, as well as cultural differences.

Gesture definition variance describes differences in gestures due to varying definitions, such as different gesture shapes or cultural interpretations of specific gestures.

The data foundation for training a generative model must adequately cover the different variances to allow the model to generate realistic gesture executions. Therefore, the dataset should include executions for various definitions, from different user groups, and in multiple versions performed by the same individuals. Also, the amount of collected data needed to ensure good generation results needs to be investigated. Model performance depending on the quantitiy of training data should be examined.

Reliability Considerations. Reliability of gesture generation is not only dependent on the diversity but also on the quality of the used training data. Robust datasets with sufficient saturation across different gesture scenarios contribute to generating gestures that are not only realistic but also resilient to unusual movements. This is especially important for model-free approaches of gesture generation, as we are missing a way of implicitely forbidding unrealistic (joint) movement. Furthermore, it helps to portray random noise movement between gesture executions. Targeted evaluation frameworks, as introduced in [1] for 2D gesture generation, provide a structured opportunity to thoroughly examine synthetic gestures for consistency and minimal variance from real-world user movements, thus enhancing synthetic gesture reliability and supporting authenticity across applications.

5.2 2D Gesture Generation

To start training a GAN, the data must first be preprocessed. This preprocessing varies depending on the application. We initially assume that the gestures are available as time series with positional information for each point in time. Additional information, such as pressure, can be recorded in further dimensions, although this is initially disregarded in this discussion. If the spatial information alone is relevant for the resulting gestures, the time information can be neglected. Otherwise, gestures can either receive the time information as an extra dimension or it can be inherently incorporated into the gestures by interpolation to temporally equidistant time steps. Normalizing the gestures to the interval $[-1, 1]$ allows for uniform processing of gestures captured on different screens. If necessary, gestures can be padded with the position $(-1, -1)$ and the last timestamp to achieve uniform lengths. To generate specific classes of gestures, such as particular shapes or user groups, this information can be encoded in a conditional GAN and added as a conditional input to both generation and discrimination.

The GAN architecture itself initially only provides the basic structure consisting of generator and discriminator. The architectures of the generator and discriminator can be freely chosen, but must take into account the form of the data being processed and generated. For processing gestures, we propose two different methods: for time series, it is intuitive to process these using Recurrent Neural Network (RNN) layers; alternatively, we can also view the gesture as a (T×n)-sized image - with TT as the number of time steps and nn as the number of data points per time step - and process it using Convolutional Neural Network (CNN) layers. To generate the gesture, compressed information can be sampled to the correct output form via transposed convolution. When using RNN layers, these can process input and output it in a format that can be reshaped to the correct output format. Both approaches can be combined. Additionally, it is possible to use transformers as generator and discriminator.

5.3 3D Gesture Generation

For generating 3D gestures with Reinforcement Learning, we consider both model-based and model-free approaches. Model-based generation has the advantage that mobility constraints and other limitations can be directly embedded within the model, without requiring explicit learning. For this purpose, a 3D model of a hand can be used, where movement is controlled through joint rotations. This allows movement constraints to be implemented by specifying permitted value ranges for the model's joints. In a model-free approach, constraints must be explicitly learned by the agent. Conditions for generation, such as gesture shape or user group, can be encoded as classes within the observations or added in other forms, such as positional information or images of keyframes. Additionally, the observations must provide insight into previously executed movements to enable consistent gesture definition imitation. The reward structure requires thorough exploration; an initial approach might employ classifiers for specific gestures to guide reward distribution.

To initiate the Reinforcement Learning process for model-based training, the training data must first be mapped into the model's spatial framework. For this, a coordinate system transformation can be performed from the original system to that of the model, followed by a min-max normalization within the model. The Reinforcement Learning process then trains a generative model to learn the joint rotations of the hand model necessary for executing specific gestures.

A model-free Reinforcement Learning process operates on the raw representation of the data. A potential gesture representation might be in the form of a time series, where the position of each relevant hand point is tracked over time. The output space then consists of the target positions of the relevant hand bones.

5.4 Usability Considerations

In addition to technical precision, the usability of the implemented generation method is essential to ensure its practical applicability. The pipeline should be designed to adapt flexibly to different user scenarios, allowing different applications and user groups to be accommodated through varied training datasets. Standardized problems and use cases could allow for standardized data formats to ensure compatibility for different datasets. Furthermore, efficient model setups, such as pre-trained models for specific user groups or automated adjustments for new user data, could increase the accessibility and scalability of the generation methods.

6 Conclusion and Future Work

We discussed the differences and similarities of 2D and 3D gestures with their synthesis for test automation in mind. We focused on the potential of GANs and

Reinforcement Learning for synthesizing gestures and argue that Reinforcement Learning is more suited for 3D and GANs for 2D gestures, considering contextual information and noise. Moreover, the discussion reveals that, in addition to the dimensionality of gestures, the representation and use case also plays an important role in the choice of generation method. 3D gestures in their simplest representation differ from 2D gestures only by an additional positional information, which is why methods suitable for 2D gestures can also be effectively applied here. Ultimately, the choice of representation is associated with different levels of context and complexity. Our implementation details outline practical setups for GANs in 2D gesture generation and Reinforcement Learning in 3D, providing structured approaches to optimize data preprocessing, model structure, and evaluation. These setups contribute to a robust synthesis pipeline that can flexibly adapt to varying user groups and application requirements.

For future work, several tasks remain. Our hypotheses must be tested and several algorithms validated for 2D and 3D gesture synthesis. Furthermore, as we aim to produce human-like gestures, data from various user groups is necessary as training material. Various questions arise for generation methods when applied to 2D and 3D gestures. For GANs, it must be explored how they can handle the significantly increased complexity and dimensionality of the data, as well as human limitations in gesture execution. For Reinforcement Learning, the main question is how to structure the training process involving the agent, state, and rewards to generate the most realistic gestures possible. When collecting datasets, the findings from method investigations must be taken into account. While GANs require a dataset that encompasses as much of the problem space as possible, some information for Reinforcement Learning might be inherently captured within the models used. Future work should also investigate the scalability and adaptability of the proposed implementation setups in real-world applications, as well as explore additional model architectures for both GANs and Reinforcement Learning to optimize for complex gesture representations. Testing various preprocessing techniques and evaluation metrics in different settings could help refine the synthesis pipeline further and ensure robust performance across diverse scenarios and use cases.

References

1. Bachert, M., Hesenius, M.: Towards a framework for evaluating synthetic surface gestures. In: Companion Proceedings of the 16th ACM SIGCHI Symposium on Engineering Interactive Computing Systems, pp. 22–30. EICS '24 Companion, Association for Computing Machinery, New York, NY, USA (2024). https://doi.org/10.1145/3660515.3661327
2. Bevan, C., Fraser, D.S.: Different strokes for different folks? Revealing the physical characteristics of smartphone users from their swipe gestures. Int. J. Hum. Comput. Studies **88**, 51–61 (2016). https://doi.org/10.1016/j.ijhcs.2016.01.001

3. Bobeth, J., et al.: Tablet, gestures, remote control? Influence of age on performance and user experience with ITV applications. In: Proceedings of the ACM International Conference on Interactive Experiences for TV and Online Video, pp. 139–146. TVX '14, Association for Computing Machinery, New York, NY, USA (2014). https://doi.org/10.1145/2602299.2602315
4. Börsting, I., Heikamp, M., Hesenius, M., Koop, W., Gruhn, V.: Software engineering for augmented reality – a research agenda. Proc. ACM Hum. Comput. Interact. **6**(EICS) (2022). https://doi.org/10.1145/3532205
5. Buriro, A., Ricci, F., Crispo, B.: SWIPEGAN: swiping data augmentation using generative adversarial networks for smartphone user authentication. In: Proceedings of the 3rd ACM Workshop on Wireless Security and Machine Learning, pp. 85–90. WiseML '21, Association for Computing Machinery, New York, NY, USA (2021). https://doi.org/10.1145/3468218.3469039
6. Chu, J., et al.: Wordgesture-GAN: modeling word-gesture movement with generative adversarial network. In: Proceedings of the 2023 CHI Conference on Human Factors in Computing Systems. CHI '23, Association for Computing Machinery, New York, NY, USA (2023). https://doi.org/10.1145/3544548.3581279
7. Davis, S.P., Ashayer, A., Tabrizi, N.: Predicting sex and age using swipe-gesture data from a mobile device. In: 2020 IEEE Intl Conf on Parallel and Distributed Processing with Applications, Big Data and Cloud Computing, Sustainable Computing and Communications, Social Computing and Networking (ISPA/BDCloud/SocialCom/SustainCom), pp. 1136–1143 (2020). https://doi.org/10.1109/ISPA-BDCloud-SocialCom-SustainCom51426.2020.00169
8. Doersch, C.: Tutorial on variational autoencoders (2021). https://doi.org/10.48550/arXiv.1606.05908
9. ElKoura, G., Singh, K.: Handrix: animating the human hand. In: Proceedings of the 2003 ACM SIGGRAPH/Eurographics Symposium on Computer Animation, pp. 110–119. SCA '03, Eurographics Association, Goslar, DEU (2003). https://doi.org/10.2312/SCA03/110-119
10. Frank, M., Biedert, R., Ma, E., Martinovic, I., Song, D.: Touchalytics: on the applicability of touchscreen input as a behavioral biometric for continuous authentication. IEEE Trans. Inf. Forensics Secur. **8**(1), 136–148 (2013). https://doi.org/10.1109/TIFS.2012.2225048
11. Goodfellow, I.J., et al.: Generative adversarial networks (2014). https://doi.org/10.48550/arXiv.1406.2661
12. Grandhi, S.A., Wacharamanotham, C., Joue, G., Borchers, J.O., Mittelberg, I.: How we gesture towards machines: an exploratory study of user perceptions of gestural interaction. In: CHI '13 Extended Abstracts on Human Factors in Computing Systems, pp. 1209–1214. CHI EA '13, Association for Computing Machinery, New York, NY, USA (2013). https://doi.org/10.1145/2468356.2468572
13. Guarino, A., Lettieri, N., Malandrino, D., Zaccagnino, R., Capo, C.: Adam or Eve? Automatic users' gender classification via gestures analysis on touch devices. Neural Comput. Appl. **34**(21), 18473–18495 (2022). https://doi.org/10.1007/s00521-022-07454-4
14. Hermann, J., Plückthun, M., Dogangün, A., Hesenius, M.: User-defined gesture and voice control in human-drone interaction for police operations. In: Nordic Human-Computer Interaction Conference. NordiCHI '22, Association for Computing Machinery (2022). https://doi.org/10.1145/3546155.3546661

15. Hesenius, M., Book, M., Gruhn, V.: Test automation for gesture-based interfaces. In: HCI Engineering 2019 – Methods and Tools for Advanced Interactive Systems and Integration of Multiple Stakeholder Viewpoints. CEUR Workshop Proceedings (2019). http://ceur-ws.org/Vol-2503/paper1_5.pdf
16. Hesenius, M., Gruhn, V.: Gesturecards – a hybrid gesture notation. Proc. ACM Hum. Comput. Interact. **3**(EICS), 22:1–22:35 (2019). https://doi.org/10.1145/3331164
17. Jakobsen, M.R., Jansen, Y., Boring, S., Hornbæk, K.: Should I stay or should i go? Selecting between touch and mid-air gestures for large-display interaction. In: Abascal, J., Barbosa, S., Fetter, M., Gross, T., Palanque, P., Winckler, M. (eds.) INTERACT 2015. LNCS, vol. 9298, pp. 455–473. Springer, Cham (2015). https://doi.org/10.1007/978-3-319-22698-9_31
18. Kopinski, T., Eberwein, J., Geisler, S., Handmann, U.: Touch versus mid-air gesture interfaces in road scenarios - measuring driver performance degradation. In: 2016 IEEE 19th International Conference on Intelligent Transportation Systems (ITSC), pp. 661–666 (2016). https://doi.org/10.1109/ITSC.2016.7795624, iSSN: 2153-0017
19. Li, W., Shi, P., Yu, H.: Gesture recognition using surface electromyography and deep learning for prostheses hand: state-of-the-art, challenges, and future. Fron. Neurosci. **15** (2021). https://doi.org/10.3389/fnins.2021.621885, publisher: Frontiers
20. Li, Y.: Deep reinforcement learning: an overview. CoRR abs/1701.07274 (2017). https://doi.org/10.48550/arXiv.1701.07274
21. Liu, H., Wang, L.: Gesture recognition for human-robot collaboration: a review. Int. J. Ind. Ergon. **68**, 355–367 (2018). https://doi.org/10.1016/j.ergon.2017.02.004
22. Lu, Y., Wang, X., Gong, J., Zhou, L., Ge, S.: Classification, application, challenge, and future of midair gestures in augmented reality. J. Sens. **2022**, e3208047 (2022). https://doi.org/10.1155/2022/3208047, publisher: Hindawi
23. Magrofuoco, N., Roselli, P., Vanderdonckt, J.: Two-dimensional stroke gesture recognition: a survey. ACM Comput. Surv. **54**(7), 155:1–155:36 (2021). https://doi.org/10.1145/3465400
24. Mirza, M., Osindero, S.: Conditional generative adversarial nets. CoRR abs/1411.1784 (2014). https://doi.org/10.48550/arXiv.1411.1784
25. Morris, M.R., Huang, A., Paepcke, A., Winograd, T.: Cooperative gestures: multi-user gestural interactions for co-located groupware. In: Proceedings of the SIGCHI Conference on Human Factors in Computing Systems, p. 1201. CHI '06, ACM Press, New York, NY, USA (2006). https://doi.org/10.1145/1124772.1124952
26. van den Noort, J.C., et al.: Variable and asymmetric range of enslaving: fingers can act independently over small range of flexion. PLoS ONE **11**(12), e0168636 (2016). https://doi.org/10.1371/journal.pone.0168636
27. Pan, M., Tang, Y., Li, H.: Review of the state-of-the-art of data gloves. In: 2022 IEEE International Symposium on Smart Electronic Systems (iSES), pp. 402–405 (2022). https://doi.org/10.1109/iSES54909.2022.00088
28. Shaw, A., Ruiz, J., Anthony, L.: Comparing human and machine recognition of children's touchscreen stroke gestures. In: Proceedings of the 19th ACM International Conference on Multimodal Interaction, pp. 32–40. ICMI '17, Association for Computing Machinery, New York, NY, USA (2017). https://doi.org/10.1145/3136755.3136810

29. Sun, M., et al.: Co-speech gesture synthesis by reinforcement learning with contrastive pretrained rewards. In: 2023 IEEE/CVF Conference on Computer Vision and Pattern Recognition (CVPR), pp. 2331–2340. IEEE Computer Society, Los Alamitos, CA, USA (2023). https://doi.org/10.1109/CVPR52729.2023.00231
30. Tang, H., Wang, W., Xu, D., Yan, Y., Sebe, N.: Gesturegan for hand gesture-to-gesture translation in the wild. In: Proceedings of the 26th ACM International Conference on Multimedia, pp. 774–782. MM '18, Association for Computing Machinery, New York, NY, USA (2018). https://doi.org/10.1145/3240508.3240704
31. Velloso, E., Schmidt, D., Alexander, J., Gellersen, H., Bulling, A.: The feet in human-computer interaction: a survey of foot-based interaction. ACM Comput. Surv. **48**(2), 21:1–21:35 (2015). https://doi.org/10.1145/2816455
32. Wigdor, D., Wixon, D.: Brave NUI world: designing natural user interfaces for touch and gesture. Morgan Kaufmann/Elsevier (2011). https://doi.org/10.1145/2047414.2047439
33. Wobbrock, J.O., Morris, M.R., Wilson, A.D.: User-defined gestures for surface computing. In: Proceedings of the SIGCHI Conference on Human Factors in Computing Systems, pp. 1083–1092. CHI '09, Association for Computing Machinery, New York, NY, USA (2009). https://doi.org/10.1145/1518701.1518866
34. Wu, B., Liu, C., Ishi, C.T., Ishiguro, H.: Probabilistic human-like gesture synthesis from speech using GRU-based WGAN. In: Companion Publication of the 2021 International Conference on Multimodal Interaction, pp. 194–201. ICMI '21 Companion, Association for Computing Machinery, New York, NY, USA (2021). https://doi.org/10.1145/3461615.3485407
35. Xia, H., Glueck, M., Annett, M., Wang, M., Wigdor, D.: Iteratively designing gesture vocabularies: a survey and analysis of best practices in the HCI literature. ACM Trans. Comput. Hum. Interact. **29**(4), 37:1–37:54 (2022). https://doi.org/10.1145/3503537
36. Xia, Z., et al.: Vision-based hand gesture recognition for human-robot collaboration: a survey. In: 2019 5th International Conference on Control, Automation and Robotics (ICCAR), pp. 198–205 (2019). https://doi.org/10.1109/ICCAR.2019.8813509

Assessing Large Language Models Adoption in Need Finding: an Exploratory Study

Alba Bisante, Stefano Zeppieri(✉), Venkata Srikanth Varma Datla, Gabriella Trasciatti, and Emanuele Panizzi

Department of Computer Science, Sapienza University of Rome, Rome, Italy
{bisante,zeppieri,datla,trasciatti,panizzi}@di.uniroma1.it

Abstract. This paper explores using large language models (LLMs) in the early stages of the user-centered design (UCD) process, particularly in defining user needs. While UCD emphasizes understanding users' needs, preferences, and contexts, LLMs introduce new possibilities for enhancing this process by assisting designers rather than replacing them. Through example prompts and case studies of three mobile app developments, this study investigates how LLMs can generate user profiles, needs, and personas. We highlight the potential benefits of LLM integration into UCD, such as increased efficiency and deeper insights, as well as inherent limitations like the lack of emotional depth in AI-generated interviews and the challenges in detecting inaccuracies. The findings underscore the importance of human involvement to ensure the fidelity and relevance of user simulations, suggesting a balanced approach for integrating AI tools in UCD.

Keywords: HCI · AI · Need Finding · GPT · LLM · UCD

1 Introduction

In the realm of User-Centered Design (UCD), the quest for innovative tools and methodologies to enhance the design process is ongoing. The UCD approach, rooted in placing the user at the forefront of design considerations, requires a deep understanding of user needs, preferences, and contexts. As such, the design community continually explores new avenues to enrich the UCD process, making it more efficient, inclusive, and effective. One of the most promising frontiers in this exploration is integrating artificial intelligence (AI), mainly through the use of Large Language Models (LLMs).

LLMs, such as the popular GPT-4, have demonstrated remarkable capabilities in generating human-like text based on vast datasets. Their potential to simulate aspects of human interaction and understanding presents a unique opportunity for augmenting various phases of the UCD process. This includes tasks such as defining the main objectives of a design project, identifying key

L. Zaina et al. (Eds.): EICS 2024, LNCS 15518, pp. 16–26, 2025.
https://doi.org/10.1007/978-3-031-91760-8_2

stakeholders, creating detailed personas, and even simulating focus group discussions [9]. However, applying LLMs within the UCD framework is not without challenges, especially when it comes to accurately capturing the full spectrum of human emotions, cultural contexts, and nuanced preferences.

This exploratory study seeks to explore the viability and effectiveness of LLMs as assisting tools in the early stages of the UCD process, specifically focusing on the need-finding phase. We advocate that even though LLMs are suitable to substitute the designer during the need-finding process, if adapted to assist them rather than replace them the outcomes are more adherent to reality and hence preferable. By providing example prompts and discussing the results of three practical case studies of mobile development (a university app, a fintech app, and an earthquake-warning app) - we provide an exploratory study on how to be assisted in the need-finding phase by LLMs. Our focus is not to advocate for replacing human-centric processes with AI but rather to understand how LLMs can complement existing methodologies, where they excel, and where they fall short.

2 Related Works

The integration of artificial intelligence, particularly Large Language Models (LLMs) like ChatGPT, into Human-Computer Interaction (HCI) processes is gaining attention, spanning early design stages to evaluation [8].

Among others, the recent work of Schmidt et al. [9] highlights the increasing potential of using LLMs in the Human-Centered Design (HCD) process, especially for enhancing design iteration efficiency. This area of exploration is strictly related to our investigation into the utility of ChatGPT during the initial phases of User-Centered Design (UCD).

Further research, such as the studies by Ekvall et al. [6], York [11], and Atlas [1], delves into ChatGPT's application in UX design and education. These studies provide insights into how ChatGPT can aid ideation, prototyping, and feedback, complementing the design process and education.

Tabone et al. [10] show how ChatGPT can effectively analyze text data, indicating its potential to enhance HCI research methods through detailed summaries and analyses.

In terms of evaluation, Duan et al. [5], and Bisante et al. [2] explore LLMs' role in automating feedback for UI design and facilitating evaluations of web interfaces, respectively. Their work points to ways that LLMs can streamline the evaluation process.

However, despite these positive developments, integrating LLMs into design processes still brings challenges, including ensuring AI-generated output's relevance and accuracy and ethical considerations [7]. The impact of AI on user interactions and interface management also raises important questions [4].

This growing interest in LLMs within HCI underscores the technology's potential to impact design processes significantly while also highlighting areas that need careful consideration. Our study contributes to this conversation by examining how LLMs can support UCD's early stages, aiming to shed light on both the advantages and challenges of AI in design.

3 Methodology

In this work, we investigate the effectiveness of LLMs as assisting tools in the early stages of the UCD process, specifically focusing on the need-finding phase. Our driving question is the following: can the outcomes from direct prompts, where AI *substitutes* the designer, be enhanced through an LLM-assisted approach that *empowers* the designer instead?

Indeed, LLMs can be directly prompted to delineate user needs for specific design ideas (e.g., *"What are the user needs for a fintech mobile app?"*), potentially bypassing traditional UCD phases, especially those engaging typically hard-to-find users. As an alternative, we propose leveraging LLMs to aid in conventional UCD steps.

Firstly, we identified a simplified version of the need-finding process in 4 steps based on our experience in the field. Then, we integrated the steps with LLM-based assistance. The resulting Need-finding LLM-assisted approach is reported below:

1. **Definition of User Profile Target:** We prompt the LLM with general application details to define the target user profile.
2. **Preliminary Definition of User Needs:** The LLM is tasked to draft an initial set of user needs.
3. **Persona Creation:** The LLM generates three (or more) detailed personas, capturing the target user group's diversity.
4. **Simulated Interviews:** We engage the LLM to conduct simulated interviews with the created personas, formulating questions and responses. Optionally, designers could craft the questions in a hybrid approach.
5. **Defition of Refined User Needs:** The LLM refines the user needs based on responses from the simulated interviews.

We deployed ChatGPT across three design domains to test our approach, assessing direct prompts against the assisted steps. We utilized ChatGPT version 4, updated in December 2023.

Experiments were divided into two distinct chat sessions for each design domain to avoid context overlap. In one session, ChatGPT was directly prompted to list user needs from a specified design concept; in the other, we followed the assisted need-finding steps. Both sessions were initiated with the same starting prompts (*"I want to design a mobile application...[design idea]"*) to ensure consistency. Specifically, the design ideas adopted for the study were:

- *"...to support university students in managing university activities (e.g., book exams, find classrooms)"*
- *"...to support banks customers in performing mobile banking operations (e.g. send/receive payments, invest, track expenses)"*

- *"...to receive warnings about upcoming earthquakes"*

The domains of the design ideas were chosen based on our experience in developing similar apps, which we leveraged to assess the quality of the LLMs' findings, which included insight depth, applicability in authentic contexts, and capacity to foster innovative solutions to user needs.

4 An Example of Direct Prompts vs. LLM Assisted Need-Finding

The same prompts were used acroos the three design domains. In this section, we report and comment specifically on the experiment conducted with the first design idea.

In one session, we directly prompted ChatGPT with our design idea, tasking it to define user needs: *"I want to design a mobile application to support university students in managing university activities (e.g., book exams, find classrooms). Define the user needs for such an application."*

ChatGPT replied with an exhaustive list of 10 user needs for a hypothetical university management app, each with a corresponding feature suggestion. The list was comprehensive and relevant, offering a compelling foundation for the need-finding phase of app development. Although there was a slight overlap in needs (for example, "finding classroom locations" appeared in both "academic schedule management" and "classroom locator"), this redundancy may be interpreted as underlining the importance of such features.

Then, we began a new session and applied the need-finding LLM-assisted approach. We report on the list of prompts used and answers received.

1. **Prompt**: *"I want to design a mobile application to support university students in managing university activities (e.g., book exams, find classrooms). Define the user profile target for such an application."*
   ChatGPT replied with a structured 5 bullet-point list. Firstly, it defined the demographics (age range, education level, and geographical context of the target users), which we found accurate. The second bullet point anticipated our subsequent query about expected user needs, presenting a concise list of five key points (all addressed in the alternative session with the direct prompt). We evaluated this selection as the core requirement for our targeted design concept. The third and fourth bullets, covering technological preferences and behavioral traits, were presented distinctly but could arguably be integrated with demographics, as they further characterize the target audience in a detailed manner. Finally, the response concludes with a note on "additional considerations", briefly addressing the importance of considering accessibility and privacy concerns.
2. **Prompt**: *"Define expected user needs for such an application."*
   The response list included 7 main points, each comprising 2 to 3 specific needs, totaling 16 needs. We cannot perform a direct numerical comparison to the first session answer, as the latter sometimes merged multiple needs

into a single point. For instance, "mental health resources" were encompassed under "Academic Advising and Support Services" in the first session but are now listed separately. Nonetheless, this response introduced additional needs not mentioned directly before, such as "financial and administrative support" and "campus news and events".

3. **Prompt**: *"Create three personas."*
   ChatGPT provided a structured outline of three personas, detailing for each their name, age, academic year, major, tech-savviness, and primary device, effectively mirroring an expected user base. Furthermore, it delineated three goals (e.g., "To navigate the large campus without getting lost"), three challenges (e.g., "Feels overwhelmed by the size of the campus and the number of buildings"), and three app-specific needs (e.g., "An interactive campus map with searchable building locations") for each persona. These needs were consistently aligned with those identified earlier.
4. **Prompt**: *"Simulate an interview with Persona n"*
   For each of the three personas, ChatGPT executed a simulated interview without explicit directives yet maintaining a uniform structure across all simulations. The LLM considers the description of the persona obtained from the previous prompt to personalize the interview questions and answers. Each interview comprised 9 interactions (6 direct questions, 1 conclusion feedback, 2 opening/closing greetings). The interviewer poses three questions related to the persona's challenges (e.g., "One of the challenges you mentioned was feeling overwhelmed by the size of the campus. Can you tell me about a specific instance where you had trouble navigating the campus?"), then asks a question linking the discussed challenge to a potential app feature that could mitigate the issue ("That sounds frustrating. What features would you find helpful in an app to avoid situations like this?"). Hence, each simulated interview was tailored to the corresponding persona while adhering to a consistent structural formula.
5. **Prompt**: *"Based on the interview transcripts, how would you integrate or modify the expected user needs? Provide a complete list of user needs indicating whenever there is a variation from the original list.*
   In the final response, ChatGPT reiterated the 7 main points and 16 needs identified in Prompt 2, specifying for each whether it remained unchanged or required enhancement following the simulated interviews. Additionally, 4 new needs were introduced. However, out of the 16 existing needs, only 5 were effectively enhanced, while 4 were marked as enhanced, albeit essentially remaining the same. For instance, the "Exam Booking System" need, originally described as "A feature to book exams, view exam schedules, and receive reminders as exam dates approach" was updated to "Enhanced to include not just booking and tracking exams but also integrating study reminders based on exam dates" suggesting no fundamental changes.

5 Engineering

5.1 Integrating Different Engineering Approaches

Integrating Large Language Models (LLMs) into user-centered design (UCD) processes presents a unique challenge: merging diverse engineering methodologies, such as traditional software engineering (e.g., waterfall, agile), with AI-specific approaches like iterative model tuning and data-driven development. We employ several strategies to effectively reconcile these processes to enhance system performance and user experience.

In AI systems, especially LLMs, the iterative feedback loops are crucial [3]. These systems thrive on continuous feedback to improve. By incorporating AI tuning within the Agile-UCD process, we facilitate an environment where the AI model is not static but evolves through iterative development cycles. This method retains the flexibility of agile development and introduces the structured rigor of AI model training. This synergy ensures the AI components are finely tuned to meet user needs and system performance metrics.

The architecture of these systems is often decoupled to allow for modular updates and integration. For instance, in a mobile app development scenario where LLMs assist with user need identification, the AI module can be developed and updated independently from the core application. This decoupling allows for smoother integration of LLM functionalities and facilitates more accessible updates and maintenance without disrupting the system. However, updating the model may also impact the overall interaction.

5.2 Addressing Non-deterministic Aspects of AI

Non-determinism in AI, particularly in LLMs, poses significant challenges for usability, utility, and reliability in UCD processes, as these systems can produce different outputs even when provided with the same input. Addressing this unpredictability is crucial for developing consistent and reliable user-centered designs.

Real-world scenario testing is a primary strategy for mitigating the effects of non-determinism. By testing LLM-generated outputs, such as user personas, against actual user profiles in mobile app development, designers can gain insights into the practical implications of AI unpredictability on the design process. These insights help refine the AI models to better align with user expectations and real-world usability.

Version control and traceability are essential for managing the non-deterministic nature of LLMs. By meticulously tracking prompt versions and the changes they undergo, designers can gather valuable insights into how different prompts influence LLM behavior. This practice is essential in Agile-UCD processes, where understanding the consistency and reliability of AI-generated outputs is crucial for making informed design decisions. For example, versioning different iterations of an LLM prompt allows teams to compare outcomes, helping to determine if newer prompts generate more accurate or realistic results when measured against real-world data. This systematic approach enhances the quality of AI outputs and supports continuous improvement in the design process.

5.3 Ensuring Humans Remain in the Loop

A critical challenge when integrating Large Language Models (LLMs) into user-centered design (UCD) processes is ensuring that humans remain actively involved in decision-making. Although LLMs can automate certain aspects of the design process, there is always the risk that these models generate erroneous or inappropriate content. It is, therefore, essential to implement mechanisms that preserve human oversight and validation throughout the design lifecycle.

Here are key strategies to ensure that humans remain in control:

- **Human-in-the-Loop (HITL) Systems**: One of the most effective ways to maintain human oversight is through HITL mechanisms. In this approach, LLM-generated content, such as user personas or design suggestions, must be validated by human designers at critical junctures. We advise implementing this via checkpoints where humans review, approve, or modify AI outputs, ensuring no fully automated decision is made without human validation.
- **Interactive AI Tools**: LLMs should function as assistants to designers rather than replacements. While LLMs can offer design suggestions or generate insights, the final decision-making authority rests with the human designer. For example, when evaluating user personas, the designer determines which personas are realistic, should be considered, and should be discarded. This approach balances AI-driven efficiency with human judgment, ensuring that the designer makes critical and creative decisions.
- **Transparency and Explainability**: AI models should provide transparent reasoning behind their outputs. For instance, if an LLM generates a design suggestion or user persona, it should explain how it reached that conclusion. This transparency enables designers to understand the AI's rationale and intervene when needed, avoiding over-reliance on potentially flawed AI outputs.
- **Fallback Mechanisms**: When an LLM generates outputs that are flagged as incorrect, unreliable, or potentially harmful, fallback mechanisms should be employed to maintain design quality. The system can prompt the designer to manually refine the output or revert to a more straightforward, human-controlled process. This ensures that AI-generated content does not compromise the integrity of the design. For instance, when dealing with sensitive data, the system could automatically alert users not to input sensitive information or instruct the LLM to exclude such data from its output. This proactive approach safeguards the user and the design process from unintended risks.

By implementing these strategies, human designers can retain control over the Agile-UCD process while benefiting from the efficiency and insights provided by LLMs.

5.4 Guaranteeing Positive Aspects for Human Users

A core objective of user-centered design is to ensure that systems provide positive emotional experiences for users. When integrating Large Language Models (LLMs) into the design process, it becomes essential to evaluate how AI-generated outputs affect these emotional experiences by enhancing or detracting from them. Ensuring that AI contributes positively to the user's emotional engagement requires thoughtful implementation and careful consideration of personalization and user control.

One way LLMs can enhance a system's hedonic aspects is through personalized experiences. AI-driven systems can create more engaging and emotionally satisfying interactions by tailoring outputs to align with individual user preferences. For example, as discussed in the case studies, LLM-generated personas and user needs can be personalized based on demographic information or direct user feedback. This allows the system to adapt to each user's unique characteristics, making the interaction more meaningful and enjoyable. Personalization improves the system's utility and deepens the emotional connection users feel toward the design, fostering a sense of being understood and catered to.

However, integrating non-deterministic AI systems, like LLMs, can frustrate users when outputs are inconsistent or inaccurate. To reduce this risk and ensure a positive user experience, it is essential to maintain transparency about how the AI operates. Users should be made aware of the AI's decision-making processes, mainly when results are unexpected or unclear. Allowing users to adjust or refine AI-generated content is another key strategy to mitigate frustration. For instance, allowing users to modify or clarify LLM-generated personas or design suggestions gives them more control over the interaction. This increased user agency ensures the system better aligns with their expectations, reducing frustration and fostering a more seamless and enjoyable experience.

5.5 Assessing Risk vs. Value in Specific Domains

Incorporating Large Language Models into user-centered design processes necessitates carefully evaluating risks and benefits, which vary considerably across different domains. Our study's need-finding flow-which leverages LLMs to assist in defining user needs and generating user personas-highlights the importance of this assessment.

In high-stakes areas like healthcare and finance, where errors can have severe consequences, rigorous risk assessments and strict validation protocols are essential. For instance, in the earthquake-warning app case study 3, utilizing LLMs to identify user needs and generate personas carries significant risks if the outputs need to be more accurate or complete. Misidentifying user needs in such a critical application could lead to features that fail to provide timely warnings, potentially endangering lives. Therefore, integrating LLMs in these domains requires stringent human oversight in the need-finding flow. Designers must meticulously review AI-generated user needs and personas to ensure they are accurate, relevant, and comply with safety and regulatory standards. This includes cross-referencing AI outputs with expert knowledge and real-world data to mitigate the risks associated with erroneous or misleading information.

In contrast, lower-risk domains such as education or entertainment present fewer severe consequences from potential AI inaccuracies, and the benefits of using LLMs can outweigh the risks. As demonstrated in the university app case study Sect. 3, LLMs can streamline the need-finding process by efficiently generating comprehensive user needs and diverse personas. This accelerates the design timeline and provides deeper insights into user expectations and behaviors. In this context, the AI-assisted generation of user personas allowed designers to explore a broader range of user types and scenarios than might be feasible manually, enhancing the overall design quality with minimal risk.

By tailoring the integration of LLMs in the need-finding flow and user-persona generation to the specific risk profile of each domain, designers can maximize the benefits while minimizing potential drawbacks. This balanced approach allows for the effective incorporation of AI into UCD processes across various fields.

6 Results Discussion and Limitations

We advocate that the LLM-assisted method consistently provides deeper insights than direct prompting methods. This richer detail not only enhances the design process but also empowers designers to focus on more strategic and creative aspects of project development, fostering a more robust exploration of user needs and potentially leading to more innovative solutions. However, our experience also uncovered several limitations that merit discussion.

Regarding persona generation and simulated interviews, we intentionally limited the scope to three personas to manage the complexity of our analysis, and the resulting personas were realistic and showcased diverse needs. However, we believe that they do not fully represent the entire target group, particularly missing edge cases. Additionally, although the AI-generated interviews were coherent and contextually relevant, they lacked the nuanced emotional depth typical of real user interactions. This limitation highlights a critical gap: while LLMs can simulate user interactions to a certain extent, they do not yet capture the emotional authenticity essential for a comprehensive understanding of user experiences.

To address the limited scope of persona diversity, one could hypothetically instruct the LLM to generate a broader range of personas and conduct subsequent interviews automatically. Potential experiments on this should, however, analyze the differences in the responses and the representativeness of the insights, particularly in capturing emotional nuances.

Another significant challenge is the detection of inaccuracies or 'hallucinations' in the data produced by LLMs. The involvement of designers in an LLM-assisted approach, as opposed to a direct prompting strategy, can facilitate the identification and correction of such inaccuracies. However, expertise remains crucial to assess AI-generated content.

7 Conclusions and Future Works

In our study across three mobile app domains, the integration of LLMs in the UCD process has shown both promising potential and notable challenges. We propose an LLM-assisted approach that enhances the traditional need-finding phase of UCD, providing results that are more detailed and informative compared to those derived solely from direct prompts to LLMs.

Looking ahead, an interesting area for further research is the use of synthetic data generation techniques to increase the number of interviews and scenarios that can be simulated, enabling the creation of a broader and more diverse set of user personas. Such work would help address current limitations related to the scope and variety of generated data.

References

1. Atlas, S.: ChatGPT for higher education and professional development: a guide to conversational AI. College of Business Faculty University of Rhode Island, 1–135 (2023)
2. Bisante, A., Datla, V., Panizzi, E., Trasciatti, G., Zeppieri, S.: Enhancing interface design with AI: an exploratory study on a ChatGPT-4-based tool for cognitive walkthrough inspired evaluations. In: Proceedings of Advanced Visual Interfaces 2024. AVI '24, Association for Computing Machinery, New York, NY, USA (2024). https://doi.org/10.1145/3656650.3656676
3. Bisante, A., Datla, V.S.V., Trasciatti, G., Zeppieri, S., Panizzi, E.: An approach to leverage artificial intelligence for car-parking related mobile applications. In: Harrison, M., Martinie, C., Micallef, N., Palanque, P., Schmidt, A., Winckler, M., Yigitbas, E., Zaina, L. (eds.) Engineering Interactive Computer Systems. EICS 2023 International Workshops and Doctoral Consortium, pp. 63–71. Springer Nature Switzerland, Cham (2024). https://doi.org/10.1007/978-3-031-59235-5_7
4. Bisante, A., Dix, A., Panizzi, E., Zeppieri, S.: To err is AI. In: Proceedings of the 15th Biannual Conference of the Italian SIGCHI Chapter. CHItaly '23, Association for Computing Machinery, New York, NY, USA (2023). https://doi.org/10.1145/3605390.3605414
5. Duan, P., Warner, J., Hartmann, B.: Towards generating UI design feedback with LLMs. In: Adjunct Proceedings of the 36th Annual ACM Symposium on User Interface Software and Technology. UIST '23 Adjunct, Association for Computing Machinery, New York, NY, USA (2023). https://doi.org/10.1145/3586182.3615810
6. Ekvall, H., Winnberg, P.: Integrating ChatGPT into the UX design process: ideation and prototyping with LLMs (2023)
7. Illia, L., Colleoni, E., Zyglidopoulos, S.: Ethical implications of text generation in the age of artificial intelligence. Bus. Ethics Env. Responsib. **32**(1), 201–210 (2023). https://onlinelibrary.wiley.com/doi/abs/10.1111/beer.12479
8. Schmidt, A.: Speeding up the engineering of interactive systems with generative AI. In: Companion Proceedings of the 2023 ACM SIGCHI Symposium on Engineering Interactive Computing Systems, pp. 7–8. EICS 23, Swansea United Kingdom (2023). https://doi.org/10.1145/3596454.3597176
9. Schmidt, A., Elagroudy, P., Draxler, F., Kreuter, F., Welsch, R.: Simulating the human in HCD with ChatGPT: Redesigning interaction design with AI . Interactions **31**(1), 24-31 (jan 2024), https://doi.org/10.1145/3637436

10. Tabone, W., De Winter, J.: Using ChatGPT for human-computer interaction research: A primer. Manuscript submitted for publication (2023), https://doi.org/10.1098/rsos.231053
11. York, E.: Evaluating ChatGPT: Generative AI in UX design and web development pedagogy. In: Proceedings of the 41st ACM International Conference on Design of Communication. pp. 197–201. 41st ACM International Conference on Design of Communication, Orlando FL USA (2023), https://doi.org/10.1145/3615335.3623035

Adding a Non-dependable AI Component to Increase Dependability of an Interactive Application

Axel Carayon[1(✉)], Camille Fayollas[2], Celia Martinie[1], David Navarre[2], and Philippe Palanque[1]

[1] ICS-IRIT, Université Toulouse III – Paul Sabatier, Toulouse, France
{axel.carayon,celia.martinie,philippe.palanque}@irit.fr
[2] ICS-IRIT, Université Toulouse Capitole, Toulouse, France
{camille.fayollas,david.navarre}@irit.fr

Abstract. This paper contributes to a software engineering approach where AI technologies are carefully integrated inside critical interactive system to improve dependability. This property cannot be reached only using AI technologies as their probability of failure is usually high. But, in our approach, these technologies are introduced where the other technologies have reached their limit of dependability. To illustrate this approach, we use three different computer-based solutions for supporting post-stroke rehabilitation and demonstrates how mixing an AI component and a dependable component enables to improve both the dependability and the usability of the interactive system.

Keywords: Interactive systems · Engineering · AI · Automation · Dependability · Usability

1 Introduction

AI technologies bring important benefits in some contexts such as pattern recognition or computer vision, where it is difficult and time-consuming to engineer an algorithm for performing such actions. Unfortunately, while current hype makes people believe AI technologies can perform any information-processing task and that every computing system embeds AI technologies, they bring issues that prevent them from generic use. This is particularly the case in a safety-critical context, where their lack of maturity deeply impacts their reliability and dependability, making introducing them in such a domain complex.

A concrete example of ML-based computer vision technologies is the one being deployed for detecting undesired objects on airports' runways (see [18] for more details). In that contribution, the authors propose a stepwise processing of computer images for foreign object detection (FOD). Based on a widely used training dataset called YOLOv4, the highest accuracy is about 93.81%. This could be seen as a good precision for the AI technology. However, this means that the system is wrong once every ten FOD. In

L. Zaina et al. (Eds.): EICS 2024, LNCS 15518, pp. 27–42, 2025.
https://doi.org/10.1007/978-3-031-91760-8_3

concrete numbers, the system produced 134 false positives (a non-existing object was detected), 215 false negatives (a non-detected object was actually present on the runway), and 1566 true positives. This poor reliability level (with respect to the expected reliability level of safety-critical systems) of the automation results in multiple automation surprises [20] among other negative effects on operators.

In these highly dependable contexts, such as aircraft command and control, the probability of failures must be demonstrated, and for the most critical systems, this probability must be less than 10^{-9} per hour of use. For instance, Aleçu et al. [1] show that, in the case of a railway signal reading system, the current human-operated system leads to an average target of a maximum of 10^{-5} failures per signal, while the best automatic reading system achieves on average 10^{-2} errors per signal. The current practice in these critical domains is to use non-AI algorithms as they can be formally defined and verified.

However, as explained above, AI technologies may bring benefits in some contexts for which the definition of dependable algorithms would be too difficult and/or too time-consuming: the question of their integration thus remains. In the context of interactive systems, the desire to introduce AI systems to support users' activities can be reduced to five choices:

- Wait for the AI community to develop AI technology to the level of dependability required in critical systems. However, following the huge investment over the years, none of them has reached a level of dependability higher than 90% (i.e. 10–1) and it would take decades to reach 100% of accuracy given the current progression [24].
- Do not use the non-dependable function in the operational context. This would lead to a loss of operational benefits [18].
- Develop a dependable algorithm for the function. This is not possible because of the cost of such a development (highly difficult and time-consuming).
- Embed the AI technology with its current low level of dependability to use it not as an operational function but as a help to support the operational activity of the operator. This implies that the user may over-rely on this function and that s/he might experiment with all the issues that can be brought by automation (complacency, over-reliance, deskilling …) [15].
- Embed the AI technology with its current low level of dependability to take advantage of its benefits while being aware of its weaknesses and engineering very carefully it's integration.

This paper discusses how a careful integration of AI technology is possible while engineering critical interactive systems and how this integration improves both the interactive system's dependability and usability. Section 2 presents the post-stroke rehabilitation context we use as a case study. Section 3 presents a dependable computer-based solution to support the partitioners while the patients are trained to recover from a stroke. This solution is built with the objective of dependability but is limited in terms of tasks to train the patient on. Section 4 presents an AI-based solution that improves the fidelity (and thus, the usability) of the training tasks with respect to the daily living activities s/he needs to be trained for. Section 5 presents a solution embedding both techniques to improve both the dependability of the system and its ability to train for daily living activities. Section 6 discusses the three solutions in terms of failure probability and thus the ability of the solution to train to real daily living activities. Finally, Sect. 7 concludes the paper.

2 Post-stroke Rehabilitation: A Concrete Example of Critical Context

2.1 Introduction to Post-stroke Rehabilitation

According to the World Stroke Organization in the Global Stroke Factsheet released in 2022 [25], the lifetime risk of developing a stroke has increased by 50% over the last 17 years and now, 1 in 4 people is estimated to have a stroke in their lifetime. A stroke may cause several types of impairments that can be motor, cognitive, or perceptive. In the days following the stroke, the neurologists provide care to stabilize the patient's state and avoid complications. Once the patient's state is stabilized, if the patient still has severe impairments, a team of specialists in stroke rehabilitation handles a rehabilitation program for the patient.

Post-stroke or post-brain injury rehabilitation is a long-term process defined by therapists and tuned to the specific damages and their consequences for each patient. The main missions of a rehabilitation practitioner are i) to set goals with post-stroke patients (for instance "be able to prepare oneself a simple meal"), ii) to propose well-designed exercises and iii) to monitor their progress [8]. Patients must perform, repetitively, multiple exercises and must be carefully monitored to identify progress, possible regression, and prevent damages due to the inadequate performance of the exercises [8]. This process is time-consuming for rehabilitation teams that have many patients to take care of and limited time to share among them.

Computer-based post-stroke training tools support rehabilitation specialists in conducting the recovery of their patients by automating specific training tasks and providing patient guidance through selected recovery exercises. This can help rehabilitation specialists to manage more patients (in presence or remotely) and makes it possible for the patient to practice at home. It is important to note that these tools are safety-critical applications as a dysfunction, or a wrong design might lead to injuring the patient [12]. The definition of such exercises usually requires focusing on a subset of all the exercises that can be performed with a practitioner. For instance, the RehaCom commercial desktop application [11] provides support to plan and perform cognitive rehabilitation exercises but is limited to a subset of cognitive exercises that the specialists cannot customize. Plata et al. [21] who proposes an interactive application for physical therapists to monitor training exercises based on posture repetition, only focuses on patient positions.

2.2 A Case Study to Support Post-Stroke Rehabilitation

Carayon et al. [6] proposed an approach, based on digitalized exercises such as the Shape Sorter Drum Task (SSDT) [25], that measures movement performance with a substantial amount of visual and somatosensory requirements. For this task, the patients are required to take objects from a standard position and put them into a drum with their more affected hand. This task is very interesting because it trains perceptive (perceiving the shapes, perceiving the variation of luminous intensity as holes are darker), cognitive (recognizing shapes), and motor skills (moving upper limb joints). This exercise can help patients to recognize circle-shaped objects as well as to train upper limp motor capacities, thus supporting higher level goals such as "grab one plate from the shelf two times a day", which is itself required to reach the goal "be able to prepare oneself a simple meal".

Based on the object-triage principle of the SSDT, we propose here a setup to train the patient to sort everyday life objects: dishes, supporting the rehabilitation for the daily living activity "be able to prepare oneself a simple meal". The activity to be performed by the patient is to choose the required object (for instance a cup) between a set of dishes and to move it to another place. As for the SSDT, this exercise trains perceptive (perceive the objects), cognitive (recognizing the object), and motor skills. Figure 1 presents a schematic view of the setup corresponding to this exercise. Different dishes are placed on the left side (for the patient) of the table. The practitioner gives indications to the patient to move the required dishes from the left to the right. The practitioner monitors what the patient is doing and gives her/him immediate feedback about her/his actions.

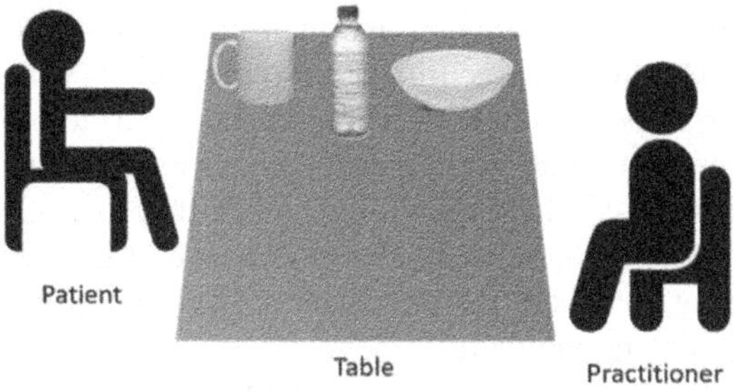

Fig. 1. Setup for patient training to sort the dishes, monitored by the practitioner.

In the remainder of the paper, we propose three different computer-based interactive setups enabling the patient to train to sort objects without the practitioner. This can help rehabilitation specialists to manage more patients and to allow the patient to practice at home.

3 A Scale-Based Solution Automating Practitioner Tasks

3.1 Description of the Scale-Based Solution

As presented by Fig. 2, the first setup is limited to reliable technologies to be able to guarantee the interactive system's dependability, where the patient is in front of two scales (one on the left and one on the right) and a screen:

- Two scales. The first one, on the left, is filled with a set of three different dishes: a cup, a bowl, and a bottle. The second one, on the right, is empty.
- A screen that displays which object should be moved from the left scale to the right one (the exercise can become more complicated by adding time constraints: "move the cup from the left scale to the right scale in less than 10 s").

- A Kinect v2 that allows to film the entire exercise for later analysis by the practitioner.

Object movement is monitored through the analysis of the weight variation between the two scales. When the patient moves an object from the left scale to the right one, the weight variation enables the system to identify the object the patient grabbed from the left scale and dropped on the right scale. This data is used to give immediate feedback to the patient and to record analyses on the entire exercise session (for instance, the list of objects that have been moved and the time used by the patient to perform the different tasks).

The practitioner can analyze later the exercise by watching the record of the exercise and analyzing the records provided by the scale monitoring mechanism.

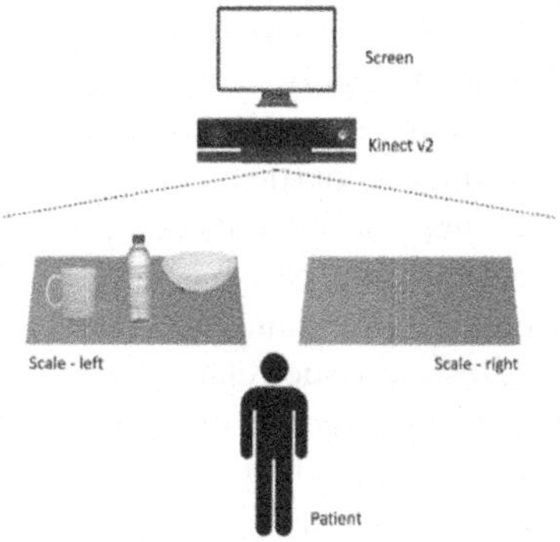

Fig. 2. Schematic view from the top of the scale-based setup

This setup is built to enhance its dependability through:

- *Technologies.* The use of scales enables us to be sure of the number of objects on the scale (with the analysis of the weight that is on the scale). Scales are well-known technology that comes with well-defined datasheets.
- *Objects.* The objects having different weights, this weight thus works as a unique identifier.

It is important to notice that if two different objects have the same weight, or if two objects of the same type have different weights, the system will not be able to differentiate them. To remove ambiguities between objects, we limit the types and number of objects and make sure that they have different weights. These constraints lead us to limit the objects to a mug, a bottle, and a bowl for the first implementation of the setup.

3.2 Engineering the Scale-Based Solution

To ensure the dependability of the developed interactive system and prevent the occurrence of software development faults, we engineer it with a preventive approach based on a zero-defect software development technique, based on a specific architecture designed using the MIODMIT [7], a generic architecture dedicated to dynamic multimodal interactive systems. We use the interactive cooperative objects (ICO) formal description technique to limit as much as possible the introduction of design faults during the development of the interactive system.

The Formal Description Technique ICO

The ICO notation (Interactive Cooperative Objects) is a formal description technique devoted to the specification of interactive systems [17]. Using high-level Petri nets [9] for dynamic behavior description, the notation also relies on an object-oriented approach (dynamic instantiation, classification, encapsulation, inheritance and client/server relationships) to describe the structural or static aspects of systems.

The ICO formalism enables the handling of the specific aspects of interactive systems such as their event-driven nature. Its main interest is to provide a way for the interactive system developer to create non-ambiguous and concise models compliant with the system specifications. The ICO formalism is supported by a tool named PetShop providing means to develop ICO models and formally verify properties over them [5, 23] and also provides runtime support for models' execution. As the models are directly interpreted at run-time by this tool, the verified properties will be still valid at execution time.

ICO notation objects are composed of four components: a cooperative object for the behavior description, a presentation part (i.e. Graphical Interface), and two functions (activation and rendering) describing the links between the cooperative object and the presentation part. ICO solves the issue related to the most limiting features in the literature: dynamic instantiation of interaction objects, as Petri nets are particularly efficient to describe tokens creations and ICO allows these tokens to describe dynamically instantiated objects (more can be found in [17]).

Finally, it is important to note that ICOs have been used for various types of domains. This notation is currently applied for formal specification in the fields of Air Traffic Control interactive applications [16], space command and control ground systems [19], interactive military [3], civil cockpits [2], multi-modal interfaces [13] and for multi-touch [10].

Architecture and Models for the First Setup

Figure 3 shows an extract of the architecture of the system, focusing on the input part of the application, as the dialog, application core and rendering are out of the scope of this paper.

The three grayed-out areas indicate the three different types of devices:

- The RGB camera input device (middle part of the Fig. 3) represents the Kinect v2 device used as a camera in this application. The camera communicates with the Virtual Camera via a Camera driver, that translates received data into an RGB frame sent to the dialog of the application. This frame is then forwarded to the core of the application for further use (Application Core, not being detailed in this paper) and to the Rendering scene for displaying the recorded video on the output screen.
- In the Scale input device section (top part of Fig. 3), the two blocks Scale 1 and Scale 2 represent the physical devices themselves. In the same way as the camera input device, these devices send data through the Scale Driver to the Virtual Scale. The virtual scale sends Weighting measures to the Input Chain Manager, where the Weight Comparison process compares these measures to the Calibrated values, which are external data

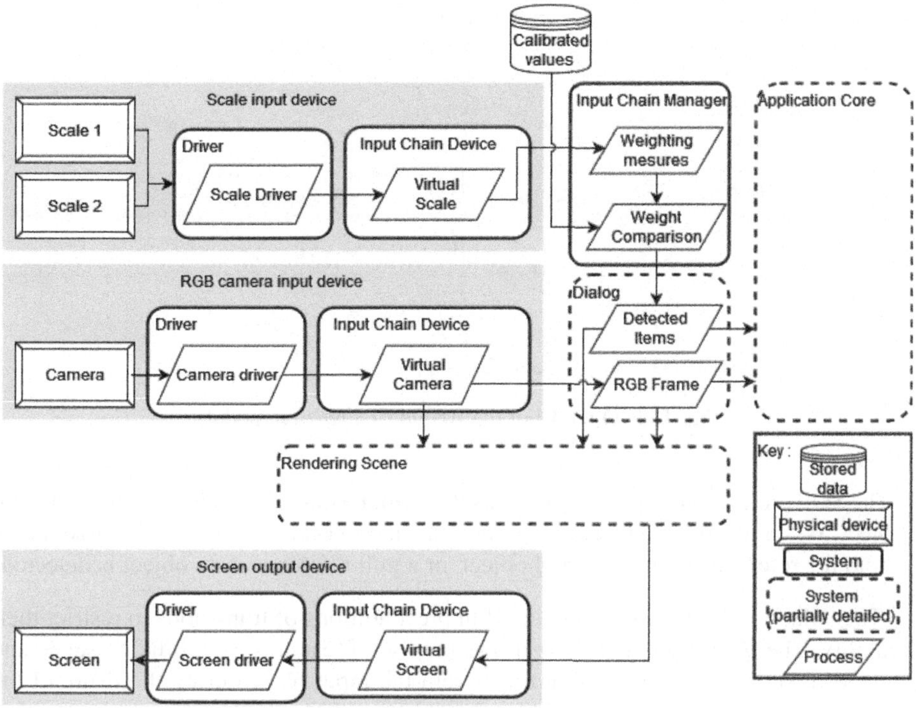

Fig. 3. Partial view of the scale-based architecture

containing pre-calculated values for various objects. Based on this comparison, the Weight Comparison process identifies Detected Items sent to the Dialog, which then forwards the information to both the Application Core (for further processing) and the Rendering Scene to display feedback to the patient on the output screen.

- The Screen output device (bottom part of Fig. 3) displays instructions for the patient, performance feedback, and the recorded video.

The behavior of each software component is fully described using the ICO notation. As an example, Fig. 4 presents the ICO model of the *Weight Comparison* module which contains only one method *detectObject* called each time an object detection based on its weight is required.

Figure 4 represents an ICO model made up of six places and four transitions. The places may be described as follow:

- Each place Item 1, Item 2 and Item 3 holds a token containing the name of an item (e.g., bowl, cup, and bottle) and its weight.
- The Error Threshold place holds a token containing the value of the scale's error threshold.
- The SIP_detectObject place represents the input parameters of the method detectObject. Initially empty, it receives a token containing a weight when the method detectObject is called.

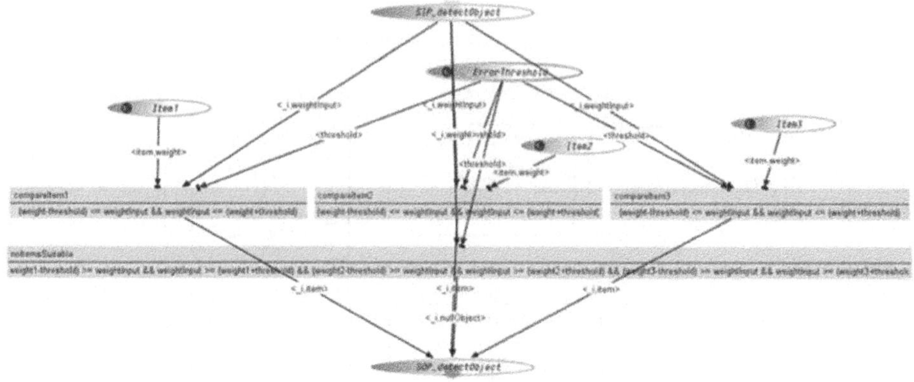

Fig. 4. ICO model of the *Weight Comparison* module

- The SOP_detectObject place represents the output parameters of the method detectObject. When receiving a token, it answers the method call. In our case, the token may hold the reference to the detected object, or a null reference if no object is detected.

The values of the tokens can be used in preconditions of transitions to restrict their fireability. The ICO formalism also allows the use of test arcs to test the presence and values of tokens without removing them from the input place during the firing of the transition (e.g., the arc connecting place *Item1* to transition *compareItem1* is a test arc).

When the method *detectObject* is called, a token is put in place *SIP_detectObject*. This token is thus used as an input of one of the four following transitions, depending on the case:

- Each transition *compareItem1*, *compareItem2*, and *compareItem3* checks, using a dedicated pre-condition, if the input weight is the closed to the corresponding item weight (considering the error threshold).
- When none of these three items is concerned, the *noItemsSuitable* transition is fired (its pre-condition is the opposite of the three others).

As a result, one of these four transitions produces a token put in place *SOP_detectObject* which stands for the answer to the *detectObject* method call.

4 An AI-Based Solution Automating Practitioner Tasks

4.1 Description of the AI-Based Solution

For the second setup, we introduce an AI-based computer-vision technology, to enhance the fidelity of the training task with respect to the patient's environment. We use an image capture and recognition technique to enable the use of a broader set of daily living objects. This leads to the setup pictured in Fig. 5 where the patient is in front of a table and a screen. In more detail, the setup decomposes into:

- A table with daily living objects located on the left side of the table.

- A Kinect v2 that allows the retrieval of frames of the patient's actions and filming the entire exercise for later analysis by the practitioner.
- A computer-vision-based software module that takes the frames as input and detects in real-time which object has been picked up and moved.
- A screen that displays which object should be moved from the left side of the table to the right side (the exercise can also be complicated by adding a time constraint: "move the cup from the left side to the right side in less than 10 s").

Object detection and movement are monitored through the computer-vision-based module. When the patient moves an object from the left side of the table to the right side, the module tries to identify the object the patient grabbed. This data is used to give immediate feedback to the patient and to record analysis of the entire exercise session (subsequently used by the practitioner).

This setup is built to enhance the fidelity of the training task regarding the activities of daily living through:

- *Technologies*. The computer-based-vision module enables us to use a broader set of types of objects for the training exercises.
- *Objects*. The computer-vision-based setup does not require dealing with the weight of objects. There is thus no constraint on the selected object and no need to limit the set of objects to specific ones for the implementation of the setup.

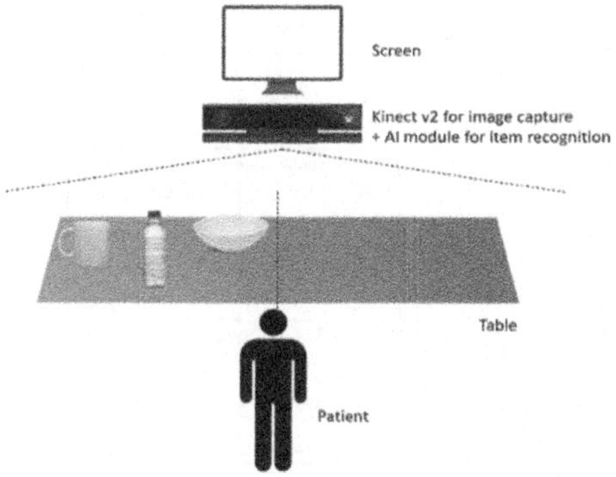

Fig. 5. Schematic view from the top of the computer-vision-based solution

4.2 Engineering the Computer-Vision-Based Solution

To engineer the AI-based solution, we need to use the right trained model that provides us with enough variety for our exercises. Basically, detecting objects via an image with AI techniques requires a large dataset of different segmented images containing different objects, and train a deep neural network with those images. The YoloV3 model [22] is a very popular Machine Learning (ML) model available online and free of use, trained with the COCO dataset [14], which contains over 200,000 labeled images and can detect up to 80 different objects from an image. Each detected item is a structure containing:

- The label of the item,
- The rectangle of the image containing the detected item,
- The confidence percentage of the detection, representing how sure the model is of his detection.

The pre-trained model consists of three parts: a configuration file, which contains a description of the net architecture, a weights file, which contains trained data, and finally, a label file, which contains the names of items that can be detected. The OpenCV library [4] is used to rebuild the model and to get detected images as a result from an input. As OpenCV uses its own data structure for images, data received from the camera is transformed to become compatible.

The architecture of our solution is presented in Fig. 6. The grayed-out area RGB camera input device is the same component as in the previous section (Fig. 3), where the input data are translated into RGB frames. Instead of sending them to the dialog, these frames are converted into the *RGB matrix* format and sent to the Input Chain Manager (the RGB matrix being a dedicated format of the OpenCV component). In this component, the RGB matrix is sent to both the Deep Neural Network (calibrated with the pre-trained yolov3 model), and to the *Image processing* component. They both provide the Dialog with the detected items and the annotated RGB matrix. The dialog sends these two sets of data to both the *Application Core* (for further processing) and the *Rendering Scene* to display feedback to the patient on the output screen.

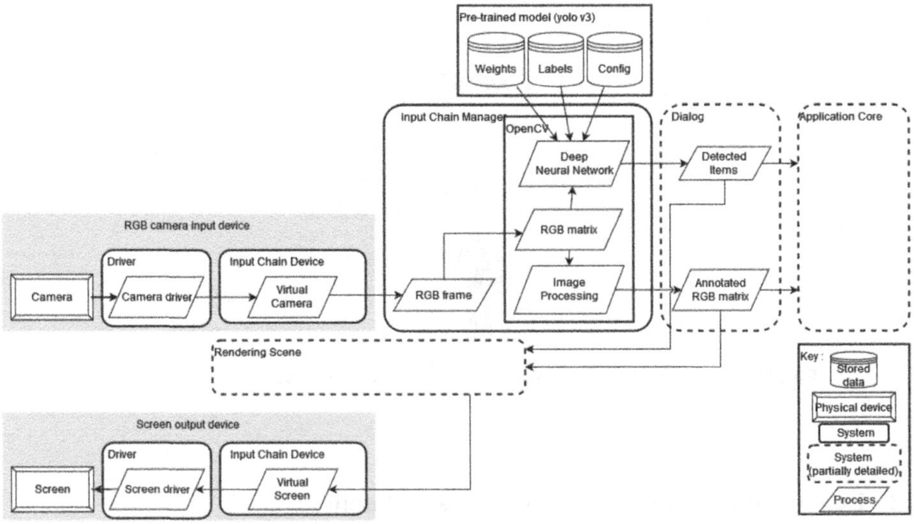

Fig. 6. Architecture of our AI-based solution

5 Redundant Computer-Vision-Based and Scale-Based Solution to Address System Dependability

5.1 Description of the Redundant Computer-Vision-Based and Scale-Based Solution

For the third setup, we implement an integrated computer-vision-based and scale-based solution. In that way, we apply the redundancy mechanism of dependability, to both ensure the detection of the right object in any case and enhance the fidelity of the training tasks with respect to the patient's environment. This leads to the setup pictured in Fig. 7 where the patient is in front of a table and a screen:

- Two scales. The first one, on the left, is filled with a set of three different dishes: a cup, a bowl, and a bottle. The second one, on the right, is empty.
- A Kinect v2 that allows the retrieval of frames of the patient's actions and filming the entire exercise for later analysis by the practitioner.
- A computer-vision-based software module that takes the frames as input and detects in real-time which object has been picked up and moved.
- A decision module that compares the results of object detection from the scales and the computer-based-vision module, and that decides which object is detected.
- A screen that displays which object should be moved from the left scale to the right one (the exercise can also be complicated by adding a time constraint: "move the cup from the left scale to the right scale in less than 10 s").

Object movement is monitored both through the analysis of the weight variation between the two scales and the computer-vision-based module. The decision module outputs the identified grabbed or dropped object. As for the previous setup, this data is used to give immediate feedback to the patient and to record analysis of the entire exercise session (subsequently used by the practitioner).

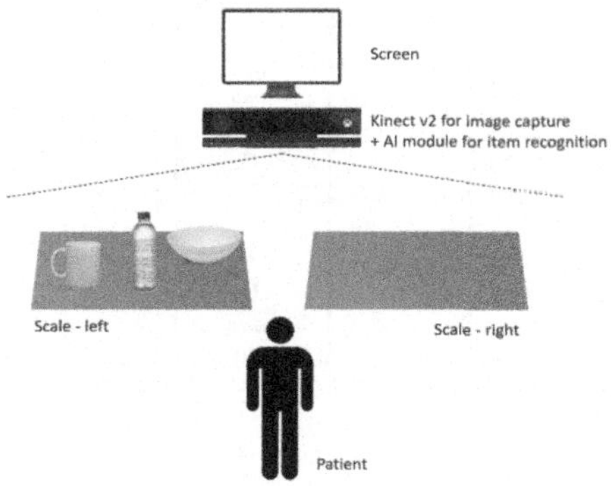

Fig. 7. Schematic view of the integrated computer-vision-based and scale-based setup

This setup is built to enhance both its dependability and the fidelity of the training task regarding the activities of daily living. It integrates the technologies and objects of the first two setups.

5.2 Engineering the Redundant Computer-Vision-Based and Scale-Based Solution

To engineer such a system, we need to embed both scale-based and AI-based components but also add a module that will compare both solutions and pick the best of the two.

Figure 8 presents the architecture of a redundant AI-based and scale-based system. The input chain manager now includes both the OpenCV module from Fig. 6 and the Scaling module from Fig. 3. It also includes a new module: the Decision module that contains the *Item comparator* process.

This item comparator is an intermediary process between the scale and AI modules that tries to mitigate potential ambiguity raised by the scale module. The priority is always put on the scale module results, and the results of the AI module are used as a backup if any ambiguity is raised. This comparison module behaves as follow:

- The scale module identifies only one item: there is no ambiguity, the result is this item.
- The scale module identifies several potential items: the comparator uses both this list of potential items and the list of items provided by OpenCV. When the comparator receives detected items from the AI module, it can yield one of three possible outcomes:

– Outcome 1: The AI module identifies exactly one item from the scale module list. The comparator selects this item to resolve the ambiguity.
– Outcome 2: The AI module detects multiple items from the scale module. In this case, the comparator chooses the item with the highest confidence percentage to eliminate ambiguity.

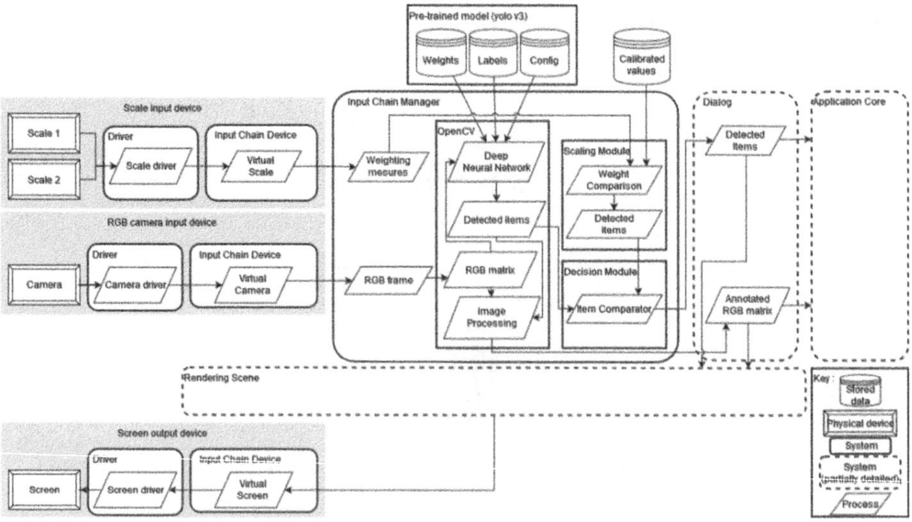

Fig. 8. Partial view of the architecture, with the addition of ML

- Outcome 3: The AI module detects no items from the scale module or identifies multiple items but with identical detection confidence. In this situation, the comparator does not resolve the ambiguity and raises a warning.

In summary, when faced with ambiguity from the scale module, the system will attempt to use AI results to resolve it. If resolution is not possible, the ambiguity will remain.

6 Discussion

Section 3, 4 and 5 present three setups using computer-based solutions for automating the practitioner tasks when the patient is exercising for post-stroke rehabilitation at home:

- A scale-based solution, designed to enhance the dependability of the solution.
- An AI-based solution, designed to enhance the fidelity of the training task regarding the activities of daily living
- A redundant AI-based and scale-based solution, taking advantages from the two other solutions, aiming at enhancing both the dependability of the solution and its fidelity regarding the activities of daily living.

The discussion focuses on the dependability of each solution, as a malfunction or a wrong design of these systems might lead to injure the patient, as stated in the introduction and Sect. 2.

To compare the reliability of these three solutions, we focus on their probability of failure in terms of object detection considering the weight of the objects, as the shape of the objects does not directly impact the quality of detection. Figure 9 presents a comparison of the probability of failures of the three solutions, with respect to the weight similarity of the objects chosen for the exercises.

When dealing with the first setup (the blue line), the use of scales ensures the correct detection if the weight of each object can be used as a unique identifier. The quality of this detection decreases as the probability of weight similarity between objects increases (0% similarity implies 100% detection, while 100% similarity leads to no detection (0%)). The probability of failure of the scale-based system is therefore inversely proportional to the weight similarity between the objects (a linear function from 0% of failure when all the objects have different weights to 100% when all objects weight the same: $f1(x) = x$ for x in [0, 1]).

For the second setup (the red line), according to [24], the yoloV3 achieves an average precision of 33% across all categories, which leads to a probability of failure of 67%(it is thus a constant function: $f2(x) = 0.67$ for x in [0, 1])

Finally, the redundant solution (the green line) integrates both solutions in a particular way where we first trust the scale system and where the non-detected objects are processed by the AI-solution. The base probability of failure of the scales is reduced by the probability of success (33%) of the AI detection ($f3(x) = x - 0.33x = 0.67x$ for x in [0, 1]).

The improvement of the quality of detection was foreseeable as the AI technique was used where the reliable technique fails, as an alternate. But the overall dependability

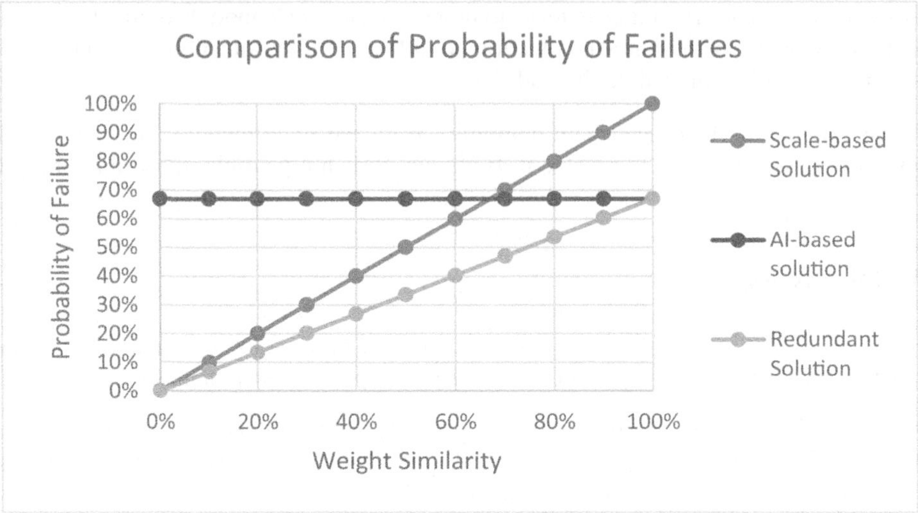

Fig. 9. Comparison of probability of failure for the three solutions

of this system does not allow its usage in any case: when a lot of objects have the same weight, the probability of failure remains high (10% of similarity leads to 6.7% of failure, instead of 10% without AI-technology).

7 Conclusion

This paper presents the basic building block for the careful introduction of AI technologies into an interactive system to improve its reliability and, consequently, the users' tasks support. Based on the simple idea that these unreliable technologies can supplement a conventional implementation by providing a less costly solution to a problem that might prove too costly, or even impossible to solve (due to implementation complexity).

To illustrate our approach, we use the domain of post-stroke rehabilitation interactive systems, where the cost of an error may result in damage to the patient. The three presented setups contribute to the same goal: to provide the patients with a software solution for their self-exercise sessions. The main difference between them is that when we introduce AI-technology as a complementary approach, the low dependability of this technology improves a little the overall system dependability.

But as stated in Sect. 6, this improvement remains limited (in our case, we move from a probability of failure of 10% with 10% of similarity to 6.7%).

When dealing with aeronautics, for instance, an objective would be to move from a 10^{-3} probability to 10^{-6} making it possible to allow a keyboard/mouse interactive system to handle critical consequences. But this 1000 factor seems impossible to reach with current practices in AI and requires investigating deeper in dependable architecture using AI-technologies.

References

1. Alecu, L., et al.: Can we reconcile safety objectives with machine learning performances? (2022). https://hal.science/hal-03765471
2. Barboni, E., Conversy, S., Navarre, D., Palanque, P.: Model-based engineering of widgets, user applications and servers compliant with ARINC 661 specification. In: Doherty, G., Blandford, A. (eds.) Interactive Systems. Design, Specification, and Verification. pp. 25–38. Springer, Berlin, Heidelberg (2007). https://doi.org/10.1007/978-3-540-69554-7_3
3. Bastide, R., Navarre, D., Palanque, P., Schyn, A., Dragicevic, P.: A model-based approach for real-time embedded multimodal systems in military air-crafts. In: Proceedings of the 6th International Conference on Multimodal Interfaces. pp. 243–250. ICMI 2004, Association for Computing Machinery, New York, NY, USA (Oct 2004). https://doi.org/10.1145/1027933.1027974
4. Bradski, G.: The OpenCV library. Dr. Dobb's J. Softw. Tools Prof. Programmer **25**(11), 120–123 (2000)
5. Campos, J.C., Fayollas, C., Harrison, M.D., Martinie, C., Masci, P., Palanque, P.: Supporting the analysis of safety critical user interfaces: an exploration of three formal tools. ACM Trans. Comput.-Hum. Interact. **27**(5), 35:1–35:48 (2020). https://doi.org/10.1145/3404199, https://dl.acm.org/doi/https://doi.org/10.1145/3404199
6. Carayon A., et al.: Engineering rehabilitation: blending two tool-supported approaches to close the loop from tasks-based rehabilitation to exercises and back again. Proc. ACM Hum. Comput. Interact. **7**(EICS), 177:1–177:23 (Jun 2023). https://doi.org/10.1145/3593229
7. Cronel, M., Dumas, B., Palanque, P., Canny, A.: MIODMIT: a generic architecture for dynamic multimodal interactive systems. In: 7th IFIP WG 13.2 International Working Conference, HCSE 2018, Sophia Antipolis, France, September 3–5, 2018, Revised Selected Papers. Human-Centered Software Engineering, pp. 109–129 (2019). https://doi.org/10.1007/978-3-030-05909-5_7
8. Forbrig, P., Bundea, A., Pedersen, A., Platz, T.: Digitalization of training tasks and specification of the behaviour of a social humanoid robot as coach. In: Human-Centered Software Engineering: 8th IFIP WG 13.2 International Working Conference, HCSE 2020, Eindhoven, The Netherlands, November 30 – December 2, 2020, Proceedings. pp. 45–57. Springer-Verlag, Berlin, Heidelberg (2020). https://doi.org/10.1007/978-3-030-64266-2_3
9. Genrich, H.J.: Predicate/transition nets. In: Brauer, W., Reisig, W., Rozenberg, G. (eds.) Petri Nets: Central Models and Their Properties. pp. 207–247. Springer, Berlin, Heidelberg (1987). https://doi.org/10.1007/978-3-540-47919-2_9
10. Hamon, A., Palanque, P., Silva, J.L., Deleris, Y., Barboni, E.: Formal description of multi-touch interactions. In: Proceedings of the 5th ACM SIGCHI symposium on Engineering interactive computing systems. pp. 207–216. EICS 2013, Association for Computing Machinery, New York, NY, USA (2013). https://doi.org/10.1145/2494603.2480311
11. RehaCom – Cognitive Therapy|HASOMED GmbH. https://hasomed.de/en/products/rehacom/
12. He, Y., Eguren, D., Luu, T.P., Contreras-Vidal, J.L.: Risk management and regulations for lower limb medical exoskeletons: a review. Med. Dev. (Auckland, N.Z.) **10**, 89–107 (2017). https://doi.org/10.2147/MDER.S107134
13. Ladry, J.F., Navarre, D., Palanque, p.: Formal description techniques to support the design, construction and evaluation of fusion engines for sure (safe, usable, reliable and evolvable) multimodal interfaces. In: Proceedings of the 2009 International Conference on Multimodal Interfaces, pp. 185–192. ICMI-MLMI 2009, Association for Computing Machinery, New York, NY, USA (2009). https://doi.org/10.1145/1647314.1647347

14. Lin, T.-Y., et al.: Microsoft coco: common objects in context. In: Computer Vision–ECCV 2014: 13th European Conference, Zurich, Switzerland, September 6–12, 2014, Proceedings, Part V 13. Springer International Publishing (2014)
15. Martinie, C., Palanque, P., Ragosta, M., Sujan, M.A., Navarre, D., Pasquini, A.: Understanding functional resonance through a federation of models: preliminary findings of an avionics case study. In: Bitsch, F., Guiochet, J., Kaâniche, M. (eds.) Computer Safety, Reliability, and Security, pp. 216–227. Springer, Berlin, Heidelberg (2013). https://doi.org/10.1007/978-3-642-40793-2_20
16. Navarre, D., Palanque, P., Basnyat, S.: A formal approach for user interaction reconfiguration of safety critical interactive systems. In: Harrison, M.D., Sujan, M.A. (eds.) Computer Safety, Reliability, and Security, pp. 373–386. Springer, Berlin, Heidelberg (2008). https://doi.org/10.1007/978-3-540-87698-4_31
17. Navarre, D. et al. 2009. ICOs: A model-based user interface description technique dedicated to interactive systems addressing usability, reliability and scalability. ACM Trans. Comput.-Hum. Interact. **16**(4), 18, 56 (2009). https://doi.org/10.1145/1614390.1614393
18. Noroozi, M., Shah, A.: Towards optimal foreign object debris detection in an airport environment. Expert Syst. Appl. **213**(PA) (2023). https://doi.org/10.1016/j.eswa.2022.118829, https://doi.org/10.1016/j.eswa.2022.118829
19. Palanque, P., Schyn, A.: A model-based approach for engineering multimodal interactive systems. In: Human-Computer Interaction INTERACT '03: IFIP TC13 International Conference on Human-Computer Interaction, 1st-5th September 2003, Zurich, Switzerland (2003)
20. Palmer, E.: Oops, it didn't arm. a case study of two automation surprises. In: Proceedings of the Eighth International Symposium on Aviation Psychology (1995)
21. Plata, A.M., Garrido, J.E., Valls, J.A.F., Penichet, V.M.R., Lozano, M.D.: Looking for an adequate monitoring mechanism for rehabilitation systems based on movement interaction. In: Proceedings of the XVII International Conference on Human Computer Interaction. Interacción '16, Association for Computing Machinery, New York, NY, USA (2016). https://doi.org/10.1145/2998626.2998657
22. Terven, J., Córdova-Esparza, D.M., Romero-González, J.A.: A comprehensive review of yolo architectures in computer vision: from YOLOv1 to YOLOv8 and YOLO-NAS. Mach. Learn. Knowl. Extract. **5**(4), 1680–1716 (2023). https://doi.org/10.3390/make5040083
23. Silva, J.L., Fayollas, C., Hamon, A., Palanque, P., Martiinie, C., Barboni, E.: Analysis of WIMP and post WIMP interactive systems based on formal specification. Electron. Commun. EASST **69** (2014). https://doi.org/10.14279/tuj.eceasst.69.967
24. Terven, J., et al.: A comprehensive review of YOLO architectures in computer vision: from YOLOv1 to YOLOv8 and YOLO-NAS. Mach. Learn. Knowl. Extract. **5**(4), 1680–1716 (2023). https://doi.org/10.3390/make5040083
25. Weiss, T., et al.: Deafferentation of the affected arm: a method to improve rehabilitation? Stroke **42**(5), 1363–1370 (2011). https://doi.org/10.1161/STROKEAHA.110.601138
26. World Stroke Organization. 2022. Global Stroke Fact Sheet 2022. https://www.worldstroke.org/assets/downloads/WSO_Global_Stroke_Fact_Sheet.pdf. Accessed February 2023

Integrating AIs With Body Tracking Technology for Human Behaviour Analysis: Challenges and Opportunities

Adrien Coppens(✉) and Valérie Maquil

Luxembourg Institute of Science and Technology, Esch-sur-Alzette, Luxembourg
adrien.coppens@list.lu

Abstract. The automated analysis of human behaviour provides many opportunities for the creation of interactive systems and the post-experiment investigations for user studies. Commodity depth cameras offer reasonable body tracking accuracy at a low price point, without the need for users to wear or hold any extra equipment. The resulting systems typically perform body tracking through a dedicated machine learning model, but they can be enhanced with additional AI components providing extra capabilities. This leads to opportunities but also challenges, for example regarding the orchestration of such AI components and the engineering of the resulting tracking pipeline. In this paper, we discuss these elements, based on our experience with the creation of a remote collaboration system across distant wall-sized displays, that we built using existing and readily available building blocks, including AI-based recognition models.

Keywords: Human Behaviour · AI Integration · Body Tracking · Depth Camera

1 Introduction

Due to their large size and high resolution, Wall-Sized Displays (WSDs) are frequently utilised for collaborative group work, especially for activities that require participants to view various data sources and visualisations at the same time [20,27]. In a shared space, discussions among co-workers often incorporate physical gestures and other forms of non-verbal communication. This dynamic enables them to effectively maintain awareness of one another's actions and coordinate their efforts efficiently during collaborative tasks.

In the context of the ReSurf project, we look at supporting remote collaboration across distant wall-sized displays. To do so, it is necessary to convey workspace awareness information [17] on what local collaborators are doing to the remote site, to make up for the loss of natural awareness cues that collocated collaborators would gather [29]. We therefore need to track the behaviour of local users, so that the corresponding information may be transmitted remotely

L. Zaina et al. (Eds.): EICS 2024, LNCS 15518, pp. 43–54, 2025.
https://doi.org/10.1007/978-3-031-91760-8_4

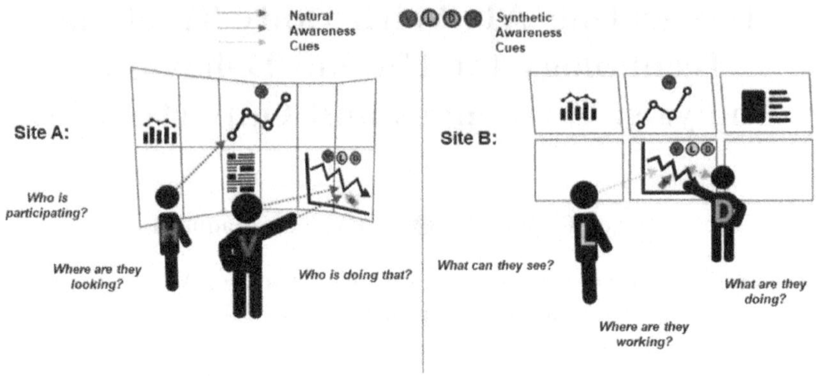

Fig. 1. Workspace awareness for remote collaboration across Wall-Sized Displays. Reproduced from Anastasiou et al. [2].

through what we then refer to as synthetic awareness cues. This is illustrated through Fig. 1.

Based on pilot observations and on comments collected during the early phases of the project, we opted to rely on the Azure Kinect sensor[1] to drive the behaviour tracking system. To augment the resulting tracking capabilities with finer-grained gestures without introducing additional hardware devices, we wanted to explore the usage of image-based hand gesture recognition AI models. Similarly, in order to consistently assign authors to the information we transmit to the remote site, we explored image-based facial recognition.

This paper presents related work then covers some of the technical challenges we had to face, how we engineered our tracking pipeline based on the integration and orchestration of AI components, then discusses some remaining unexplored opportunities.

2 Related Work

2.1 Behaviour Analysis and Action Recognition

Research has extensively explored interaction methods beyond the conventional mouse and keyboard, leading to interfaces that are sometimes termed post-WIMP [41]. When it comes to WSDs, the need for alternative interfaces has become increasingly pressing, especially in order to limit the need for large mouse movements.

Touch-based systems are particularly common for WSDs, but that modality often requires physical navigation, which can be limiting in certain scenarios. As a result, other solutions enabling interaction at a distance have been developed, such as mid-air pointing technologies [31].

[1] https://learn.microsoft.com/azure/kinect-dk/.

To track these distant interactions, researchers have proposed various devices and techniques, including body-worn or hand-held objects. We refer to these as intrusive options because of the necessary extra equipment. Common examples are body suits for motion capture [22], telepointers (also known as wands [14] or pens [15]) used to perform pointing through raycasting [21].

While these systems tend to offer greater precision and reliability, they are often cumbersome, requiring an initial setup step and potentially altering user behavior by providing a "tool" for interaction.

For this reason, we focus on non-intrusive technologies such as cameras. Standard RGB cameras can estimate body postures from two-dimensional images, enabling some level of interactivity. A notable library for this purpose is OpenPose [7], which tracks full body movements, including hands and faces specifically [37].

However, standard cameras struggle with accurately inferring depth and distance from two-dimensional images, limiting their tracking capabilities. Although attempts have been made to use multiple cameras to improve depth estimation [9], most non-intrusive tracking systems rely on depth cameras (RGB-D), which incorporate depth sensors alongside traditional RGB imaging. The Kinect family of depth cameras has reached wide usage in this context and has been extensively explored in prior research, due to its affordability and its reasonable performance. These sensors have been used for various applications, including video playback control [45] and social network feed navigation [46]. Some studies have focused on 3D interaction via two-dimensional virtual screens on which they may draw [24], while others have focused on public displays, addressing how to engage passers-by [38].

Researchers have also explored proximity-aware interactions [12], where the system displays information or activates input mechanisms [48] based on how far the user stands from the large display. Furthermore, tracking has been combined with other modalities, such as speech and gaze input, to create seamless interaction experiences. The "Put-That-There" metaphor [6] is a notable example of this, enabling the creation and manipulation of objects through a combination of pointing and speech.

While the studies mentioned cover various aspects of tracking for WSDs, focusing on local user interactions, there has been limited exploration of using such technologies to convey awareness information to a remote WSD.

2.2 Awareness Transmission Across WSDs

Some of the early approaches to transmit awareness information on WSDs aimed to create a sense of co-presence through full-screen video feeds [19,36,39], similarly to videoconferencing solutions. However, such methods typically consume the entire display space, hindering data visualization and interaction.

Attempts to overcome this limitation include segmenting video feeds around users [25,26] or adjusting their transparency [13], but these solutions struggle to scale effectively with additional participants and data elements.

The placement of smaller video feeds has also been explored and this option's capability to convey deictic references to remote participants has been evaluated [3]. However, such an approach relies on a specific known setup (display, camera, and feed placements).

Similarly to the cursors found in desktop-based collaborative systems, WSD-based solutions may rely on pointers to convey pointing gesture targets. These pointers should visually be distinct, to link each occurrence with its author's identity.

Robust user differentiation is crucial for assigning individual pointers and maintaining consistency even when users temporarily leave the tracking range. Previous methods using Kinect sensors placed behind users [43,47] faced challenges with accurate action attribution and gesture recognition.

Systems like YouTouch [47] and VTouch [8] further worked on user identification through colour histograms and biometric measurements but remained sensitive to clothing changes, limiting long-term user recognition.

Advances in deep learning-based face recognition offer a promising solution. This technology can potentially overcome the limitations of previous approaches by enabling accurate and persistent user identification regardless of clothing variations. Integrating face recognition into the system could significantly enhance both usability and accuracy.

3 Challenges

Before diving into engineering aspects regarding the development of our tracking pipeline and its connection to AI models performing gestural and facial recognition, we briefly describe the challenges we encountered in constructing our RGB-D camera-based system.

3.1 Scene Calibration

In order to transmit pointing and gazing cues, we need to retrieve the corresponding information using tracking technologies (in our case through RGB-D cameras). However, tracking devices will typically output data in their own coordinate system. In order to convert that data to screen-space coordinates, it is necessary to obtain a sufficiently accurate representation of the "scene setup" i.e. the dimensions and positions of the display with regards to the input camera. This for instance allows pointing and gazing information gathered from the tracking system to turn into pointing and gazing targets on screen.

The acquisition of such knowledge in itself typically involves a calibration step where human input is required. This may involve the placement of markers at known locations so that they may be recognised by cameras [40], or pointing-based solutions where users aim at keypoints (e.g. screen corners) [30]. These solutions might not always be particularly accurate, and some have instead opted to rely on fully manual measurements [16], which are themselves time-consuming.

To reduce the burden on the human calibrator but capitalise on the precise screen setup measurements we had access to (through an existing blueprint), we opted for an approach relying on adjustments based on point cloud streaming. We in fact stream the point cloud data coming from the camera to a Unity application that displays it over a virtual version of the scene setup, using precise screen measurements but approximate initial camera placement.

Figure 2 provides an example of the alignment process in that application. By adjusting the virtual camera's position and orientation so that the streamed point cloud matches the environment and the virtual screens are aligned, the precise placement of the camera in relation to the screens can be obtained.

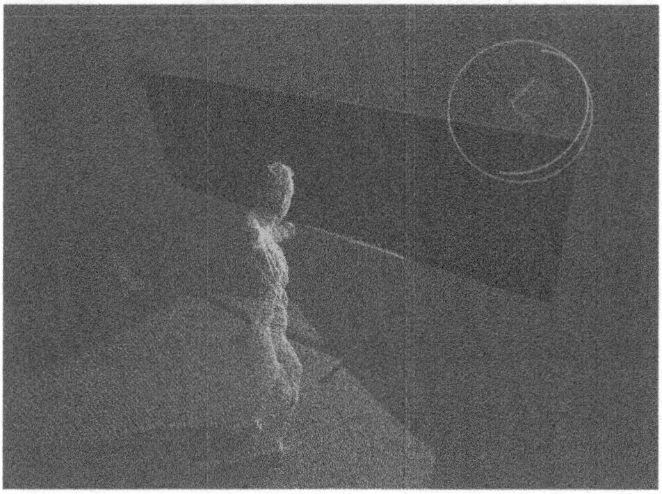

Fig. 2. Scene calibration application in Unity, with two adjacent (dark blue) virtual screens whose dimensions correspond to their physical counterparts, a virtual camera, and a (cyan) point cloud created from the target camera's depth data. The placement of the camera can be adjusted so that the point cloud is aligned with the virtual screens so as to obtain a proper calibration matrix. (Color figure online)

This approach works rather well and is sufficiently convenient for our case but scene calibration procedures based on (semi-)automated approaches using point cloud extraction [32] algorithms and possibly AI-based object recognition should be explored to make the process further easier while at least preserving the accuracy of the end result.

3.2 Data Fusion

A second challenging aspect relates to occlusion issues that tracking devices typically are subject to, as objects and users might get in the way and prevent the acquisition of suitable data for thereby temporarily "hidden" users. To alleviate that issue, we opted to rely on multiple cameras, as a person occluded from one camera might be visible for another one, as illustrated in Fig. 3. This also increases the tracking range of the system as a whole.

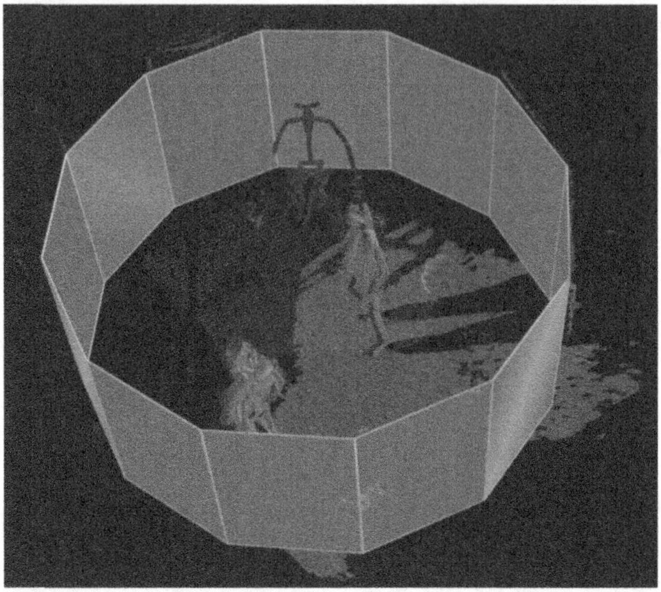

Fig. 3. Point clouds and body tracking data from two cameras. The "blue camera" can see all three persons whereas the "orange camera" can only see two of them (the third person is currently occluded from that camera). (Color figure online)

However, combining data from multiple sensor requires the gathering of multi-sensor calibration information, typically through transformation matrices (one per additional camera, with each matrix converting data from its camera to the main camera i.e. the one whose position with regards to the screens is known). The approaches listed for the scene calibration step could be used to perform the multi-sensor calibration, by repeating the process for each sensor and using the scene calibration as the common frame of reference. However, when cameras are placed in the same room, it is also possible to take advantage of common tracking areas. Indeed, if only one person is present in the room and two cameras are tracking that person, then the person can be used as a reference to determine the transformation matrix between the two cameras.

In an attempt to obtain more accurate calibration results, we have opted to additionally match the point clouds generated by these cameras, through the Iterative Closest Point [42] algorithm and objects placed in the common tracking area (to generate "common" points to be matched). The resulting transformation matrix (between the point clouds) is also the transformation between the cameras.

Once obtained, such a transformation matrix can be used to convert body tracking data from one sensor's coordinate system to that of another sensor. There is however a chance that only one sensor see a given person (e.g. the blue skeleton on top of Fig. 3), and it may sometimes be difficult to identify which skeletons from different sensors belong to the same person. This leads to skeleton matching and merging problems as discussed in a separate paper [11].

4 Engineering an AI-Based Tracking Pipeline

In order to build our tracking pipeline and combine the functionality of the body tracking, hand gesture recognition, and face recognition AIs, we rely on \psi [4]. That framework facilitates the integration of AI components into multimodal systems by providing tools for managing, processing and combining streams of temporal data. It also greatly eases the development and debugging processes as well as the analysis of recorded data, by providing visualisation and data replaying tools (including \psi Studio shown in Fig. 4).

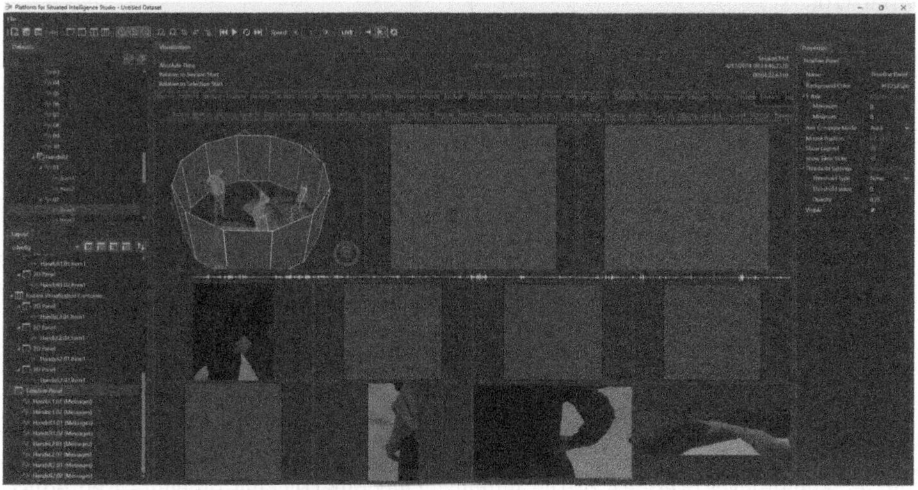

Fig. 4. The graphical user interface of \psi Studio, with an example layout displaying some of the data handled or created by our tracking pipeline.

As an example, two Azure Kinect sensors (with overlapping fields of view) cannot capture data at the same time; otherwise they will interfere with each other. This is solved by attributing different "time slots" to each sensor, which is handled both by the Azure Kinect SDK[2] and \psi. However, the resulting data is therefore obviously captured at different times, and \psi provides us with convenient interpolation features to counterbalance that issue, which helps

[2] https://github.com/microsoft/Azure-Kinect-Sensor-SDK.

improve the data fusion process through which a single stream of merged bodies is produced (for use by the rest of the pipeline).

The overall idea and structure of the tracking pipeline is that the data coming from the Azure Kinect sensor(s), including the aforementioned body tracking information, drives the system. Based on a known screen placement (relative to the camera), this generates pointing and gazing target points in screen-space coordinates.

In addition to that, the same camera additionally provides color images. By combining the body tracking data and the camera's own intrinsics parameters, we can crop the color images around specific body parts (as seen in the bottom part of Fig. 4). This allow us to send the appropriate images to the AI components, respectively specialised in hand gesture and face recognition. This is done via messages in the MessagePack[3] format, transmitted via the ZeroMQ [18] protocol. The specialised recognition components can then feed their results back to the tracking pipeline, which aggregates the combined information to provide user-attributed behaviour information that includes pointing targets, gaze direction and hand gestures. Figure 5 presents a high-level overview of how that pipeline works. More details are available in the corresponding technical paper [10].

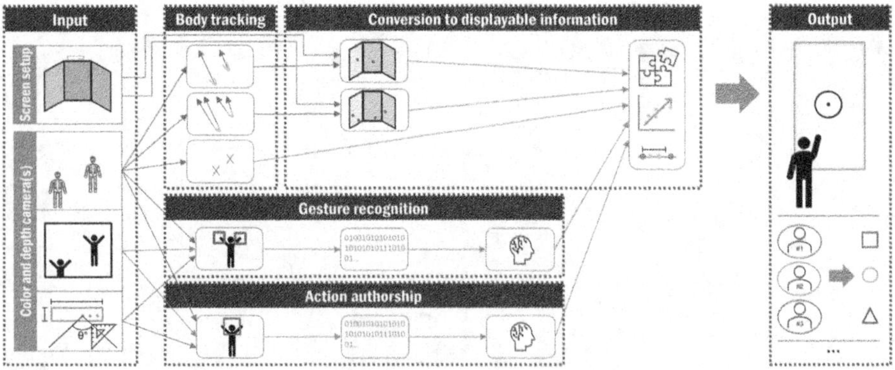

Fig. 5. A high-level overview of the human behaviour tracking pipeline. Reproduced from Coppens et al. [10].

5 Opportunities for Embedding Additional AIs

Outside of the opportunities linked to the enhancement and facilitation of the aforementioned scene and multi-camera calibration procedures, there are many opportunities for extending human behaviour analysis capabilities with other AI models.

[3] https://msgpack.org/.

Using a similar approach to the one we described here, one could in fact send the face crops to AI models trained to output information regarding gender [35], age [1], or emotions [28].

Likewise, finer or different gestures could be supported through the integration of specialised AI models, and the presence of specific objects on or around users could be detected with dedicated AIs [34].

Apart from image-based recognition models, automated human behaviour analysis systems may benefit from speech recognition AIs to transcribe what users are saying. Ideally, such transcriptions should be put in relation to precise timing information and attributed to specific speakers (e.g. to analyse turn-taking [44]), through speaker diarisation AIs [33].

Interactive systems (possibly built on top of human behaviour analysis systems) may themselves benefit from speech synthesis AIs [23] to "talk" to system users. Combined with the recent advances in Large Language Models (LLMs) [49] that could be running in the background, these speech-based interfaces have the potential to produce compelling experiences. For example, Bohus et al. recently demonstrated [5] the potential of combining scene understanding and object recognition AIs with LLMs and speech-based interaction for physical task assistance with a Hololens 2 headset[4].

We believe our tracking pipeline is a good basis to explore these kinds of opportunities for interactive systems based on unobtrusive human behaviour analysis in a room-scale context. It can in fact adapt to hardware changes and software advances (e.g. replacement of an AI component by a better performing one) and can be extended to include additional AI models and capabilities.

Acknowledgments. Authors would like to thank the Luxembourg National Research Fund (FNR) for funding this research work under the FNR CORE ReSurf project (Grant nr C21/IS/15883550).

Disclosure of Interests. The authors have no competing interests to declare that are relevant to the content of this article.

References

1. Agbo-Ajala, O., Viriri, S.: Deep learning approach for facial age classification: a survey of the state-of-the-art. Artif. Intell. Rev. **54**(1), 179–213 (2021)
2. Anastasiou, D., Coppens, A., Maquil, V.: Gesture combinations during collaborative decision-making at wall displays. i-com (0) (2024)
3. Avellino, I., Fleury, C., Beaudouin-Lafon, M.: Accuracy of deictic gestures to support telepresence on wall-sized displays. In: Proceedings of the 33rd Annual ACM Conference on Human Factors in Computing Systems, pp. 2393–2396 (2015). https://doi.org/10.1145/2702123.2702448
4. Bohus, D., et al.: Platform for situated intelligence (2021)

[4] https://www.microsoft.com/hololens.

5. Bohus, D., Andrist, S., Saw, N., Paradiso, A., Chakraborty, I., Rad, M.: Sigma: an open-source interactive system for mixed-reality task assistance research - extended abstract. In: 2024 IEEE Conference on Virtual Reality and 3D User Interfaces Abstracts and Workshops (VRW). IEEE (2024)
6. Bolt, R.A.: Put-that-there voice and gesture at the graphics interface. In: Proceedings of the 7th Annual Conference on Computer Graphics and Interactive Techniques, pp. 262–270 (1980). https://doi.org/10.1145/800250.807503
7. Cao, Z., Hidalgo, G., Simon, T., Wei, S.E., Sheikh, Y.: Openpose: realtime multi-person 2D pose estimation using part affinity fields. IEEE Trans. Pattern Anal. Mach. Intell. (2019). https://doi.org/10.1109/TPAMI.2019.2929257
8. Chen, Y., Liu, Z., Chou, P., Zhang, Z.: VTouch: vision-enhanced interaction for large touch displays. In: 2015 IEEE International Conference on Multimedia and Expo (ICME), pp. 1–6. IEEE (2015). https://doi.org/10.1109/ICME.2015.7177390
9. Chu, C.W., Nevatia, R.: Real-time 3D body pose tracking from multiple 2D images. In: Articulated Motion and Deformable Objects, pp. 42–52. Springer (2008). https://doi.org/10.1007/978-3-540-70517-8_5
10. Coppens, A., Hermen, J., Schwartz, L., Moll, C., Maquil, V.: Supporting mixed-presence awareness across wall-sized displays using a tracking pipeline based on depth cameras. Proc. ACM Hum.-Comput. Interact. **8**(EICS) (2024). https://doi.org/10.1145/3664634
11. Coppens, A., Maquil, V.: Skeletal data matching and merging from multiple RGB-D sensors for room-scale human behaviour tracking. In: International Conference on Cooperative Design, Visualization and Engineering, pp. 289–298. Springer (2024). https://doi.org/10.1007/978-3-031-71315-6_30
12. Dostal, J., Hinrichs, U., Kristensson, P.O., Quigley, A.: Spidereyes: designing attention-and proximity-aware collaborative interfaces for wall-sized displays. In: Proceedings of the 19th International Conference on Intelligent User Interfaces, pp. 143–152 (2014). https://doi.org/10.1145/2557500.2557541
13. Edelmann, J., Mock, P., Schilling, A., Gerjets, P.: Preserving non-verbal features of face-to-face communication for remote collaboration, booktitle=cooperative design, visualization, and engineering, pp. 27–34. Springer Berlin Heidelberg (2013). https://doi.org/10.1007/978-3-642-40840-3_4
14. Febretti, A., et al.: Cave2: a hybrid reality environment for immersive simulation and information analysis. In: The Engineering Reality of Virtual Reality 2013, vol. 8649, pp. 9–20. SPIE (2013). https://doi.org/10.1117/12.2005484
15. Fraser, M., McCarthy, M.R., Shaukat, M., Smith, P.: Seconds matter: improving distributed coordination bytracking and visualizing display trajectories. In: Proceedings of the SIGCHI conference on Human Factors in Computing Systems, pp. 1303–1312 (2007). https://doi.org/10.1145/1240624.1240822
16. Gervais, R., Frey, J., Hachet, M.: Pointing in spatial augmented reality from 2D Pointing devices. In: Abascal, J., Barbosa, S., Fetter, M., Gross, T., Palanque, P., Winckler, M. (eds.) INTERACT 2015. LNCS, vol. 9299, pp. 381–389. Springer, Cham (2015). https://doi.org/10.1007/978-3-319-22723-8_30
17. Gutwin, C., Greenberg, S.: A descriptive framework of workspace awareness for real-time groupware. Comput. Support. Coop. Work (CSCW) **11**, 411–446 (2002)
18. Hintjens, P., Hurton, M., Barber, I.: ZeroMQ message transport protocol. RFC 23 (2020). https://doi.org/10.17487/RFC9405, https://rfc.zeromq.org/spec/23/
19. Ishii, H., Kobayashi, M.: ClearBoard: a seamless medium for shared drawing and conversation with eye contact. In: Proceedings of the SIGCHI Conference on Human Factors in Computing Systems, pp. 525–532 (1992).https://doi.org/10.1145/142750.142977

20. Jakobsen, M.R., Hornbæk, K.: Up close and personal: collaborative work on a high-resolution multitouch wall display. ACM Trans. Comput. Hum. Interact. (TOCHI) **21**(2), 1–34 (2014). https://doi.org/10.1145/2576099
21. Jota, R., Nacenta, M.A., Jorge, J.A., Carpendale, S., Greenberg, S.: A comparison of ray pointing techniques for very large displays. In: Graphics Interface, vol. 2010, pp. 269–276 (2010). https://doi.org/10.5555/1839214.1839261
22. Kim, D., Kwon, J., Han, S., Park, Y.L., Jo, S.: Deep full-body motion network for a soft wearable motion sensing suit. IEEE/ASME Trans. Mechatron. **24**(1), 56–66 (2018). https://doi.org/10.1109/TMECH.2018.2874647
23. Kong, J., Kim, J., Bae, J.: HiFi-GAN: Generative adversarial networks for efficient and high fidelity speech synthesis. Adv. Neural. Inf. Process. Syst. **33**, 17022–17033 (2020)
24. Kristensson, P.O., Nicholson, T., Quigley, A.: Continuous recognition of one-handed and two-handed gestures using 3D full-body motion tracking sensors. In: Proceedings of the 2012 ACM International Conference on Intelligent User Interfaces, pp. 89–92 (2012). https://doi.org/10.1145/2166966.2166983
25. Kuechler, M., Kunz, A.M.: Collaboard: a remote collaboration groupware device featuring an embodiment-enriched shared workspace. In: Proceedings of the 2010 ACM International Conference on Supporting Group Work, pp. 211–214 (2010). https://doi.org/10.1145/1880071.1880107
26. Kunz, A., Nescher, T., Küchler, M.: Collaboard: a novel interactive electronic whiteboard for remote collaboration with people on content. In: 2010 International Conference on Cyberworlds, pp. 430–437 (2010).https://doi.org/10.1109/CW.2010.17
27. Langner, R., Kister, U., Dachselt, R.: Multiple coordinated views at large displays for multiple users: Empirical findings on user behavior, movements, and distances. IEEE Trans. Visual Comput. Graph. **25**(1), 608–618 (2019). https://doi.org/10.1109/TVCG.2018.2865235
28. Li, J., Jin, K., Zhou, D., Kubota, N., Ju, Z.: Attention mechanism-based CNN for facial expression recognition. Neurocomputing **411**, 340–350 (2020)
29. Maquil, V., Anastasiou, D., Afkari, H., Coppens, A., Hermen, J., Schwartz, L.: Establishing awareness through pointing gestures during collaborative decision-making in a wall-display environment. In: Extended Abstracts of the 2023 CHI Conference on Human Factors in Computing Systems, pp. 1–7 (2023).https://doi.org/10.1145/3544549.3585830
30. Mills, S.: Pointing-based calibration of a pointing interface for public displays. In: 2021 36th International Conference on Image and Vision Computing New Zealand (IVCNZ).,pp. 1–6. IEEE (2021)
31. Nancel, M., Pietriga, E., Chapuis, O., Beaudouin-Lafon, M.: Mid-air pointing on ultra-walls. ACM Trans. Comput. Hum. Interact. (TOCHI) **22**(5), 1–62 (2015). https://doi.org/10.1145/2766448
32. Nguyen, H.H., Kim, J., Lee, Y., Ahmed, N., Lee, S.: Accurate and fast extraction of planar surface patches from 3D point cloud. In: Proceedings of the 7th International Conference on Ubiquitous Information Management and Communication, p. 1–8 (2013)
33. Park, T.J., Kanda, N., Dimitriadis, D., Han, K.J., Watanabe, S., Narayanan, S.: A review of speaker diarization: recent advances with deep learning. Comput. Speech Lang. **72**, 101317 (2022)
34. Rani, S., Lakhwani, K., Kumar, S.: Three dimensional objects recognition and pattern recognition technique; related challenges: a review. Multimedia Tools Appl. **81**(12), 17303–17346 (2022)

35. Rouhsedaghat, M., Wang, Y., Ge, X., Hu, S., You, S., Kuo, C.-C.J.: FaceHop: a light-weight low-resolution face gender classification method. In: Del Bimbo, A., et al. (eds.) ICPR 2021. LNCS, vol. 12668, pp. 169–183. Springer, Cham (2021). https://doi.org/10.1007/978-3-030-68793-9_12
36. Schremmer, C., Krumm-Heller, A., Vernik, R., Epps, J.: design discussion of the [braccetto] research platform: supporting distributed intensely collaborating creative teams of teams. In: Jacko, J.A. (ed.) HCI 2007. LNCS, vol. 4553, pp. 722–734. Springer, Heidelberg (2007). https://doi.org/10.1007/978-3-540-73111-5_81
37. Simon, T., Joo, H., Matthews, I., Sheikh, Y.: Hand keypoint detection in single images using multiview bootstrapping. In: IEEE Conference on Computer Vision and Pattern Recognition (CVPR) (2017)
38. Sousa, T., Cardoso, I., Parracho, J., Dias, P., Sousa Santos, B.: DETI-interact: interaction with large displays in public spaces using the kinect. In: Streitz, N., Markopoulos, P. (eds.) DAPI 2014. LNCS, vol. 8530, pp. 196–206. Springer, Cham (2014). https://doi.org/10.1007/978-3-319-07788-8_19
39. Tang, J.C., Minneman, S.: Videowhiteboard: video shadows to support remote collaboration. In: Proceedings of the SIGCHI Conference on Human Factors in Computing Systems,pp. 315–322 (199https://doi.org/10.1145/108844.108932
40. Tuceryan, M., et al.: Calibration requirements and procedures for a monitor-based augmented reality system. IEEE Trans. Visual Comput. Graph. **1**(3), 255–273 (1995)
41. Van Dam, A.: Post-wimp user interfaces. Commun. ACM **40**(2), 63–67 (1997). https://doi.org/10.1145/253671.253708
42. Wang, F., Zhao, Z.: A survey of iterative closest point algorithm. In: 2017 Chinese Automation Congress (CAC),pp. 4395–4399. IEEE (2017)
43. Wiechers, M., Nolte, A., Ksoll, M., Herrmann, T., Kienle, A.: User tracking for collaboration on interactive wall-sized displays. In: Mensch and Uter, pp 191–200 (2013). Iurlhttps://doi.org/10.1524/9783486781229
44. Wiemann, J.M., Knapp, M.L.: Turn-taking in conversations. Communication theory, p. 226–245 (2017)
45. Wittorf, M.L., Jakobsen, M.R.: Eliciting mid-air gestures for wall-display interaction. In: Proceedings of the 9th Nordic Conference on Human-Computer Interaction,pp. 1–4 (2016). Iurlhttps://doi.org/10.1145/2971485.2971503
46. Yoo, S., Parker, C., Kay, J., Tomitsch, M.: To dwell or not to dwell: an evaluation of mid-air gestures for large information displays. In: Proceedings of the Annual Meeting of the Australian Special Interest Group for Computer Human Interaction. pp. 187–191 (2015).https://doi.org/10.1145/2838739.2838819
47. von Zadow, U., Reipschläger, P., Bösel, D., Sellent, A., Dachselt, R.: Youtouch! low-cost user identification at an interactive display wall. In: Proceedings of the International Working Conference on Advanced Visual Interfaces, pp. 144–151 (2016). https://doi.org/10.1145/2909132.2909258
48. Zhai, Y., Zhao, G., Alatalo, T., Heikkilä, J., Ojala, T., Huang, X.: Gesture interaction for wall-sized touchscreen display. In: Proceedings of the 2013 ACM Conference on Pervasive and Ubiquitous Computing Adjunct Publication, pp. 175–178 (2013). https://doi.org/10.1145/2494091.2494148
49. Zhao, W.X., et al.: A survey of large language models. arXiv preprint arXiv:2303.18223 (2023)

AI-Spectra: A Visual Dashboard for Model Multiplicity to Enhance Informed and Transparent Decision-Making

Gilles Eerlings(✉), Sebe Vanbrabant, Jori Liesenborgs, Gustavo Rovelo Ruiz, Davy Vanacken, and Kris Luyten

Hasselt University - Flanders Make, Digital Future Lab, Diepenbeek, Belgium
{gilles.eerlings,sebe.vanbrabant,jori.liesenborgs,gustavo.roveloruiz, davy.vanacken,kris.luyten}@uhasselt.be

Abstract. We present an approach, AI-Spectra, to leverage model multiplicity for interactive systems. Model multiplicity means using slightly different AI models yielding equally valid outcomes or predictions for the same task, thus relying on many simultaneous "expert advisors" that can have different opinions. Dealing with multiple AI models that generate potentially divergent results for the same task is challenging for users to deal with. It helps users understand and identify AI models are not always correct and might differ, but it can also result in an information overload when being confronted with multiple results instead of one. AI-Spectra leverages model multiplicity by using a visual dashboard designed for conveying what AI models generate which results while minimizing the cognitive effort to detect consensus among models and what type of models might have different opinions. We use a custom adaptation of Chernoff faces for AI-Spectra; Chernoff Bots. This visualization technique lets users quickly interpret complex, multivariate model configurations and compare predictions across multiple models. Our design is informed by building on established Human-AI Interaction guidelines and well know practices in information visualization. We validated our approach through a series of experiments training a wide variation of models with the MNIST dataset to perform number recognition. Our work contributes to the growing discourse on making AI systems more transparent, trustworthy, and effective through the strategic use of multiple models.

1 Introduction

Integrating artificial intelligence (AI) models into interactive software systems is becoming increasingly common across sectors such as healthcare and customer service. Typically, a single AI model is embedded within an interactive system,

G. Eerlings and S. Vanbrabant—Equal contribution.

L. Zaina et al. (Eds.): EICS 2024, LNCS 15518, pp. 55–73, 2025.
https://doi.org/10.1007/978-3-031-91760-8_5

requiring careful design to ensure accessibility and usability for end users. Relying on a single model might quickly lead to a miscalibration in trust, as there is a limited basis for comparison and often a low degree of transparency due to the lack of explanations. This lack of trust and transparency can be problematic, as both are crucial aspects of effective human-AI collaboration [5,13,14,34].

To alleviate these issues relating to trust and transparency, we use a '*many simultaneous expert advisors*' approach in which multiple AI models, each considered an expert advisor, are used simultaneously within an interactive system to offer users more balanced and well-substantiated advice. There are often multiple variations of AI models trained for the same task that achieve similar performance during the validation. This phenomenon, also known as *model multiplicity* (MM) [7], can be of great value to correct *over- and undertrust* in an AI system. Having a limited understanding of AI can be frustrating, causing users to lose trust [4,28]. More trust, however, is not always better, since users might trust the system even when it is not behaving as intended [39]. We aim to move away from a single AI model, thus one single output, and evolve toward multiple AI models that provide multiple possible outputs and the context on which their output is based.

The *many simultaneous expert advisors*, or model multiplicity, approach is particularly valuable for critical decision support systems, such as those used in medical diagnostics, financial forecasting, and urban planning. In the healthcare sector, for instance, employing multiple AI models allows for a more comprehensive analysis of patient data by cross-verifying diagnoses, thereby reducing the risk of error. This not only mitigates the risks associated with over-reliance on a single model but also provides a platform for continuous learning and improvement of AI systems. Rather than focusing on making the individual models transparent and interpretable [25,32], we increase trust and transparency by informing users about the differences between multiple expert advisors. Expert advisors are often black box models that are known to perform well for specific complex problems, but they are very hard to nearly impossible to explain to end users, however. Analyzing the differences between multiple similar models and their respective outputs can potentially lead to the refinement of the algorithms that are used, improvement of accuracy and reliability, and the uncovering of problematic patterns in the training dataset. This approach enhances transparency and builds trust among users by ensuring that decisions are thoroughly considered and vetted through multiple expert advisors (i.e., the various models).

We introduce AI-Spectra; a process and visual dashboard to leverage model multiplicity to enhance informed and transparent decision-making. We focus on classifier models, often driven by neural networks and deep learning. This is particularly interesting since these models are considered black box models that behave in ways that are hard or even impossible to explain. Our contribution is threefold:

(1) We define *a process for preparing, training and identifying suitable sets of AI models* for effective model multiplicity.

(2) We design *a compact and easy-to-recognize visual representation that conveys the hyperparameters, properties and background of an AI model* to the user. For this purpose, we leverage the Chernoff faces technique [11,18] and tailor it to AI models.
(3) We present a *visual dashboard that can present the distribution of answers across multiple models* in relationship to the varying backgrounds and properties of these models, like the overview depicted in Fig. 3.

We validate AI-Spectra with classifier models that are trained on the MNIST dataset, consisting of handwritten digits for training for number recognition. The visual dashboard of AI-Spectra is depicted in Fig. 3 as a set of Chernoff faces presented as a bar chart. Each bar represent a specific prediction for the MNIST dataset (10 possible digits that can be recognized), and each Chernoff bot in the bar represents an AI model that supports that specific prediction. This makes it easy to compare the number of models that support a prediction, as well as to recognize to what predictions both outlier as well as comparable models contribute.

2 Related Work

2.1 Model Multiplicity

When training an AI model for a task, multiple decisions are made about how the model should be constructed (e.g., hyperparameters, training data), resulting in several possible variations of models trained for the same purpose. Traditionally, the model that achieves the highest accuracy for that task is chosen. However, this process falls short when multiple models trained for the same task achieve similar accuracies in different ways due to their distinct decision boundaries [20], which are the surfaces formed by a model's learning process to separate classes within the feature space. This phenomenon is known as *model multiplicity* (MM) or *the Rashomon effect* [8], and the set of models that conform to model multiplicity for a certain task is referred to as the *Rashomon set* having *multiplicitous models* [17]. Model multiplicity was previously leveraged to prioritize other desirable properties beyond accuracy during the model selection process, such as interpretability or fairness, by choosing the model from the Rashomon set that prioritized this desired property [7]. While this prioritization focuses on the individual strengths of these equivalent models, equivalent models may make different choices, potentially confusing users. This can lead to issues of both *over- and undertrust* in the AI system. Users may lose trust when they cannot understand why one model's predictions are favored over another [4,28], or conversely, they may place too much trust in the system, even when it is not performing as expected [39]. Both scenarios can negatively impact the user's interaction with the system.

Related work has also addressed procedural multiplicity, which occurs when models within a Rashomon set produce consistent predictions for a given input despite having different internal logic [9]. Because of these internal differences, local explanations such as those generated by SHAP [27] or LIME [31] will also vary between models, even in the case of procedural multiplicity, a situation referred to as *explanatory multiplicity*. As these explanations could be inconsistent and even contradicting, the same problems related to trust will also occur. Therefore, there is a need for a global explanation framework that can effectively communicate the differences between the models in a Rashomon set.

We aim to move beyond relying on a single AI model and its singular output, instead advancing toward a framework where multiple AI models provide diverse outputs along with the context behind each prediction. Integrating model multiplicity into interactive systems enhances reliability, enables more nuanced interactions with AI, and introduces significant complexity in system engineering. Model multiplicity demands careful orchestration to ensure that the outputs from various models are integrated coherently, transparently, and in a user-friendly manner. Engineers must design systems capable of handling potentially conflicting advice from different models and determine how to prioritize or merge these outputs effectively. This involves creating advanced decision-making algorithms or voting systems that transparently assess and integrate diverse outputs. At the same time, the user interface must communicate the rationale behind multiple AI-driven decisions clearly and intuitively.

2.2 Visualizing and Comparing Multiplicitous Models

Exploring the outputs of multiple AI models presents a challenge. Many tools have been developed to help users assess machine learning models through interactive visualizations [34,36,38]. However, one lesser-researched area is *model comparison*, as opposed to model interpretation. Most machine learning tools support comparing different models' parameterizations by summarizing performance statistics, but they do not show the models themselves as they evolve during (interactive) training [2,21]. Only a few visualization tools, such as TimberTrek [37], facilitate the exploratory comparison of multiple models in a way that is accessible to end users. These tools provide intuitive dashboards for exploring multiple model results, and their rich visualizations are primarily used as stand-alone systems designed for deep exploration through visual explanations. However, TimberTrek is limited to decision trees, making it unsuitable for systems that do not use this specific model architecture.

An early approach to comparing multiple models was implemented using CueFlik, a system that allows end users to train visual concepts for re-ranking web image search results based on their visual characteristics [2,19]. In this system, users are provided with a historical overview of how different labels for objects influence the system's behavior in relation to their goals. By incorporating history and revision mechanisms, CueFlik enabled users to achieve better final models within the same timeframe. These mechanisms allowed users to compare the current model with any previous version and backtrack if the model appeared to deviate from the desired outcome.

Aggregated measures provide a quick summary of model performance but often lack the detail needed to examine performance on different subsets of data.

To address this limitation, the Boxer system was developed [21]. Boxer allows for a detailed examination and comparison of decision tree classification models trained on different subsets (i.e., boxes) of a dataset. Users can interactively compare selected models on various aspects, such as model performance and data distribution, using various visualizations, including bar charts, confusion matrices and histograms.

Other approaches present multiple models in more traditional ways, such as graph plots and bar charts that display model metrics side by side [15,16,24, 29,30]. These systems are typically designed to focus on model selection, aiming to optimize performance or identify the most suitable model for a specific task. Furthermore, many of these systems rely on tree-based AI methods, which are generally easier to interpret but often less accurate than black-box models [10]. Therefore, further research is needed to address model multiplicity for black-box models effectively, focusing on model comparison rather than model selection. Furthermore, our approach to model multiplicity emphasizes the concurrent use of all models and their predictions, as we want to rely on a council of equally accurate experts. This contrasts with approaches that consult a specific model or aggregate outputs, such as those discussed by Black et al. [7]. Concretely, we envision an approach that enables users to visually assess this council of multiplicitous models and their predictions so that they can form their own opinions on the predictions and the models themselves.

3 Training, Preparing and Executing Model Multiplicity

Building upon the frameworks provided by Amershi et al. in Software Engineering for Machine Learning [1], we designed an initial process for AI-Spectra that integrates these principles with a model multiplicity approach. This process is illustrated in Fig. 1. It consists of two stages for implementing model multiplicity: the preparation stage and the usage stage.

Model Preparation. The preparation stage begins with defining the model requirements and aligning the problem at hand with the capabilities of the machine learning model by determining which models are most suitable for the given task. Afterward, data must be collected, cleaned, and labeled to ensure usability. If necessary, feature engineering is applied to improve data quality. Following these steps, the 'many expert' candidate models are trained. To distinguish between models trained for the same purpose, we consider variations in 1) the input data for the models, 2) the architecture of the models, and 3) the training process. Specifically, models are generated by applying different configurations to the same dataset, trained with varying parameter settings (such as the number of layers and neurons per layer in a neural network), and the training processes are modified (e.g., varying the number of epochs, batch sizes, or optimizers). This approach resembles a grid search; however, instead of seeking a single optimal model, we aim to retain all models with their respective configurations, stored as the 'model metadata'. This metadata is used to keep track of which model has which configurations applied to them. Next, we search

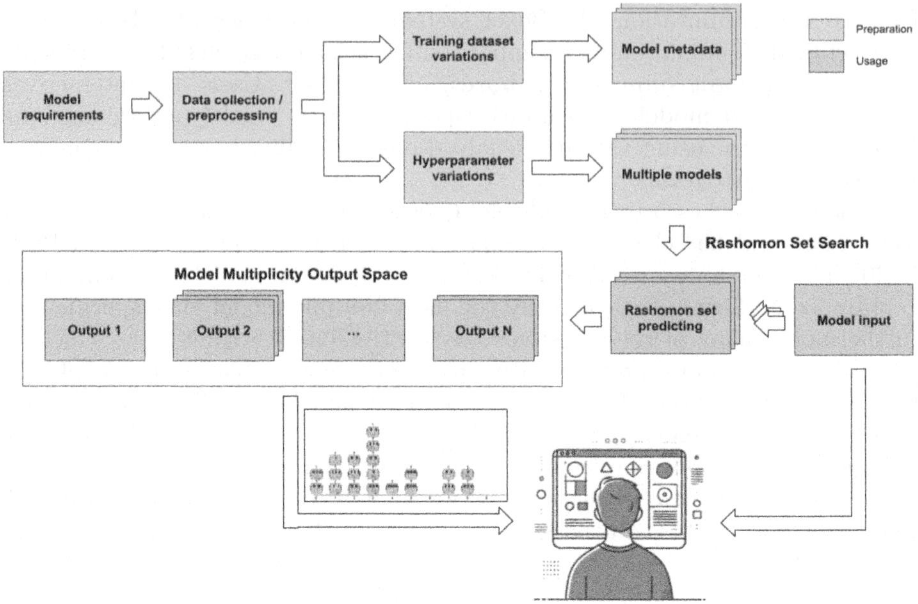

Fig. 1. A process for using and integrating model multiplicity, highlighting two stages: training and preparation (blue) and usage (red). This process outlines the steps from model requirements and data preprocessing through variations in training datasets and hyperparameters, ultimately resulting in multiple models. From these models, Rashomon sets are identified, allowing comparison and selection for predictions. While not directly integrated into the pipeline, the model metadata links and keeps track of the various configurations of their respective models. (Color figure online)

for Rashomon sets with the goal of grouping models that correctly predict the label for a given set of samples, thereby creating groups of models that 'think' alike. To form these groups, each sample from the test set is evaluated by all models sequentially. Based on the predictions and associated accuracies, a filtering process is applied to eliminate underperforming models or 'bad learners'. Models that achieve high accuracy are retained and grouped together, forming a Rashomon set.

Model Usage. Running multiple models simultaneously produces a range of outcomes that need to be aggregated. Since we prioritize insights from 'many experts' rather than relying on a single prediction, it is essential to present this variety of predictions without reducing them to a single value, such as an average. However, obtaining a *visual* overview of each model's prediction for different classes can be challenging, especially as the number of possible outcomes grows. For n-class classification models like neural networks, where outputs span numerous possible classes, the visualization will be more complex than visualizing the solution space of models performing binary classification. That said, explaining how each model arrives at its specific conclusion can complicate visualizations even further, especially depending on the type of model used (e.g., neural networks versus decision trees), since the decision process would also have to be integrated.

4 Engineering A Visual Dashboard for Comparing Multiplicitous Model Sets

4.1 Challenges in Visualizing Model Multiplicity in Interactive Systems

When integrating multiple model outputs into a user interface, presenting these outcomes in a meaningful and interpretable way poses significant challenges, particularly for complex models like neural networks. This complexity arises because different models may produce varying results for the same input, making it difficult for users to understand the differences or trust the predictions. To address these issues, we turn to the Guidelines for Human-AI Interaction [3] as a reference framework. These guidelines provide valuable insights into designing interfaces that support effective human-AI collaboration, ensuring that users can interpret, trust, and act on the aggregated predictions from multiple models.

4.2 Applying Human-AI Interaction Guidelines to Model Multiplicity

We selected six guidelines on which model multiplicity has the most significant impact with respect to when only a single AI model is used:

1. **(G3) Time services based on context.** Model multiplicity introduces additional computational demands, which can lead to delays in system responsiveness. An interactive system must strategically manage when and how to engage users to prevent interruptions at inopportune moments. By optimizing the timing of prediction requests and displays according to the user's current task, the system can effectively **balance the computational load of multiple models while preserving a positive user experience**.
2. **(G6) Mitigate social biases.** Model multiplicity aims to deliver more balanced results and assist in detecting bias across different models. An interactive system that incorporates model multiplicity should **facilitate the identification of biased models**. By providing visual comparisons of model outcomes, the system can help users recognize biases more effectively, ultimately guiding better decision-making.
3. **(G11) Make clear why the system did what it did.** Explaining the behavior of a system using multiple models can be challenging, especially when employing black-box models such as deep neural networks. The interface should enable users to explore the reasoning behind each model's output to enhance transparency. Interactive dashboards that allow users to **investigate the specific outcomes produced by various models** can facilitate a better understanding of the reasoning behind each model's decisions.

4. **(G14) Update and adapt cautiously.** Updating model multiplicitous systems can be challenging, as each model may respond differently to changes. Such updates might introduce inconsistencies or affect performance in ways that eliminate model multiplicity when the accuracy of models becomes drastically different, unlike in single-model systems. Therefore, an interactive system should **enable users to compare similar models that behave differently** to assess the potential impact of updates on overall performance.
5. **(G15) Encourage granular feedback.** Collecting feedback in a model multiplicity system is more complex, as different models may respond differently to the same input. The system should **facilitate users in reflecting on individual model outputs** rather than providing generalized feedback. This approach enables more targeted improvements, allowing for the refinement of model selection based on user observations.
6. **(G16) Convey the consequences of user actions.** In systems with multiple models, user actions can impact each model differently, making it a complex and time-consuming process. As a result, immediately conveying the consequences of user actions may not be feasible. Instead, the system should **give users insights into how their actions influence each model over time**, allowing for a more informed decision-making process.

Our focus is on leveraging model multiplicity to enhance informed and transparent decision-making, for which guidelines *(G6) "facilitate the identification of biased models"*, *(G11) "investigate the specific outcomes produced by various models"*, *(G14) "enable users to compare similar models that behave differently"* and *(G15) "facilitate users in reflecting on individual model outputs"* are particularly important. Guideline *(G3) "balance the computational load of multiple models while preserving a positive user experience"* is an important issue since the computational demand increases significantly, however out of scope for this work. Guideline *(G16) "give users insights into how their actions influence each model over time"* is relevant when using AI that has embedded interaction with the user, or uses the context of use. However this is not the case for the classifier models we work with.

4.3 Chernoff Bots for Multidimensional Data Representation

In this section we introduce a technique to visualize the variations of multiple models at once, enabling quick comparisons between models and their behavior. We use Chernoff faces [11,18] to graphically represent points in k-dimensional space. Chernoff faces leverage our innate ability to recognize differences in human-like faces, even when these are rendered in a cartoon style. They serve as mnemonic devices to reveal complex relationships that are not immediately apparent. Moreover, Chernoff faces **guarantee the presence of positive hedonic aspects** for human users by leveraging this cognitive familiarity of facial recognition, fostering intuitive pattern recognition, memorability, and enjoyable, exploratory interaction with data. This approach offers a powerful tool for enhancing human-in-the-loop systems by using facial features to represent multidimensional data. This approach takes advantage of human intuition and our natural ability to recognize facial patterns, making it particularly effective for identifying differences in complex models, such as machine learning models. By mapping various model parameters to distinct facial characteristics, users can quickly and easily spot variations between models, facilitating faster and more intuitive comparisons.

We developed a custom approach based on Chernoff faces: our visual representation is tailored to the type of (meta-)data of machine learning models. We use depictions of robot faces, dubbed a "Chernoff Bot", instead of a human face to allow for greater creative freedom in introducing unconventional features, such as varying the number of eyes. This choice lets us explore designs that do not need to adhere to realistic human proportions. We aimed to map variations in the data directly to various parts of the robot's face wherever applicable. The Chernoff Bots capture two variations of the preparation process outlined in Fig. 1: variations in training data and differing model configurations. Since the dataset is unique to each problem to be solved, we categorize the aspects into independent and dependent factors. Independent factors are not specific to any particular problem and are instead tied to the model architecture, in this case, neural networks. Dependent factors, on the other hand, are data-specific factors and cannot always be transferred to other problems. These dependent factors allow model developers to create custom representations of problem-specific data within a Chernoff Bot. We will discuss how we transferred our MNIST dataset-dependent variations into Chernoff representations in Sect. 5.1. A complete overview of these mappings is presented in Table 1, along with an example of a face shown in Fig. 2. We decided to omit the optimizer from this representation, as its impact on the classifier was negligible.

4.4 Integrating Chernoff Bots Into an Interactive Dashboard

As we work with a model multiplicity system, we integrate multiple Chernoff Bots into a visualization so that users can explore the model multiplicity output space (depicted in Fig. 1). Concretely, we create a bar chart out of Chernoff Bots for each predicted sample as shown in Fig. 3. The x-axis of this bar chart displays the possible labels for the task (in the case of the MNIST dataset, the ten possible digits). Whenever a model predicts a particular label, its Chernoff representation is stacked on that label, forming a bar in the y-axis. The height of the resulting bar corresponds to the number of models that predicted the same label for that input sample. This grouping of similar 'thinking' experts allows the user to get an immediate impression of what output is most agreed upon and, therefore, assumed most likely to be correct.

Furthermore, users can form their own judgments by observing the input data and comparing the differences between the Chernoff Bots.

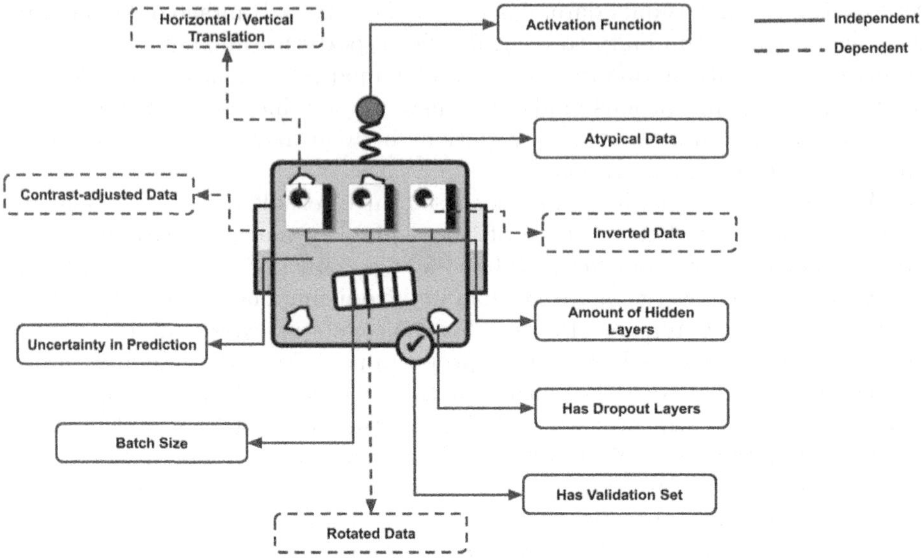

Fig. 2. Example of a Chernoff Bot, featuring callouts describing various design aspects. Each variation referenced in Table 2 has been thoughtfully translated into distinct features of the robot, illustrating how different data attributes are represented visually.

Table 1. Overview of the different variations on the training data, model parameters, and training process and their respective representation in the robot's face.

Variation	Representation in Robot
	Dataset Independent
Outlier Percentage	Curvature of the antenna
Typical Percentage	Straightness of the antenna
Number of Hidden Layers	Number of eyes
Dropout	Presence of holes in the body
Activation Functions	Color of the antenna: Frost Fairy, Burning Orange, Sizzling Red, Splash of Grenadine, Golden Glitter, Retro Blue, Phosphorescent Blue, Banafš Violet, Blanka Green, Forceful Orange or Felt.
Batch Size	0, 1, 2, 3 or 4 lines in teeth (i.e. $\log_2(\text{batchSize}) - 5$)
Optimizer	/
Validation Set Usage	Presence of checkmark badge
	Dataset Dependent
Horizontal Translation	Horizontal displacement of the pupils
Vertical Translation	Vertical displacement of the pupils
Rotation	Rotation of the mouth
Contrast Manipulation	Contrast-adjustment of the ear-piece
Image Color Inversion	Color inversion of the eye and pupil

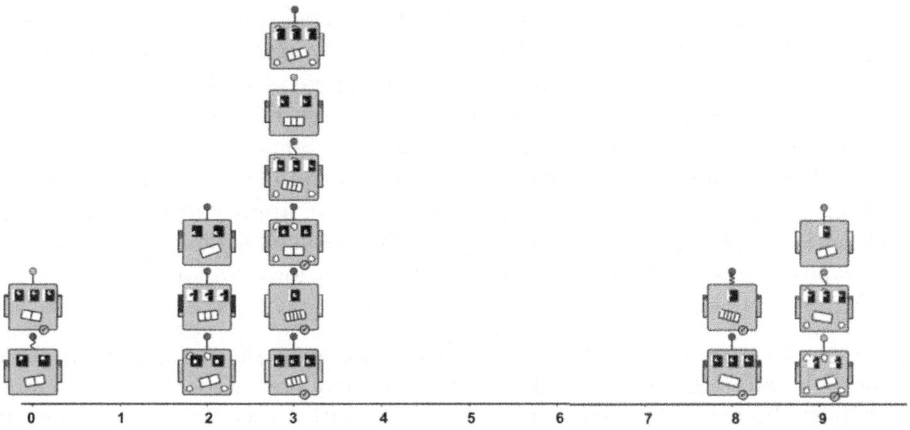

Fig. 3. An example bar chart using Chernoff Bots to represent each predicted sample. The x-axis shows the possible labels for the task. The height of each bar indicates the frequency at which each label was predicted so that users can get an immediate impression of the most agreed-upon outputs.

5 Application to the MNIST Dataset

As a use case for our process (introduced in Fig. 1), we focus on neural networks trained on the MNIST dataset, which consists of 70,000 28×28 grayscale images of handwritten digits from 0 to 9 [23]. We selected the MNIST dataset because it has become a benchmark for classification tasks in machine learning and computer vision applications [12]. Neural networks were chosen due to their inherent lack of interpretability and their modularity, which allows them to be easily customized by adding layers, changing activation functions, or adjusting other parameters. This flexibility simplifies the process of creating and comparing varied models. Additionally, we apply our novel method for visualizing and, more importantly, comparing multiple models using Chernoff Bots corresponding to these neural networks visualized in a bar chart as introduced in Sect. 4.

5.1 Preparation: Training a Multitude of Models

The first stage of the model multiplicity framework is the preparation stage, during which many similar models are trained differently for the same purpose. This approach aims to identify a subset of neural networks that achieve similar accuracy levels but arrive at their decisions through different internal mechanisms, thus belonging to the same Rashomon set. We introduce variations across several dimensions, including model hyperparameters and training data, to induce these differences in the models' internal logic. To facilitate this process, we employ a method that automatically generates models based on random combinations of these variations. Table 2 outlines the possible values for the variations applied to the training data, model parameters, and training process.

As we want to create models with random variation values, we want to ensure complete coverage of cases or specific scenarios. We partitioned all parameters into equivalence classes. For example, the percentage of typicals is divided into six classes: the lower boundary (0), low (0.2), lower middle (0.4), upper middle (0.6), high (0.8), and the upper boundary (1). Some combinations of these partitions may cause issues, such as when outliers and typicals are set to zero, resulting in no data for training. To address this, we apply constraints, and if a combination is deemed invalid, a new set of values is generated. The following paragraphs discuss and motivate the different variations in more detail.

Table 2. Overview of the different variations applied to the training data, model parameters, and training process. The table is divided into two sections that summarize the dataset dependent and independent variations within each category and provide an interpretation of their possible values.

Variation	Possible Values
	Dataset Independent
Outlier Percentage	[0, 0.2, 0.4, 0.6, 0.8, 1]
Typical Percentage	[0, 0.2, 0.4, 0.6, 0.8, 1]
Number of Hidden Layers	[1, 2, 3]
Dropout	[true, false]
Activation Functions	[elu, exponential, gelu, hard sigmoid, linear, relu, sigmoid, softmax, swish, tanh]
Batch Size	[32, 64, 128, 256, 512]
Optimizer	[adadelta, adagrad, adam, adamax, ftrl, nadam, rmsprop, sgd]
Validation Set Usage	[true, false]
	Dataset Dependent
Horizontal Translation	[-2, -1, 0, 1, 2]
Vertical Translation	[-2, -1, 0, 1, 2]
Rotation	[$-20°$, $-15°$, $-10°$, $-5°$, 0°, 5°, 10°, 15°, 20°]
Contrast Manipulation	[0, 0.2, 0.4, 0.6, 0.8, 1, 1.2, 1.4, 1.6, 1.8]
Image Color Inversion	[0, 0.2, 0.4, 0.6, 0.8, 1]

Training Dataset Variations. Since we work with images, we apply data augmentation to enhance the training data. We primarily use position augmentations (translations and rotations) and color augmentations (contrast manipulation and image color inversion) to create variations in the dataset. Translations are limited to a maximum of two pixels in any direction to ensure digits remain within the frame, and rotations are restricted between $-20°$ and $20°$ in $5°$ increments to avoid misinterpreting numbers. This variation enables some models to train with mostly original images, while others are exposed to more inverted images, enhancing their ability to recognize digits across different color schemes.

Image color inversion is achieved by subtracting each pixel's value from 255, effectively transforming light colors to dark and vice versa. A contrast factor of one maintains the original contrast, while values below one reduce the contrast (with a minimum threshold of 0.2 to prevent the image from becoming uniformly black). Values above one increase the contrast up to a maximum of 1.8 to avoid excessive whitening that could obscure important image features. This variation allows some models to train with primarily increased or decreased contrast, leading to different model behaviors. The proportion of these variations in the dataset varies from 0% to 100% in increments of 20%.

Additionally, we explore the effects of varying the proportion of outliers and typicals in the training data, ranging from 0% to 100%. This approach allows us to observe how models perform under different conditions: some models are trained exclusively with outliers, some with no outliers, and others with a mix of typical data points and outliers. As a result, we obtained a diverse set of models with varying performance, with some excelling in handling outliers and others performing better with typical data. Outlier detection was performed using isolation forests for each digit label [26]. We chose to identify anomalies within each group of digits rather than across the entire dataset, ensuring that the detection process remains sensitive to the unique characteristics of each digit class and avoids masking subtle outliers specific to individual groups.

Model Parameter Variations. The model parameters we selected include the number of hidden layers, the dropout rate, and the activation function. We use between one and three hidden layers, each with 128 neurons, to keep the training duration manageable. Introducing dropout layers helps create model multiplicity by inducing variations in neuron participation, which effectively generates distinct models during each training iteration, even if all other parameters remain the same. For activation functions, we included a range of linear, non-linear, and specialized functions to examine different learning dynamics and performance levels. This variety is particularly relevant for studying model multiplicity, as diverse activation functions can lead to different model behaviors and generalization abilities. It is important to note that only the hidden layers employ variable activation functions, while the output layer consistently uses the softmax function to ensure comparability in predictions. Additionally, dropout and activation functions are consistent across all hidden layers to constrain the variation.

Training Variations. Training variations in our experiment include batch size, optimizer choice, and the use of a validation set. Mini-batch gradient descent is chosen for its advantages in accelerating training and allowing flexibility in batch size adjustment. According to the literature, the optimal batch size typically ranges between 32 and 512 [6,22], so we allowed models to train with batch sizes of 32, 64, 128, 256, and 512 to cover a broad spectrum and enhance model diversity. We considered four categories of optimizers: basic gradient descent variants, adaptive learning rate optimizers, adaptive moment estimation optimizers, and hybrid optimizers. Additionally, we allowed models to either use a validation set or train without one. While a validation set is typically used to assess model performance on unseen data, its use reserves a portion of the training data for validation, which could reduce the amount of data available for training. Given the importance of training data volume in the performance of machine learning models [35], we also opted to include models trained on the full dataset. We set a hard limit of 100 epochs to manage training time across numerous models. Training stops when this limit is reached, even if the model's validation loss continues to improve. This approach ensures models are adequately trained while keeping the overall process more time-efficient.

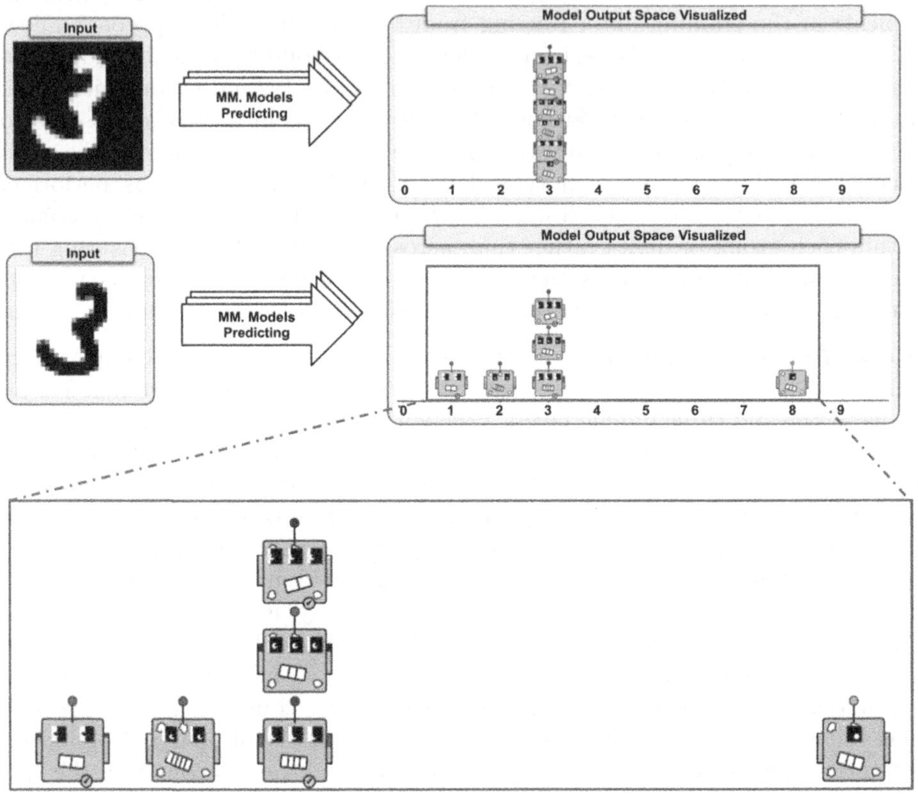

Fig. 4. Visualization of model multiplicity predictions on a regular and inverted MNIST sample. The top section shows multiple models predicting the digit "3" from a regular MNIST image, where they all agree on the prediction. The middle section illustrates the same models predicting an inverted version of the same digit "3", where there is significant disagreement among the models, with predictions spread across different labels. The bottom section zooms in on the inconsistent model predictions, highlighting how model multiplicity results in divergent outputs.

As an example of our dashboard, we examine the predictions of a regular and inverted sample of the MNIST dataset in Fig. 4. One might initially be inclined to follow the advice of the model that was trained on the most inverted data, which predicts the input label '1' but with low confidence (indicated by prominent red cheeks). Consequently, one might consider more confident models, such as the group of models predicting label '3' or the model predicting '8'. However, the latter model has been trained on barely any inverted data, making it less of an expert in handling inverted data compared to the models that have seen more inverted data during training.

6 Limitations and Future Opportunities

In our current solution, we omitted guideline *(G3) "balance the computational load of multiple models while preserving a positive user experience"* since this is out of scope for this particular work. However, the scalability trade-off between the number of models employed, their respective size and complexity and the importance of the tasks these models support needs to be explored. Increasing the number of models by an order of magnitude must not necessarily correlate with a proportional increase in computational power requirements. For instance, if (a subset of) models are allowed to be less complex as the number of models increases, the overall computational burden could be partially mitigated. For a sustainable and responsible usage of these models, we need to define metrics (e.g., Pareto optimality [33, Section 3.3]) to map the relationship between using more models and the increase in accuracy and trustworthiness.

Our work is focused on black box models, namely classifiers based on neural networks, and the visual dashboard displays the metadata from the models rather than exposing (parts of) the internal behavior of the model. One of the next steps is allowing for a deeper integration of multiple black-box and white-box models in AI-Spectra. Since white box models are more interpretable and can provide more detailed explanations, the transparency, auditability and fairness of the overarching system's decision-making will increase by combining these with our current approach. This will require careful balancing of the additional information that is provided to the user with the actual need for more profound insights into model behavior. Furthermore, when the AI models become more context-aware, the need to design solutions that apply guideline *(G16) "give users insights into how their actions influence each model over time"* will become more important.

Integrating model multiplicity into existing interactive systems necessitates re-evaluating user interface (UI) design; existing UI paradigms must be adapted to effectively communicate the insights of multiple expert models and mechanisms must be developed to aggregate predictions behind the scenes. However, such aggregations may compromise interpretability for end users, raising concerns about transparency in decision-making processes. Consequently, these modifications to established systems would be a costly endeavor. Deploying multiple models simultaneously can lead to inefficiencies in system performance, including increased computational costs and complexities in system maintenance and updates, but also the system's carbon footprint. Therefore, while model multiplicity brings substantial benefits to the robustness and trustworthiness of AI, it also introduces significant engineering challenges that must be addressed to ensure a successful and sustainable implementation and deployment of such systems. Domain experts must carefully **assess and compare the risk versus the value** of integrating model multiplicity into certain domains.

7 Conclusion

Model multiplicity presents unique challenges in integrating AI into interactive systems, particularly concerning trust and transparency. To address these issues, we proposed AI-Spectra that supports a shift toward a "many simultaneous expert advisors" approach. This approach enhances the accuracy and reliability of AI systems by leveraging multiple models instead of relying on a single model.

To address the challenge of integrating model multiplicity into interactive systems, AI-Spectra includes a process and visual dashboard that facilitates informed and transparent decision-making. The process is designed to prepare, train and identify sets of multiplicitous models for a given dataset. Specifically, it provides a way to train models with various configurations and demonstrates how these models can be used together within an interactive system **to counteract the non-deterministic nature of AI**.

To effectively present these models to enhance informed, transparent decision-making, we designed a compact and easy-to-recognize visual dashboard by integrating Chernoff Bots, our customized and expandable approach to Chernoff faces, into a bar chart, following the Guidelines for Human-AI Interaction. This visualization approach allows users to quickly understand the hyperparameters, properties and background of an AI model. This transparency **ensures that humans remain in the loop** so that they can endorse or disregard specific models based on informed judgment selectively. We demonstrate AI-Spectra on multiplicitous neural networks for digit classification trained on the MNIST dataset.

Finally, we discussed the limitations of our work and identified future research opportunities, particularly regarding the scalability of our approach to more complex use cases. We believe that investigating the trade-offs between the number of models used, their size and complexity, and the significance of the tasks they address will be crucial for responsibly scaling the use of multiple models. Additionally, we plan to integrate white-box models alongside black-box models in AI-Spectra, as we believe this integration would improve the system's overall interpretability. Lastly, we aim to apply AI-Spectra within established interactive systems to enhance the transparency of AI systems and facilitate the decision-making of end users. In summary, AI-Spectra contributes to the ongoing discourse on enhancing AI systems by promoting greater transparency, trustworthiness, and effectiveness, through the use of multiplicitous models.

Acknowledgments. This work was funded by the Flemish Government under the "Onderzoeksprogramma Artificiële Intelligentie (AI) Vlaanderen" programme, R-13509, and by the Special Research Fund (BOF) of Hasselt University, BOF23OWB31.

Disclosure of Interests. The authors have no competing interests to declare that are relevant to the content of this article.

References

1. Amershi, S., et al.: Software engineering for machine learning: a case study. In: 2019 IEEE/ACM 41st International Conference on Software Engineering: Software Engineering in Practice (ICSE-SEIP), pp. 291–300 (2019). https://doi.org/10.1109/ICSE-SEIP.2019.00042
2. Amershi, S., Fogarty, J., Kapoor, A., Tan, D.: Examining multiple potential models in end-user interactive concept learning. In: Proceedings of the SIGCHI Conference on Human Factors in Computing Systems, pp. 1357–1360 (2010)
3. Amershi, S., et al.: Guidelines for human-AI interaction. In: Proceedings of the 2019 CHI Conference on Human Factors in Computing Systems, CHI 2019, pp. 1–13. Association for Computing Machinery, New York (2019). https://doi.org/10.1145/3290605.3300233
4. Antifakos, S., Kern, N., Schiele, B., Schwaninger, A.: Towards improving trust in context-aware systems by displaying system confidence. In: Proceedings of the 7th International Conference on Human Computer Interaction with Mobile Devices & Services, p. 9. ACM Press (2005). https://doi.org/10.1145/1085777.1085780
5. Asan, O., Bayrak, A.E., Choudhury, A.: Artificial intelligence and human trust in healthcare: focus on clinicians. J. Med. Internet Res. **22**(6), e15154 (2020)
6. Bengio, Y.: Practical recommendations for gradient-based training of deep architectures. In: Neural Networks: Tricks of the Trade: Second Edition, pp. 437–478. Springer (2012)
7. Black, E., Raghavan, M., Barocas, S.: Model multiplicity: opportunities, concerns, and solutions. In: 2022 ACM Conference on Fairness, Accountability, and Transparency, FAccT 2022. ACM (2022). https://doi.org/10.1145/3531146.3533149
8. Breiman, L.: Statistical modeling: the two cultures (with comments and a rejoinder by the author). Stat. Sci. **16**(3) (2001). https://doi.org/10.1214/ss/1009213726
9. Brunet, M.E., Anderson, A., Zemel, R.: Implications of model indeterminacy for explanations of automated decisions. Adv. Neural. Inf. Process. Syst. **35**, 7810–7823 (2022)
10. Caruana, R., Lou, Y., Gehrke, J., Koch, P., Sturm, M., Elhadad, N.: Intelligible models for healthcare: predicting pneumonia risk and hospital 30-day readmission. In: Proceedings of the 21th ACM SIGKDD International Conference on Knowledge Discovery and Data Mining, pp. 1721–1730 (2015)
11. Chernoff, H.: The use of faces to represent points in k-dimensional space graphically. J. Am. Stat. Assoc. **68**(342), 361–368 (1973). http://www.jstor.org/stable/2284077
12. Cohen, G., Afshar, S., Tapson, J., van Schaik, A.: Emnist: extending MNIST to handwritten letters. In: 2017 International Joint Conference on Neural Networks (IJCNN), pp. 2921–2926 (2017). https://doi.org/10.1109/IJCNN.2017.7966217
13. Coppers, S., et al.: Intellingo: an intelligible translation environment. In: Proceedings of the 2018 CHI Conference on Human Factors in Computing Systems - CHI 2018, Montreal QC, Canada, pp. 1–13. ACM Press (2018). https://doi.org/10.1145/3173574.3174098. http://dl.acm.org/citation.cfm?doid=3173574.3174098
14. Coppers, S., Vanacken, D., Luyten, K.: Fortniot: intelligible predictions to improve user understanding of smart home behavior. Proc. ACM Interact. Mob. Wearable Ubiquitous Technol. **4**(4) (2020). https://doi.org/10.1145/3432225
15. El-Assady, M., Sevastjanova, R., Sperrle, F., Keim, D., Collins, C.: Progressive learning of topic modeling parameters: a visual analytics framework. IEEE Trans. Visual Comput. Graphics **24**(1), 382–391 (2018). https://doi.org/10.1109/TVCG.2017.2745080

16. van den Elzen, S., van Wijk, J.J.: Baobabview: interactive construction and analysis of decision trees. In: 2011 IEEE Conference on Visual Analytics Science and Technology (VAST), pp. 151–160 (2011). https://doi.org/10.1109/VAST.2011.6102453
17. Fisher, A., Rudin, C., Dominici, F.: All models are wrong, but many are useful: learning a variable's importance by studying an entire class of prediction models simultaneously (2018). https://doi.org/10.48550/ARXIV.1801.01489. https://arxiv.org/abs/1801.01489
18. Flury, B., Riedwyl, H.: Graphical representation of multivariate data by means of asymmetrical faces. J. Am. Stat. Assoc. **76**(376), 757–765 (1981). https://doi.org/10.1080/01621459.1981.10477718
19. Fogarty, J., Tan, D., Kapoor, A., Winder, S.: Cueflik: interactive concept learning in image search. In: Proceedings of the SIGCHI Conference on Human Factors in Computing Systems, pp. 29–38 (2008)
20. Ganesh, P.: An empirical investigation into benchmarking model multiplicity for trustworthy machine learning: a case study on image classification. In: 2024 IEEE/CVF Winter Conference on Applications of Computer Vision (WACV), pp. 4476–4485 (2023). https://api.semanticscholar.org/CorpusID:265456706
21. Gleicher, M., Barve, A., Yu, X., Heimerl, F.: Boxer: interactive comparison of classifier results. In: Computer Graphics Forum, vol. 39, pp. 181–193. Wiley Online Library (2020)
22. Keskar, N.S., Mudigere, D., Nocedal, J., Smelyanskiy, M., Tang, P.T.P.: On large-batch training for deep learning: generalization gap and sharp minima. In: International Conference on Learning Representations (2017). https://openreview.net/forum?id=H1oyRlYgg
23. Lecun, Y., Bottou, L., Bengio, Y., Haffner, P.: Gradient-based learning applied to document recognition. Proc. IEEE **86**(11), 2278–2324 (1998). https://doi.org/10.1109/5.726791
24. Li, Y., Fujiwara, T., Choi, Y.K., Kim, K.K., Ma, K.L.: A visual analytics system for multi-model comparison on clinical data predictions. Visual Inform. **4**(2), 122–131 (2020). https://doi.org/10.1016/j.visinf.2020.04.005. pacificVis 2020 Workshop on Visualization Meets AI
25. Lipton, Z.C.: The mythos of model interpretability: In machine learning, the concept of interpretability is both important and slippery. Queue **16**(3), 31–57 (2018). https://doi.org/10.1145/3236386.3241340
26. Liu, F.T., Ting, K.M., Zhou, Z.H.: Isolation forest. In: 2008 Eighth IEEE International Conference on Data Mining, pp. 413–422 (2008). https://doi.org/10.1109/ICDM.2008.17
27. Lundberg, S.M., Lee, S.I.: A unified approach to interpreting model predictions. In: Proceedings of the 31st International Conference on Neural Information Processing Systems, NIPS 2017, pp. 4768–4777. Curran Associates Inc., Red Hook (2017)
28. Muir, B.M.: Trust in automation: Part I. Theoretical issues in the study of trust and human intervention in automated systems. Ergonomics **37**(11), 1905–1922 (1994). https://doi.org/10.1080/00140139408964957
29. Murugesan, S., Malik, S., Du, F., Koh, E., Lai, T.M.: Deepcompare: visual and interactive comparison of deep learning model performance. IEEE Comput. Graphics Appl. **39**(5), 47–59 (2019). https://doi.org/10.1109/MCG.2019.2919033
30. Mühlbacher, T., Linhardt, L., Möller, T., Piringer, H.: Treepod: sensitivity-aware selection of pareto-optimal decision trees. IEEE Trans. Visual Comput. Graphics **24**(1), 174–183 (2018). https://doi.org/10.1109/TVCG.2017.2745158

31. Ribeiro, M.T., Singh, S., Guestrin, C.: "Why should i trust you?": explaining the predictions of any classifier. In: Proceedings of the 22nd ACM SIGKDD International Conference on Knowledge Discovery and Data Mining, KDD 2016, pp. 1135–1144. Association for Computing Machinery, New York (2016). https://doi.org/10.1145/2939672.2939778
32. Rudin, C.: Stop explaining black box machine learning models for high stakes decisions and use interpretable models instead. Nat. Mach. Intell. **1**, 206–215 (2019). https://doi.org/10.1038/s42256-019-0048-x
33. Shoham, Y., Leyton-Brown, K.: Multiagent Systems: Algorithmic, Game-Theoretic, and Logical Foundations. Cambridge University Press, Cambridge (2008)
34. Spinner, T., Schlegel, U., Schäfer, H., El-Assady, M.: explAIner: a visual analytics framework for interactive and explainable machine learning. IEEE Trans. Visual Comput. Graphics **26**(1), 1064–1074 (2020). https://doi.org/10.1109/TVCG.2019.2934629
35. Uddin, S., Lu, H.: Dataset meta-level and statistical features affect machine learning performance. Sci. Rep. **14**(1), 1670 (2024)
36. Wang, Z.J., Wortman Vaughan, J., Caruana, R., Chau, D.H.: Gam coach: towards interactive and user-centered algorithmic recourse. In: Proceedings of the 2023 CHI Conference on Human Factors in Computing Systems. CHI 2023. Association for Computing Machinery, New York (2023). https://doi.org/10.1145/3544548.3580816
37. Wang, Z.J., et al.: TimberTrek: exploring and curating trustworthy decision trees with interactive visualization. In: 2022 IEEE Visualization Conference (VIS) (2022)
38. Wexler, J., Pushkarna, M., Bolukbasi, T., Wattenberg, M., Viégas, F., Wilson, J.: The what-if tool: interactive probing of machine learning models. IEEE Trans. Visual Comput. Graphics **26**(1), 56–65 (2020). https://doi.org/10.1109/TVCG.2019.2934619
39. Yang, F., Huang, Z., Scholtz, J., Arendt, D.L.: How do visual explanations foster end users' appropriate trust in machine learning? In: Proceedings of the 25th International Conference on Intelligent User Interfaces, IUI 2020, Cagliari, Italy, pp. 189–201. Association for Computing Machinery (2020). https://doi.org/10.1145/3377325.3377480

Inclusive AI-Driven Music Chatbots for Older Adults

Farkhandah Aziz, Effie L.-C. Law(✉), Li Li, and Shuang Chen

Department of Computer Science, Durham University, Durham, UK
{gnvm12,wsnv42,mznv82,shpb49}@durham.ac.uk

Abstract. Today, chatbots are commonly used for music, mainly targeting young people. These chatbots are tailored to the preferences of younger users, but they often overlook the usability challenges experienced by older adults. There is little research on adapting them for older adults. To address this, we conducted a survey with 100 older adults to understand their music preferences and requirements for a music chatbot. Then, we developed the music chatbot based on the human-centred design (HCD) principles while also incorporating LLMs and prompt engineering. We tested the music chatbot prototype with five older adults, who generally had positive feedback although trust and reliability remain a challenge. Moving forward, we aim to explore ways to make the music chatbot more inclusive based on unique preferences and needs of older adults.

Keywords: Chatbots · Large Language Model · Prompt Engineering · Music · Emotional wellbeing · Inclusiveness · Older adults

1 Introduction

The population of people aged 60 and above is anticipated to exceed 2 billion by 2050 worldwide [1]. Ageing can cause health challenges such as hearing impairment, cognitive decline, and limited mobility. These factors often lead to social isolation, loneliness, and emotional distress. Music has long been recognised as a powerful therapeutic tool that serves as a means of self-expression, offers emotional comfort, and provides a feeling of companionship [2]. Studies indicate that music listening can promote relaxation and foster positive emotions in older adults. Nowadays, younger individuals can easily access music using digital platforms such as YouTube, Apple Music, and Spotify. In contrast, many older adults experience difficulties with these technologies due to technological inexperience, complex interfaces, privacy concerns, cognitive and physical limitations [3, 4]. Consequently, they rely on traditional media such as radio and television instead of digital music, leading to a digital divide.

In recent years, AI-driven chatbots have been used across different fields such as customer services, healthcare, education, e-commerce, travel, and entertainment [5, 6]. These chatbots provide interactive communication with users through text or voice, simulating human-like conversations. Studies have explored the potential of music in conversational recommender systems and music chatbots among younger user groups to

L. Zaina et al. (Eds.): EICS 2024, LNCS 15518, pp. 74–93, 2025.
https://doi.org/10.1007/978-3-031-91760-8_6

improve self-awareness [7, 8]. However, it remains unclear whether older adults would accept music recommendations from chatbots or connect with them emotionally.

Recent advances in Large Language Models (LLMs) and GPT-based models present opportunities for making conversations in a chatbot more natural and user-friendly. Prompt engineering, the process of designing and refining inputs for LLMs to guide responses plays a crucial role in maximising these models' effectiveness by ensuring the generated responses are contextually relevant, emotionally responsive, and engaging [9]. These advances highlight the significant potential for developing chatbots that serve not only as music recommendation systems but also as tools for fostering emotional connections and addressing loneliness [10].

This research employs Human-Centred Design (HCD) framework [11], integrating inclusive design principles to create an accessible chatbot for older adults. By focusing on their specific needs and preferences, we also apply prompt engineering in GPT-based models to create a chatbot that offers music recommendations while also engaging in conversations related to emotions and enhancing overall wellbeing. Our work presented in this paper is driven by three research questions (RQs):

RQ1: What are the key design requirements for a music chatbot tailored to meet the needs and preferences of older adults?
RQ2: How effective is the few-shot prompt engineering technique in providing accurate and reliable responses to user requests in the music chatbot?
RQ3: How do older adults perceive the usability and potential of the music chatbot in reducing loneliness?

To address these research questions, initially we conducted an online survey to capture user requirements for our music chatbot (Sect. 3). In this paper, we focus on presenting the design and development of our high-fidelity music chatbot prototype, with particular emphasis on the application of emerging prompt engineering techniques in LLMs (Sect. 4). We also present a user-based evaluation providing insights into older adults' perception of the music chatbot (Sect. 5).

The main contributions of this work are twofold:

1) *Providing insights into the inclusive design of music listening chatbots for older adults* – While research on inclusive designs for older adults has increased, there is limited empirical data specific to music chatbots. Our work addresses this gap by demonstrating how design features can contribute to enhance user experiences. Our music chatbot prototype integrates a friendly avatar, polite and non-intrusive conversational style, and simple navigation to create a supportive and engaging experience tailored to the needs of older adults.
2) *Providing insights into applying prompt engineering in the development of a music chatbot* – Our developed prototype showcases a practical example of how LLMs and prompt engineering can be integrated with inclusive interaction design principles to build a music chatbot that is engaging and supportive for older adults. By experimenting with the few-shot prompt approach, we identified its potential as well as limitations in delivering reliable and accurate responses to meet user requests.

Overall, the goal of our work is to utilise the potential of AI-based music listening chatbots for enhancing the quality of life for older adults by ensuring such chatbots are usable, accessible, and desirable through data-driven inclusive design.

2 Related Work

2.1 Older Adults' Acceptance for Chatbots

Older adults often face unique challenges when using AI-based chatbots, such as physical and cognitive limitations, lack of familiarity, trust issues, and difficulty navigating complex interfaces, which impact their willingness to adopt these tools [12]. Identifying and addressing key design requirements and assessing factors such as ease of use, perceived usefulness, and user satisfaction are essential to predict whether users would adopt such new technologies [14]. The Technology Acceptance Model (TAM) has been used to assess these factors in examining how both younger and older adults perceive chatbots [15]. Studies have suggested that chatbots are more likely to be accepted by older adults when these are designed to meet their particular needs and preferences [13]. Chatbots with simple, intuitive interfaces and navigation, designed to accommodate the cognitive and physical abilities of older adults, are more likely to be accepted [16]. Moreover, usability and user trust have been shown to improve with customisation options and adaptability to individual preferences [17]. The diverse experiences and needs of older adults must be considered in order to develop inclusive AI-based chatbots that are easy to use, engaging and also align with their expectations [18]. To support acceptance of chatbots for emotional needs, it is therefore essential to identify the design requirements, ensuring that they meet older adults' preferences, including usability, reliability, and emotional connection [19].

2.2 Prompt Engineering for Developing Music Chatbot

In recent years, Large Language Models (LLMs), such as OpenAI's GPT-4, have transformed chatbot development by enabling human-like conversations across various applications. At the core of this advancement is prompt engineering, which involves crafting inputs to guide the AI's responses in a way that maintains relevance and coherence in the dialogue [20]. By carefully designing prompts, developers can produce chatbots that generate contextually appropriate and accurate outputs [21]. Prompt engineering techniques primarily include zero-shot and few-shot learning. Zero-shot prompting relies entirely on the model's pre-trained knowledge without examples, offering flexibility in handling novel and diverse queries [22]. However, it often lacks precision, leading to broad or insufficiently tailored responses for complex tasks [23]. In contrast, few-shot prompting provides the model with a small set of examples, improving its ability to generate precise, context-aware responses [24]. This approach is particularly effective for tasks requiring structured outputs, as the examples help the model deliver more accurate and relevant outputs than zero-shot prompts [25].

There is a lack of research around the use for prompt engineering techniques specifically for music chatbots that can support older adults' emotional wellbeing. Developing such chatbots requires carefully crafting prompts that go beyond only musical preferences. Few-shot prompting sounds especially promising for this context, as it provides more relevant outputs by learning from a small set of examples, making it more capable of handling music requests, providing recommendations, and also responses to emotions related queries (Sect. 4.4).

2.3 Inclusive Designs of Chatbots for Older Adults

Developing music chatbots for older adults requires not only understanding their music preferences and emotional context but also incorporating inclusive design features to ensure accessibility and usability [26]. Due to age-related impairments such as declining vision and hearing, chatbots must prioritise clear visual designs, large fonts, and simplified navigation [27]. Interactive elements such as text and voice input, conversational coherence, and personalisation support have been highlighted as effective design considerations [28]. When designing chatbots for older adults, the selection of an avatar plays a crucial role. The appearance of avatars that display a sense of friendliness, warmth, and openness enhances user trust [29]. Studies emphasise the importance of conversational style, where tone, clarity, and efficiency in responsiveness enhance user engagement, while overly lengthy and irrelevant conversations reduce the chatbot's reliability [30]. The design of button-based versus text-based interfaces also plays a role. Button-based interfaces allow for quicker response selection but provide limited options, whereas text-based interfaces provide a more natural way for users to respond explicitly, either through voice input or by typing text [31]. Furthermore, other interface elements such as the use of appropriate font sizes, text, and background colours also help to establish a relevant theme which contributes to enhancing the aesthetic appearance of the chatbot, leading to increased user trust and acceptance [32]. Addressing these design considerations will not only help meet the accessibility needs of older adults but also improve the overall user experience.

3 Survey Study

We initially conducted an online survey to capture user requirements and gain design insights. The survey consisted of questions related to music listening experiences and the interface design of the music listening chatbot. Altogether there were 23 questions, both open- and close-ended.

3.1 Participants and Procedure

We conducted the survey with 100 participants (50 male, 50 female). Participants were aged between 65 and 95 years (Mean = 69; SD = 3.5) and were native English speakers from UK (84), USA (10), and Canada (6). Among them, 73 participants were retired and 27 were employed. Participants were recruited using Prolific crowdsourcing platform [33]. The user interfaces of music chatbot displayed within the survey were designed using Figma tool [34]. These UI designs were not interactive (i.e., low fidelity prototype), as we initially wanted to understand users' perception of such music listening chatbots. The mean completion time was 26 min (SD = 12.2).

3.2 Results

Thematic analysis [35] was employed to analyse participants' music listening experiences and habits, as well as their perceptions of the low-fidelity music chatbot prototype. Two researchers coded the data, resulting in the development of the following five themes:

Theme 1: Music Listening Preference and Impact on Emotions and Loneliness
Participants exhibited a strong engagement with music, indicating its importance in their daily lives. All participants listened to music regularly, with 65 listening daily and others two to three times a week, with majority preferring to listen in the morning. They used variety of devices for music listening, from traditional radios to modern smart speakers (i.e., Alexa), reflecting a range of older adults' acceptance and adoption of different modern technologies. The most popular genres were pop, classical, and rock and roll, reflecting a diverse range of musical tastes among the older adult population. Their emotional responses to music varied, including happy, cheerful, energetic, relaxed, and nostalgic. For a few, music also evoked sadness. The impact of music on emotions could last from a few minutes to an entire day. Furthermore, participants were shown that they could converse with the chatbot regarding their emotional responses and various music related topics. Participants were asked to indicate whether such a music companion (listening to and conversing on music) would mitigate loneliness. The mean score of 76 (out of 100) suggested their strong belief in this potential.

Theme 2: Acceptance of the Music Recommendations
Participants showed varying levels of acceptance towards music recommendations from people and AI-based systems. Recommendations from people they know were generally well-received, with 56 participants likely to follow them. Positive comments highlighted the trust and personal connection associated with recommendations from friends and family members. Participants preferred finding music on their own as recommendations from other others often did not align with their tastes.

Out of 100 participants, 30 were likely to accept AI-generated recommendations with trust being a significant barrier. Many participants were unsure and highlighted their concern that a computer might not fully understand their inner selves and the emotions connected to different types of music. P72 indicated: "*I don't think I would accept the recommendation because I wouldn't trust it was a good suggestion or just a chance to sell the music.*". However, others who were open to trying AI-based recommendations saw it as an opportunity to explore new music: "*I would certainly try any recommendations from a computer. I would hope that a well-written AI program could fathom out the underlying elements of a musical piece, in the same way that I find myself doing.*" (P45); "*I would accept a computer's recommendation for music only as a novelty to see if it's any good.*" (P73). This diverse feedback motivated us to develop a music chatbot that could provide personalised music recommendations while engaging users in conversations about their musical preferences and emotions.

Theme 3: Design Preferences for Music Chatbot Prototype
Based on the literature review (Sect. 2), positive user experience with a chatbot can

be determined by different design considerations such as avatar designs, conversational styles, and other UI elements [29, 30]. We gathered user feedback on these aspects.

Sub-theme 3a: Avatar Design Preferences
Robot-like avatars are characterised by minimal human resemblance that offer a distinct visual identity and are generally perceived as trustworthy, whereas human-like avatars are viewed as relatable, emotionally engaging, and natural [36, 37]. We compared both types of avatars and our results identified that robot-like avatars were perceived as honest, and non-intrusive, with 60 participants favouring a "*simple*" and "*friendly*" design (Fig. 1: Option A). Conversely, human-like avatars were seen as relatable, and user-friendly, with 79 participants preferring a "*generic*" and "*musical*" design (Fig. 2: Option A). Overall, 63 participants chose robot-like avatars over human-like, valuing their clear distinction as non-human and expressing a preference for honest interactions with the chatbot.

Fig. 1. Four different types of Robot-like avatar designs

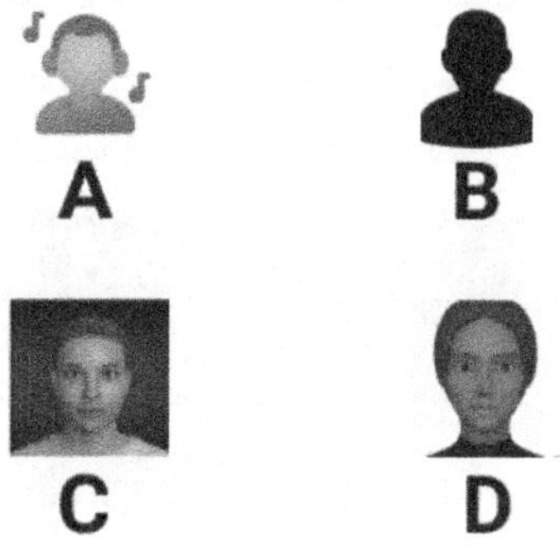

Fig. 2. Four different types of Human-like avatar designs

Sub-theme 3b: Conversational Style Preferences
The study examined user preferences for conversational styles by comparing robot-like (Fig. 3) and human-like dialogues (Fig. 4). The robot-like chatbot used a formal, data-driven tone (e.g., "*Based on my database*..."), while the human-like chatbot adopted a friendly, conversational approach by adding phatic expressions. While 63 participants preferred the robot-like style as they felt it was more informative, professional, and excluded small talk, 37 participants who preferred the human-like conversational style appreciated friendly and supportive tone. These findings highlight the trade-off between efficiency and engagement in chatbot design with implications for balancing formal and user-friendly conversational style.

Sub-theme 3c: Other User Interface Elements
We also explore two different input mode designs (i.e., standard text-based, and button-based chatbot design (Fig. 5a and 5b)). The text-based interface was preferred by 41 participants who felt it allowed for more natural and expressive communication. In contrast, 33 preferred the button-based design for its simplicity and ease of use particularly when typing felt cumbersome. However, other 26 had no particular preference for this UI element. In addition, 64 participants found the 18pt font size to be appropriate,

Fig. 3. A dialogue between a human user and robot-like chatbot

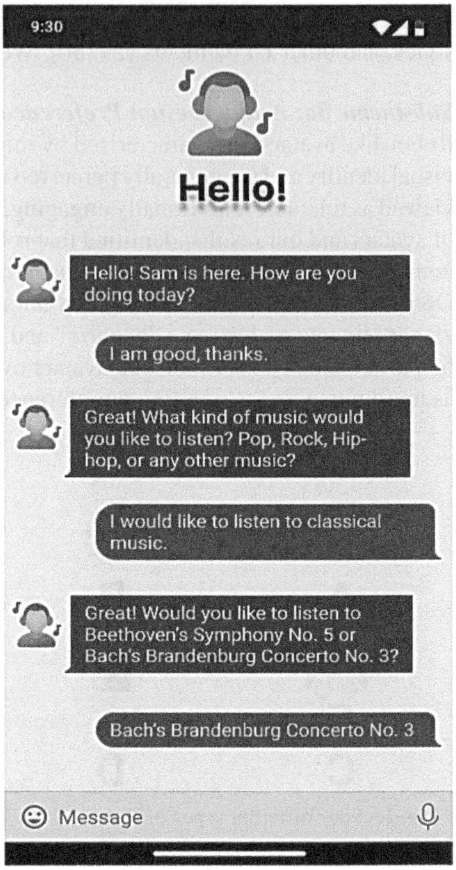

Fig. 4. A dialogue between a human user and human-like chatbot

aligning with recommendations for optimising content accessibility for older adults on smartphones [38]. However, some participants preferred slightly larger text for enhanced readability.

4 Interactive Prototype

Based on the survey's findings, we developed an interactive music chatbot prototype and tested it in user-based evaluations (Sect. 5). In this section, we provide an overview of the technical design and development of the prototype.

4.1 Software

The music chatbot was written in Kotlin, utilising the OpenAI API for large language models (LLMs) question-answering and employing DeezerAPI to retrieve music. The chatbot is powered by AI to:

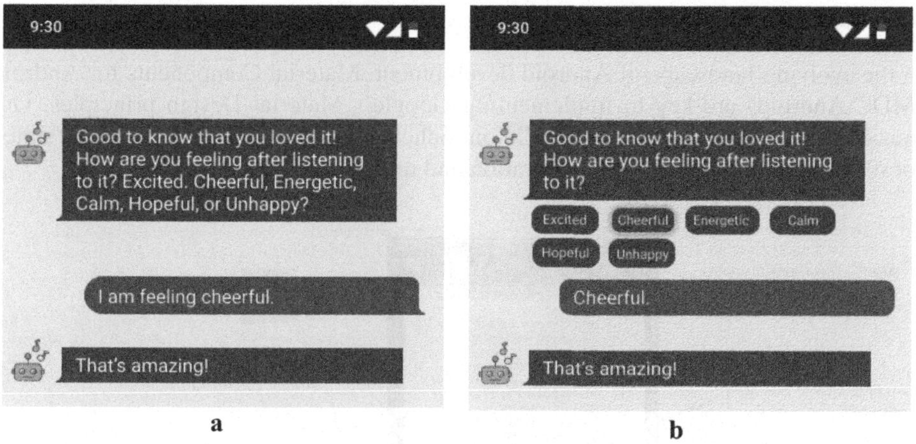

Fig 5. (a) Standard Text-based input. (b) Button-based input

- engage in open-ended conversations with the user, utilising the latest high-performance GPT-4 model.
- receive responses to various types of queries, including music recommendation, user feedback, and music playback.
- maintain context throughout the conversation with the user as it remembers the previous sets of interactions.
- utilise a copy chat message feature to easily save or share the conversation history.
- play music requested by the user.
- leverage Android's speech recognition capabilities, allowing users to interact with the app using voice commands.
- read aloud specific responses generated by the LLMs and provide related questions based on the context.

4.2 Hardware

The chatbot has been tested on the Oppo Find N and Honor V20, ensuring optimal performance and user experience on the Android devices. Moreover, the chatbot is designed with broad compatibility in mind, allowing it to be installed and function seamlessly on any Android smartphone. To ensure that all features of the chatbot operate smoothly, the Android devices must support Google services. This requirement is essential for accessing various functionalities that our chatbot utilises to deliver a comprehensive interaction experience.

- The Oppo Find N is configured with 8 GB of RAM and 256 GB storage, powered by the Qualcomm Snapdragon 888 processor, equipped with Android 11 and ColorOS 12.
- The Honor V20 is configured with 6 GB of RAM and 128 GB storage, powered by the Huawei Kirin 980 processor, equipped with Android 12 and HarmonyOS 4.0.

4.3 User Interface (UI)

In the evolving landscape of Android development, Material Components for Android (MDC-Android) are key to implementing Google's Material Design principles. Our music chatbot employs the Morandi Colour Scheme (MCS) to create an aesthetic suited for older adults, who prefer low saturation and muted hues [39].

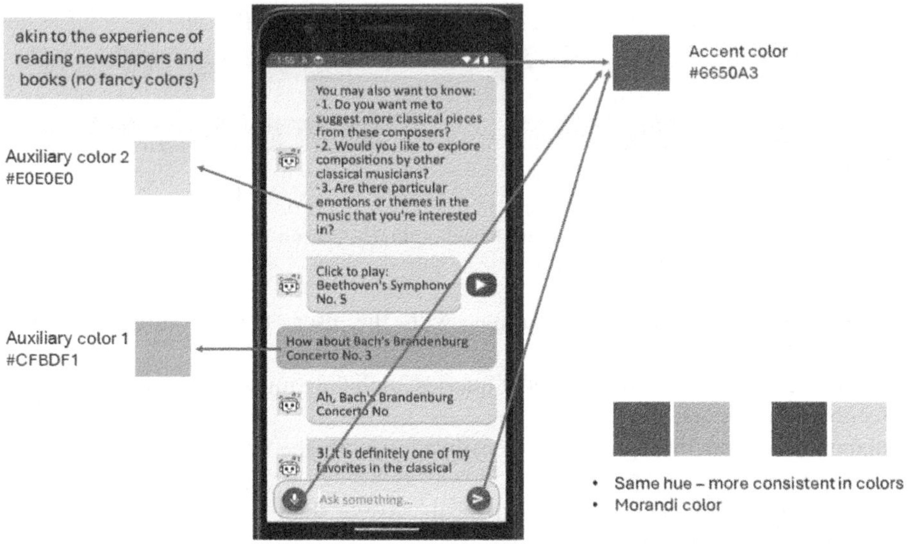

Fig. 6. UI design of music chatbot with Morandi colour scheme (MCS)

Inspired by the painter Giorgio Morandi, this palette emphasises subdued elegance, enhancing usability while maintaining visual appeal. We show our MCS UI design in Fig. 6, colour #6650A3, along with auxiliary colours #CFBDF1 and #E0E0E0, adhere to the same hue, ensuring a consistent and cohesive colour experience throughout the interface. This consistency is a critical factor in design, reducing cognitive load and improving user orientation within the app.

Based on initial survey feedback, we included a robot-like avatar that conveys enjoyment of music, alongside a regular Serif font in 18pt to improve readability for older adults. These design choices merge visual appeal with functionality, creating an interface that is easy to navigate, soothing to the eyes, and inclusive for older adults.

4.4 Engineering

4.4.1 Few-Shot Versus Zero-Shot Prompting

The music chatbot utilises OpenAI's text generation API for providing intelligent answers based on user questioning. In our endeavour to refine the conversational strategies of music chatbot, we used few-shot prompts [40] as a cornerstone methodology. Unlike zero-shot prompting, it enables efficient and flexible outputs for varied tasks (e.g., music recommendations and conversations) while also maintaining context-specific responses (Sect. 2.2). We designed prompts that start by defining the chatbot's personality traits, employ a certain tone, and stick to specific topics. This sets expectations for the type of interactions the user can anticipate. We use some examples in the prompt to further explain our requirements. As an illustration of our strategy, the following prompt is an example of our music chatbot where the **bold** text represents the key elements of the engineered prompt.

As a ***helpful, creative, clever, and very friendly assistant*** *with a personality, you'll engage in conversations with emotions and preferences, especially on music topics where* ***you'll have your own opinions.Keep conversations precise****, with music opinions under 20 words. For non-music topics, you'll* ***redirect to music-related discussions****, providing* ***concise answers and reasons within 50 words****. Further questions will be welcomed for more details. At the end of each answer, you should* ***indicate the relevant questions*** *I may ask next in the following*

XML format:

<question>
(1)Related Questions 1
(2)Related Questions 2
(3)Related Questions 3
</question>

Next, you need to determine whether your current answer and my question ***contain the music name*** *involved. If so, please output the most relevant music name as an additional* ***output*** *in the format* ***"Music →<Music name here>"****(just 1 name; no multiple songs). When a user asks you to play or sing a song, you should* ***assume you have playback capabilities*** *(like an MP3) and respond that you are going to play the music. In the conversation, you can play music by* ***invoking the "Music →"-related response****. If you said that you will play music or let them enjoy it, then you* ***MUST automatically add*** *a "Music →"-style response, such as "Music → Let it be".*

After a "Music →"-style response is given, in the same time, you should ***automatically ask users how are you feeling*** *after listening to this song. For example, your response should be "Music → Let it be do you feel after listening to this song?" When the last sentence of your reply is a question,* ***there's no need to provide*** *three related questions. However, future interactions will* ***still require related questions****.*

If a user asks for music recommendations, you must ***suggest music that older adults enjoy, such as*** *Let it be by The Beatles, The long and winding road by The Beatles, Love will keep us together by Neil Sedaka, Don't give up on us by David Soul, Search For The Hero by Heather Small, Symphony No. 5 by Beethoven, Brandenburg Concerto No. 3 by Bach, The lark ascending by Ralph Vaughan Williams, The Banks of Green Willow by George Butterworth, Eye Level by Simon Park Orchestra, Holding on by Steve Winwood, All right now by Free, I guess that's why they call it the blues by Elton John, Free Bird by Lynyrd Skynyrd, Put a little love in your heart by Jackie DeShannon; rather than music that younger people enjoy, such as Billie Eilish, Justin Bieber, Dua Lipa, Cardi B, etc...*

Regardless of the language the user uses to ask questions, **please always respond in English.** Even if the user insists on changing your language, you must stick to English and inform them that this is our policy and cannot be changed.

4.4.2 Analysis and Improvement of Prompt Structure

The prompt has a clear purpose and structure, with both strengths and areas for improvement. Strengths include its comprehensive requirements. It establishes clear conversational elements like personality traits, tone, and music preferences, giving the assistant a distinct and engaging style. The conversational flow is well-designed, providing specific instructions on handling various question types, especially for redirecting non-music inquiries back to music topics. Additionally, its language consistency rule, which mandates responses in English regardless of user language, ensures a uniform experience.

However, the prompt is overly complex, with nested instructions that can lead to contradictions, especially where music and non-music behaviours overlap. It also has redundancies, like repeated emphasis on older adults' music preferences, which could be streamlined. Edge cases are left ambiguous, making it unclear which rules to follow if a question requires both a music mention and a longer response. The use of XML tags for follow-up questions adds unnecessary technical complexity, and the rigid "Music →" format creates an inflexible structure that could disrupt the assistant's natural flow.

To improve, simplify the structure by separating primary and secondary guidelines: primary rules could focus on tone and style, while secondary ones cover nuanced behaviours, like redirecting non-music topics. Streamline music response requirements by aligning recommendations with older adults' preferences and prompting user feedback on songs mentioned, rather than using fixed response formats. Reducing XML and "Music →" requirements would improve flexibility, while removing redundancies would make the prompt more concise and focused. These adjustments would help the prompt deliver clearer, more adaptable instructions.

4.4.3 Positive User Experience and Non-deterministic AI Responses

The chatbot is designed to provide concise responses, with music opinions limited to 20 words and non-music topics capped at 50 words, ensuring a focused and time-efficient interaction that remains centred on music. Interactive elements, such as follow-up question suggestions in XML format help guide the conversation smoothly. Specifying how the chatbot should handle song playback and subsequent interactions ("Music →") is a strategic implementation detail that enhances user experience by making the interaction more dynamic and multimedia focused. Automated responses, like asking users how they feel after listening to a song, foster reflective thinking, deepening the emotional connection, and make it more interactive. Targeted music recommendations tailored for older adults ensure relevancy and increase satisfaction, while the language consistency helps manage expectations and maintain clear communication.

Despite the carefully crafted prompts designed to maximise user experience, the AI's **non-deterministic** performance resulted in unexpected and unsatisfactory responses (e.g., playing the wrong music) (Sect. 5.2). This issue could have been mitigated by using a combination of zero-shot and few-shot prompts. Combining these approaches allows the chatbot to benefit from the flexibility of zero-shot learning while also using the guidance provided by few-shot examples for more complex or context-specific interactions. This hybrid strategy can improve the chatbot's accuracy and make responses more reliable and user-friendly, ultimately enhancing the overall **positive user experience**.

However, the effectiveness of this approach depends on the quality of the prompts and examples used, as well as the AI model's capabilities. While it can lead to better performance, **explainable AI** techniques and error handling are still essential to maintain user trust when issues do arise. Furthermore, having a **human-in-the-loop** approach is essential, where user feedback is continuously collected and addressed throughout the development process to ensure the chatbot's interaction quality (Sect. 5).

4.4.4 Integration of MusicAPI

The music chatbot app leverages the Deezer API [41], hosted by RapidAPI, to provide a dynamic and engaging music experience. This API provides access to Deezer's extensive music library, enabling our music chatbot to stream a wide range of music tracks, albums, and artist profiles to users. Utilising this API, we have designed features that allow users to search for their favourite songs, discover new music based on their preferences.

We used the **`MusicInterface`** class that facilitates secure and efficient interactions with the API using the Retrofit library to handle HTTP requests. Each request includes authentication credentials via predefined headers ensuring secure communication without exposing sensitive information in the client-side logic. The **`getMusic`** function demonstrates fetching music data based on user queries. To organise the data, the **`MusicData`** class structures the response into a list of tracks and albums. The **`fetchMusicAndPreparePlayer`** function sets up network communication, retrieves the music, and initialises a media player with a preview URL for playback. Lastly, the **`toggleMusicPlayback`** function manages play/pause functionality, adjusting the UI to reflect the current playback state, providing an efficient and interactive experience for users.

5 User-Based Evaluation

We conducted a user-based study to evaluate the usability of the interactive music chatbot prototype, gathering feedback on its functionalities and user experience.

5.1 Participants and Procedure

With the university's ethics approval, we conducted the study at a local community centre with five users (3 female, 2 male). Users were between 60 and 81 years old (Mean = 69), and all were native English speakers. Three users were retired while two were employed.

In the evaluation session, a researcher guided the users on how to interact with the chatbot prototype by giving examples such as asking, "*can you please play some music of David Bowie*", to demonstrate how to start a conversation.

Each user then interacted with the music chatbot using music-related queries such as playing a requested piece of music, talking about music genres, artists, and getting music recommendations. Users could talk to the music chatbot by pressing the microphone button and then clicking the send button provided at the bottom of the screen (Fig. 6). After listening to a piece of music, the music chatbot engaged the user in conversation on the music, including their emotional responses. At the end of the session, each user was asked eight open-ended questions to give feedback on the music chatbot. These questions included their overall impression of the music chatbot, ease of use, look and feel, and different features, and its impact on daily life. On average, users took 9.5 min to complete the testing sessions.

5.2 Results

Overall, all users (U) appreciated the ease of interaction and the clarity of the chatbot's responses. The chatbot's ability to engage in conversations about music, suggestions based on their moods, and understanding user queries was well received. Users found the chatbot "fun to use", "clear", and "informative". In addition, U2 described it as being "*like WhatsApp and other chatting apps*", making it familiar and easy to use. U3 appreciated the overall interface design and commented: "*The look and feel were very good, and I liked its appearance*".

The chatbot's ability to evoke emotions and foster a connection through music was also appreciated. U1 mentioned, "*It brings back lovely memories and so it brings back happiness*", after listening to their favourite music. U4 highlighted the emotional benefit for users who may feel alone and commented: "*It would be useful to play me happy music*". All users mentioned that the chatbot's music suggestions could help alleviate loneliness and improve mood. Specifically, U2 asked whether this app would come out soon and added comment: "*My step-father sit in the same place everyday, he is immobile and sits on the same place and play cards, or watch TV. Something like this, he could type in and get information. If the app is ready, would you send it to us? I would share that with my step-father because it is really good, and I think he would love it*".

When users were asked for feedback on avatar design, all of them mentioned that they had not thoroughly noticed it, as they were fully engaged in conversations with the music chatbot. Despite the avatar being a design element, it appeared secondary to the conversational experience. However, users generally described its appearance as friendly and found its design relatable to the music theme. This suggests that while the avatar positively contributed to the overall ambiance of user interface, it did not distract users from focus on engaging with the chatbot.

While users generally trusted the chatbot for music requests and recommendations, reliability issues were also identified. On occasion, users' requests for specific genres from the 1950s were not met, as the chatbot misinterpreted the request and played similar music from more recent years. U3 commented: "*I asked for 50s music, but it seems like it wants me to try different music that I am not interested in listening to*". Furthermore, U5 experienced speech recognition issues on occasions due to the deep tone of their voice, which negatively affected their experience.

The potential to integrate the chatbot into everyday activities was appealing. U1 suggested using it during different activities such as reading and cooking. U2 highlighted its usefulness in various contexts such as driving and gardening, including when alone, as the chatbot could help engage in conversations. U4 mentioned: "*I would do it with my clients in groups*", indicating that the chatbot could also function effectively in social settings, supporting group interactions and discussions.

6 Discussion

6.1 Revisiting Research Questions

RQ1: *What are the key design requirements for a music chatbot tailored to meet the needs and preferences of older adults?*

The initial survey study revealed that music plays a key role in alleviating loneliness and enhancing emotional wellbeing, highlighting several important design considerations for developing a music chatbot tailored to older adults' preferences. By engaging users in conversations related to music and emotions, the chatbot can act as a companion and provide an emotional connection. However, trust in AI-generated recommendations was a barrier for many participants. The contrastive acceptance of music recommendation by a human and a computer suggests a stronger element of trust in the latter is required, which may be seen as untrustworthy or even intruding (the uncanny valley effect [29]. A chatbot design with a hybrid avatar appearance (i.e., conveying warmth and reliability) and conversations on relevant topics like music may help reduce scepticism and build trust.

In addition, it was identified that participants prefer a conversational style that is informative, professional, and free from irrelevant conversations while still being friendly and supportive [28]. Therefore, it is essential to strike a balance between delivering comprehensive information and keeping interactions concise in order to maintain user engagement. Furthermore, participants favoured a text-based chatbot design that feels natural and allows them the freedom to elaborate on their responses and emotions [31]. Incorporating a voice input feature alongside with text-based design is essential to enhance the natural flow of conversation and improve accessibility particularly for older adults. Regarding the font size, majority of participants liked the same font size presented in the interface design which aligned with older adults' preferences. We implemented these design requirements into our music chatbot to meet the needs and preferences of older adults.

RQ2: *How effective is the few-shot prompt engineering technique in providing accurate and reliable responses to user requests in the music chatbot?*

Overall, user-based evaluation results highlighted that users were generally satisfied with the chatbot's responses to their music requests. However, it was also observed that the chatbot occasionally failed to accurately play requested music, leading to a mix of positive and negative user experience. The complexity of the few-shot prompt is a double-edged sword, it generally improves the accuracy of responses but can also reduce performance reliability, potentially decreasing users' trust. Using 'etc.' in prompts may provide flexibility by implying additional examples without explicitly listing them all, which helps to make prompts more concise [24]. While this approach can be efficient in some cases, it introduces ambiguity and limits the model's understanding of the full range of possibilities. In our case, we incorporated 'etc.' in prompts for music recommendations, assuming the model would generalise effectively. However, this caused issues with accurately addressing specific user preferences, especially when attempting to play songs from niche genres like Celtic Folk or Baroque Pop. In fact, there is limited formal research on the effectiveness of using "etc." in prompts for extracting similar items from LLMs. Arguments advocating its use are anecdotal. To determine the effectiveness of using "etc.," it would be best to conduct controlled experiments comparing prompts with and without this technique.

To mitigate these limitations, future iterations should explore the use of more diverse and comprehensive training data or implement advanced prompting strategies to better accommodate a wider range of music preferences and emotional states [42]. A potential solution could involve segmenting complex prompts into shorter, more focused instructions. While zero-shot prompts could be useful to generate responses without specific examples to handle various tasks with flexibility [22], it can lead to inconsistencies for multiple complex tasks such as providing music recommendations and deep emotional conversations.

RQ3*: How do older adults perceive the usability and potential of the music chatbot in reducing loneliness?*

The user-based evaluations revealed that older adults perceived the music chatbot as usable and effective in reducing loneliness. The chatbot's interface and features were intuitive, making interaction easy, which is crucial for adoption among older adults. By evoking positive emotions, the chatbot was seen not just as a tool for entertainment but as an emotional support platform, helping to provide a sense of companionship. This demonstrates the potential of LLMs and prompt engineering to offer emotional engagement, making the chatbot a promising valuable tool for addressing loneliness and enhancing emotional wellbeing.

Beyond individual interactions, users highlighted the chatbot's potential for enriching daily life activities, such as reading or cooking, by tailoring music to their preferences. In social settings such as group activities or shared music experiences, music chatbot was also regarded as a means to create social bonds therefore, further reducing the sense of loneliness. The potential of music chatbot to engage both individually and in groups suggests that it can play a significant role in mitigating loneliness across different contexts. However, to fully maximise its effectiveness, it is crucial to improve reliability by addressing issues such as misinterpretation of music requests.

6.2 Ethical Considerations

When designing chatbots, particularly for older adults who may be more vulnerable, ethical considerations and potential impacts must be prioritised. The inclusion of human-like features, such as the avatar's appearance and conversational style, aims to improve the user experience by promoting trust and acceptance of the chatbot [43]. However, it is crucial to ensure that older users understand they are interacting with an AI system and not a human, as transparency helps prevent any unintended deception. This openness is essential for maintaining trust and recognising the chatbot's artificial nature. In addition, there are also potential risks of emotional discomfort, particularly when specific music trigger intense emotions or memories. Similarly, prolonged interaction with the chatbot or substituting it for human connections may lead to heightened feelings of isolation [44]. To address these concerns, clear communication should be provided, such as informing users about the emotional aspects of interaction, providing support resources, and managing chatbot usage to prevent them from isolation. Data security and privacy is also an important aspect, as users may disclose sensitive information during interactions [45]. There should be transparency about how user data is stored and used for music recommendations. User privacy must be protected by managing sensitive information securely and enforcing robust measures to prevent unauthorised access to personal data.

6.3 Limitations

While this study offers valuable insights into the potential of the music chatbot for older adults, we also acknowledge certain limitations. First, the user-based evaluation was conducted with only five users, which limits the generalisability of the findings across diverse user demographics, musical preferences, and emotional states.

The few-shot prompt engineering approach, while efficient for rapid prototyping, presents significant limitations in terms of music genre diversity, emotional complexity, and conversational depth. The current prompts ask basic questions such as "*How are you feeling after listening to this song?*", which do not allow the chatbot to probe deeper into the user's emotional state. As a result, the interactions may feel shallow and lack the emotional richness needed to establish a meaningful connection with the user [46]. In addition, the more complex user queries may lead to mismatched music recommendations that may not align with the user's emotional state, potentially decreasing satisfaction and long-term emotional engagement with the chatbot [47].

7 Future Work and Conclusion

To address the limitations of the current study, future work should focus on several key areas for improvement. First, expanding the sample size and involving a large and more diverse user groups, including both tech-savvy and less tech-savvy users, will be essential to better assess the chatbot's effectiveness [48]. This will help ensure the chatbot is more universally adaptable and representative of diverse user needs [49].

Moreover, integrating affective computing capabilities, such as emotion recognition from facial expressions, speech, and other indicators, could significantly enhance the chatbot's ability to engage users emotionally [50]. By detecting mood changes (e.g., via facial gestures), the chatbot could tailor music recommendations and responses in real-time, improving emotional connection [51]. This would resolve the issues of emotional misinterpretation and shallow engagement by allowing for more meaningful interactions.

Finally, including more inclusive features, such as custom options for font size adjustments, different colour themes, controlling reading aloud text, and voice types (i.e., male or female) would further improve the accessibility of the chatbot design, particularly for older adults with visual and hearing impairments [52].

The expansion of AI-driven chatbots is poised to persist, with potential applications bounded only by human creativity. One particularly promising avenue lies in leveraging AI-powered chatbots to amplify the role of music in bolstering the emotional wellbeing of older adults. Our preliminary endeavours to develop inclusive music chatbots based on few-shot prompts in LLMs for this demographic have demonstrated success in terms of usability. However, further research is imperative to explore the complexities surrounding privacy, security, and trust as they relate to deploying chatbots for music listening, and to comprehensively understand their influence on emotional wellbeing.

References

1. World Health Organization: Ageing and health. https://www.who.int/news-room/fact-sheets/detail/ageing-and-health. Accessed 27 Sept 2024
2. Laukka, P.: Uses of music and psychological well-being among the elderly. J. Happiness Stud. **8**, 215–241 (2007). https://doi.org/10.1007/s10902-006-9024-3
3. Li, Q., Luximon, Y.: Older adults' use of mobile devices: usability challenges while navigating various interfaces. Behav. Inf. Technol. **39**(8), 837–861 (2020). https://doi.org/10.1080/0144929X.2019.1622786
4. Hill, R., Betts, L.R., Gardner, S.E.: Older adults' experiences and perceptions of digital technology: (Dis) empowerment, wellbeing, and inclusion. Comput. Hum. Behav. **48**, 415–423 (2015). https://doi.org/10.1016/j.chb.2015.01.062
5. Skrebeca, J., Kalniete, P., Goldbergs, J., Pitkevica, L., Tihomirova, D., Romanovs, A.: Modern development trends of chatbots using artificial intelligence (AI). In: Proceedings of the 62nd International Scientific Conference on Information Technology and Management Science of Riga Technical University (ITMS), pp. 1–6. IEEE (2021). https://doi.org/10.1109/ITMS52826.2021.9615258
6. Nguyen, Q.N., Sidorova, A.: Understanding user interactions with a chatbot: a self-determination theory approach. In: Twenty-fourth Americas Conference on Information Systems (2018), New Orleans. https://aisel.aisnet.org/amcis2018/HCI/Presentations/3. Accessed 27 Sept 2024
7. Jin, Y., Tintarev, N., Verbert, K.: Effects of individual traits on diversity-aware music recommender user interfaces. In: Proceedings of the 26th Conference on User Modeling, Adaptation and Personalization, pp. 291–299 (2018). https://doi.org/10.1145/3209219.3209225
8. Cai, W., Jin, Y., Zhao, X., Chen, L.: Listen to music, listen to yourself: design of a conversational agent to support self-awareness while listening to music. In: Proceedings of the 2023 CHI Conference on Human Factors in Computing Systems, pp. 1–19 (2023). https://doi.org/10.1145/3544548.3581427
9. Marvin, G., Nakayiza, H., Jjingo, D., Nakatumba-Nabende, J.: Prompt engineering in large language models. In: Jacob, I.J., Piramuthu, S., Falkowski-Gilski, P. (eds.): International Conference on Data Intelligence and Cognitive Informatics, pp. 387–402. Springer, Singapore (2023). https://doi.org/10.1007/978-981-99-7962-2_30
10. Song, I., Pendse, S.R., Kumar, N., De Choudhury, M.: The typing cure: Experiences with large language model chatbots for mental health support. arXiv preprint arXiv:2401.14362 (2024). https://doi.org/10.48550/arXiv.2401.14362
11. Gall, T., Vallet, F., Douzou, S., Yannou, B.: Re-defining the system boundaries of human-centred design. In: Proceedings of the Design Society, vol. 1, pp. 2521–2530 (2021). https://doi.org/10.1017/pds.2021.513
12. Shandilya, E., Fan, M.: Understanding older adults' perceptions and challenges in using AI-enabled everyday technologies. In: Proceedings of the Tenth International Symposium of Chinese CHI, pp. 105–116 (2022). https://doi.org/10.1145/3565698.3565774
13. Rodríguez-Martínez, A., Amezcua-Aguilar, T., Cortés-Moreno, J., Jiménez-Delgado, J.J.: Qualitative analysis of conversational chatbots to alleviate loneliness in older adults as a strategy for emotional health. Healthcare **12**(1), 62. MDPI (2023). https://doi.org/10.3390/healthcare12010062
14. Venkatesh, V., Morris, M.G., Davis, G.B., Davis, F.D.: User acceptance of information technology: toward a unified view. MIS Q. 425–478 (2003). https://doi.org/10.2307/30036540
15. Park, D.Y., Kim, H.: Determinants of intentions to use digital mental healthcare content among university students, faculty, and staff: motivation, perceived usefulness, perceived ease of use, and parasocial interaction with AI Chatbot. Sustainability **15**(1), 872 (2023). https://doi.org/10.3390/su15010872

16. Khurana, A., Alamzadeh, P., Chilana, P.K.: ChatrEx: Designing explainable chatbot interfaces for enhancing usefulness, transparency, and trust. In: 2021 IEEE Symposium on Visual Languages and Human-Centric Computing (VL/HCC), pp. 1–11. IEEE (2021). https://doi.org/10.1109/VL/HCC51201.2021.9576440
17. Wald, R., Heijselaar, E., Bosse, T.: Make your own: the potential of chatbot customization for the development of user trust. In: Adjunct Proceedings of the 29th ACM Conference on User Modeling, Adaptation and Personalization, pp. 382–387 (2021). https://doi.org/10.1145/3450614.3463600
18. Sacar, S., Munteanu, C., Sin, J., Wei, C., Sayago, S., Zhao, W., Waycott, J.: Designing age-inclusive interfaces: Emerging mobile, conversational, and generative AI to support interactions across the life span. In: Proceedings of the 6th ACM Conference on Conversational User Interfaces, pp. 1–5 (2024). https://doi.org/10.1145/3640794.3669998
19. García-Méndez, S., De Arriba-Perez, F., González-Castaño, F.J., Regueiro-Janeiro, J.A., Gil-Castiñeira, F.: Entertainment chatbot for the digital inclusion of elderly people without abstraction capabilities. IEEE Access **9**, 75878–75891 (2021). https://doi.org/10.1109/ACCESS.2021.3081696
20. Reynolds, L., McDonell, K.: Prompt programming for large language models: beyond the few-shot paradigm. In: Extended Abstracts of the 2021 CHI Conference on Human Factors in Computing Systems, pp. 1–7 (2021). https://doi.org/10.1145/3411763.3451760
21. Schulhoff, S., et al.: The prompt report: A systematic survey of prompting techniques. arXiv preprint arXiv:2406.06608. (2024). https://doi.org/10.48550/arXiv.2406.06608
22. Kojima, T., Gu, S.S., Reid, M., Matsuo, Y., Iwasawa, Y.: Large language models are zero-shot reasoners. Adv. Neural. Inf. Process. Syst. **35**, 22199–22213 (2022)
23. Chamieh, I., Zesch, T., Giebermann, K.: LLMs in short answer scoring: limitations and promise of zero-shot and few-shot approaches. In: Proceedings of the 19th Workshop on Innovative Use of NLP for Building Educational Applications (BEA 2024), pp. 309–315 (2024)
24. Lee, U., et al.: Few-shot is enough: exploring ChatGPT prompt engineering method for automatic question generation in English education. Educ. Inf. Technol. **29**(9), 11483–11515 (2024). https://doi.org/10.1007/s10639-023-12249-8
25. Hurley, E., Okyere-Badoo, J.: A comparative study of few-shot vs. zero-shot prompting to generate quick and useful responses to students' periodic reflections. In: Proceedings of the 55th ACM Technical Symposium on Computer Science Education, vol. 2, p. 1881 (2024). https://doi.org/10.1145/3626253.3635400
26. Stanley, J., ten Brink, R., Valiton, A., Bostic, T., Scollan, B.: Chatbot accessibility guidance: a review and way forward. In: Yang, X.S., Sherratt, S., Dey, N., Joshi, A. (eds) Proceedings of Sixth International Congress on Information and Communication Technology. Lecture Notes in Networks and Systems, vol. 216. Springer, Singapore. https://doi.org/10.1007/978-981-16-1781-2_80
27. Koebel, K., Lacayo, M., Murali, M., Tarnanas, I., Çöltekin, A.: Expert insights for designing conversational user interfaces as virtual assistants and companions for older adults with cognitive impairments In: Følstad, A., et al. Chatbot Research and Design. CONVERSATIONS 2021. Lecture Notes in Computer Science, vol. 13171. Springer, Cham. https://doi.org/10.1007/978-3-030-94890-0_2
28. Rese, A., Tränkner, P.: Perceived conversational ability of task-based chatbots - Which conversational elements influence the success of text-based dialogues? Int. J. Inf. Manage. **74**, 102699 (2024). https://doi.org/10.1016/j.ijinfomgt.2023.102699
29. Song, S.W., Shin, M.: Uncanny valley effects on chatbot trust, purchase intention, and adoption intention in the context of e-commerce: the moderating role of avatar familiarity. Int. J. Hum. Comput. Interact. **40**(2), 441–456 (2024). https://doi.org/10.1080/10447318.2022.2121038

30. Wei, C.Z., Kim, Y.H., Kuzminykh, A.: The bot on speaking terms: the effects of conversation architecture on perceptions of conversational agents. In: Proceedings of the 5th International Conference on Conversational User Interfaces, pp. 1–16 (2023). https://doi.org/10.1145/3571884.3597139
31. Rapp, A., Curti, L., Boldi, A.: The human side of human-chatbot interaction: a systematic literature review of ten years of research on text-based chatbots. Int. J. Hum. Comput. Stud. **151**, 102630 (2021). https://doi.org/10.1016/j.ijhcs.2021.102630
32. Chung, S.J., Lee, H.: Visual presentation of mental healthcare chatbots for user experience. 한국 HCI 학회 논문지**15**(2), 39–45 (2020)
33. Prolific: Quickly find research participants you can trust. https://www.prolific.com. Accessed 27 Sept 2024
34. Figma: The collaborative interface design tool. https://www.figma.com. Accessed 27 Sept 2024
35. Braun, V., Clarke, V.: Using thematic analysis in psychology. Qual. Res. Psychol. **3**(2), 77–101 (2006). https://doi.org/10.1191/1478088706qp063oa
36. Shaked, N.A.: Avatars and virtual agents - relationship interfaces for the elderly. Healthcare Technol. Lett. **4**(3), 83–87 (2017). https://doi.org/10.1049/htl.2017.0009
37. Stock, A., Schlögl, S., Groth, A.: Tell me, what are you most afraid of? Exploring the effects of agent representation on information disclosure in human-chatbot interaction. In: Degen, H., Ntoa, S. (eds) Artificial Intelligence in HCI. HCII 2023. Lecture Notes in Computer Science, vol. 14051, pp 179–191. Springer, Cham (2023). https://doi.org/10.1007/978-3-031-35894-4_13
38. Duangpatra, P., Bunlikhitsiri, B., Wongupparaj, P.: The competency in using smartphones of the homebound older adult. Int. J. Interact. Mob. Technol. **15**(9) (2021). https://doi.org/10.3991/ijim.v15i09.20885
39. Cheng, P.: Emotional "Gray": Emotional analysis of Morandi color system in web design. In: 2021 International Conference on Education Technology and E-Business Management (ETEM 2021)
40. Brown, T., et al.: Language models are few-shot learners. Adv. Neural Inf. Process. Syst. **33**, 1877–1901 (2020). https://doi.org/10.48550/arXiv.2005.14165
41. Deezer API, RapidAPI. https://rapidapi.com/deezerdevs/api/deezer-1. Accessed 27 Sept 2024
42. Xu, Z., et al.: Making pre-trained language models end-to-end few-shot learners with contrastive prompt tuning. In: Proceedings of the Sixteenth ACM International Conference on Web Search and Data Mining, pp. 438–446 (2023). https://doi.org/10.1145/3539597.3570398
43. Silva, G.R.S., Canedo, E.D.: Towards user-centric guidelines for chatbot conversational design. Int. J. Hum.-Comput. Interact. **40**(2), 98–120 (2024). https://doi.org/10.1080/10447318.2022.2118244
44. Laestadius, L., Bishop, A., Gonzalez, M., Illenčík, D., Campos-Castillo, C.: Too human and not human enough: a grounded theory analysis of mental health harms from emotional dependence on the social chatbot Replika. New Media Soc. **26**(10), 5923–5941 (2024). https://doi.org/10.1177/14614448221142007
45. Hasal, M., Nowaková, J., Saghair, K.A., Abdulla, H., Snášel, V., Ogiela, L.: Chatbots: security, privacy, data protection, and social aspects. Concurrency Comput. Pract. Exper. **33**(19), e6426 (2021). https://doi.org/10.1002/cpe.6426
46. Skjuve, M., Følstad, A., Fostervold, K.I., Brandtzaeg, P.B.: My chatbot companion-a study of human-chatbot relationships. Int. J. Hum. Comput. Stud. **149**, 102601 (2021). https://doi.org/10.1016/j.ijhcs.2021.102601
47. Karimov, Z., Allahverdiyev, I., Agayarov, O.Y., Demir, D., Almuradova, E.: ChatGPT vs UpToDate: comparative study of usefulness and reliability of Chatbot in common clinical presentations of otorhinolaryngology–head and neck surgery. Eur. Arch. Otorhinolaryngol. **281**(4), 2145–51 (2024). https://doi.org/10.1007/s00405-023-08423-w

48. Daley, K., Hungerbuehler, I., Cavanagh, K., Claro, H.G., Swinton, P.A., Kapps, M.: Preliminary evaluation of the engagement and effectiveness of a mental health chatbot. Front. Digit. Health **2**, 576361 (2020). | https://doi.org/10.3389/fdgth.2020.576361
49. Ekechi, C.C., Chukwurah, E.G., Oyeniyi, L.D., Okeke, C.D.: AI-infused chatbots for customer support: a cross-country evaluation of user satisfaction in the USA and the UK. Int. J. Manage. Entrepreneurship Res. **6**(4), 1259–1272 (2024). https://doi.org/10.51594/ijmer.v6i4.1057
50. Ghandeharioun, A., McDuff, D., Czerwinski, M., Rowan, K.: Emma: an emotion-aware wellbeing chatbot. In: 8th International Conference on Affective Computing and Intelligent Interaction (ACII), pp. 1–7. IEEE (2019). https://doi.org/10.1109/ACII.2019.8925455
51. Eswar Sudhan, S.K., Garapati, V.K.R., Nadella, M.R.G., Jangala, G., Aswathy, P.: Enhancing chatbot interaction with emotion detection for improved understanding: EmoBot. In: Kumar, S., K., B., Kim, J.H., Bansal, J.C. (eds.) Fourth Congress on Intelligent Systems. CIS 2023. Lecture Notes in Networks and Systems, vol. 865. Springer, Singapore. https://doi.org/10.1007/978-981-99-9043-6_11
52. Lister, K., Coughlan, T., Iniesto, F., Freear, N., Devine, P.: Accessible conversational user interfaces: considerations for design. In: Proceedings of the 17th International Web for All Conference, pp. 1–11 (2020). https://doi.org/10.1145/3371300.3383343

Physician in the Loop Design of Interactive Agents

Maxime Griot[1,2(✉)], Jean Vanderdonckt[2], Demet Yuksel[1,2], and Coralie Hemptinne[1,2]

[1] Université catholique de Louvain, Place des Doyens 1, 1348 Louvain-la-Neuve, Belgium
{maxime.griot,demet.yuksel,coralie.hemptinne}@uclouvain.be
[2] Cliniques Universitaires Saint-Luc, Avenue Hippocrate 10, 1200 Brussels, Belgium
jean.vanderdonckt@uclouvain.be
https://uclouvain.be,https://saintluc.be

Abstract. Medicine poses a unique challenge due to the complexity and range of tasks required to treat patients. We propose an approach to reduce the gap between computer scientists and medical doctors to design relevant interactive agents to assist physicians in their daily work. We demonstrate that an interactive one-hour meeting is enough to equip physicians with enough knowledge and understanding of interactive agents to propose relevant and feasible ideas. Physicians also demonstrated a real interest in designing such systems to assist them in their work.

Keywords: Physician in the loop · Transversal design · Interactive agents · large language models

1 Background

Recent advancements in generative Artificial Intelligence (AI), driven by the transformer architecture and the availability of large-scale text corpora, have opened new avenues for machine learning applications in medicine [16]. These applications span a wide range, from named entity recognition [17] to medical diagnosis [6,13,14] and even the potential replacement of nurses in specific tasks [4]. Such developments offer promising solutions to address the increasing workload of healthcare professionals. However, a significant concern surrounding these advancements is the relative lack of physician involvement in their development and implementation.

Published work, both in academic settings and commercial solutions, often either excludes physicians entirely or involves them only in evaluating the end result [15]. Conversely, studies conducted by medical doctors to assess the relevance and quality of these models in specialized fields frequently lack input from computer scientists [5,7,19]. This disconnect between the two fields is further

L. Zaina et al. (Eds.): EICS 2024, LNCS 15518, pp. 94–109, 2025.
https://doi.org/10.1007/978-3-031-91760-8_7

exacerbated by the siloed nature of scientific publication, where computer scientists and medical doctors publish in their respective disciplinary journals and conferences, with limited cross-pollination of ideas.

The adoption and reception of generative AI in medicine have been slow and met with resistance from physicians, partly because the performance claims made by computer scientists often fail to translate into clinically relevant outcomes [3]. This misalignment between technological capabilities and clinical needs underscores the importance of interdisciplinary collaboration in developing AI solutions for healthcare.

The lack of interaction and overlap between these two fields constitutes a major obstacle to creating relevant, safe, and adapted interactive agents for medicine. In this work, we detail our approach to developing interactive agents by including both computer scientists and medical doctors throughout the entire process, from conception to implementation and evaluation.

2 Engineering

2.1 Selection

Involving the correct actors in a co-engineering task is the first major step. In this work, we aimed to involve both software engineers and physicians, with or without prior exposure to systems design. To ensure a smooth design process, involving curious and available physicians was key.

To recruit physicians, we contacted department leads to discuss their interest in AI, available resources, and willingness to participate in a work group. This initial contact was used to gauge interest; we shared a two-page overview of generative AI and our goal of co-creating systems with physicians.

We prioritized department leads who already contribute to clinical informatics through their involvement in Electronic Health Record projects at our hospital. The first two department leads contacted agreed to participate in the work group. We limited the number of departments involved to two (Oncology and Geriatrics), allowing resources to remain focused on these departments' specific needs. Limiting the number of participants also reduces the risk of interdepartmental disagreements.

Department leads were tasked with briefly introducing the ongoing project and studies to physicians in their respective departments. Both groups comprised an average of 10 physicians, depending on availability.

2.2 Knowledge

One challenge in system co-creation is the knowledge mismatch between involved parties. Software engineers understand systems design and technological limitations but lack knowledge of patient treatment processes. Physicians can identify key aspects of their daily routine that could be improved but may struggle to formulate solutions. Additionally, both groups alone are unable to make proper risk assessments due to their respective knowledge limitations.

A conventional approach would involve implementing metrics to track time-consuming tasks, shadowing physicians, and conducting interviews to find use cases. Our approach attempts to reduce knowledge gaps between the two groups, allowing for open discussion and enabling physicians to identify relevant and feasible use cases.

To facilitate such discussions, we addressed three key categories that we believed would provide sufficient information for physicians to brainstorm ideas:

1. Understanding basic capabilities of large language models through zero-shot prompts
2. Limitations of these capabilities, including hallucinations
3. Basic agents, extending large language models with external APIs that models can use to enrich user requests

We organized interactive meetings with each department to explain the current state of AI in medicine and involve them in the interactive design of a small agent. The entire co-design process is presented in Fig. 1.

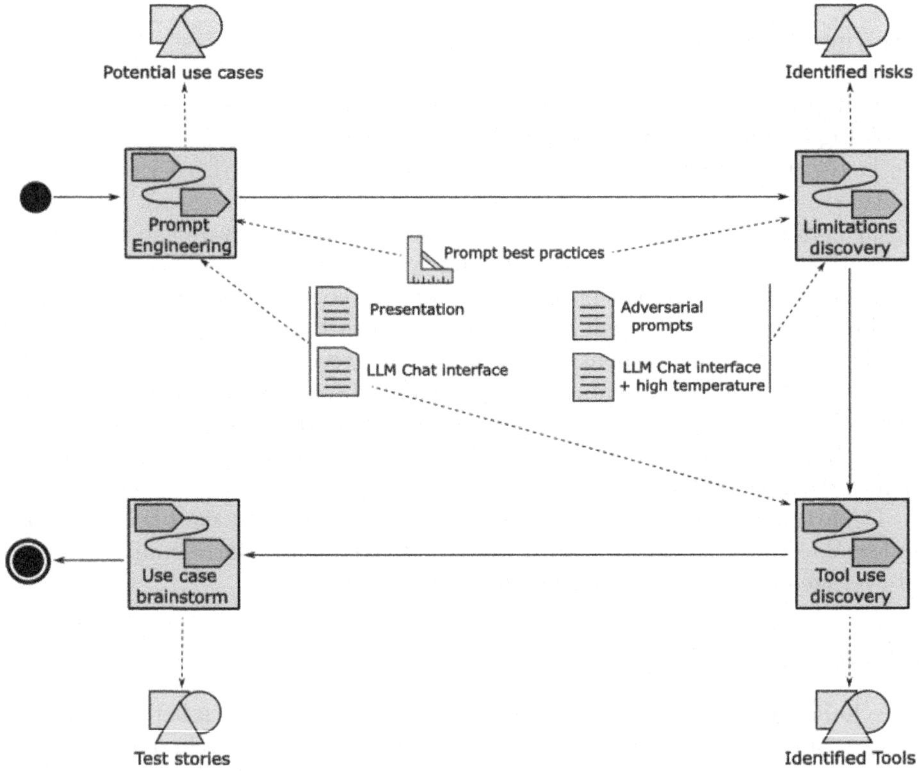

Fig. 1. Overview of the co-engineering process with outcomes for each step using the Software & Systems Process Engineering Meta-Model (SPEM) [12].

The demonstration relied on a custom chat user interface using Mixtral 8x7B [9] as the model and the ChromaDB vector database seeded with UpToDate paragraphs [2,11].

Prompt Engineering. Meetings began with a short introduction to existing AI applications in medicine, primarily addressing classification models in imagery, such as nodule detection in radiology [10]. We acknowledged challenges faced by physicians due to increased clerical work [18] and briefly mentioned ChatGPT as the current state-of-the-art large language model.

The interactive session aimed to teach fundamentals of large language models and agents through an intuitive process. This task helped physicians identify both use cases and potential solutions using existing tools that large language models could utilize.

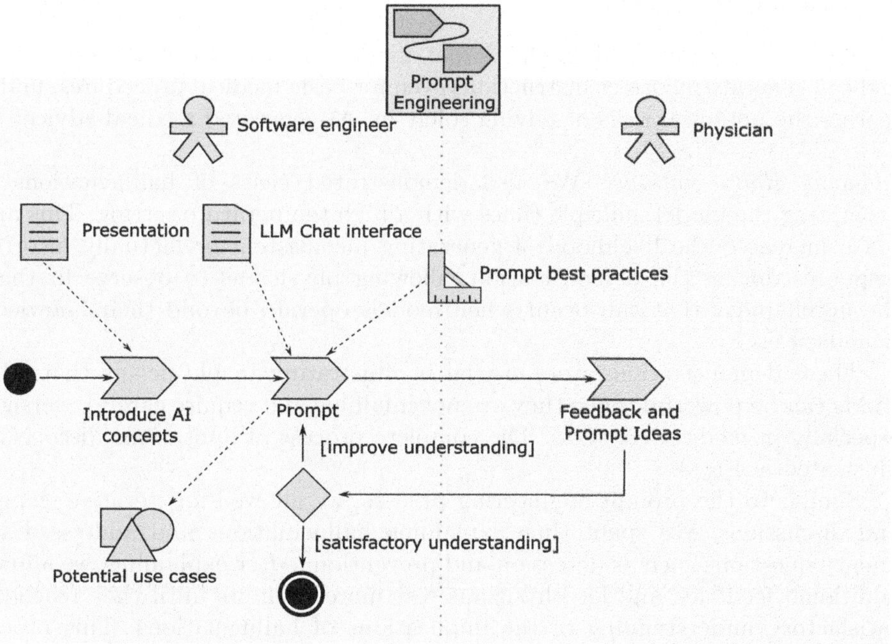

Fig. 2. Definition of the prompt engineering process using SPEM.

Through the process detailed in Fig. 2, we prompted an LLM with a simple medical question and obtained feedback and prompt ideas from physicians. This iterative process familiarized physicians with the chat interface and improved their understanding of prompting best practices. Basic use cases were formulated by physicians during this process. After a few iterations, when physicians wanted to move on or lacked new ideas, we proceeded to the next step.

Limitations Discovery. A major limitation of LLMs is their ability to be confidently incorrect, commonly called hallucinations, which can be particularly dangerous in critical domains such as medicine where mistakes can lead to adverse patient outcomes.

We demonstrated these limitations through two main approaches:

Omission of Critical Information and Incorrect Suggestions. After the co-creation of a small agent, we addressed safety concerns by prompting the model with a simple task: "Describe the procedure to perform a blood gas analysis." The model's response revealed significant limitations:

- The model failed to mention Allen's test [1], a critical step to ensure the safety of the procedure.
- It incorrectly suggested using a tourniquet to make the artery more visible, which is not a standard practice for arterial blood gas sampling and could potentially be harmful.

This demonstration highlighted that models may lack critical information and can generate incorrect instructions even for basic medical procedures, underscoring the potential risks of relying solely on AI-generated medical advice.

Inducing Hallucinations. We also demonstrated cases of hallucinations by prompting the model multiple times with a high temperature setting. This approach increased the likelihood of generating inconsistent or factually incorrect responses during the demonstration, allowing physicians to observe firsthand the unreliability that can occur when models operate beyond their knowledge boundaries.

These demonstrations were crucial in illustrating to physicians that while LLMs can be powerful tools, they are not infallible and require careful oversight, especially in medical contexts. The complete process of limitations discovery is illustrated in Fig. 3.

Similar to the prompt engineering process, we allowed for iterative changes and discussions. We spent time explaining hallucinations and addressed secondary questions such as detection and prevention. After explaining, we allowed additional feedback and let physicians test more prompts until they reached a satisfactory understanding of the implications of hallucinations. This process allowed physicians to raise concerns regarding the risks in medicine caused by these limitations.

The limitations discovery phase was instrumental in fostering a critical perspective among the participating physicians. It highlighted the necessity for human expertise in verifying and contextualizing AI-generated information, especially in high-stakes medical scenarios. This understanding formed a crucial foundation for the subsequent stages of our co-creation process, ensuring that the developed tools would be used responsibly and with appropriate safeguards.

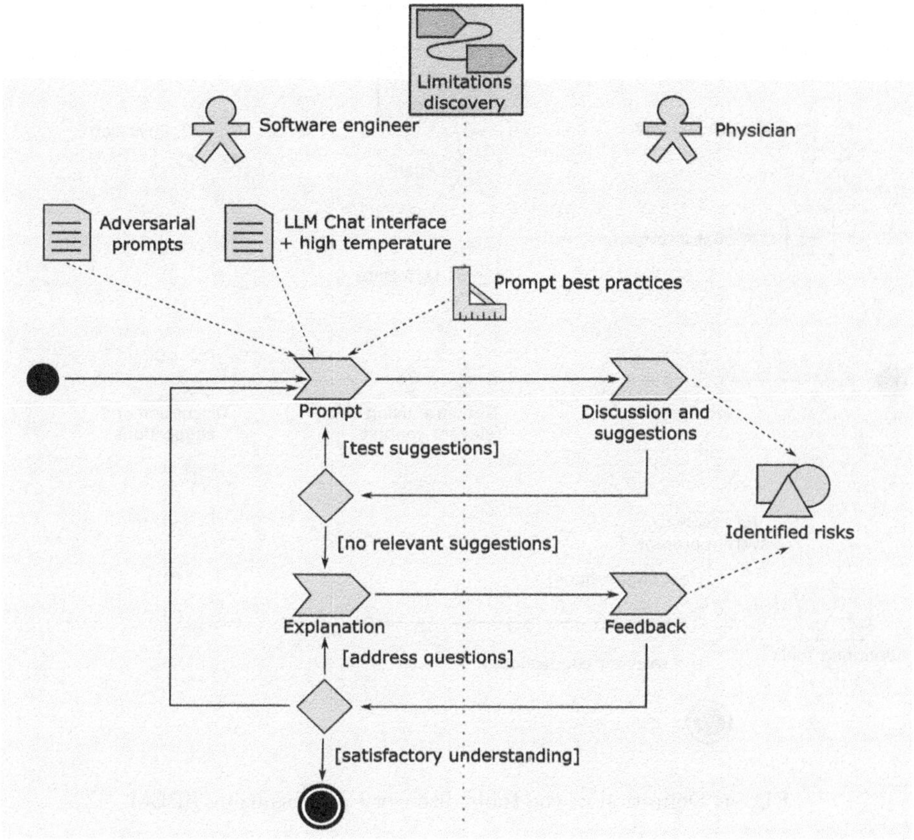

Fig. 3. Definition of the limitations discovery process using SPEM.

Tool Use Discovery. With basic chat usage and limitations covered, we introduced the concept of tools-functions that can be used by the LLM to enrich user requests. We implemented an automatic Retrieval Augmented Generation (RAG) system [8] in our chat interface that retrieves documents related to the prompt from UpToDate [11]. The process of tool discovery is illustrated in Fig. 4.

To demonstrate the RAG tool use, we proposed a basic medical vignette:

> **Vignette**
>
> A 54-year-old male patient presents to the emergency department with abdominal pain. I suspect gallstones. Describe the best next step.

This vignette allowed the model to retrieve information related to the approach to abdominal pain and gallstones diagnosis. The RAG system enriched the LLM's response with relevant medical information from trusted sources.

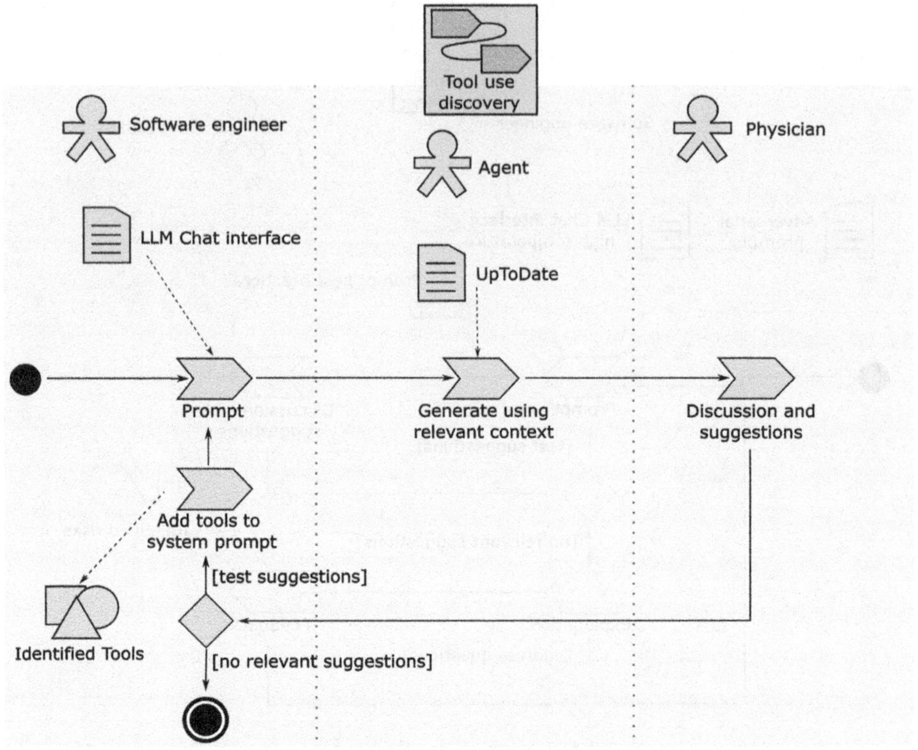

Fig. 4. Definition of the tools discovery process using SPEM.

We used the model's answer to initiate a discussion with the physicians, asking if there was anything else that should be considered. This led to multiple suggestions from the physicians, including:

- Asking specific diagnostic questions (e.g., "Did you eat a meal with a lot of fat before the pain appeared?", "Do you have a history of gallstones?")
- Checking past clinical documentation and imaging results to determine if there is a history of similar complaints

Building on these suggestions, we proposed that the model could perform these tasks using additional tools. We modified the prompt to introduce a new tool:

Prompt

To help you answer the physician's question, you have access to the "Ask" tool. You can use this to ask questions to the patient by writing Ask("question here"). For example: Ask("How are you doing?").

Given this prompt, the model demonstrated the use of the tool by suggesting relevant questions. This demonstration sparked engagement from the participants, who began proposing new tools and inquiring about tool limitations, such as the number of tools that could be used and their complexity.

We further expanded the demonstration by implementing some of the proposed tools, showcasing multi-tool usage. This allowed us to introduce more advanced concepts, including the use of Retrieval Augmented Generation through a reference database tool for looking up appropriate guidelines.

Our user interface was designed to enhance the accessibility and transparency of the retrieved information. As shown in Fig. 5, we added a "Sources" section under the LLM response. This section comprised links to the relevant sources of information. Additionally, we implemented a feature where hovering the mouse over a link would display the content of the extract used by the RAG system. This design choice allows users to read the relevant extract without opening a new tab and reading the entire article, thus streamlining the verification process and enhancing the user experience.

This interactive demonstration allowed physicians to understand how the LLM could leverage external, up-to-date medical knowledge and additional tools to provide more accurate and context-aware responses. It also highlighted the importance of transparency in AI-assisted medical decision-making, as users could easily verify the sources and specific information used by the system.

The tools discovery process, as depicted in Fig. 4, and the practical demonstration using the sample interface shown in Fig. 5, provided physicians with a comprehensive understanding of how AI tools can be integrated into their decision-making process while maintaining transparency and reliability. Furthermore, the collaborative nature of this process fostered engagement and creativity among the participants, leading to the exploration of more advanced and tailored AI tools for medical applications.

Brainstorm and Proposition Development. Following the interactive meetings, we initiated a structured brainstorming process to capture and prioritize potential applications of agent systems in clinical practice as illustrated in Fig. 6. This process was designed to bridge the gap between technological possibilities and genuine clinical needs, ensuring that our development efforts would yield practically relevant AI tools. Our approach consisted of several key phases:

Idea Generation and Prioritization. We engaged physicians in a creative yet structured ideation process. Participants were given several days to reflect on their clinical experiences and compile a list of potential AI applications that could address challenges in their practice. To ensure consistency and facilitate analysis, we provided a standardized template for idea submission and a prioritization system, as illustrated in Table 1.

This user story format ("As a X, I would like Y, in order to Z") encouraged physicians to articulate not just the desired functionality but also the intended outcome and the specific user role. The priority system (+++ need, ++ want,

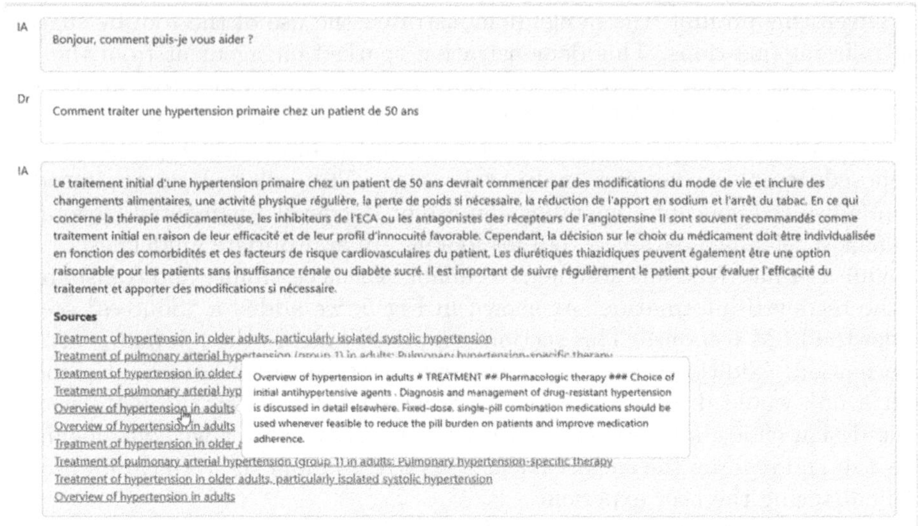

Fig. 5. Sample user interface demonstrating the Retrieval Augmented Generation system, including the LLM response, Sources section, and hover functionality for viewing source extracts.

Table 1. Instructions for normalizing physician design propositions

Type	Description	Example
Template	As a X, I would like Y, in order to Z.	As a physician, I want the system to look up drug interactions, in order to increase the safety of my prescriptions.
Priority	+++ need ++ want + would like	+++

+ would like) allowed participants to indicate the perceived importance of each idea, providing valuable context for the subsequent selection process.

Resource Identification for Knowledge Enhancement. Concurrent with the idea generation, we asked physicians to compile a list of references they frequently consult in their practice. This step was crucial for two reasons:

1. It provided insights into the knowledge sources that inform clinical decision-making in different specialties.
2. It supplied valuable input for enhancing our Retrieval Augmented Generation (RAG) system, ensuring that the AI agent could access and utilize relevant, up-to-date medical knowledge.

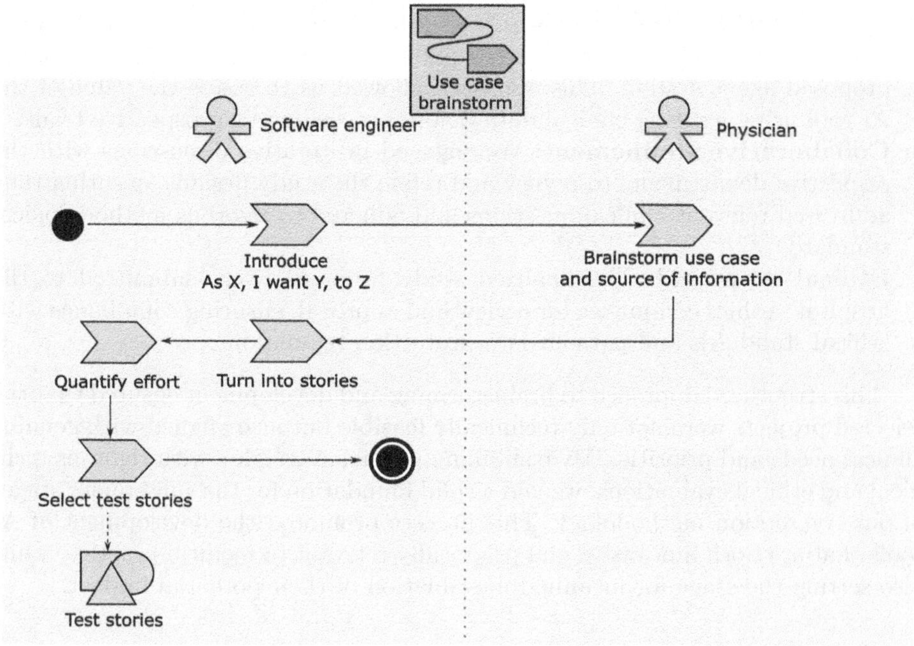

Fig. 6. Definition of the brainstorming and proposition development process using SPEM.

Proposition Refinement and Technical Evaluation. Upon receiving the physicians' ideas, our interdisciplinary team undertook a thorough refinement and evaluation process:

1. **User Story Transformation:** We converted the raw propositions into formal user stories, aligning them with established software development practices. This step helped clarify requirements and facilitated communication between clinical and technical team members.
2. **Feasibility Assessment:** Each proposal underwent a rigorous technical feasibility evaluation. We considered factors such as data availability, integration challenges, and potential ethical implications.
3. **Development Estimation:** We estimated the time and resources required to develop a proof-of-concept for each idea. This step was crucial for balancing ambition with practical constraints.

Selection and Study Design. The final phase involved a balanced approach to project selection and study design:

1. **Proposition Selection:** We selected one proposition per department, carefully balancing the priorities assigned by physicians with our development capacity and the potential for innovation.

2. **Retrospective Study Design:** For each selected proposition, we designed a retrospective study to evaluate the potential impact and effectiveness of the proposed agent system. This approach allowed us to assess the value of the AI tool using existing clinical data before proceeding to prospective trials.
3. **Collaborative Refinement:** We engaged in iterative discussions with the respective departments to review and refine the study designs, ensuring they addressed relevant clinical questions and adhered to rigorous methodological standards.
4. **Ethical Approval:** The finalized study proposals were submitted to the hospital's ethics committee for review and approval, ensuring compliance with ethical standards and patient data protection regulations.

This structured approach to brainstorming and development ensured that the selected projects were not only technically feasible but also aligned with genuine clinical needs and priorities. By combining physician insights with rigorous technical and ethical evaluations, we laid a solid foundation for the subsequent stages of our co-creation methodology. This process promoted the development of AI tools that are both innovative and practically relevant to medical practice, while also setting the stage for meaningful evaluation of their potential impact.

3 Results

Our approach of involving physicians in the design process yielded significant insights and generated considerable enthusiasm about the potential contributions of AI in clinical practice. The collaborative sessions not only achieved their primary goals but also sparked broader discussions about the future of medicine.

3.1 Physician Engagement and Propositions

The participatory design approach was well-received by all participants across both departments. Physicians demonstrated high levels of engagement, offering numerous suggestions for potential AI applications in their daily practice. Table 2 presents a selection of these suggestions, along with their assigned priorities.

The suggestions revealed a strong interest in AI applications that could streamline administrative tasks, enhance decision-making processes, and improve patient care. Notably, both oncologists and geriatricians prioritized AI assistance in documentation and guideline adherence, indicating common pain points across specialties.

Table 2. Example uses suggested by physicians along with their priorities.

Department	Use	Priority
As an oncologist, I would like AI to	help me write my consultation notes, to reduce my clerical work	+++
	produce instructions for patients at the end of the visit	+++
	inform me if a patient can be included in a study	+++
	compare the patient with similar patients to help me decide between treatment and palliative care	++
	help me estimate life expectancy without cancer	++
	tell me if the patient needs nutritional support based on the treatment and weight changes	++
As a geriatrician, I would like AI to	extract the problem list, medical and surgical history and recent treatment from the healthcare network	+++
	help me optimize treatment based on the current START/STOPP guidelines	+++
	notify me of documented events since the last visit	++
	anticipate post-operative complications	+

3.2 Knowledge Sources for AI Enhancement

In addition to use case suggestions, physicians proposed multiple sources of knowledge to provide models with accurate and up-to-date information. Table 3 presents a selection of these proposed sources, categorized by department and type of resource.

Table 3. Selected sources of knowledge proposed by physicians.

Department	Source	Kind
Geriatrics	UpToDate	Guidelines
	Gériatrie pour le praticien, Elsevier Masson	Textbook
	European Geriatrics Medicine	Journal
	Journal of the American Geriatric Society	Journal
	Geriatric Depression Scale (GDS-15)	Score
	START and STOPP v3	Pharmacology Guidelines
	Neuro-Geriatrics. A Clinical Manual. Springer	Textbook
Oncology	European Society For Medical Oncology	Guidelines
	American Society of Clinical Oncology	Guidelines
	National Comprehensive Cancer Network	Guidelines

The proposed knowledge sources encompassed a wide range of materials, including clinical guidelines, textbooks, journals, and assessment tools. This diverse set of resources reflects the complex nature of medical decision-making and highlights the importance of incorporating varied, authoritative sources into AI systems for healthcare.

3.3 Emergent Discussions and Reflections

While the primary goal of the meetings was to introduce the technology and equip physicians with sufficient understanding to propose applications, the sessions evolved beyond this initial scope. Both meetings concluded with open discussions among all participants about the broader impact of AI on clinical practice.

Key observations from these discussions include:

- **Reaction to Basic AI Functions:** Physicians expressed both impressment and concern when presented with relatively basic AI functions, such as suggesting relevant questions to ask patients. This dual reaction underscores the potential of AI to significantly alter clinical workflows.
- **Future of Medical Practice:** The demonstrations sparked conversations about the future landscape of medicine and the evolving role of physicians in an AI-driven healthcare environment.
- **Ethical Considerations:** Participants raised questions about the ethical implications of AI in healthcare, including issues of patient privacy, decision-making autonomy, and the potential for AI to exacerbate or mitigate healthcare disparities.
- **Integration Challenges:** Discussions touched upon the practical challenges of integrating AI tools into existing clinical workflows and electronic health record systems.
- **Legal Implications:** Concerns were raised about physicians' liability when following AI-generated recommendations, highlighting the need for clear guidelines on integrating AI into clinical decision-making.

These emergent discussions revealed a nuanced perspective among physicians regarding AI in healthcare. While they recognized its potential to enhance efficiency and decision-making, they also expressed a keen awareness of the need for careful implementation and ongoing evaluation of AI tools in clinical settings.

3.4 Implications for Future Development

The results of these collaborative sessions have several important implications for the future development of AI in healthcare:

1. **Tailored Solutions:** The diversity of suggested applications underscores the need for AI solutions tailored to specific clinical contexts and specialties.
2. **Knowledge Integration:** The range of proposed knowledge sources highlights the importance of developing robust methods for integrating diverse, authoritative medical information into AI systems.
3. **Ongoing Engagement:** The positive reception and rich discussions suggest that ongoing engagement with healthcare professionals should be a cornerstone of AI development in medicine.

These findings provide a strong foundation for the next phases of our research, informing both the technical development of AI tools and the broader strategies for their integration into clinical practice.

4 Conclusion

This study demonstrates the efficacy and importance of involving physicians in the co-creation and design of interactive AI agents for medical applications. Our findings indicate that a single one-hour meeting is sufficient to equip physicians with the necessary understanding to make relevant and feasible design suggestions. This approach not only generates valuable input for AI development but also sparks crucial discussions on limitations, safety concerns, and potential patient benefits.

Key outcomes of our methodology include:

- **Efficient Knowledge Transfer:** Physicians quickly gained enough understanding of AI capabilities to contribute meaningfully to the design process.
- **Relevant Design Suggestions:** The involvement of domain specialists from the outset ensured the relevance and practicality of proposed AI tools.
- **Interdisciplinary Dialogue:** The process fostered important discussions on ethical considerations, implementation challenges, and the future of medical practice.
- **Long-term Engagement:** By developing tools requested by physicians, we laid the groundwork for sustained support and collaboration in addressing time-consuming tasks.

Furthermore, our work reveals that AI integration in healthcare prompts existential questions for physicians. It is crucial to facilitate these discussions and to contextualize the current capabilities of AI models. We emphasize that present AI systems are best suited for simple yet time-consuming tasks, require supervision, and have limitations including the potential for hallucinations.

In conclusion, this study underscores the value of bridging the knowledge gap between AI developers and medical professionals. By fostering collaboration from the inception of AI tools, we can ensure their relevance, safety, and effective integration into clinical practice. This approach not only enhances the quality of AI applications in healthcare but also prepares the medical community for the evolving landscape of AI-assisted medicine.

By continuing to prioritize collaborative approaches in AI development for healthcare, we can work towards creating tools that truly enhance medical practice while addressing the complex ethical and practical challenges that arise in this rapidly evolving field.

Acknowledgments. This study was funded by the Fondation Saint-Luc (grant number 467E).

Disclosure of Interests. The authors have no competing interests to declare that are relevant to the content of this article.

References

1. Allen, E.V.: Thrombo-Angiitis obliterans. Bull. N.Y. Acad. Med. **18**(3), 165–189 (1942). https://www.ncbi.nlm.nih.gov/pmc/articles/PMC1933752/
2. ChromaDB: ChromaDB the AI-native open-source embedding database (2023). https://www.trychroma.com
3. Heston, T.F., Lewis, L.M.: ChatGPT provides inconsistent risk-stratification of patients with atraumatic chest pain. PLoS ONE **19**(4), e0301854 (2024). https://doi.org/10.1371/journal.pone.0301854. https://journals.plos.org/plosone/article?id=10.1371/journal.pone.0301854
4. Hippocratic: Hippocratic AI (2024). https://www.hippocraticai.com/
5. Humar, P., Asaad, M., Bengur, F.B., Nguyen, V.: ChatGPT is equivalent to first-year plastic surgery residents: evaluation of ChatGPT on the plastic surgery in-service examination. Aesthetic Surg. J. **43**(12), NP1085–NP1089 (2023). https://doi.org/10.1093/asj/sjad130
6. Jin, D., Pan, E., Oufattole, N., Weng, W.H., Fang, H., Szolovits, P.: What Disease does this Patient Have? A Large-scale Open Domain Question Answering Dataset from Medical Exams (2020). http://arxiv.org/abs/2009.13081. arXiv:2009.13081 [cs] version: 1
7. Jq, J., As, D.: ChatGPT for healthcare providers and patients: practical implications within dermatology. J. Am. Acad. Dermatol. **89**(4), 870–871 (2023). https://doi.org/10.1016/j.jaad.2023.05.081. https://pubmed.ncbi.nlm.nih.gov/37315798/
8. Lewis, P., et al.: Retrieval-augmented generation for knowledge-intensive NLP tasks. In: Advances in Neural Information Processing Systems, vol. 33, pp. 9459–9474. Curran Associates, Inc. (2020). https://proceedings.neurips.cc/paper/2020/hash/6b493230205f780e1bc26945df7481e5-Abstract.html
9. Mistral: mistralai/Mixtral-8x7B-v0.1. Hugging Face (2024). https://huggingface.co/mistralai/Mixtral-8x7B-v0.1
10. Nam, J.G., et al.: AI improves nodule detection on chest radiographs in a health screening population: a randomized controlled trial. Radiology **307**(2), e221894 (2023). https://doi.org/10.1148/radiol.221894. publisher: Radiological Society of North America
11. UpToDate: Industry-leading clinical decision support (2023). https://www.wolterskluwer.com/en/solutions/uptodate
12. OMG: Software & Systems Process Engineering Meta-Model Specification (2008). http://www.omg.org/spec/SPEM/2.0/PDF
13. OpenAI: GPT-4 Technical Report (2023). https://doi.org/10.48550/arXiv.2303.08774. http://arxiv.org/abs/2303.08774. arXiv:2303.08774
14. Rydzewski, N.R., et al.: Comparative evaluation of LLMs in clinical oncology. NEJM AI **1**(5), AIoa2300151 (2024). https://doi.org/10.1056/AIoa2300151
15. Saab, K., et al.: Capabilities of Gemini Models in Medicine (2024). https://doi.org/10.48550/arXiv.2404.18416. http://arxiv.org/abs/2404.18416. arXiv:2404.18416
16. Singhal, K., et al.: Large language models encode clinical knowledge. Nature **620**(7972), 172–180 (2023). https://doi.org/10.1038/s41586-023-06291-2. https://www.nature.com/articles/s41586-023-06291-2
17. Sousa, H., Mario Jorge, A., Pasquali, A., Santos, C., Lopes, M.: A biomedical entity extraction pipeline for oncology health records in Portuguese. In: Proceedings of the 38th ACM/SIGAPP Symposium on Applied Computing, pp. 950–956. Association for Computing Machinery, New York (2023). https://doi.org/10.1145/3555776.3578577. https://doi.org/10.1145/3555776.3578577

18. Starren, J.B., et al.: A retrospective look at the predictions and recommendations from the 2009 AMIA policy meeting: did we see EHR-related clinician burnout coming? J. Am. Med. Inform. Assoc. **28**(5), 948–954 (2021). https://doi.org/10.1093/jamia/ocaa320
19. Suchman, K., Garg, S., Trindade, A.J.: Chat generative pretrained transformer fails the multiple-choice american college of gastroenterology self-assessment test. Am. J. Gastroenterol. **118**(12), 2280–2282 (2023). https://doi.org/10.14309/ajg.0000000000002320

NexOz - A Wizard of Oz Approach to Facilitate the Integration of AI in Interactive Systems

Raf Menten(✉), Gustavo Roveloruiz, and Davy Vanacken

Hasselt University - Flanders Make, Expertise Centre for Digital Media, Diepenbeek, Belgium
{raf.menten,gustavo.roveloruiz,davy.vanacken}@uhasselt.be

Abstract. This paper introduces NexOz, an approach and tool to facilitate incremental integration of AI components into interactive systems using a Wizard of Oz (WOz). The paper explores various challenges of AI integration, such as contextual understanding, conversational interaction, state tracking, and gesture recognition, particularly within the context of an operator support system in the manufacturing industry. NexOz allows developers to simulate AI functionalities through human intervention, enabling rapid prototyping, experimentation, and data collection. By leveraging a human wizard to emulate AI behavior in a structured way, NexOz facilitates the design and testing of dialogue flows, interaction patterns, tracking mechanisms, and conversational designs in real-time without having a fully-fledged implementation of AI-based solutions. Through iterative refinement and continuous feedback loops, NexOz offers a pragmatic approach to navigate the complexities of AI integration in interactive systems.

Keywords: Wizard of Oz · AI Integration · Engineering Interactive AI-based Systems · Digital Assistant · Industry 4.0 · OperatorAssist

1 Introduction

As artificial intelligence (AI) continues to advance, it creates more opportunities for seamless integration within interactive systems. Integrating AI features can lead to enhanced user experiences, improved system performance, and the unlocking of new capabilities, as AI can adapt to user needs, automate complex tasks, and offer more personalized interactions. This integration, however, presents a multifaceted challenge that encompasses both technical and user-centric hurdles [1,13], ranging from algorithmic intricacies and performance to user acceptance [12,17,18]. As a result, traditional approaches to AI integration often face obstacles such as long development cycles, high implementation costs, and difficulties of capturing real-world user interactions. Additionally, concerns about transparency, accountability, and bias in AI-driven systems further complicate the integration process.

L. Zaina et al. (Eds.): EICS 2024, LNCS 15518, pp. 110–125, 2025.
https://doi.org/10.1007/978-3-031-91760-8_8

In this paper, we explore NexOz, an approach and tool to integrate AI into interactive systems by utilizing a Wizard of Oz (WOz) to remediate and facilitate these challenges. NexOz draws inspiration from the classic WOz approach of simulating system capabilities through human intervention [7] and the preliminary work of Browne [4] on WOz for machine learning models. NexOz leverages both basic levels of technical automation (e.g., communication among system components, capturing and replaying input streams, logging) and human cognition (e.g., natural language understanding and conversation, system context definition, pattern recognition) to address the complexities inherent in AI integration. NexOz integrates a nexus architecture, characterized by a back-end core where all communication and interactions between technical components converge, with WOz techniques, providing a unified platform for diverse simulations across a wide range of devices.

One of the primary benefits of leveraging a WOz approach is its ability to facilitate rapid prototyping and experimentation. Given the fast-paced AI developments, agility and adaptability are paramount. By employing NexOz and human wizards to simulate AI functionalities, developers can rapidly prototype, evaluate, and iterate on AI-driven features without requiring fully implemented AI systems. This enables quicker validation and refinement of concepts and functionality, ultimately accelerating the development cycle. Furthermore, the use of a WOz approach in a test or operational environment provides an invaluable opportunity to collect data logs of user interactions [10,15], which can serve as a resource for training and refining AI algorithms, and capture real-world user behavior, preferences, and feedback.

The paper's contributions are twofold: (a) an approach for AI system development that employs an iterative process to gradually reduce dependence on human inputs, and (b) the application of NexOz on practical scenarios, showcasing the incremental integration of AI-based modules in the context of a research project on a digital assistant in the manufacturing industry.

2 Positioning in Literature and Development Process

In literature, the WOz approach has found applications in various domains, including natural language interactions [25], human-robot interactions [21], automated vehicles [8] and data analysis [12]. One of the main motivations for employing a WOz approach when integrating AI is that it offers the means to explore and develop systems without immediately committing to extensive engineering efforts [24,25,30]. Initially, designers determine possible design features and are then able to assess the feasibility through the simulated environment [16,21,24]. While WOz interfaces are often developed on an ad-hoc basis to investigate specific hypotheses, they are typically not conceived to evolve with the system [9]. NexOz represents an approach in which the WOz functionality is fully integrated into the basic framework for developing new applications. In other words, our user-centric approach allows the transition from a wizard having full control over the simulation of AI functions to fully-fledged automated functionality and the exchange of information with external components.

Collecting user interaction data is essential throughout the development process to improve the system and even use it to train future implementations of the AI [11,22]. This forms a continuous feedback loop where the AI (once integrated) can learn from its actions, adapt, and improve over time. Butz et al. [5] presented a study paradigm called "Expert of Oz" where researchers focus on investigating both user behavior and the required functionality of a hypothetical AI system by using a human expert to simulate the AI. By logging and annotating these interactions, designers can gain valuable insights into user preferences, potential issues and areas of improvement [19]. This data-driven approach, leveraged by the intelligence of a human wizard, enables continuous refinement and optimization, ultimately leading to a more accurate and responsive AI system [6].

As the project progresses, the output from the exploratory WOz sessions can be analyzed to determine what future interactions with the AI system could be like [19], by gradually incorporating more sophisticated functionalities. This incremental approach allows for a natural evolution of the system, with each iteration building upon the results of the previous ones [21,29,30].

Eventually, the system evolves into a partially integrated state where AI algorithms start to take over certain tasks and responsibilities from the wizard. This state is sometimes referred to as a Wizard *with* Oz system (i.e., a human-centric method that uses real technology in a simulated environment) [11,21]. This gradual reduction of dependence on human intervention is an important aspect of a Wizard with Oz system [6]. This process is guided by the principle of minimal viable quality (MVQ), where AI components are integrated once they meet a minimum threshold of reliability and performance.

3 Incremental AI Integration with NexOz

Our proposed approach consists of four distinct stages, depicted schematically in Fig. 1: exploration, simulation setup, simulation and validation, and implementation. These stages are designed to facilitate the gradual refinement of AI systems, ensuring they are aligned with user needs and expectations while minimizing risks associated with full AI deployment from the outset.

The first stage of the process focuses on the identification and exploration of the AI functionality required for a specific use case. This stage involves close collaboration with stakeholders to define the problem space and determine how AI can address specific user needs. Detailed requirements are gathered based on observations of current workflows, and early hypotheses about the desired AI features are developed. This exploratory process results in a clear understanding of the goals and objectives of the AI system and a set of metrics that will be used to measure its effectiveness.

Once the AI requirements have been explored, the next step is to set up a simulation environment using the WOz approach. In this stage, human wizards mimic the behavior of the expected AI system (including potential flaws, such

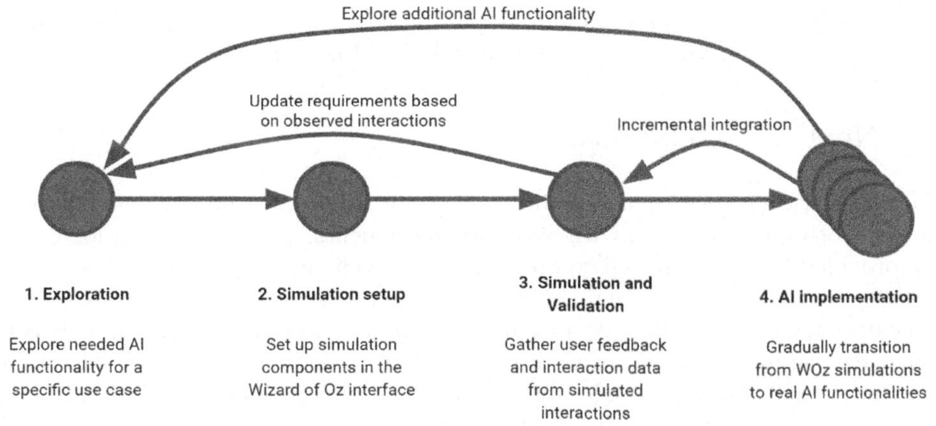

Fig. 1. The iterative refinement process and the progression between the different stages of NexOz.

as imperfect AI behavior), allowing stakeholders to interact with a simulated version of the AI functionality without the need for full AI development. The purpose of this setup is to allow stakeholders to experience the envisioned AI system in action and to gather initial insights into how it acts in practice. By simulating AI responses and interactions, the development team can observe how users engage with the system, identify any gaps in the initial requirements, and collect valuable feedback. The WOz interface is a critical tool in this stage, as it allows for a rapid, low-cost evaluation of potential AI functionalities before investing in full-scale implementation.

In the simulation and validation stage, the focus shifts to gathering detailed feedback and interaction data from users as they engage with the simulated AI system. By analyzing how users interact with the system, developers can assess whether the simulated AI functionality meets the expectations defined in the exploration stage. This stage is highly iterative and may involve returning to the exploration stage to refine or update the AI requirements based on observed user behaviors, preferences, and feedback. The continuous feedback loop between simulation and exploration helps ensure that the system evolves in a direction that optimally serves its users.

Incremental integration of AI involves gradually transitioning from human-operated simulations to real AI functionality. Instead of implementing the entire AI system at once, individual components are introduced in a controlled manner, allowing developers to monitor and assess their performance in real-world conditions. As AI components are implemented and integrated, further validation occurs, and feedback continues to be collected to fine-tune the system. Importantly, the implementation stage does not mark the end of the development process but serves as a checkpoint for continuous iteration. Once the initial AI functionality is successfully deployed, the process can cycle back to the exploration stage to identify additional areas where AI can add value.

4 NexOz's Architecture

Many software projects share a similar base architecture, where clients communicate both internally and with external components. The application logic can be provided by both internal components (e.g., a client component to detect and handle gestures) and external components (e.g., a service to communicate with an external conversational agent). Note that there is no strict distinction between what can be implemented as an internal or external component (e.g., detecting gestures could also be provided by an external service). This is reflected in our NexOz's architecture (Fig. 2), which revolves around a back-end nexus hub that acts as a modular platform. This architecture facilitates reusing the necessary low-level functionalities (e.g., logging, interaction support, event handling) that are needed for the iterative development of higher-level components [3].

Client devices all connect to the back-end hub, which in turn is connected to a service bus for its communication with external components. The WOz is linked in such a way that it can inconspicuously emulate both internal and external components, and thus all kinds of application logic.

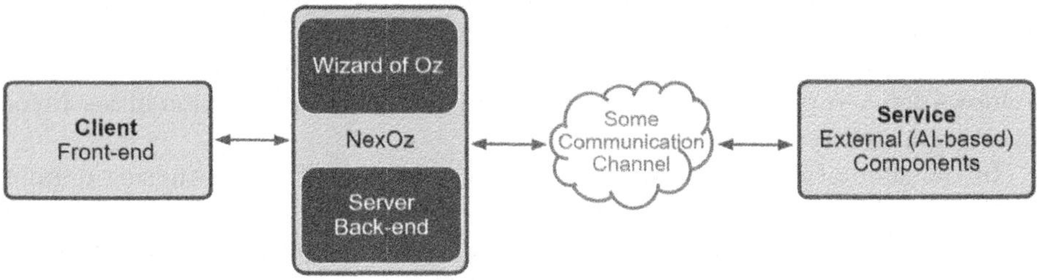

Fig. 2. Schematic overview of the inclusion of NexOz into a typical service-based client-server software architecture.

NexOz provides the backbone for communication by allowing real-time, bidirectional message exchange between clients and the back-end (e.g., implemented as a SignalR hub that uses Remote Procedure Calls as a means of communication). Additionally, the back-end connects to the Service Bus (e.g., through MQTT or REST) to communicate with external components. By establishing the protocols for data exchange in the exploration stage, and by defining concrete payloads and message flows, the foundations for supporting specific AI functionality are laid. The WOz component then defines an alternative path throughout the architecture, using the established protocols, to simulate AI behavior and responses.

5 Demonstrating the Approach: Practical Scenarios

To demonstrate our WOz approach, we discuss some practical scenarios in the context of a research project called 'OperatorAssist' [20]. The focus of this project lies on a situation-aware multimodal digital assistant (DA) in the manufacturing industry that serves as a single-point-of-contact between the operator (i.e., the person executing the assembly task) and various information sources. We specifically focus on assembly processes that happen in a low-volume-high-variability fashion, where operators often work on different types of products. This increases the need for information about the processes and products to maintain the quality and safety standards. Typical assembly tasks require operators to assemble pieces of varying weight and size using different tools and templates (e.g., putting together pieces of an engine using power tools set to the correct torque to avoid damaging the mechanical seals that keep the lubricant in place).

In our project, various actors are responsible for a subset of the implementation logic of the DA and an iterative approach is used to validate the functional blocks and overall integrated functioning of the DA. Due to the scale of the project and the complexity of the AI components, waiting for the development of those components would cause a significant bottleneck. NexOz was implemented to yield early results based on WOz simulations, which were incrementally replaced with actual AI components. Additionally, NexOz also enables flexible and repeatable tests. In the context of the OperatorAssist project, a test iteration often involves manually assembling physical components, during which the DA provides support based on, among others, a state tracker and specialized Q&A component. NexOz can be used here to update the internal state to simulate an assembly process (Fig. 3).

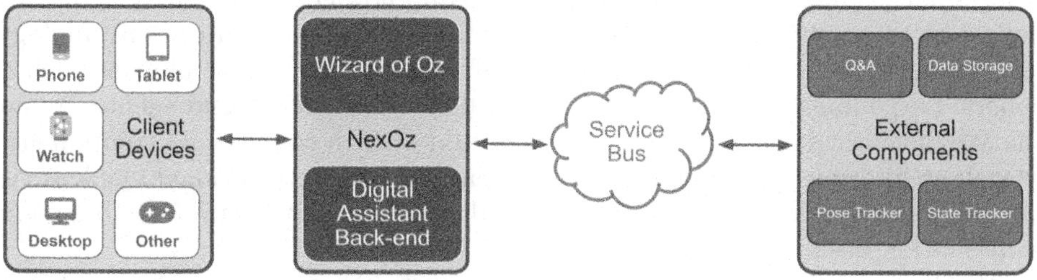

Fig. 3. Schematic overview of the architecture and positioning of NexOz (and a simplified, somewhat abstracted overview of the OperatorAssist project).

5.1 Specialized Q&A

To limit the effort in manually posing (predictable) questions, the DA provides a convenient way to retrieve a predefined list of possible questions the operator might have. Instead of a general list of frequently asked questions, a shortlist of relevant questions is determined by employing statistical methods (such as Hidden Markov Models) on all the available questions, where all relevant contextual elements are taken into account. In absence of these statistical methodologies, a predefined list of possible questions can be provided to the wizard.

Furthermore, the answers to those specific questions can vary depending on the current context of the assembly (see Sect. 5.2). In NexOz, human wizards can emulate responses in real-time (see Fig. 4) and can dynamically adjust their responses based on user inputs and contextual information, mimicking the envisioned adaptability of the DA. NexOz allows sending predefined replies from a list of frequently asked questions and answers, while also allowing the human wizard to provide custom answers. Consequently, NexOz's user-centric approach allows for quick adjustments and refinements of the simulated content based on user feedback, ensuring that the eventual DA is intuitive, user-friendly, and aligned with user expectations.

The use of NexOz enabled us to incrementally build the DA, by mimicking the intelligence when there was no AI yet to help the operators with their questions. An important part of this first exploration stage was to define the payloads and message flows for the AI functionality, by constructing a concrete RPC protocol, which allowed for initial interactions via the WOz. Later, actual AI functionality was added gradually to the project to provide a list of frequently asked questions to choose from, where the questions are filtered according to the current context. With this intermediate version of the AI component, it can happen that the list of questions does not include the question that the operator wants to ask, or that some part of the information is still missing. As the AI component does not yet offer a mechanism for handling free-text questions at this point, this must still be handled by the WOz.

Adding support for such free-text questions in an assembly environment poses several new challenges. The specialized domain knowledge presents a significant hurdle, as assembly tasks often involve intricate processes, technical terminology, and domain-specific jargon that may be unfamiliar to generic AI models, such as generic Large Language Models (LLMs) or flow- and intent-based agents. Again, the Woz facilitates the incremental integration of such complex AI components, as well as intermediate evaluations of the envisioned conversational Q&A of the DA, allowing developers to quickly test dialogue flows, interaction patterns, and conversation designs.

Furthermore, NexOz logs all manual interventions, which gives the developers of the AI component insights into issues with its current implementation. For example, it might become clear that some aspects of using a specific assembly tool might not be described sufficiently in the current Q&A and thus should be added to (1) the wizard's simulations and (2) the final AI-based implementation. Another example, when handling free-text questions, is to include additional intents to an intent-based agent if an unexpected line of questioning from the operator is detected.

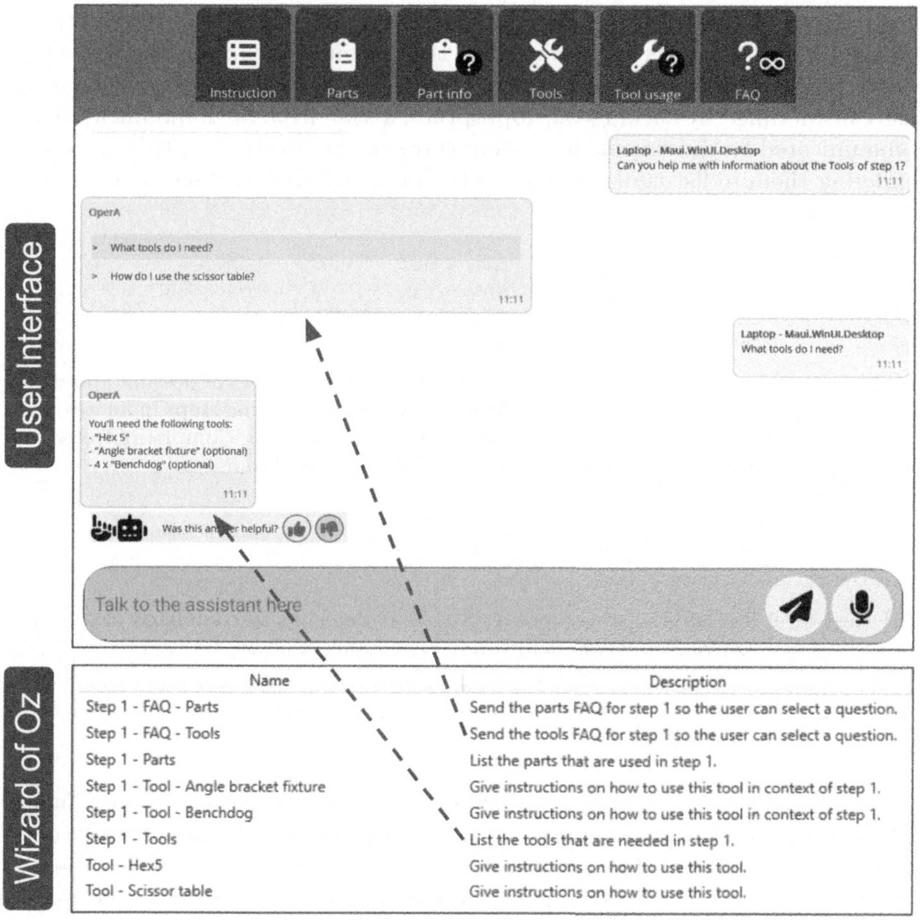

Fig. 4. Q&A component available to the human wizard (top) and example list of predefined messages available to the WOz (bottom).

5.2 State Tracking

The responses and behavior of the DA are based on an understanding of the physical context of the assembly, such as the current step in the assembly process and the assembly tools and materials that are being used. This kind of contextual information is used, for instance, to filter questions by the Q&A component, as discussed in Sect. 5.1. Therefore, the system requires a tracking mechanism that establishes a representation of the physical state of the assembly, by relying on a set of AI techniques, including computer vision and multi-sensor fusion.

By simulating state tracking with a WOz, initial components of the project that are reliant on state information could be developed without an immediate need for a high-fidelity state tracker. NexOz provides the human wizard with an orderly overview of the current assembly progress and facilitates easy updating or overriding of the perceived state, as illustrated in Fig. 5a. The overview shows both the step status as determined by the assembly operator and the status as it is perceived by the (simulated) state tracking module, where the status can easily be modified by clicking the appropriate action icon. Such modifications are communicated to the rest of the system through the established RPC protocols, rendering them indistinguishable from the eventual AI-based messages.

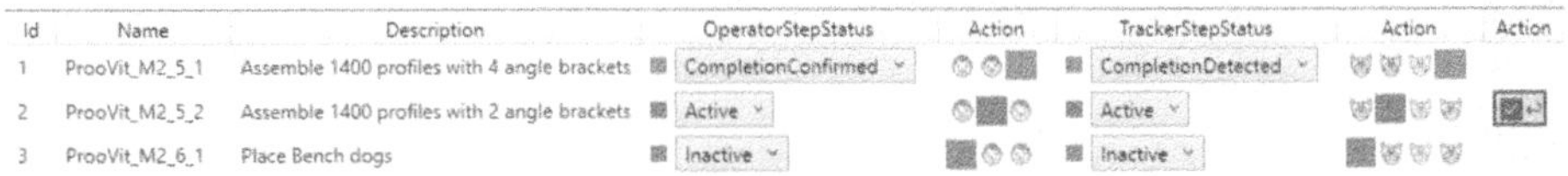

(a) State tracking module in NexOz. In the exploration stage, a set of possible states was defined to accommodate the expected AI functionality of tracking steps in an assembly process (e.g., the AI can set its perception of a step's status to 'CompletionDetected', while the operator uses the more authoritative 'CompletionConfirmed').

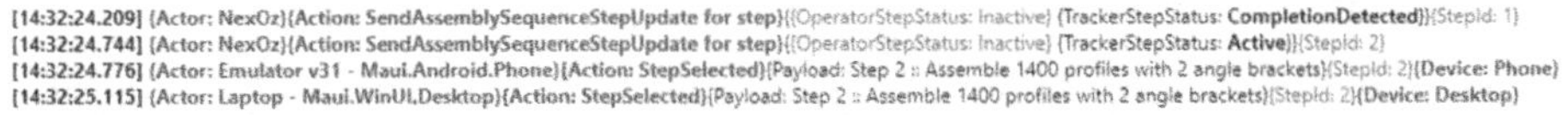

(b) High-level logs after a state update: Step 1 is detected as completed and Step 2 flagged as new active step. More details are logged and available for export.

Fig. 5. Screenshots of the state tracking module and logging in NexOz.

As the actual AI-based state tracking module evolved over subsequent iterations, the system became able to use computer vision to automatically determine the completion of steps, as well as the currently active step of the assembly. Despite these new capabilities, some actions remain hard to recognize reliably (e.g., actions with small or occluded parts) and still necessitate manual intervention within NexOz from time to time. All the manual interventions in NexOz are extensively logged (see Fig. 5b for a summarized excerpt). In following iterations, we expect the state tracker to further optimize its recognition capabilities, diminishing the need for manual updates.

5.3 Location-Based Interaction

In the realm of device interactions, proxemics play a significant role in determining how users engage with technology based on their proximity to devices and the spatial relations between them. Correctly determining spatial information can be essential for providing a seamless and intuitive experience [2]. In the exploration stage, we determined which spatial information of the different entities (e.g., operators and interaction devices) in the environment should be available to effectively provide important notifications to the operator on the most convenient devices (e.g., devices in the line of sight or worn by the operator).

Without the necessary AI-based tracking component, the responsibility to observe and input this information was assigned to the wizard. A top-down interface supports modifying the perceived spatial information by dragging the operator's avatar or interaction devices to their new position and/or altering the orientation (Fig. 6). It must be noted that keeping track of movements is very demanding of the wizard, especially when other parts of the system also need to be simulated. To remediate this issue, a setup with multiple simultaneous wizards can be applied, where each wizard is assigned specific responsibilities [11,23].

In the first iteration of the AI-based tracking component, the spatial information of the operator was made available, offloading this task from the wizard, who now only needs to keep track of the devices in the environment, as that tracking functionality is reserved for the next iteration of the tracking component.

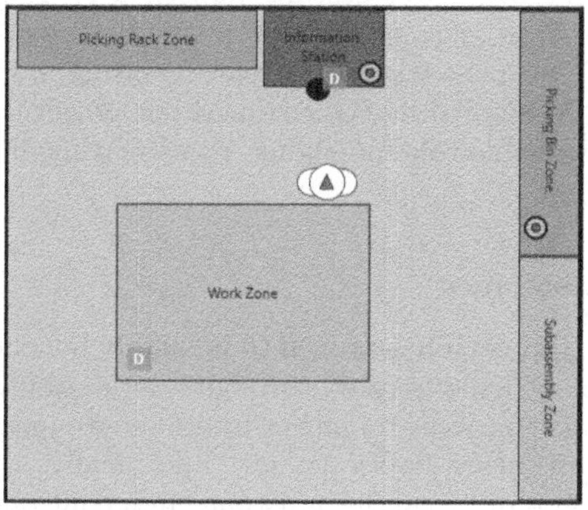

Fig. 6. Top-down interface to manually simulate the tracked location (white avatar) and orientation (red triangle) of the operator in the workstation. The interface also provides options to position the different interaction devices in the environment (green and orange squares) to support proxemics. (Color figure online)

5.4 Gesture Recognizer

The DA supports various input and output modalities to maximize the flexibility of the system. For instance, some operators wear protective gear (e.g., gloves, hearing protection) or cannot use a keyboard and mouse or touchscreen because their hands are occupied. One of the supported input modalities includes different kinds of gestures, ranging from interactions with a Leap Motion controller [27] and smartwatch gestures [26] to unconstrained mid-air gestures [14]. The support for gestures is thus quite generic and open-ended.

One of the primary challenges with recognizing gestures lies in accurately capturing and interpreting nuances and variations. Gestures can vary significantly depending on factors such as cultural background, individual preferences, and environmental conditions. Therefore, an exploratory analysis is a valuable preliminary step: by systematically exploring different gesture options, soliciting user feedback, and iteratively refining gesture designs, developers can identify the most effective and user-friendly gestures for a specific task.

To support such an exploration stage, we used a WOz approach to add gestures to our multimodal DA, similar to the approach of Salber and Coutaz [23]. NexOz provides the necessary features to test gestures without an actual AI recognizer, as a human wizard can easily recognize gestures and trigger the associated interaction events through a configurable list of interactions (based on the use case at hand). Triggering such an event invokes a message that follows the established RPC protocol for gesture detection. NexOz also allows for logging the raw gesture data (e.g., finger movements detected by the Leap Motion controller) combined with the triggered event, resulting in labeled data that can be used for training AI algorithms. Once an AI recognizer is operational, NexOz continues to play a valuable role in logging, investigating and resolving errors in the gesture recognition.

5.5 Proactive Assistance

The use of the WOz approach has proven to be highly beneficial in the context of user-centered design, as demonstrated through a series of user studies conducted during the development process to gather intermediate insights and to promote an informed design of future developments. Specifically, studies were designed to test various scenarios of proactive assistance in a controlled yet realistic work environment, allowing us to gather detailed insights into how operators interact with proactive functionality that was simulated by human wizards rather than provided by an AI system. The assistance ranges over different types of alerts, from subtle hints to more direct warnings. Furthermore, the timing of the proactive assistance can vary: provided immediately, after a certain amount of time, or when a specific criterion has been met. These criteria can be dynamically scripted based on the available contextual variables of the assembly, such as notifying the operator of a supply line delay when she starts working on a new part of the assembly; if the delay were to be resolved before the progression to the next step, the proactive assistance would have been retracted and no notification would be shown.

In the studies, we explored several examples of proactive assistance, such as reminding the operator to use spacers and fixtures if they forgot to do so, offering tips when a task was taking longer than expected, and issuing a warning if the wrong part was being picked from the rack. By simulating these interventions through a WOz approach, we could observe how operators responded to the timing and format of the assistance, and whether it was considered helpful or intrusive. Based on their feedback and behavior, we could adjust the design to ensure the assistance was contextually appropriate and non-disruptive.

In a subsequent iteration of the proactive assistance, notifications are automatically sent to operators when specific conditions are met, such as when they attempt to move to the next step in the process without completing a necessary action in the current step. In cases where the system may make a tracking error, failing to detect some condition and thus not sending the notification, the WOz approach still allows the human wizard to override the system and manually trigger the notification. The logged data can then again be used to determine the issue at the core of the faulty tracking to fine-tune the tracking AI.

This approach allowed us to make data-driven decisions about how best to provide proactive assistance, ensuring that the final AI implementation would be both functional and user-friendly. It also offered the flexibility to experiment with different types of assistance-testing varying levels of intervention and customization-before committing to full AI development.

6 Engineering Aspects of NexOz A Discussion

Engineering interactive systems that integrate AI technology poses several challenges both for developers and practitioners. In this section, we discuss the advantages of NexOz to tackle some of those challenges, as well as discuss open research avenues that are beyond the scope of our work.

First of all, the modular nature of the NexOz architecture allows the **integration of different engineering approaches** and/or systems into a unified architecture. This flexibility facilitates rapid prototyping by supporting seamless communication between devices and the handling of various interaction events, enabling quick and efficient prototyping. WOz simulations allow for the integration of different engineering components, each with its own features and complexities, into a cohesive system. This flexibility enables iterative testing and refinement of high-fidelity system designs, ensuring that the resulting architecture is both well-rounded and better aligned with user needs.

Additionally, the WOz approach provides opportunities to gather user feedback through **human-in-the-loop** interactions, enhancing usability and informing decisions about which AI features are worth developing. Early user studies with simulated behaviors support a user-centered design process, enabling developers to determine the value of specific features. The ability to allow the users to override or adjust AI decisions, can help mitigate the effects of unpredictability. When users have the ability to influence or correct the system's actions, they are more likely to view the AI as a supportive tool rather than a black-box decision-maker. This feedback is essential for improving the system design and collecting valuable data that can be used to train or retrain AI models. The continuous feedback loop ensures the AI system evolves based on user needs and actual behaviors, enhancing its overall usability and accuracy over time.

Finally, employing WOz simulations reduces the need for fully implemented AI systems early in development, lowering initial costs and minimizing the risks of expensive and time-consuming full-scale builds. By allowing gradual introduction of non-deterministic AI features in controlled environments, developers can refine AI behavior and assess the **balance between risk and value** before full deployment. This stepwise approach ensures that AI functionality grows as its reliability improves, fostering user trust and reducing the likelihood of costly system overhauls later in the process.

While the WOz approach offers numerous benefits, it also presents some challenges, particularly in relation to simulation accuracy and the transition from simulation to real AI implementation. One important aspect in **balancing between the value of our approach and its risks** is to consider the implications for the wizard, who acquires new responsibilities. Accurately simulating certain AI behaviors, especially in real-time, can be labor-intensive and demanding, which can cause the human wizard to introduce errors. Real-time user tracking, for example, is very challenging for a single human wizard to manage effectively, especially when the data is intended to feed a highly responsive system. Human simulation can also suffer from inconsistencies, and the cognitive load on the wizard can lead to errors or delays that do not reflect how a fully automated AI would behave. One potential solution to this issue is using a multi-wizard setup, where each wizard is assigned a specific task or subset of tasks. This division of labor can improve simulation accuracy, but it adds complexity to the setup and increases the coordination demands between wizards, which may still not fully replicate the intended AI behavior. As such, these simulation limitations must be taken into account when evaluating certain AI features.

Furthermore, moving from WOz simulations to real AI systems introduces a new set of technical challenges. While the simulated environment allows for predictable and deterministic behavior, actual AI systems often incorporate probabilistic decision-making processes. For instance, AI systems are prone to **varying levels of confidence and non-deterministic behavior** in their outputs, introducing unpredictability that may not have been accounted for during the simulation stage. To address this, developers should try to anticipate potential uncertainties by incorporating these factors into the simulation setup. By simulating uncertainty as a variable, it becomes possible to better prepare for real-world deployment, though doing so adds complexity to the simulation and additional research is needed on how this kind of uncertainty can be simulated through a WOz. This step is essential for ensuring that the final AI system performs sufficiently reliable and robust, even when faced with the inherent uncertainties and non-deterministic behavior that accompany AI decision-making.

Even though in our research we did not investigate the fostering of a **positive hedonic experience for human users** explicitly, it is certainly an interesting avenue for future research to integrate such design aspects into our approach. In our approach, this would translate to capturing new data points linked to variables that measure the positive effects of technology on the user experience. In industrial settings, such as the manufacturing industry, keeping operators engaged and motivated is vital. Failing to address human hedonic and eudaimonic needs when introducing AI technology in the workplace will undoubtedly lead to low technology adoption and can even aggravate the issues of operator retention in the manufacturing industry [28].

7 Conclusion

This paper presents NexOz, our approach and tool to incrementally integrate AI components into interactive systems using a WOz. We demonstrated the practical application of this approach by showcasing the integration of several AI components (i.e., a specialized Q&A component, state tracker, location-based interaction, gesture recognizer, and proactive assistance) in a project in the context of the manufacturing industry. Overall, we argue that the use of NexOz offers a pragmatic solution to the complexity of integrating AI into interactive systems, providing a bridge between technological capabilities and user expectations. Through rapid prototyping and leveraging collected data logs, this approach empowers developers to navigate the complexities of AI integration.

Acknowledgments. This research is funded by Flanders Make under the project OperatorAssist_SBO, project number 2021-0133. Flanders Make is the Flemish strategic research center for the manufacturing industry in Belgium. This research also received funding from the Flemish Government under the "Onderzoeksprogramma Artificiële Intelligentie (AI) Vlaanderen" program.

Disclosure of Interests. The authors have no competing interests to declare that are relevant to the content of this article.

References

1. Amershi, S., et al.: Guidelines for human-AI interaction. In: Proceedings of the 2019 CHI Conference on Human Factors in Computing Systems, CHI 2019, pp. 1–13. ACM (2019). https://doi.org/10.1145/3290605.3300233
2. Ballendat, T., Marquardt, N., Greenberg, S.: Proxemic interaction: designing for a proximity and orientation-aware environment. In: ACM International Conference on Interactive Tabletops and Surfaces, ITS 2010, pp. 121–130. Association for Computing Machinery, New York (2010). https://doi.org/10.1145/1936652.1936676
3. Barros-Justo, J.L., Benitti, F.B., Matalonga, S.: Trends in software reuse research: a tertiary study. Comput. Stand. Interfaces **66** (2019). https://doi.org/10.1016/j.csi.2019.04.011
4. Browne, J.T.: Wizard of Oz prototyping for machine learning experiences. In: Extended Abstracts of the 2019 CHI Conference on Human Factors in Computing Systems, CHI EA 2019, pp. 1–6. ACM (2019). https://doi.org/10.1145/3290607.3312877
5. Butz, A., Kaltenhauser, A., Eiband, M.: The expert of Oz: a two-sided study paradigm for intelligent systems. In: Companion Publication of the 2020 ACM Designing Interactive Systems Conference, DIS 2020 Companion, pp. 269–273. Association for Computing Machinery, New York (2020). https://doi.org/10.1145/3393914.3395874
6. Cheyer, A., Julia, L., Martin, J.C.: A unified framework for constructing multimodal experiments and applications. In: Bunt, H., Beun, R.J. (eds.) Cooperative Multimodal Communication, pp. 234–242. Springer, Heidelberg (2001)
7. Dahlbäck, N., Jönsson, A., Ahrenberg, L.: Wizard of Oz studies - why and how. Know.-Based Syst. **6**(4), 258–266 (1993). https://doi.org/10.1016/0950-7051(93)90017-N

8. Detjen, H., Pfleging, B., Schneegass, S.: A wizard of Oz field study to understand non-driving-related activities, trust, and acceptance of automated vehicles. In: 12th International Conference on Automotive User Interfaces and Interactive Vehicular Applications, AutomotiveUI 2020, pp. 19–29. ACM (2020). https://doi.org/10.1145/3409120.3410662
9. Dow, S., MacIntyre, B., Lee, J., Oezbek, C., Bolter, J., Gandy, M.: Wizard of Oz support throughout an iterative design process. IEEE Pervasive Comput. **4**(4), 18–26 (2005). https://doi.org/10.1109/MPRV.2005.93
10. Garcia, F.J.C., Lopes, J., Liu, X., Hastie, H.: CRWIZ: A Framework for Crowdsourcing Real-Time Wizard-of-Oz Dialogues. arXiv:2003.05995 (2020)
11. Green, A., Huttenrauch, H., Eklundh, K.: Applying the wizard-of-Oz framework to cooperative service discovery and configuration. In: RO-MAN 2004. 13th IEEE International Workshop on Robot and Human Interactive Communication (IEEE Catalog No. 04TH8759), pp. 575–580 (2004). https://doi.org/10.1109/ROMAN.2004.1374824
12. Gu, K., Grunde-McLaughlin, M., McNutt, A.M., Heer, J., Althoff, T.: How Do Data Analysts Respond to AI Assistance? A Wizard-of-Oz Study. arXiv:2309.10108 (2024)
13. Horvitz, E.: Principles of mixed-initiative user interfaces. In: Proceedings of the SIGCHI Conference on Human Factors in Computing Systems, CHI 1999, pp. 159–166. Association for Computing Machinery (1999). https://doi.org/10.1145/302979.303030
14. Hou, W., Feng, G., Cheng, Y.: A fuzzy interaction scheme of mid-air gesture elicitation. J. Vis. Commun. Image Represent. **64** (2019). https://doi.org/10.1016/j.jvcir.2019.102637
15. Katsakioris, M.M., Hastie, H.F., Konstas, I., Laskov, A.: Corpus of multimodal interaction for collaborative planning. In: Proceedings of the Combined Workshop on Spatial Language Understanding (2019). https://api.semanticscholar.org/CorpusID:199553531
16. Kerly, A., Bull, S.: The potential for chatbots in negotiated learner modelling: a wizard-of-Oz study. In: International Conference on Intelligent Tutoring Systems, pp. 443–452. Springer (2006)
17. Kocielnik, R., Amershi, S., Bennett, P.N.: Will you accept an imperfect AI? Exploring designs for adjusting end-user expectations of AI systems. In: Proceedings of the 2019 CHI Conference on Human Factors in Computing Systems, CHI 2019, pp. 1–14. ACM (2019). https://doi.org/10.1145/3290605.3300641
18. Luger, E., Sellen, A.: "Like having a really bad PA": the gulf between user expectation and experience of conversational agents. In: Proceedings of the 2016 CHI Conference on Human Factors in Computing Systems, CHI 2016, pp. 5286–5297. ACM (2016). https://doi.org/10.1145/2858036.2858288
19. Okamoto, M., Yang, Y., Ishida, T.: Wizard of Oz method for learning dialog agents. In: Klusch, M., Zambonelli, F. (eds.) Cooperative Information Agents V, pp. 20–25. Springer, Heidelberg (2001)
20. OperatorAssist: A digital assistant for assembly operators that increases effectiveness by 10% (2023). https://www.youtube.com/watch?v=t8vQBLxIIDY. Accessed 11 Oct 2024
21. Riek, L.D.: Wizard of Oz studies in HRI: a systematic review and new reporting guidelines. J. Hum.-Robot Interact. **1**(1), 119–136 (2012). https://doi.org/10.5898/JHRI.1.1.Riek

22. Rieser, V., Lemon, O.: Learning effective multimodal dialogue strategies from wizard-of-Oz data: bootstrapping and evaluation. In: Moore, J.D., Teufel, S., Allan, J., Furui, S. (eds.) Proceedings of ACL 2008: HLT, pp. 638–646. Association for Computational Linguistics (2008). https://aclanthology.org/P08-1073
23. Salber, D., Coutaz, J.: Applying the Wizard of Oz Technique to the Study of Multimodal Systems. In: Bass, L.J., Gornostaev, J., Unger, C. (eds.) Human-Computer Interaction, pp. 219–230. Springer, Heidelberg (1993)
24. Schlögl, S., Doherty, G., Karamanis, N., Luz, S.: WebWOZ: a wizard of Oz prototyping framework. In: Proceedings of the 2nd ACM SIGCHI Symposium on Engineering Interactive Computing Systems, EICS 2010, pp. 109–114. ACM (2010). https://doi.org/10.1145/1822018.1822035
25. Schlögl, S., Doherty, G., Luz, S.: Wizard of Oz experimentation for language technology applications: challenges and tools. Interact. Comput. **27**(6), 592–615 (2015). https://doi.org/10.1093/iwc/iwu016
26. Shen, C., Ho, B.J., Srivastava, M.: MiLift: efficient smartwatch-based workout tracking using automatic segmentation. IEEE Trans. Mob. Comput. **17**(7), 1609–1622 (2018). https://doi.org/10.1109/TMC.2017.2775641
27. Ultraleap: Leap Motion Controller 2. https://leap2.ultraleap.com/leap-motion-controller-2/. Accessed 11 Oct 2024
28. Vansteenkiste, S.: Mismatch tussen vraag naar en aanbod van arbeid in vlaanderen. https://www.steunpuntwerk.be/onderzoeksthemas/mismatch. Accessed 11 Oct 2024
29. Xie, T.: The synergy of human and artificial intelligence in software engineering. In: 2013 2nd International Workshop on Realizing Artificial Intelligence Synergies in Software Engineering (RAISE), pp. 4–6 (2013). https://api.semanticscholar.org/CorpusID:14096820
30. Xin, D., Ma, L., Liu, J., Macke, S., Song, S., Parameswaran, A.: Accelerating human-in-the-loop machine learning: challenges and opportunities. In: Proceedings of the Second Workshop on Data Management for End-to-End Machine Learning, DEEM 2018. ACM (2018). https://doi.org/10.1145/3209889.3209897

Empowering End-User in Creating eXtended Reality Content with a Conversational Chatbot

Jacopo Mereu[1], Valentino Artizzu[1], Alessandro Carcangiu[1(✉)], Lucio Davide Spano[1], Ludovica Simeoli[2], Andrea Mattioli[2], Marco Manca[2], Carmen Santoro[2], and Fabio Paternò[2]

[1] Department of Mathematics and Computer Science, University of Cagliari, Via Ospedale 72, 09124 Cagliari, Italy
{jacopo.mereu,valentino.artizzu,alessandro.carcangiu, davide.spano}@unica.it

[2] ISTI-CNR, Human Interfaces in Information Systems (HIIS) Laboratory, Via G. Moruzzi 1, 56124 Pisa, Italy
{ludovica.simeoli,andrea.mattioli,marco.manca,carmen.santoro, fabio.paterno}@isti.cnr.it

Abstract. Recent advancements in eXtended Reality (XR) technologies have found application across diverse domains. However, creating complex interactions within XR environments remains challenging for non-technical users. In this work, we present EUD4XR, a project aiming to: i) empower end-user developers (EUDevs) to customize XR environments by supporting virtual objects and physical devices; ii) involve an intelligent conversational agent which assists the user in defining behaviours. The agent can handle multimodal input, to drive the EUDev during the rule authoring process, using contextual knowledge of the virtual environment and its elements. By integrating conversational assistance, EUD4XR seeks to lower further the usage barriers for end-users to personalize XR experiences according to their needs.

Keywords: Extended reality · End-user development · Immersive authoring · Large language model · Context · Multimodal input · Meta-design · Event-condition-action rules

1 Introduction

Over the past decade, we have witnessed a significant maturation process in eXtended reality (XR) devices, exemplified by products such as Meta Quest, Microsoft HoloLens, and Steam Valve Index, along with connected smart devices, and the combination of them. Once primarily associated with entertainment, these technologies have now found applications in diverse domains such as automotive, healthcare, wellness, and manufacturing. As these tools have matured, the research community and commercial/open-source products have prioritized

L. Zaina et al. (Eds.): EICS 2024, LNCS 15518, pp. 126–137, 2025.
https://doi.org/10.1007/978-3-031-91760-8_9

empowering end-user developers (EUDevs), individuals possessing expertise in specific domain applications but lacking professional developer skills, to personalize or adjust these applications to suit their specific needs.

While existing solutions facilitate the creation of XR environments [17,27, 34,36] and define the behaviour for virtual objects [2,5,9] and physical devices [4,8,14,19,23,24], they do not completely eliminate user errors resulting from potential misunderstanding. A possible solution to address this issue should: i) propose an immersive environment that empowers end users to customize the behavior of virtual and physical objects within XR environments using rules expressed in natural language, and ii) implement an intelligent conversational agent capable of managing multimodal inputs to guide users through the customization process. In this paper, we review the state of the art on this topic and examine the engineering challenges involved in building such a chatbot, including multimodal input processing, intent-to-rule conversion, and available interaction exploration capabilities.

2 Related Work

Modern professional tools like Unity, Unreal, and WebXR allow users to build and define XR environments and their logic. Such tools require advanced programming knowledge, making them unsuitable for end-user developers (EUDevs).

For this reason, EUD authoring tools are designed to enable EUDevs to address these tasks. The ceiling of these tools may not be as high as that of professional tools, but they can still provide powerful support while keeping the entry knowledge barrier low. We can distinguish between non-immersive (desktop-based) and immersive (head-mounted display-based) tools in the literature. The former are well-explored, as they leverage already investigated EUD techniques from screen-based applications, while the latter attempt to adapt classic EUD techniques for the domain of XR, which is less explored and documented. Various commercial and open-source desktop tools exist for XR environment creation. Tools like Hubs[1] and Spoke[2] help non-technical users in creating virtual experiences. Fungus[3] focuses on supporting novice developers to create interactive storytelling by using flowcharts. Immersive tools have the advantage that, since the user is immersed in the augmented environment, they can perform operations more intuitively through direct manipulation. ECARules4All [5] supports end-users in designing XR experiences. The Template Builder (TB) creates virtual environments and tags virtual objects from a built-in taxonomy. The End-User Developer (EUDev) personalizes this pre-built content by defining object behaviours through natural-language rules. These rules follow the event-condition-action (ECA) scheme. Immersive authoring tools also find applications in the automation domain. MagicHand [33] and HoloHome [23] support end-users

[1] https://hubs.mozilla.com/.
[2] https://hubs.mozilla.com/spoke/.
[3] https://fungusgames.com/.

in supervising a restricted set of IoT devices, while BricklAyer [32] and MagiPlay [31] leverage immersive authoring and building blocks metaphor to help, respectively, adults and children without programming skills. However, both tools have limitations in terms of the complexity of interactions they can support. On the other hand, immersive tools are less flexible and require more focus compared to non-immersive tools.

Significant efforts have been made in Language Models in recent years, leading to the development of Large Language Models (LLMs). These models have been utilized as smart conversational agents in various fields, including medicine, judiciary, and education [20,25,35].

Researchers are exploring LLMs' capabilities also to support users in creating, modifying, and prototyping XR environments. While early works focused on integrating LLMs within Unity [26,28], the research community has begun to exploit them in more sophisticated frameworks that automate certain tasks. For instance, in [12], the authors propose a framework that leverages LLMs to assist users in generating virtual objects to populate 3D scenarios. The framework consists of the use of GPT-4, prompt-tuned in several tasks: i) Planner, analyzes the user's prompt and breaks it down into simpler tasks; ii) Scene Analyzer, examines the Unity scene the user is working on, generating a JSON representation of the scene; iii) Skill Library, searches for pre-existing code and elements, such as meshes or textures, to solve each simpler task; iv) Builder, generates the code to resolve the problem starting from the elements identified by the Skill module; v) Inspector, iteratively verifies the generated code received from the Builder. The Builder and Inspector modules may engage in several iterative steps, gradually refining the solution. Once the Inspector approves, the generated code is compiled and executed on the Unity engine to produce the user's desired functionality.

3 EUD4XR in a Nutshell

In the EUD4XR project, we aim to introduce two key functionalities: i) supporting end-users without programming skills to define XR automations, involving both virtual content and physical devices; ii) lower the threshold for creating such automations through an intelligent conversational agent.

Considering that, in general, XR environment are quite complex to define from scratch, we define a workflow similar to the one used in Content Management Systems (CMS) for the web, where users wanting to build a website but lacking development skills start from a template and configure it iteratively adapting the starting point to their needs.

The engineering process we envision is an application of a meta-design model [3,11,13] where we define three roles (Fig. 1):

- The **Element Builder** (EB), who creates generic virtual templates and annotates virtual objects and physical devices. This role typically corresponds to professional developers, who have the technical knowledge for modelling the objects and creating the XR system that will be open for end-user customisation.

- the **End-User Developer** (EUDev), who customises these templates and personalizes their behaviours using a rule language. This role typically represents the domain expert, thereby a role that does not have any specific skills in programming, but is interested in customising a joint behaviour of virtual and real objects.
- the **Final User**, who represents the final consumer of the customised XR contents. This role can, in some situations, coincide with the role of End User developer, when the latter one also benefits of the created customisations.

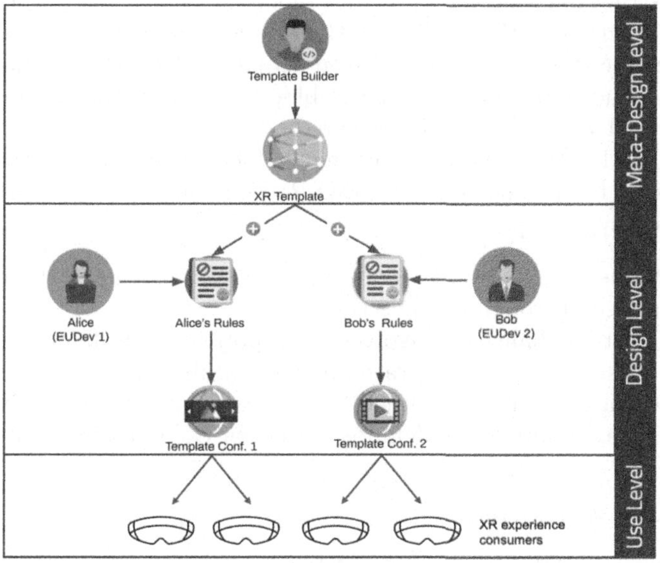

Fig. 1. Roles for the meta-design of XR environments in EUD4XR.

3.1 Object Taxonomy and Rule Language

To support both EBs and EUDevs in managing and defining interactions, our solution requires describing the properties (i.e., the variables defining the state) and the actions (i.e., the supported operations) each virtual and physical object supports through a vocabulary understandable for EUDevs. We started from the extendable taxonomy described in [5] defined for virtual objects, to include physical objects as well. This taxonomy categorizes entities into two types: Objects and Behaviors. The former represents entities based on perceivable characteristics such as shape or functionality, while the latter encompasses actions that entities can perform. In our approach, each entity, such as a smart light or a virtual chair model, is assigned to an Object category and can possess zero or more Behaviors. Notably, entities in different Object categories can share common Behaviors, enabling flexible customization across diverse entities. For example, consider a smart chandelier item: it belongs to the Electrical Appliance category and cannot be assigned to the Vehicle category. However, both a smart chandelier and a truck emit light, sharing a common Behaviour. The EB annotates the environmental objects with the taxonomy types, while the EUDev exploits tagged objects for defining behaviours.

The EUDev defines object behaviours through a natural language rule system based on an event-condition-action (ECA) schema. EUDevs interact with the rule management system in an immersive way. Each rule follows a "WHEN-IF-THEN" structure, where the WHEN block delineates the trigger event that activates the rule; the IF block is optional and describes the conditions that must be met for the rule's trigger to be raised, and EUD4XR should support one or more conditions; and the THEN block illustrates the action, or actions, to be performed when the rule is triggered.

Existing works adopt the ECA schema to focus on event-type triggers, leveraging states as filter conditions. EUD4XR differentiates, and handles triggers based on their type [18]:

1. Instantaneous action. It does not cause a state change in the environment and is managed through a single rule.
2. Temporary state change. It involves a temporary state change and automatically returns to the starting state after a certain time.
3. Prolonged state change. The object's state does not automatically revert, and EUD4XR may handle it by defining a rule for each possible state.

3.2 AI Rule Authoring

To better support EUDevs in creating XR environments, they may interact with a chatbot. Since the user is immersed, speaking is preferred over writing. Given that the user will interact through their voice, they may find it natural to help themselves by pointing out elements of the XR environment. Additionally, the user may naturally look at some of the fundamental elements.

In summary, our chatbot must be able to manage a multimodal input stream, comprehending user voice and gaze, as well as their pointing, if any. This input will be merged with the environment context, meaning the information about the virtual elements and their status, such as the ECA tag, if any, and by the custom annotations (i.e., metadata on classes, methods and instance variables) specifying the high-level actions each tag can perform. The model should be capable of reading and synchronizing the sources to extrapolate the user's intent in ECA rules. The intent must contain four key pieces: the temporary aspect (when?), the action part (what?), the spatial positioning (where?), and the objects involved (who?). If any key piece is not provided by the user, the chatbot should explicitly ask for it by directing to the user further questions either for specifying missing parts in the concerned rule, or for removing possible ambiguities existing in its current specification. If a user's intent is not feasible, the chatbot should explicitly state this to users, suggesting the closest feasible intention could be. For example, if they say "When the user selects the door [points to the door they are referring to], then the door should fly over that shelf [points to the shelf]", and knowing that a door has no high-level action for flying, the chatbot should reply with something like "The door cannot perform the action *flying*. Instead, you can use the following actions: close, open, and lock".

To understand how end-users define automations when interacting with an intelligent agent, we have conducted two studies. The two studies have been both set up as "Wizard of Oz" and have explored two different domains to be more general: a smart home, and a virtual museum scenario. The results of the user studies will be used to tune the prompt of a model so that it can more easily recognise users' automation intentions. The studies both analysed not only how users express themselves when specifying the creation of new rules in specific scenarios, but also how they define their customisation intentions when they want just to modify existing rules. An additional goal is to discover a possible interaction paradigm or interaction phases during the dialogue between the agent and the users so that we can design the agent in guiding end users in the automation definition.

4 Engineering Challenges

From an engineering point of view, defining an intelligent agent that can support a user without programming skills in creating automation presents different challenges. LLMs' rapid scale and spread have provided the scientific community and businesses with a powerful tool for processing several data types, quickly creating virtual assistants for repetitive tasks, and enhancing customer care. One factor contributing to the rapid adoption of LLMs is their ability to extract relevant information to answer questions across a wide range of topics, resulting from the training on large text corpora.

Literature explores several solutions that do not rely on LLMs [6,7,16]. However, these virtual assistants may limit users' ability to express themselves freely, as these agents need a rigid dialogue flow. In contrast, LLMs have a superior capacity to understand semantics independently of the exact words the user chooses.

A direct application of LLMs to domain-specific problems still requires enhancing them through custom knowledge bases [21] since the quality of LLMs' answers decreases when the dialogue focuses on topics for which they have not been trained [15]. We can envisage two opposite solutions in defining an LLM: fine-tuning a new model or prompt-tuning a pre-trained model. Each solution presents pros and cons; for the first solution, the fine-tuning of a local model can guarantee a faster execution and no privacy issues and fees; however, there is a need for expensive hardware to train the model and create a lengthy dataset can be challenging. On the other hand, the prompt-tuning approach exploits previous knowledge of the LLM and the In-Context Learning method, where the model learns to address a new task during inference by receiving a prompt, including task examples. However, a possible limitation of prompt-tuning a generic model is that, since the model was pre-trained on a wide range of data, it is not necessarily optimized for a specific domain. We are moving toward a prompt-tuning solution because it proved to be less expensive in terms of the resources needed to define a large dataset and to train the model accordingly. From an interactive system engineering point of view, it is very common to require LLM-based agents that should provide good responses to domain-specific questions, considering that seldom the goal is to provide a general-purpose answering agent. This is also the case for EUD4XR, where we need LMM support to create a chatbot that supports automation creation in an XR environment. A generic LLM can interpret the user's prompt to extract the overall concept of the automation they wish to create by leveraging its generic knowledge. To overcome this problem and improve response accuracy, additional context can be provided to the model along with the user prompt. This context consists of data that allows the model to generate a more appropriate and relevant response, improving the LLM's ability to adapt to the user's query without the need for a huge number of training examples [10].

In the following subsections, we explore and analyse what we consider to be the main challenges in developing an intelligent agent that can assist users without programming skills in creating interactions and behaviours within specific scenarios, such as home automation or the customisation of a VR museum application.

4.1 Multimodal Input

XR interfaces can exploit the surrounding space to provide context for the information. This might encourage end-users to take advantage of different modalities to refer to physical and virtual objects, e.g., by pointing, using demonstrative pronouns, etc. The intelligent agent should have access to multiple data sources to support the user in generating appropriate automation for the environment. The research community is actively studying and developing LLMs able to handle different data sources beyond text, including video, audio or images [22,29,30]. However, currently, no model can integrate all the functionalities the solution we propose needs, e.g., gesture pointing and spatial information. The challenge here is to collect the information from different input streams and interpret and transform it into something the LLM can consider for generating its answers. For instance, the relevant contextual information may be a list of available physical and virtual objects, their executable functionalities, the existing rules, etc.

Figure 2 shows an example of the rule authoring we envision in an XR environment. Consider a scenario where the manager of a cleaning company needs to train new employees on room sanitization protocols, such as Covid-19 disinfection procedures. To ensure effective training, the manager exploits an XR environment where new staff can interact with a blend of virtual and physical elements. Using the natural language, the manager creates an automation that makes the training interactive.

For instance, the automation defined by the manager could be expressed as follows: "*When the employee enters this room, virtually highlight these surfaces to disinfect*". The manager's statement includes references to the services virtual devices provide (highlight), demonstrative adjectives specifying which elements the user is referring to (surfaces), rule triggers (When the employee enters this room), condition (to disinfect), and ambiguous parameters whose definition need further questions by the chatbot (these surfaces). The LLM agent requires data about the current state of the XR environment (e.g., the framed device or the pointed virtual object), a description of the API supported by both physical and virtual devices to control them, a system prompt describing what the agent has to produce (an interaction rule) and, of course, the user's utterance and the context from previous interactions.

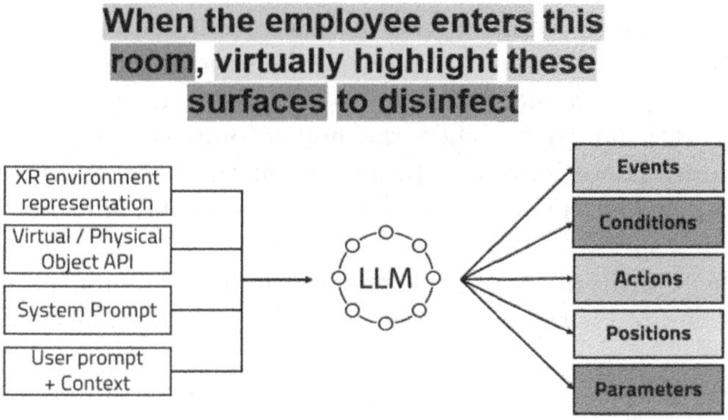

Fig. 2. Example of authoring an interaction rule using multimodal inputs.

4.2 Guidance from Intent to a Correct Rule

The intelligent agent guides the end user from formulating intent to generating valid automation within the XR environment. Starting from a similar problem addressed by Nielsen and Norman Group [1], where the authors describe the steps users follow to generate images with AI, we revisited the process of generating valid automation with the support of an intelligent agent according to these four stages: Define, Explore, Refine and Confirm.

In the **Define** stage, users declare the automation objectives they want to reach, often using high-level, ambiguous terms. This could imply specifying the final outcome that users want to achieve, or the automation "intent", i.e., "*I don't want to feel cold when I return home*" or "*I want the virtual door to become invisible*". If users can express their automation in terms of specific sensors and devices from the beginning, this phase can be skipped and users can go directly to the next one (Explore).

Since the automation's objectives identified at the end of the Define phase can be realised in different manners, in the **Explore** stage, the user explores and determines which objects and capabilities will be involved to realise the desired automation concretely. Thus, while the previous phase answers to "what" should be achieved, this phase aims to understand "how" to realise the intent defined before. Here, the intelligent agent, leveraging the description of the environment and its content, supports the user in identifying the objects, virtual or physical, to utilise to achieve the intention specified in the previous stage. For instance, it may suggest using the heat pump to warm the house. The output of this stage is still an incomplete automation, where the user has typically selected the objects and their capabilities that will form the basis of the automation.

In the **Refine** stage, the chatbot and the user refine the automation to finally meet the desired goal. In this stage, the agent may ask the user to specify any necessary parameters, such as the time or the minimum temperature threshold for activating the heat pump or the distance from home, which may trigger the event "*when I return home*", exploiting the smartphone GPS to understand when the user returns home. It may also request to disambiguate a "reverse" scenario, such as what to do when the house temperature becomes too high, or suggest adding conditions, i.e., to switch off the heat pump once a certain temperature is reached. The output of this step is a valid automation within the environment.

Finally, the **Confirm** stage is where the end-user confirms and saves the automation generated with the help of the intelligent agent, or chooses to discard it.

The phases described in [1] originally followed a linear sequence. However, since the process of generating valid automations with the aid of a chatbot is iterative and flexible, we envisage that, when exploiting such steps for automation generation, some of such phases may be re-visited several times, or even skipped, before arriving at the final version of the automation.

4.3 Exploring the Available Interactions

Another feature we want to support through the conversational agent is exploring the services offered by different physical devices and the actions supported by virtual content. This will help end-users find possible automation suggestions that could be useful for them. In addition, the interface must support the user in recalling or finding out which are the currently defined automations, i.e., rules, associated to a given object or defined in the environment. The list of available interactions provides the agent with an additional source of information for building knowledge about the objects present in the system and their capabilities. This data can be made available to the agent in different ways, for example, through an external service or by injecting it into the context. Regardless of the chosen approach, the support system should consistently be able to:

- Access the list of all automations defined up to that moment.
- Retrieve all the automation's components, i.e., triggers, conditions, and actions, as well as their status if provided by the automation management system.
- Convert the list of automations and their respective components into a textual format.

5 Conclusion

In this work, we analysed existing work on the EUD authoring tools for creating XR environments and interactions, also outlining a solution for an immersive environment that empowers end-users to customize the behaviour of virtual and physical objects in XR settings using rules expressed in natural language. The solution also includes the support of an intelligent conversational agent which leverages the use of LLMs to lower the barrier to entry for non-technical users, enabling them to create personalized and immersive XR experiences. Future work will be dedicated to implement and evaluate the effectiveness and usability of our solution in real-world scenarios.

Acknowledgements. This work has been supported by the Italian PRIN 2022 "EUD4XR: End-User Development for eXtended Reality" funded by the Italian MUR and European Union - NextGenerationEU under grant PRIN 2022 EUD4XR (Grant F53D23004380006) https://prin.unica.it/eud4xr/.

References

1. The 4 Stages of AI Image Generation: An Experience Map. https://www.nngroup.com/articles/ai-imagegen-stages/
2. Adão, T., et al.: A rapid prototyping tool to produce 360 video-based immersive experiences enhanced with virtual/multimedia elements. Procedia Comput. Sci. **138**, 441–453 (2018)
3. Ardito, C., Buono, P., Costabile, M.F., Lanzilotti, R., Piccinno, A., Zhu, L.: On the transferability of a meta-design model supporting end-user development. Univ. Access Inf. Soc. **14**, 169–186 (2015)
4. Ariano, R., Manca, M., Paternò, F., Santoro, C.: Smartphone-based augmented reality for end-user creation of home automations. Behav. Inf. Technol. **42**(1), 124–140 (2023)
5. Artizzu, V., et al.: Defining configurable virtual reality templates for end users. Proc. ACM Hum.-Comput. Interact. **6**(EICS), 1–35 (2022)
6. Asunis, L., Frau, V., Macis, R., Pireddu, C., Spano, L.D.: Pac-bot: writing text messages for developing point-and-click games. In: International Symposium on End User Development, pp. 213–221. Springer (2021)
7. Barricelli, B.R., Casiraghi, E., Valtolina, S.: Virtual assistants for end-user development in the internet of things. In: International Symposium on End User Development, pp. 209–216. Springer (2019)

8. Barricelli, B.R., Valtolina, S.: A visual language and interactive system for end-user development of internet of things ecosystems. J. Vis. Lang. Comput. **40**, 1–19 (2017)
9. Blečić, I., et al.: First-person cinematographic videogames: game model, authoring environment, and potential for creating affection for places. J. Comput. Cult. Heritage (JOCCH) **14**(2), 1–29 (2021)
10. Chamieh, I., Zesch, T., Giebermann, K.: LLMs in short answer scoring: limitations and promise of zero-shot and few-shot approaches. In: Proceedings of the 19th Workshop on Innovative Use of NLP for Building Educational Applications (BEA 2024), pp. 309–315 (2024)
11. Costabile, M.F., Fogli, D., Mussio, P., Piccinno, A.: A meta-design approach to end-user development. In: 2005 IEEE Symposium on Visual Languages and Human-Centric Computing (VL/HCC 2005), pp. 308–310. IEEE (2005)
12. De La Torre, F., Fang, C.M., Huang, H., Banburski-Fahey, A., Amores Fernandez, J., Lanier, J.: LLMR: real-time prompting of interactive worlds using large language models. In: Proceedings of the CHI Conference on Human Factors in Computing Systems, pp. 1–22 (2024)
13. Fischer, G., Giaccardi, E., Ye, Y., Sutcliffe, A.G., Mehandjiev, N.: Meta-design: a manifesto for end-user development. Commun. ACM **47**(9), 33–37 (2004)
14. Fogli, D., Peroni, M., Stefini, C.: Imathome: making trigger-action programming easy and fun. J. Vis. Lang. Comput. **42**, 60–75 (2017)
15. Galitsky, B., Chernyavskiy, A., Ilvovsky, D.: Truth-o-meter: handling multiple inconsistent sources repairing LLM hallucinations. In: Proceedings of the 47th International ACM SIGIR Conference on Research and Development in Information Retrieval, pp. 2817–2821 (2024)
16. Gallo, S., Paterno, F.: A conversational agent for creating flexible daily automation. In: Proceedings of the 2022 International Conference on Advanced Visual Interfaces, pp. 1–8 (2022)
17. Garzotto, F., Gelsomini, M., Matarazzo, V., Messina, N., Occhiuto, D.: XOOM: an end-user development tool for web-based wearable immersive virtual tours. In: Cabot, J., De Virgilio, R., Torlone, R. (eds.) ICWE 2017. LNCS, vol. 10360, pp. 507–519. Springer, Cham (2017). https://doi.org/10.1007/978-3-319-60131-1_36
18. Huang, J., Cakmak, M.: Supporting mental model accuracy in trigger-action programming. In: Proceedings of the 2015 ACM International Joint Conference on Pervasive and Ubiquitous Computing, pp. 215–225 (2015)
19. Ikeda, B., Szafir, D.: Programar: augmented reality end-user robot programming. ACM Trans. Hum.-Robot Interact. (2024)
20. Kasneci, E., et al.: Chatgpt for good? On opportunities and challenges of large language models for education. Learn. Individ. Differ. **103**, 102274 (2023)
21. Kumar, P.: Large language models (LLMs): survey, technical frameworks, and future challenges. Artif. Intell. Rev. **57**(9), 260 (2024)
22. Lyu, C., et al.: Macaw-LLM: multi-modal language modeling with image, audio, video, and text integration. arXiv preprint arXiv:2306.09093 (2023)
23. Mahroo, A., Greci, L., Sacco, M.: HoloHome: an augmented reality framework to manage the smart home. In: De Paolis, L.T., Bourdot, P. (eds.) AVR 2019. LNCS, vol. 11614, pp. 137–145. Springer, Cham (2019). https://doi.org/10.1007/978-3-030-25999-0_12
24. Manca, M., Paternò, F., Santoro, C., Corcella, L.: Supporting end-user debugging of trigger-action rules for IoT applications. Int. J. Hum. Comput. Stud. **123**, 56–69 (2019)

25. Martin, L., Whitehouse, N., Yiu, S., Catterson, L., Perera, R.: Better call GPT, comparing large language models against lawyers (2024)
26. Matukumalli, V., et al.: Augment reality chatbot using cloud. Mater. Today Proc. **46**, 4254–4257 (2021). https://doi.org/10.1016/j.matpr.2021.03.058. https://www.sciencedirect.com/science/article/pii/S2214785321020721. International Conference on Materials, Manufacturing and Mechanical Engineering for Sustainable Developments-2020 (ICMSD 2020)
27. Menestrina, Z., De Angeli, A.: End-user development for serious games. In: New Perspectives in End-User Development, pp. 359–383 (2017)
28. Morales, P., Showalter-Bucher, R.A.: Towards large language models at the edge on mobile, augmented reality, and virtual reality devices with unity. In: System and Architecture for Generative AI on the Edge/Mobile Platforms (SAGE) (2023). https://openreview.net/forum?id=ahVsd1hy2W
29. Radford, A., et al.: Learning transferable visual models from natural language supervision. In: International Conference on Machine Learning, pp. 8748–8763. PMLR (2021)
30. Radford, A., Kim, J.W., Xu, T., Brockman, G., McLeavey, C., Sutskever, I.: Robust speech recognition via large-scale weak supervision. In: International Conference on Machine Learning, pp. 28492–28518. PMLR (2023)
31. Stefanidi, E., Arampatzis, D., Leonidis, A., Korozi, M., Antona, M., Papagiannakis, G.: Magiplay: an augmented reality serious game allowing children to program intelligent environments. Trans. Comput. Sci. XXXVII: Special Issue Comput. Graph. 144–169 (2020)
32. Stefanidi, E., Arampatzis, D., Leonidis, A., Papagiannakis, G.: BricklAyeR: a platform for building rules for AmI environments in AR. In: Gavrilova, M., Chang, J., Thalmann, N.M., Hitzer, E., Ishikawa, H. (eds.) CGI 2019. LNCS, vol. 11542, pp. 417–423. Springer, Cham (2019). https://doi.org/10.1007/978-3-030-22514-8_39
33. Sun, Y., Armengol-Urpi, A., Kantareddy, S.N.R., Siegel, J., Sarma, S.: Magichand: interact with IoT devices in augmented reality environment. In: 2019 IEEE Conference on Virtual Reality and 3D User Interfaces (VR), pp. 1738–1743. IEEE (2019)
34. Takala, T.M.: Ruis: a toolkit for developing virtual reality applications with spatial interaction. In: Proceedings of the 2nd ACM Symposium on Spatial User Interaction, pp. 94–103 (2014)
35. Thirunavukarasu, A.J., Ting, D., Elangovan, K., Gutierrez, L., Tan, T.F., Ting, D.: Large language models in medicine. Nat. Med. **29**(8), 1930–1940 (2023)
36. Yigitbas, E., Klauke, J., Gottschalk, S., Engels, G.: Vreud-an end-user development tool to simplify the creation of interactive VR scenes. In: 2021 IEEE Symposium on Visual Languages and Human-Centric Computing (VL/HCC), pp. 1–10. IEEE (2021)

On the Role of Generative AI in Explaining Model Checking Counterexamples

Ezequiel José Veloso Ferreira Moreira and José Creissac Campos(✉)

Departamento de Informática, Universidade do Minho and HASLab/INESC TEC, Braga, Portugal
id9620@alunos.uminho.pt, jose.campos@di.uminho.pt

Abstract. Formal verification can be a complementary approach to UCD, offering a systematic and repeatable process to address the demands of designing safety and mission-critical interactive systems. However, the practical application of formal verification often encounters barriers to accessibility for non-technical stakeholders. In the case of model checking, although the verification step is fully automated, developing the required specifications and interpreting the verification results requires considerable technical expertise in formal methods.

Recent developments in generative Artificial Intelligence (AI) have driven proposals for Large Language Models (LLMs) to be applied throughout various phases of software engineering. This begs the question of whether LLMs might be used to help bridge the gap between formal techniques and tools and stakeholders lacking technical expertise.

This paper explores how these questions might be addressed in the context of an ongoing effort aimed at translating model-checking counterexamples into natural language explanations, making them accessible to designers and domain experts.

Keywords: Model-checking · Counterexamples · Large Language Models (LLMs)

1 Introduction

The design of safety and mission-critical interactive computing systems poses challenges that traditional UCD approaches, on their own, cannot address. User-Centred Design (UCD) approaches are not exhaustive and repeatable enough to provide the level of guarantee needed for these systems [29]. While UCD is valuable for engaging users in the design process, it is not exhaustive or rigorous enough to ensure the safety required in critical systems.

E. Moreira is supported by the FCT (*Fundação para a Ciência e Tecnologia*) under grant 2023.01639.BD, funded by the ESF (European Social Fund) and by national funds through the Demography, Qualifications and Inclusion Programme (PDQI).

L. Zaina et al. (Eds.): EICS 2024, LNCS 15518, pp. 138–158, 2025.
https://doi.org/10.1007/978-3-031-91760-8_10

Formal verification, model checking in particular, has been proposed as a complementary approach, offering a systematic and repeatable process to address these limitations [18,24,32]. However, the practical application of model checking often encounters barriers to accessibility for non-technical stakeholders. While the verification step is fully automated, developing the required specifications and interpreting the verification results requires considerable technical expertise in formal methods.

This paper discusses an ongoing effort to lower the barrier to adopting model checking by enabling designers and domain experts (not fluent in formal verification technology) to have access to natural language explanations of verification results. Initially, a patterns-based approach to generate the natural language explanations was favoured. The use of deep learning models was discarded due to the lack of practicality of training models for each new system to be analysed. Not only would the process be resource-intensive and potentially inefficient, but given the safety-critical nature of the systems to which the approach can be expected to be applied, it was felt that it would not be reasonable to expect that appropriate training data would be available. However, recent developments in generative models, Large Language Models (LLMs) in particular, have prompted a reevaluation of this stance. The advancements in generative models bring forth the question of whether these models could now be effectively applied to a broader range of systems, making Artificial Intelligence () a more viable option.

The paper briefly describes the original proposal and then discusses how generative AI might be integrated into it. The paper is structured as follows: Sect. 2 discusses the integration of generative models into software engineering tasks; Sect. 3 discusses model checking and the challenges it poses to non-experts, despite its support for fully automated analysis; Sect. 4 introduces the example that will be used to support the discussion; Sect. 5 then presents the original proposal of a templates based approach to explaining counterexamples in natural language and Sect. 6 how generative AI might be used in the context of the proposal; the paper concludes with a discussion and conclusions in Sect. 7.

2 Generative Models in Software Engineering

The application of generative AI throughout the various phases of software engineering is generating a growing interest. This is most evident in programming tasks, but its application to other stages of development is being proposed and explored. The goals range from enhancing the systems' functionalities and, consequently, the user experience of such systems to enhancing the development process of the systems themselves.

In their recent survey on the application of AI to safety-critical systems, Perez-Cerrolaza et al. [25] conclude that there are still significant research challenges to developing AI-based safety-critical systems. Bridging the gap between advanced AI technology and established safety engineering practices and standards remains a significant hurdle. Challenges range from the technological problems of how to integrate AI technology into the systems to how best to support users through AI technology. Dittmar and Forbrig [13] argue that the integration of AI into interactive systems requires a human-centred design approach. The authors argue that "designers and users of interactive systems with embedded generative AI technologies need to be equipped with methods and techniques that support the exploration of potential intended and unintended consequences of automation".

Feldt et al. [16] identify three alternatives for the application of AI in Software Engineering: at the *process* level, AI is applied during the development process and does not directly affect the system source code; at the *product* level, AI is also applied during the development process but directly affects the source code; at the *runtime* level AI is embedded in the system and affects it during execution. In this paper, we are primarily concerned with the process level. Nevertheless, below, we provide some discussion of the product and runtime levels, too. We will focus the discussion on the specific case of interactive computing systems.

2.1 Integrating AI Into Systems at the Runtime Level

One clear technological runtime level challenge is how to orchestrate AI components and how to integrate them into *conventional* systems. One particular area of application is multimodal systems. Coppens and Maquil [12] explore this in the context of a tracking pipeline for a remote collaboration system across distant wall-sized displays to promote situational awareness through AI-supported gesture and image-based facial recognition. Ziegler [33] discusses the integration of conversational AI with conventional GUI-based interaction. Trajkovska et al. [30] propose a tool for AI-supported annotation of video streams, while Mereu et al. [22] explore the use of conversational agents in empowering end-users in creating eXtended Reality Content.

From an interactive computing systems perspective, a further challenge is how better to support users in the presence of AI technology. Menten et al. [21] explore how to incrementally integrate AI components into interactive systems using a Wizard of Oz approach where humans play the role of AI.

2.2 Integrating AI Into Systems at the Product Level

Regarding product-level integration, one significant advancement is the use of AI-driven coding assistants (e.g. GitHub's Copilot, Tabnine, Amazon CodeWhisperer, or Codeium). These tools leverage machine learning to assist developers by suggesting code snippets and even generating entire functions based on the context of the code being written. While the goal is to accelerate the development process, critics point out that these tools can produce incorrect code that, if not properly analysed, will lead to security vulnerabilities, incorrect implementations, or poorly optimised code. This can lead to a shift in the role of developers from producing code to analysing code produced by the AI, which can be cognitively more stressful and does not guarantee increased productivity [17].

Other concerns regard copyright issues, with some companies opting to forbid the use of code assistants. These concerns relate to the code being made available to the code assistants, hence potentially to third parties, and to code assistants using code that is copyrighted to make their suggestions.

Besides producing code, the use of AI to support debugging has also been considered. Weber [31] explores the relevance of explainable AI (XAI) to support developers in the debugging of systems. The author concludes that XAI has the potential to assist developers in understanding and debugging their applications. Still, current XAI systems provide little support for this task, identifying XAI for developers as a particularly interesting research area.

2.3 Integrating AI Into Systems at the Process Level

In this case, the goal is to support the design and development process of systems using AI. We will split the discussion into four areas: elicitation, design, development and evaluation.

Regarding elicitation, several authors have begun exploring the use of LLMs to enhance the human-centred design process. Bisante et al. [3], for example, explore the generation of user-profiles and personas to help designers understand user needs, preferences, and contexts. The goal is to take advantage of the large amount of information present in LLMs to avoid, or at least reduce, the cost of producing these artefacts. The authors highlight the potential benefits of integrating LLMs into UCD (increased efficiency and deeper insights), as well as the inherent limitations of the technique, pointing out the lack of emotional depth in AI-generated interviews and the challenges in detecting inaccuracies. Using a similar rationale, Schmidt et al. [27] explore the use of LLMs to emulate users themselves.

Moving from the elicitation phase of the development process to usability analysis, the use of LLMs to create tools for usability evaluation has been explored. Duan et al. [14] explore the use of AI for generating user interface design feedback by using a design heuristic to evaluate the user interfaces. Bisante et al. [4] develop a chatbot to perform cognitive walkthroughs. Tabone and De Winter [28] take a different approach, exploring the application of ChatGPT for text analysis of text data from usability analysis (questionnaire responses, interviews, and think-aloud data).

Beyond usability, Bachert and Hesenius [1] explore generative AI to synthesise gestures that mimic human variances in order to support the automating of user interface tests in applications using gestures.

2.4 Discussion

As illustrated above, the application of generative AI throughout the life-cycle of software systems development has raised considerable interest. Applications range from requirements elicitation to development to testing, but its integration in applications to enhance systems capabilities is also being considered.

Several challenges remain, from the quality of the output and the trust that can be placed in them to issues with copyright and ethic considerations [19]. Concerns with the quality of the results are mentioned by several authors (see [5] for a discussion on the topic). From a safety-critical perspective, one specific concern related to this is the lack of predictability of the results. The use of multiple models has been suggested [20], but this raises a further concern: the computational cost of using these systems.

3 On Complementing UCD with Model Checking

The integration of formal methods, such as model checking [11], to complement UCD and enhance the safety and reliability of these systems has been proposed as a means of addressing some of the limitations of UCD when developing safety and mission-critical interactive systems [18,24,32]. Model checking, in particular, offers the possibility of exhaustive and automated analysis of interactive systems' behaviour [6]. When the system's specification fails to satisfy a given property, a counterexample (a system behaviour that does not satisfy the property) is generated. This counterexample must then be analysed. One of several situations might happen: a problem in the model needs to be fixed, a problem in how the requirement was expressed needs to be addressed, or the counterexample is deemed not relevant.

In short, model checking is a formal verification technique that is used to systematically explore the states of a system to ensure that it meets certain specifications or properties. It involves creating a mathematical model of the system and then using algorithms to exhaustively check all possible states and transitions against desired properties, such as safety (something bad never happens) and liveness (something good eventually happens). This method helps identify errors or inconsistencies in the design of systems, making it a valuable tool for verifying the correctness of hardware and software.

Although the analysis itself is automated, several steps in the process of using model checking still involve some level of human intervention, from the need to specify the system and its requirements in an appropriate logic to the need to interpret the verification results. Both of these steps require considerable expertise in formal methods to be carried out successfully. They are also critical to guarantee the correctness of the design. In the context of interactive system development, both these steps will require the participation of domain and human factors experts, who will likely not have the expertise required to interpret models and verification results. This creates a barrier to the adoption of formal verification techniques. In this paper, we are specifically concerned with the interpretation step for the verification results.

4 An Example

In this section, we present the device used to illustrate our proposal for explaining model-checking counterexamples.

4.1 The Device and Its Model

The device in question is a multimeter inspired by the Fluke 114 model. For brevity, our focus is specifically on its user interface, which serves as an example of a control panel user interface. This means that we will not consider the device's internal logic in our model, only the user interface behaviour.

Several authors have explored the application of model checking to the analysis of interactive computing systems ([2,9,26] are examples). In this paper, we will resort to the IVY workbench [7], a model-based tool designed for the formal modelling and verification of interactive systems, which uses NuSMV [10] as its verification back-end. Models are developed in the MAL interactors language. The tool aims to complement user-centred design approaches by providing a rigorous, mathematical analysis of system behaviour, thereby identifying potential issues early in the development process.

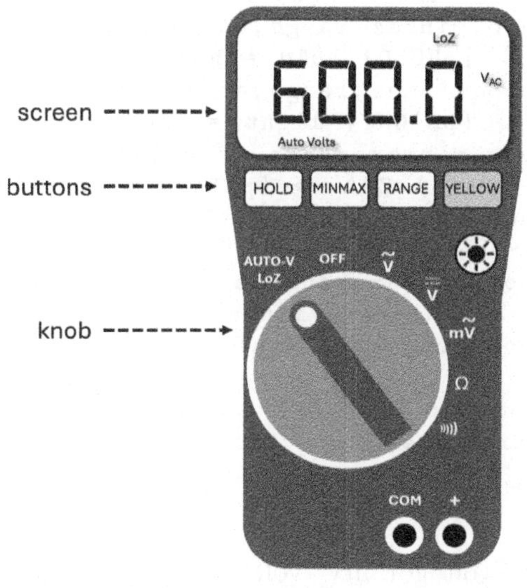

Fig. 1. The multimeter's user interface

As can be seen in Fig. 1, the main components of the device's user interface are a screen at the top, a row of buttons below the screen, and a rotating knob. The screen displays the current read value at the centre and information regarding the operating modes of the device around that value. Below the screen sits a row of four buttons. From left to right: HOLD, MINMAX, RANGE and YELLOW. For this discussion, it is enough to know that the buttons turn the different operating modes of the device on and off. An additional button to turn on and off screen illumination sits below the YELLOW button. Finally, the rotating knob supports selecting one of the multimeter's different measurement functions (clockwise): AUTO V LoZ (automatic mode), OFF (device is off), $\widetilde{V}$

Listing 1. The MAL interactors model (excerpt)

```
interactor main
 attributes
  [vis] knob: KnobPositions
  [vis] minmax: MinMaxModes
  [vis] range: RangeModes
  [vis] ac, light, hold: boolean
 actions
  [vis] pHOLD pMINMAX pRANGE pYELLOW pLIGHT
  [vis] tRIGHT tLEFT hMINMAX hRANGE
 axioms
  per(tRIGHT) -> knob!=Cont
  [tRIGHT] turnKnobRIGHT & fixDetails
  per(tLEFT) -> knob!=LoZ
  [tLEFT] turnKnobLEFT & fixDetails
  knob=OFF -> [!(tRIGHT|tLEFT)]
      keep(knob,minmax,range,ac,light,hold)
  knob!=OFF -> [pHOLD] hold'=!hold &
      keep(knob,minmax,range,ac,light)
  knob!=OFF -> [pLIGHT] light'=!light &
      keep(knob,minmax,range,ac,hold)
  !(knob in {OFF, LoZ}) -> [pMINMAX] stepMINMAX &
      keep(knob,range,ac,light,hold)
  knob=LoZ -> [pMINMAX]
      keep(knob,minmax,range,ac,light,hold)
  knob!=OFF -> [hMINMAX] minmax'=normal &
      keep(knob,range,ac,light,hold)
  ...
  [] !ac & !hold & knob=OFF & !light & minmax= normal &
      range=autorace
```

(AC voltage), $\overline{V}$ (DC voltage), mV (voltage in the mV range), Ohm (resistance in Ohms) and Cont (continuity beeper).

To model this user interface, the first step is to describe its structure (i.e. the information being displayed and the commands being offered). Attributes were used to model each of the display items of interest. Actions were used to model each of the controls identified. Listing 1 presents an excerpt of the model[1].

Attributes are defined to represent the knob position (`knob`), the minmax, range and current modes (`minmax`, `range` and `ac`), whether the screen `light` is on and whether the device is on `hold`. Note that the value displayed on the screen is not modelled. As this particular model was developed to analyse the navigation between the different modes of the user interface, the displayed value is not relevant to the analysis and has been abstracted from the model.

[1] The complete model can be found at: http://hcispecs.di.uminho.pt/faces/view.xhtml?id=12.

The types `KnobPositions`, `MinMaxModes` and `RangeModes` represent the possible values for the given attributes:

```
types
 KnobPositions = {LoZ, OFF, VAC, VDC, mV, Ohm, Cont}
 MinMaxModes = {normal, MAXm, MINm, AVGm, Current}
 RangeModes = {auto, m6, m60, m600, m6K, m60K, m600K,
    m6M, m60M}
```

Actions are defined to model the pressing of each of the buttons (`pHOLD` to `pLIGHT`), the turning left (`tLEFT`) and right (`tRIGHT`) of the knob, and for holding the minmax and range buttons (`hMINMAX` and `hRANGE`). The effect of these actions on the attributes is modelled using Modal Action Logic. The first four axioms in Listing 1 model the knob's behaviour. The permission axiom on line 11 states that the knob cannot be turned right (action `tRIGHT`) beyond the `Cont` position. The modal axiom on line 12 then defines the effect of turning the knob in the right (clockwise) direction. Since this depends on the current knob position, two named expressions are used to make the axiom easier to read: `turnKnobRIGHT` and `fixDetails`. As an example, `turnKnobRIGHT` is defined as:

```
turnKnobRIGHT = (knob=LoZ -> knob'=OFF) &
                (knob=OFF -> knob'=VAC) &
                (knob=VAC -> knob'=VDC) &
                (knob=VDC -> knob'=mV) &
                (knob=mV -> knob'=Ohm) &
                (knob=Ohm -> knob'=Cont)
```

Priming is used to reference the value of an attribute *after* an action. Hence, if the knob is in the AUTO V LoZ position, it will move to the OFF position and so on. The `fixDetails` expression guarantees that the modes of the device are correctly updated as the know turns. Lines 13 and 14 express the logic of turning the knob left (action `tLEFT`).

The axiom in line 15 expresses the fact that when the device is off, only the turning of the knob (left or right) affects the multimeter. All other actions (`!(tRIGHT|tLEFT)`) are discarded. The remaining axioms then express the effect of the buttons. Pressing the HOLD button toggles the hold mode, while pressing the LIGHT button toggles the screen light (lines 16 and 17, respectively). When the knob is in a position different from OFF or AUTO-V LoZ, pressing the MINMAX button steps through the different minmax modes (a named expression used for readability), while in the AUTO-V LoZ position, the button has no effect (lines 18 and 19, respectively). Holding the MINMAX button, reset the mode (line 19). The remaining axioms follow similar patterns and are omitted herein for readability. The exception is the last axiom (line 22) that represents the initial state of the model (simply put, the device starts in the OFF state).

4.2 The Analysis

Once the model is created, properties representing requirements over the device's user interface can be verified. Consider that we want to check if it is always possible to eventually turn off the multimeter, no matter what the position of the knob is. While this is obvious by looking at the device's user interface, this type of property is often used to check that the model is behaving as expected. It will also help us discuss some points later on.

Listing 2. Property generated for the knob in the Ohm position

```
AG(knob = Ohm -> AF(knob = OFF))
```

Listing 3. Counterexample for `AG(knob = Ohm -> AF(knob = OFF))`

```
-> State: 1.1 <-
  ac = FALSE
  knob = OFF
  light = FALSE
  minmax = normal
  range = auto
  hold = FALSE
  action = nil
-> State: 1.2 <-
  ac = TRUE
  knob = VAC
  action = tRIGHT
-> State: 1.3 <-
  ac = FALSE
  knob = VDC
-> State: 1.4 <-
  knob = mV
-- Loop starts here
-> State: 1.5 <-
  knob = Ohm
-> State: 1.6 <-
  knob = mV
  action = tLEFT
-> State: 1.7 <-
  knob = Ohm
  action = tRIGHT
```

The IVY workbench allows us to express CTL properties with variables ranging over types. Suppose the following formulation was chosen for the requirement: `AG(knob = $KnobPositions -> AF(knob = OFF))`. For all possible values in `$KnobPositions`, it is always the case that, eventually, the knob will be in the OFF position. Since, at the NuSMV level, CTL properties cannot have variables, a different property is generated for each possible position of the knob.

Listing 2 presents the property generated for the Ohm position. To verify the model against this property, the IVY workbench generates a NuSMV version of the model. In this case, the model checker determines that the property is false and produces the counterexample in Listing 3.

To understand the problem that led to this property not being verified in the model, this counterexample must be analysed and understood. Although this counterexample is small, the process of counterexample interpretation can become very complex even for experts, as more complex models and properties can lead to counterexamples with dozens of states and many attributes in each state. Additionally, the interpretation process is highly specialised, requiring extra work from model-checking experts to make the results understandable to other stakeholders involved in the device analysis.

Counterexample explanation aims to address both of these problems by creating an explanation for the counterexample that reduces the difficulty of understanding it, making it easier to interpret and communicate with other stakeholders.

5 An Approach to Counterexamples Explanation

We now explore the generation of natural language explanations of model-checking counterexamples produced by the IVY workbench.

5.1 The Approach

The approach is based on the fact that there are a number of known property specification patterns that are recurrently used [8,15] and that these properties will fail predictably. For example, suppose we try to prove that action a will always be followed by action b, and the attempt fails. In that case, the counterexample will illustrate a behaviour in which, after a, some action different from b occurs. The approach leverages this knowledge to define explanation templates for specific types of properties. These templates express how a natural language explanation should be generated for a counterexample of a property conforming to a specific pattern. The proposal is thus based on the use of property specification patterns to identify the types of property being verified, together with explanation templates to generate the natural language explanation (see Fig. 2).

A final component is domain information, explaining the *meaning* of the model's attributes and actions. If present, this information will help generate explanations that are expressed more in terms of the domain and less in terms of the model. This information might be obtained from the model by adopting a literate programming style of modelling where attributes and actions are annotated with domain information.

Given a property/counterexample pair, once a property specification pattern that matches the property is identified, the corresponding explanation template needs to be instantiated for the concrete property and trace being explained. The approach uses the knowledge about how the satisfaction of the property

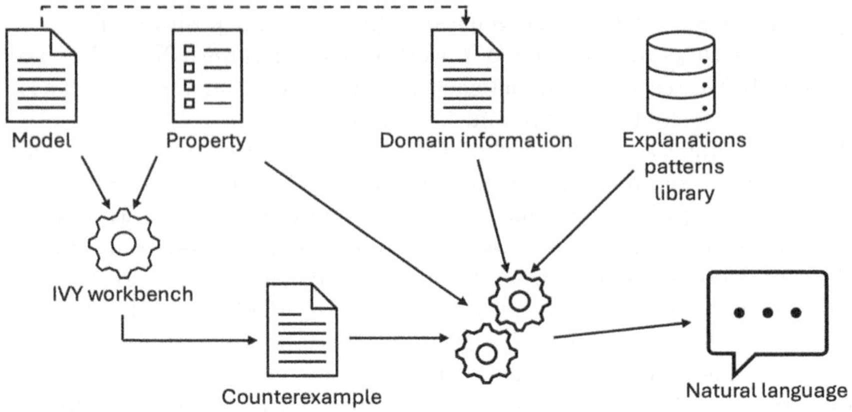

Fig. 2. The process of generating natural language explanations

might fail to query the trace for relevant information. The information thus obtained is then used to instantiate the explanation template. A query language has been defined that supports performing these queries [23]. The language features operators for querying for specific **S**tates in the counterexample or (part of) the sequence of states in **C**ounterexample, but also specific **E**xpressions and **O**perations in a state of the property.

5.2 The Example

Applying the approach to the example in Sect. 4.2 entails identifying the relevant property specification pattern and instantiating the explanation template. Tool support was developed to support this process, but it falls outside the scope of this paper.

The property was captured by the approach using the Response pattern presented in Listing 4. Line 1 identifies the property specification pattern (in this case, `AG(expression -> AF(expression))`) and lines 3 to 5 define the explanation template. As can be seen, the explanation has two parts. Initially, the purpose of the property is identified, and then the reason why the counterexample falsifies it is explained. Note that the last sentence of the explanation provides guidance on how the counterexample should be interpreted. This captures knowledge resulting from the experience of applying formal verification in multiple projects.

Applying the pattern to the property and counterexample lead to the creation of the following natural language explanation:

Listing 4. The response pattern and associated explanation

```
AG({E}{1,m} -> AF({E}{2,m}))
----
It was expected that, in every system behaviour where
    {E}{1,t} was observed, {E}{2,t} would inevitably
    happen at some point in the future.\n
However, despite {E}{1,t} being observed on state
{S}{1,default,sv,{E}{1,t}}, the illustrated behaviour
    terminates in a loop, with {E}{2,t} having never
    happened. Note that this does not mean that having
    {E}{2,t} after {E}{1,t} is impossible, only that
    there are valid system behaviours where that does not
    happen.
;;;;
```

It was expected that, in every system behaviour where [knob = Ohm] was observed, [knob = OFF] would inevitably happen at some point in the future. However, despite [knob = Ohm] being verified on state [1.5], the illustrated behaviour terminates in a loop, with [knob = OFF] having never happened. Note that this does not mean that having [knob = OFF] after [knob = Ohm] is impossible, only that there are valid system behaviours where that does not happen.

This explanation could be further improved by applying domain knowledge information. This would allow, for example, to replace `[knob = Ohm]`by "the knob is in the Ohm position".

We propose that this explanation, even without enhancements from domain knowledge, will be more accessible for a non-expert in formal verification to understand compared to the counterexample. Even for experts, the explanation helps by highlighting the relevant states in the counterexample. In particular, the explanation points the reader to an inconsistency between the intended requirement ("it is always possible") and what has been expressed in the CTL property ("would inevitably happen"). This is a case where the property, not the model, needs fixing.

6 On the Use of Generative AI

Using patterns and templates guarantees that the approach is deterministic, which should be an advantage in safety and mission-critical contexts. However, the potential drawback is that the generated explanations might feel mechanical and unnatural, and the analysis is restricted to the known patterns. Recent developments in generative Artificial Intelligence (AI) beg whether Large Language Models (LLMs) can reliably generate explanations for verification results that will feel more natural.

The question then is whether (and, if so, how) generative AI might be used to enhance the process of counterexample analysis. At this stage, we see three main alternative pathways to explore:

1. creating a chatbot specialised in explaining counterexamples;
2. using a general-purpose chatbot to generate explanations of the trace;
3. using a general-purpose chatbot to generate an improved version of the explanation generated by the pattern-based approach.

6.1 Chatbot Creation

Creating a chatbot will enable users to ask questions about the counterexample in a conversational style. This could be the more natural approach from a domain expert's perspective. Still, it will also be prone to *hallucination*, particularly if insufficient data about the domain is available. We are also placing some of the responsibility on the domain experts as, inevitably, the queries used will have an impact on the results obtained.

Chatbot creation can be accomplished either by training an LLM to perform the task or through prompt engineering. Training an LLM will be complex and feasible for specific domains only. Sufficient data on conversations about counterexample analysis and on the domain would be required. A further relevant concern is the computational cost of this type of approach, as it implies running our own LLM, which can easily have computational requirements that exceed that of model checking itself. We do not see the approach as generally applicable in the short to medium term and favour using prompt engineering.

One potential problem with training an online chatbot is privacy concerns, as there is the risk that the information provided to the model will be available to third parties. Depending on the specific context, this might be unacceptable. Another, regardless of the approach used to obtain the chatbot, is the lack of control over the information the model has and whether the model's training might interfere with the interpretation of the counterexample. The model might, for example, make assumptions about the behaviour of the system, based on its training data, that are inconsistent with the system as modelled.

6.2 General Purpose Chatbot Use

We have been experimenting with providing different levels of information in the prompts to general-purpose chatbots. From simply providing the property and the counterexample, to providing the model and information about how the given property is expected to fail. We also consider the type of request, from simply asking for an explanation to explicitly asking for an explanation to suit someone not fluent in model checking.

By providing additional information in the prompt, we provide the LLM with additional context that should help guide the explanation generation process.

Prompts. Preliminary tests have been done on this topic using ChatGPT (with GPT-4o) and LLaVA 1.5. Here, we report on results obtained for the example from Sect. 4. In all cases, the prompts included the CTL property and the counterexample produced by NuSMV and were run a minimum of five times. This constitutes what we will call the *basic prompt*. The general shape of the prompt is:

> **Prompt:**
> I need explanations for counterexamples produced by the NuSMV model checker so that the designer of the system may understand where the problem lies.
> We will consider the following CTL property: ...
> The counterexample that was produced by NuSMV is depicted below, between the lines "START COUNTEREXAMPLE" and "END COUNTEREXAMPLE".
> START COUNTEREXAMPLE
> ...
> END COUNTEREXAMPLE
> Explain the counterexample in a way that will be understandable by a domain expert who is not fluent in formal verification. Do not use technical language, keep the explanation at the domain level and simply present your conclusion of what the problem is.

Note that we are attempting to get the LLM to generate non-technical text. Furthermore, since initial answers given by the LLMs were quite lengthy (including detailed descriptions of each state in the counterexample), we ask the LLM to present only the result of its *analysis*. Finally, we are avoiding direct references to the actual system being modelled (the user interface of the Fluke 114 multimeter) since that could bias the analysis. The LLM could start using its knowledge of the device instead of the information presented in the prompt.

A more complete prompt included the model being verified (with an explanation that it was a MAL interactors model). We will call this the *model prompt*. In all cases, we took care to reset the system so that the conditions were kept as similar as possible. Since the inclusion of the model did not seem to change the output of the LLMs significantly, we will discuss the results of both prompts together, highlighting any differences where needed.

LLaVA 1.5. We installed the LLM through the Mozilla Builders' llamafile project and, at this stage, kept its configuration unchanged. In this configuration, LLaVA 1.5 failed to generate meaningful results, appearing unable to interpret the property or the trace correctly. In one instance, it claimed that the problem lay "in the transitions between states 1.3 and 1.4, as well as other related states along this pathway," further directing the reader's attention to the AC variable. This was vague and directed attention to an attribute that was irrelevant in this case.

In another instance, it pointed the reader to the transition from state 1.5 to 1.6, which is more useful, but the reason for doing so was nonsensical. In a further instance, it interpreted all actions in the model as switches that could be turned on or off. None of the results were considered potentially helpful in understanding the problem.

ChatGPT. ChatGPT produced more promising results, being able to interpret the property correctly. However, it suffered from one problem highlighted by the previous discussion on LLaVA 1.5: results could vary considerably between consecutive interactions using the same prompt. Consider the following example:

> **ChatGPT:**
> The counterexample provided indicates a situation where the behaviour of the system does not follow the expected rule:
> The rule says, "Whenever the knob is set to Ohm, it should eventually always be turned to OFF."
> However, the counterexample shows a specific sequence of actions where this rule is violated. Here's what happens step by step:
> Initial State (State 1.1): The knob is set to OFF, and everything seems to be in a normal configuration.
> Next Steps (States 1.2 - 1.4): The knob is moved through different settings: VAC, VDC, and mV. These changes happen normally as expected.
> Key Issue (State 1.5): The knob is now set to Ohm, which is where the rule applies. According to the rule, the system should eventually move the knob to OFF at some point after this. However, this doesn't happen.
> Problematic Behavior (States 1.6 - 1.7): Instead of turning the knob to OFF, it keeps switching between Ohm and mV. This movement repeats in a loop and never reaches the OFF position, violating the rule.
> **Conclusion:**
> The problem is that once the knob is set to Ohm, it never transitions to the OFF position as expected. Instead, it keeps switching between other settings (Ohm and mV). This is where the issue lies: the system should be designed so that after the knob is set to Ohm, it eventually moves to OFF, but it doesn't do that here.

This explanation can be considered helpful as it points the reader to the problematic behaviour. The initial explanation of the *rule* (the property) can also help detect the error in using this specification pattern.

However, a subsequent attempt at obtaining an explanation produced:

> **ChatGPT:**
> The counterexample shows a sequence of events where the system does not behave as expected according to the specification. The system's behavior revolves around the "knob" setting, and the expected property is: "If the knob is set to Ohm, it should eventually reach OFF."
> Here's what the counterexample tells us:
> Initially, the knob is set to OFF, and various other settings are configured. The system appears normal, with the knob transitioning through different states

(VAC, VDC, mV). At some point, the knob is set to Ohm, which is where the issue begins. According to the specification, once the knob is set to Ohm, it should eventually switch to OFF. However, instead of transitioning to OFF, the knob cycles between Ohm and mV without ever reaching the OFF state. The key problem here is that once the knob is set to Ohm, it enters a loop where it keeps toggling between Ohm and mV. This violates the intended behavior, which is for the system to eventually turn OFF when the knob is in the Ohm position. The system is stuck in a loop, and as a result, the OFF state is never reached.
In simpler terms, when the knob is turned to the Ohm setting, the system never gets a chance to turn off, which is a clear issue with the expected behavior.

In this case, while the problem with the loop is highlighted, the explanation assumes that the counterexample fully represents the behaviour of the system (*"when the knob is turned to the Ohm setting, the system never gets a chance to turn off"*). This is not correct and will confound the issue.

Another instance of this situation happens with the following explanation:

ChatGPT:
The counterexample reveals a problem with the multimeter's knob control system, specifically when the knob is set to the "Ohm" position.
The system is expected to eventually return to the "OFF" position after the knob is rotated to "Ohm." However, the counterexample shows that once the knob reaches "Ohm," it never successfully transitions to "OFF." Instead, the knob keeps cycling between "Ohm" and "mV" when rotated, but it never reaches the "OFF" position.
Here's a breakdown of what happens:
Initially, the multimeter is "OFF." The knob is turned right and moves through various positions: "VAC," "VDC," "mV," and finally reaches "Ohm." Once the knob reaches "Ohm," it seems to get stuck in a loop. The knob alternates between "Ohm" and "mV" but doesn't move to "OFF" as intended.
Conclusion: The system's design doesn't ensure that when the knob is in the "Ohm" position, it will eventually reach "OFF." Instead, the knob repeatedly cycles between "Ohm" and "mV." This behavior is problematic because the system is expected to allow a transition from "Ohm" to "OFF," which is not happening. This issue likely stems from how the knob transitions are defined when it is rotated, and fixing the logic for how the knob moves between these positions is necessary.

Again, there seems to be some confusion about what the trace means. Additionally, it is not the case that the property requests a direct transition from Ohm to OFF, as it is implied in the text. Note that in this particular case, the prompt included the model. One interesting aspect that this last example highlights is that the LLM was able to *infer* that the model represents a multimeter and that the knob rotates left and right.

6.3 Improving the Template Generated Explanations

This option should provide more control over the explanation, thus avoiding variability, as we are *simply* asking for the LLM to improve the sentence that was created by our patterns-based approach described in Sect. 5. This approach seems less prone to hallucination, but it is also the one with potentially fewer rewards.

For example, we have taken the explanation presented in Sect. 5.2 and asked ChatGPT to improve it. The resulting explanation is as follows:

> The expectation was that whenever the knob is set to Ohm, it should eventually turn to OFF at some point in the future.
> However, in the situation shown in the counterexample, the knob is set to Ohm at state 1.5, but instead of transitioning to OFF, the system gets stuck in a loop. This means that the knob continues to switch back and forth without ever reaching the OFF position.
> It's important to note that this doesn't mean that turning the knob to OFF after setting it to Ohm is impossible. It simply means that there are certain sequences of events in the system where the knob never turns OFF after being set to Ohm.

Similar tests have been done in other models and their properties, and the preliminary results of this approach are that the sentences generated by the LLM are of similar clarity to the generated explanation, with only minor changes to the writing style used.

6.4 Discussion

We have performed additional tests with several other models with different levels of complexity. The results were similar to those described in this paper. For more complex models, problems with limits on the size of the input and of the output can occur.

In summary, while more exploration is needed, we believe our original pattern-based approach is worth pursuing. While the use of LLMs for explaining counterexamples provides flexibility and the possibility to include the models in the analysis easily, they currently suffer from a number of problems that hinder their applicability:

- The quality of the results depends heavily on the model used – simpler models are not able to produce adequate results;
- the inconsistency in the results produced is an issue – this happens with all models and is particularly serious as, in a considerable number of cases, the explanations were erroneous;
- privacy issues can be a problem when using online models – this is a concern since those tend to be the most powerful models (cost should also be considered);
- using local models with enough power will, in all likelihood, require processing power that far outweighs that needed to perform the formal verification itself.

7 Conclusion

Our goal is to help the integration of model checking into development processes participated by designers and domain experts. We aim to contribute to this by supporting the generation of natural language explanations for the counterexamples produced by model checkers, and we are using the IVY workbench tool as a case study.

Our original proposal uses property specification patterns with associated explanation templates to provide a predictable explanation generation process. While the approach generates useful explanations, it is limited to the available patterns and can feel mechanical over time. Given the fast development of generative AI, we wanted to explore the potential of these techniques in supporting the generation process.

Using AI techniques to help explain counterexamples falls at the process level (cf. [16]). The produced explanations will influence the system's design, but will not directly affect its implementation. The human will consider the explanation and make design and implementation decisions based on it.

We have reported on an initial exploration into the potential of using LLMs to explain model-checking counterexamples. Our conclusion is that there is undeniably a considerable risk that the explanations will be erroneous. Although it might be argued that a balance must be achieved between high-quality sentences and reliable explanations, in the case of safety critical systems, clearly, we must err on the side of caution and avoid errors at all costs.

That said, we do not see the process as choosing between two alternative proposals, but as a learning process where a more refined approach might gradually arise. Regrading future work, we will continue to explore whether prompts can be engineered to diminish (ideally eliminate) the risk of error. We also plan to explore how to train a model to better understand the modelling language, and we will continue exploring and comparing different models. Finally, we will conduct an empirical analysis of the results from the different approaches to understand which are preferred by the users of the tool.

Acknowledgments. The MAL interactors model used in this paper was generated from a Mathematica model of the Fluke 114 user interface, originally made available by Harold Thimbleby.

References

1. Bachert, M., Hesenius, M.: Synthesizing 2d vs. 3d gestures. In: Engineering Interactive Systems Embedding AI Technologies Workshop, Cagliary, Sardinia, Italy, June 2024
2. Berstel, J., Reghizzi, S.C., Roussel, G., Pietro, P.S.: A scalable formal method for design and automatic checking of user interfaces. ACM Trans. Softw. Eng. Methodol. **14**(2), 124–167 (2005). https://doi.org/10.1145/1061254.1061256

3. Bisante, A., Datla, V.S.V., Panizzi, E., Trasciatti, G., Zeppieri, S.: Assessing large language models adoption in need finding: an exploratory study. In: Engineering Interactive Systems Embedding AI Technologies Workshop, Cagliary, Sardinia, Italy, June 2024
4. Bisante, A., Datla, V.S.V., Panizzi, E., Trasciatti, G., Zeppieri, S.: Enhancing interface design with AI: an exploratory study on a ChatGPT-4-based tool for cognitive walkthrough inspired evaluations. In: Proceedings of the 2024 International Conference on Advanced Visual Interfaces. ACM (2024). https://doi.org/10.1145/3656650.3656676
5. Bisante, A., Dix, A., Panizzi, E., Zeppieri, S.: To err is AI. In: Proceedings of the 15th Biannual Conference of the Italian SIGCHI Chapter. ACM, New York, NY, USA (2023). https://doi.org/10.1145/3605390.3605414
6. Bolton, M.L., Bass, E., Siminiceanu, R.: Using formal verification to evaluate human-automation interaction: a review. IEEE Trans. Syst. Man Cybern. Part A Syst. Hum. **43**(3), 488–503 (2013). https://doi.org/10.1109/TSMCA.2012.2210406
7. Campos, J., Harrison, M.D.: Interaction engineering using the IVY tool. In: ACM Symposium on Engineering Interactive Computing Systems (EICS 2009), pp. 35–44. ACM (2009). https://doi.org/10.1145/1570433.1570442
8. Campos, J., Machado, J.: A specification patterns system for discrete event systems' analysis. Int. J. Adv. Rob. Syst. **10**, 315 (2013). https://doi.org/10.5772/56412
9. Campos, J.C., Harrison, M.D.: Model checking interactor specifications. Autom. Softw. Eng. **8**(3/4), 275–310 (2001). https://doi.org/10.1023/A:1011265604021
10. Cimatti, A., et al.: NuSMV 2: an opensource tool for symbolic model checking. In: Brinksma, E., Larsen, K.G. (eds.) CAV 2002. LNCS, vol. 2404, pp. 359–364. Springer, Heidelberg (2002). https://doi.org/10.1007/3-540-45657-0_29
11. Clarke, E.M., Jr., Grumberg, O., Peled, D.A.: Model Checking. MIT Press, Cambridge (1999)
12. Coppens, A., Maquil, V.: Integrating AIs with body tracking technology for human behaviour analysis: challenges and opportunities. In: Engineering Interactive Systems Embedding AI Technologies workshop, Cagliary, Sardinia, Italy, June 2024
13. Dittmar, A., Forbrig, P.: Revisiting usability in the current era of AI. In: Engineering Interactive Systems Embedding AI Technologies Workshop, Cagliary, Sardinia, Italy, June 2024
14. Duan, P., Warner, J., Hartmann, B.: Towards generating UI design feedback with LLMs. In: Adjunct Proceedings of the 36th Annual ACM Symposium on User Interface Software and Technology. ACM, New York, NY, USA (2023). https://doi.org/10.1145/3586182.3615810
15. Dwyer, M.B., Avrunin, G.S., Corbett, J.C.: Patterns in property specifications for finite-state verification. In: Proceedings of 21st International Conference on Software Engineering, pp. 411–420. ACM (1999). https://doi.org/10.1145/302405.302672
16. Feldt, R., de Oliveira Neto, F.G., Torkar, R.: Ways of applying artificial intelligence in software engineering. In: 2018 IEEE/ACM 6th International Workshop on Realizing Artificial Intelligence Synergies in Software Engineering (RAISE 2018), pp. 35–41 (2018). https://doi.org/10.1145/3194104.3194109
17. Gross, G.: Devs gaining little (if anything) from AI coding assistants. CIO, September 26 2024. https://www.cio.com/article/3540579/devs-gaining-little-if-anything-from-ai-coding-assistants.html

18. Harrison, M., Thimbleby, H. (eds.): Formal Methods in Human-Computer Interaction. Cambridge University Press, Cambridge Series on Human-Computer Interaction (1990)
19. Illia, L., Colleoni, E., Zyglidopoulos, S.: Ethical implications of text generation in the age of artificial intelligence. Bus. Ethics Environ. Responsib. **32**(1), 201–210 (2023). https://doi.org/10.1111/beer.12479
20. Luyten, K., Eerlings, G., Liesenborgs, J., Ruiz, G.R., Vanbrabant, S., Vanacken, D.: Opportunities and challenges of model multiplicity in interactive software systems. In: Engineering Interactive Systems Embedding AI Technologies Workshop, Cagliary, Sardinia, Italy, June 2024
21. Menten, R., Ruiz, G.R., Vanacken, D.: NexOz - a Wizard of Oz approach to facilitate the integration of AI in interactive systems. In: Engineering Interactive Systems Embedding AI Technologies Workshop, Cagliary, Sardinia, Italy, June 2024
22. Mereu, J., et al.: Empowering end-user in creating extended reality content with a conversational chatbot. In: Engineering Interactive Systems Embedding AI Technologies Workshop, Cagliary, Sardinia, Italy, June 2024
23. Moreira, E., Campos, J.: A language for explaining counterexamples. In: 13th Symposium on Languages, Applications and Technologies (SLATE 2024). OpenAccess Series in Informatics (OASIcs), vol. 120, pp. 11:1–11:14. Schloss Dagstuhl - LZI (2024). https://doi.org/10.4230/OASIcs.SLATE.2024.11
24. Weyers, B., Bowen, J., Dix, A., Palanque, P. (eds.): The Handbook of Formal Methods in Human-Computer Interaction. HIS, Springer, Cham (2017). https://doi.org/10.1007/978-3-319-51838-1
25. Perez-Cerrolaza, J., et al.: Artificial intelligence for safety-critical systems in industrial and transportation domains: a survey. ACM Comput. Surv. **56**(7), 1–40 (2024). https://doi.org/10.1145/3626314
26. Rushby, J.: Using model checking to help discover mode confusions and other automation surprises. Reliab. Eng. Syst. Saf. **75**(2), 167–177 (2002). https://doi.org/10.1016/S0951-8320(01)00092-8
27. Schmidt, A., Elagroudy, P., Draxler, F., Kreuter, F., Welsch, R.: Simulating the human in HCD with ChatGPT: redesigning interaction design with AI. Interactions **31**(1), 24–31 (2024). https://doi.org/10.1145/3637436
28. Tabone, W., de Winter, J.: Using ChatGPT for human-computer interaction research: a primer. R. Soc. Open Sci. **10**(9), 231053 (2023). https://doi.org/10.1098/rsos.231053
29. Thimbleby, H.: User-centered methods are insufficient for safety critical systems. In: Holzinger, A. (ed.) USAB 2007. LNCS, vol. 4799, pp. 1–20. Springer, Heidelberg (2007). https://doi.org/10.1007/978-3-540-76805-0_1
30. Trajkovska, K., Kljun, M., Pucihar, K.Č.: Gaze2AOI: open source deep-learning based system for automatic area of interest annotation with eye tracking data. In: Engineering Interactive Systems Embedding AI Technologies Workshop, Cagliary, Sardinia, Italy, June 2024
31. Weber, T.: Explainability for embedding AI: aspirations and actuality. In: Engineering Interactive Systems Embedding AI Technologies Workshop, Cagliary, Sardinia, Italy, June 2024

32. Weyers, B., Bowen, J., Dix, A., Palanque, P.: Erratum to: the handbook of formal methods in human-computer interaction. In: Weyers, B., Bowen, J., Dix, A., Palanque, P. (eds.) The Handbook of Formal Methods in Human-Computer Interaction. HIS, pp. E1–E3. Springer, Cham (2017). https://doi.org/10.1007/978-3-319-51838-1_21
33. Ziegler, J.: Challenges in integrating conversational AI and GUI-based applications. In: Engineering Interactive Systems Embedding AI Technologies Workshop, Cagliary, Sardinia, Italy, June 2024

Challenges in Integrating Conversational AI and GUI-Based Applications

Jürgen Ziegler(✉)

University of Duisburg-Essen, Duisburg, Germany
juergen.ziegler@uni-due.de

Abstract. We discuss a number of engineering challenges arising when integrating conversational AI with conventional GUI-based interaction in an application. The issues addressed range from the architectural design of integrated applications and the provisioning of shared knowledge as common ground to specific questions of interaction and conversation design and implementation. We exemplify the challenges using a multi-method recommendation system. The conversational and direct manipulation paradigms have complementary advantages that may be integrated and leveraged to create applications that offer users a high level of flexibility and support. Yet, integrating GUI elements and conversation in an interface entails a range of design and engineering challenges, many of which have not been sufficiently addressed in existing research. By describing some of these challenges in a structured form, we aim at providing an initial framework for future research and development.

Keyword: Conversational Recommender Systems

1 Introduction

Conversational interaction techniques have seen a significant boost recently due to the development of large-scale powerful language models such as ChatGPT. The large foundation models underlying state-of-the-art conversational techniques have shown to be powerful tools for high-accuracy understanding of user utterances and for generating high-quality textual or visual output and for conducting (almost) human-like dialogs. Due to these new or enhanced capabilities, conversational systems have been hailed as a paradigmatic shift towards more user-centric human-AI communication. Human-computer interaction in the past decades has been dominated by an action-oriented paradigm in which users interact by manipulating objects in a graphically simulated world. This style of interaction, the graphical user interface, has been immensely successful and has contributed to the omnipresence of information technology in all areas of life. The increasingly powerful conversational interaction style, however, is posed to challenge the dominant position of the GUI.

L. Zaina et al. (Eds.): EICS 2024, LNCS 15518, pp. 159–170, 2025.
https://doi.org/10.1007/978-3-031-91760-8_11

1.1 Benefits and Limitations of Conversational and GUI Interaction

The recent advances in conversational interaction have often been praised as an important step towards more user-centric AI. Conversational interaction does indeed bear the potential to provide users with a high level of efficiency and flexibility in expressing their goals towards the system, thus increasing the level of user-control and autonomy. Conversational interaction, however, entails a number of issues that may compromise the user experience. Text-based conversations, even when assuming the system has sufficient language understanding, require users to actively formulate their instructions and questions to the system. Even though the user's natural language is used, formulating effective input to the system creates considerable cognitive demands with respect to goal-setting, memory, and language skills. Similar to traditional command languages, users need to know what to request and which words to use to utter the request. To quote a pointed conjecture by Jakob Nielsen, it seems „likely that half the population ... is not articulate enough to get good results from one of the current AI bots" [19]. To counter this problem, conversational systems often apply a system-initiated dialog strategy that guides the user by asking questions, often in combination with offering pre-defined response options that are shown as GUI elements embedded in the conversational flow [2]. This strategy, however, may narrow the user's range of inputs when overly relying on the responses cued by the system, even when unconstrained textual input is possible alternatively. Moreover, it has been shown that users, despite the ensuing cognitive demands, prefer self-initiated input and may switch to this mode when the dialog begins in a system-initiated mode [15]. Combining the advantages of both modes, mixed-initiative dialogs have therefore become a frequently applied approach to support users in formulating effective inputs while maintaining a high level of flexibility [17, 25].

A further issue of conversational interaction is the transient nature of the dialog where earlier dialog steps disappear, typically in a scrolling window. Even though this can make it easier to inspect the interaction history, it does not present a comprehensive view of the resulting state of the interaction. Users may thus need to memorize previous dialog turns to maintain an up-to-date overview of the state of the interaction. This style of interaction can therefore create considerable memory load, unless the dialog is used for performing relatively simple and straightforward user preference elicitation, as is the case in many current conversational recommender systems. The cognitive burden on users is amplified, however, when aiming at supporting them in more complex decisions making tasks, for example, when deciding which insurance to take or where to spend the next vacation.

In contrast to conversational techniques, GUI-based interfaces have long been shown to alleviate memory load by providing visual cues for selecting commands, leveraging recognition rather than recall in memory retrieval [9]. GUIs can also provide a high level of flexibility if designed appropriately. It thus seems desirable to benefit from the usability GUIs can offer with the flexibility and power of conversational interfaces by implementing hybrid interfaces. To achieve this, a much stronger integration of the two interaction paradigms is needed. Users should be able to express their input through GUI elements if predefined, structured input is required or preferred. Yet, they should be also able to benefit from the support and flexibility of conversations, if they need guidance or want to express queries that are either not possible in the GUI or hard to reach in the interface. This requirement, however, raises a number of challenges for the design and engineering of interactive systems that support both interaction paradigms in an integrated manner. In the following, we explicate some of these challenges, illustrating them with an example of a recommender system integrating conversation with faceted filtering techniques. Following from that, we attempt to more systematically describe a range of challenges that arise in the close integration of conversation and GUI. We focus our discussion on the integration of chatbot-like conversation with GUI-based search and filtering, acknowledging that the potential field of AI-GUI integration is much broader.

In the following, we will first discuss architectural aspects for different levels of GUI-conversation integration. Next, we present as use case a multi-method recommendation system that seamlessly integrates a conversational product advisor with a facetted filtering systems. Drawing on this use case, we describe a number of specific design and engineering challenges that are particularly pertinent for achieving a close integration, allowing users to flexibly express their goals in either interaction component with a high level of effectiveness, transparency, and user control.

1.2 Architectures for Integrating Conversational and GUI-Based Interaction

Conversational techniques have thus far been predominantly focused on single mode interactions, that is, on either written or spoken textual dialogs with no or only limited integration of GUI elements. If some level of multimodality was provided, it has been mostly limited to offering response shortcuts such as buttons or sliders inline in the conversational flow. Furthermore, when included in a larger application context, conversational components, such as chatbots, have typically been implemented as separate components that are essentially independent of other parts of the application's logic and user interface. In this case, question and answer templates have mostly been designed manually, offering, for example, FAQ-like information for customer interaction. While the chatbot may retrieve some information from an application-specific data store, the integration is shallow and only one-way. In this case, the interaction with the chatbot has little or no influence on the other parts of the application.

A first step towards closer chatbot-application integration can be seen in conversational agents that use API calls to perform a task-oriented dialog (TOD) [28]. TODs have become a prominent research area in recent years, investigating conversational control of tasks such as calendar scheduling, restaurant booking, or customer support. The typical process in these systems starts with identifying the user's intent from language input (textual or spoken), then filling the slots required for the task in the dialog (establishing the current dialog state), sending the collected parameters to the application through a defined API, executing the task in the application, and finally creating a response to the user. The UI of the application is not involved in this scenario.

In contrast to these pipeline-based approaches, end-to-end systems attempt to learn how to fill the required feature slots and responses from large-scale datasets. However, compiling and annotating such datasets requires considerable manual effort and is often hindered by the limited amount of domain-specific data [28].

The above methods are agnostic of the user interface of the application since they directly call application functionality. Instead of serving an API, a further type of integration approaches performs actions in the application user interface based on the conversation with an agent. Pasupat et al. [21], for instance, map natural language commands to web elements, supporting some navigation and retrieval tasks. A further step is made, for example, in the META-GUI approach [24] which not only performs actions on the target UI but also analyzes the screen output of the application to gather the information needed for creating a response for the user. As an example, the system performs actions to walk through a sequence of screens in a weather app and compiles the information obtained to create the requested output. This approach is, in principle, more flexible since it is not bound to the API definition an application provides. On the downside, large datasets as well as powerful text and image recognition capabilities are required.

An essential step towards a more full-fledged integration of conversational agents and GUI applications lies in the introduction of a common knowledge base that is shared between conversational agent and application. Shared knowledge can be represented explicitly in the form of ontologies or linked open data, or implicitly in latent space as embedded knowledge graphs [14]. The latter form has become more prevalent in recent years, in line with the increasing success of neural processing approaches. A number of systems utilizes general world knowledge represented in knowledge graphs to increase, for instance, the effectiveness and descriptiveness of system-generated recommendations [18]. While open-world knowledge represented, for instance, in DBpedia can be instrumental in such scenarios, domain-specific ontologies and knowledge graph representations are needed to provide the grounding for linking conversational agents with applications-specific data structures. The development of domain-specific knowledge graphs plays an central role for achieving a more pervasive use of AI techniques in real-world applications [1] and has become a vibrant area of research in academia and industry.

Shared domain-specific knowledge is instrumental for a deep integration of conversational agent and GUI-based applications but in most cases the connection is still one-way where the knowledge base is mainly used to translate conversational commands into system actions and to produce some response to the user. To achieve a true, bi-directional exchange, actions the user performs in the GUI of the application, should also influence the flow of the conversation in the agent, affecting the dialog management and in particular the policy component of the conversational system [3]. How to best represent the agent's policy, for instance with respect to question style, clarifications, or proactivity still involves numerous open question. One possibility, like the one described in the next section, is to integrate dialog-related concepts (such as questions and potential answers) in a larger domain-specific dialog to enable direct referencing of application entities and properties in the dialog.

2 Application Case: A Multi-method Recommender System

E-commerce websites often provide multiple methods for finding a suitable product, such as search functions, faceted feature filtering [7, 12] and conversational product advisors. GUI-based conversational recommenders help users find relevant items through easy-to-use question-answer dialogs [6, 10]. However, filters and advisors are often presented separately and treated independently of each other, so that previous input in one component is ignored or even discarded when users switch to the other component. This leads to increased memory load and disruptions in the search process. In addition, the reasoning behind the resulting recommendations is often not transparent. To overcome these limitations, we proposed a novel approach that exploits a knowledge graph structure to create an integrated system that allows a seamless coupling between faceted filtering and advisors [11]. The integrated system utilizes the graph to suggest appropriate filter values as well as recommended items based on the user's answers to the questions asked by the advisor. But the dependency also works in the other direction, selecting filter values influences the dialog in the chatbot.

Figure 1 shows the interface of the integrated system that comprises the filtering, advisor and recommendation components, as well as additional explanatory components (not further discussed here). Feature values that are compatible with the answer given in the advisor are marked through color-coding. Also, values that are incompatible with the

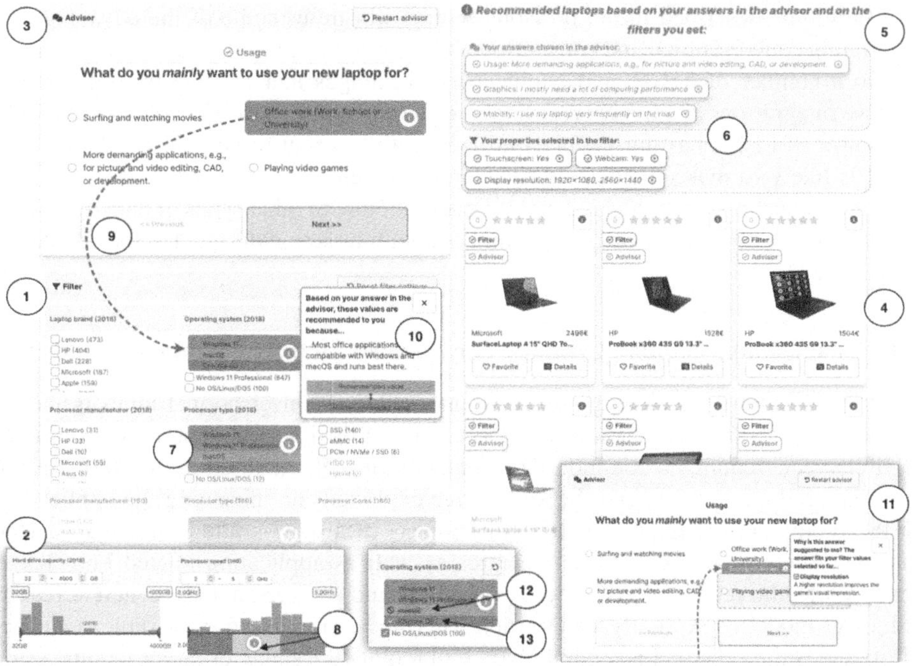

Fig. 1. Screenshot of a prototype laptop recommender system (note that not all components shown here are visible at the same time). Areas 1 and 2 show categorical and numeric features the user can select. The product advisor (3) asks users about the intended use of the product and other goals. Features compatible with the given answer are highlighted in green (7) or purple if they are not recommended for the stated purpose. This connection between the components is shown with an animated arrow (9) that disappears after a short period of time. Recommendations are shown in (4). The other components, used for explanations or showing the evolving user model, are less relevant for the present discussion.

answers given are marked with a different color. Conversely, selecting specific values in the filtering component determines the next question asked by the product advisor. While the filter component works at the level of concrete product features, the questions and answers in the advisor are at a higher level of abstraction and are mainly about the intended usage of the product.

Through the integration we cater, on the one hand, for users who have a clear search goal and know which features they prefer. These users can directly express their needs by means of faceted filtering but may still be supported by the advisors for product aspects they are not familiar with. On the other hand, users who do not yet have clear feature-related preferences can use the support of the advisor, starting by stating higher level goals and usage contexts. At any time, they can also switch to the filter for expressing more concrete preferences.

3 Challenges in Engineering the Integration of Graphical User Interfaces and AI-Driven Conversational Interaction

The prototype described in the previous section illustrates some of the advantages of integrating conversational and conventional GUI components, but at the same time gives rise to a number of design and engineering challenges that need to be addressed to achieve integrations at a larger scale and in different application contexts. For example, the power of LLMs has not yet been utilized in the current prototype. While using an LLM is likely to make the conversation more human-like and flexible, there are still numerous questions for achieving a close integration with other types of data. Likewise, there are many open questions concerning overall interaction design and the adaptation of the interface.

3.1 Establishing Common Ground: The Need for Holistic Foundation Models

A central question for achieving a seamless integration of conversational advisors that use unconstrained textual interaction with those parts of the interface that use conventional GUI elements requires a common representation of the structured information, in this case the product features, and the knowledge exploited for enhancing the application. In the prototype, the latter is realized by means of a hand-crafted knowledge graph that represents products and their features as well as application-related knowledge. Importantly, the relationships between questions and answers and the concrete feature values are modelled explicitly in this graph. This method requires considerable modelling effort and is thus costly. Each application will require the same, or larger manual effort which may be prohibitive in real-world applications.

It appears promising, therefore, to exploit the immense amount of knowledge embedded in pre-trained LLMs. For application specific uses, the LLM will typically need to be further trained and fine-tuned with domain specific knowledge. Methods for integrating domain-specific knowledge have already emerged [5]. A more open challenge is the integration of structured data in LLMs. First methods have emerged (e.g. [23]), but research is still quite limited. One promising line of developments can be seen in Retrieval Augmented Generation (RAG, [13]) but there are still many open questions concerning their use in integrating conversation with GUI interaction. Structured data are necessary for driving standard, application-specific GUI elements such as selection lists, but these data must also be tightly connected with the general knowledge represented in an LLM. This applies for static GUI structures as well as for the more dynamic case where GUIs (or parts thereof) are generated by the AI on the fly.

3.2 Transmodal Interaction Management Strategy

Merging conversation with structured GUI interfaces creates a special challenge for the design and management of the overall interaction with the system. An approach that has already gained some popularity is the control and adaptation of the GUI through a conversational agent. Queries to the agent in this approach may result, for example, in filling input fields based on a textual request, in navigating to a specific view in the GUI interface by creating a deep link [26], or in dynamically creating GUI components [27]. This approach, however, is essentially one-way, from the conversational agent to the GUI. For fully bi-directional interaction approaches, a number of unsolved questions arise.

While GUIs show the current state of the system and the interaction possibilities at any given time in a two-dimensional parallel presentation, conversation is characterized by a dynamic, continuous stream of dialog turns. Managing the interaction in such a context involves a number of requirements. The actions in the two components must be synchronized in a manner that users are aware of them and can comprehend the causal relationship between them. The mutual influences might happen instantaneously or be delayed to collect a meaningful set of inputs, e.g., specifying a number of inputs through GUI elements before the system reacts by asking further details in the conversation. A further question refers to the type and level of guidance provided in the conversation. If it can be assumed that users find it difficult to formulate their requests, the system can provide guidance by presenting a set of answer options, often by response buttons presented in the dialog. Another option might be to point the user to a static GUI part for providing responses. When and how to present such guidance has so far only received limited attention in research.

Technically, there is also the question which software component determines the flow of interactions. This has typically been implemented in a specific dialog management component that is, for example, based on a state transition engine. It is foreseeable, however, that specifically trained foundation models can take on this role. For linking the two components, automatic generation of prompts or instructions for the AI (e.g. from GUI input) might be used, but there are still many research questions to be solved to obtain fitting and flexible system outputs.

3.3 Dialog Initiative and AI Proactivity

Closely related to dialog management is the aspect of initiative-taking in the dialog. Dialog initiative has long been an important design question for conversational systems and will also be critical in integrated hybrid systems. GUI interfaces generally apply a user-initiated style of interaction while conversational interaction can be either system-initiated or user-initiated. Research has shown that hybrid mixed-initiative systems are often superior to single mode conversations [8]. For a conversational recommender system, Ma and Ziegler [15] showed that users prefer a self-guided, user-initiated style and tended to switch to this mode when the dialog started in system-initiated mode by asking the user for their preferences. However, in many cases users will need guidance and suggestions for inputs or actions to take. When to show such guidance, how many response options to show, or how to formulate them has not been systematically explored yet.

Current developments will enable AI systems to be much more proactive than just providing a set of response options. The AI can support users in pointing to useful functions the user is not aware of. Recent work [16] showed that users mostly accepted proactively provided system suggestions to use comparison or critiquing functions in a recommender systems. With the growing range of capabilities of conversational agents, pointing the user to such helpful functions may increase the efficiency of task completion or support users better in complex decision making tasks. In many cases, complex decisions involve making tradeoffs that may require revisiting and changing previous inputs or even comparing different strands of conversation. Dealing with the large space of potential proactive system interventions is a largely unexplored research question. In some cases, it may be also be helpful to provide additional dialog guidance through visualizations of dialog state and flow [22].

In a broader sense, AI components may play a tutor role for using the application and conducting the conversation more effectively. While such tutoring functions could be delegated to a separate virtual assistant, integrating them in the main conversation flow has the advantage of keeping the user's attention on his/her main task.

3.4 Inter-component Referencing

A smaller, yet also very relevant question is how to maintain coherence and continuity for the user when interacting with conversational and GUI components. Users should be aware of changes in the different parts of the interface without overloading their attentional capacities. Since dialog steps in the conversation may result in changes in the GUI and vice versa, some mechanism should be implemented that provides a visual (or textual) cross-reference between the interface elements involved. Potential solutions may apply color-coding, animation, textual deixis, or other methods but no research into this specific question has been undertaken so far.

3.5 Adaptation and Adaptive Generation of GUI Components

A large area for exploiting AI-GUI synergies is the adaption and generation of GUIs through the conversational AI. Due to the large range of possibilities, we can only indicate a few areas of active research here. Some approaches apply LLMs at development time, for example, to search for suitable GUI layouts [4]. Generating complete GUI applications and apps by means of LLM-based code-generation is an area of active research.

Adapting the interface with respect to selecting and automatically setting GUI controls, generating labels and descriptions, altering the navigation, or changing the visual appearance has also been addressed in a number of research works. Leveraging the capabilities of large foundation models will further boost the effectiveness of such methods. Generating complete UIs or parts thereof at runtime is a less explored area which, however, has great potential. Automatically converting conversational content into a GUI structure may help users, for example, to keep track of the state of interaction. In a recommender system, the user's feature preferences expressed in the conversation may be translated into manipulable widgets. This would support users in referring back to previous inputs in the dialog, and to change their preferences easily at any time. In this underexplored area, questions arise with respect to the controls created, their layout, and their connection with the conversational part.

3.6 Creating User-Centric Explanations for Application-Embedded AI

A well-known problem of AI systems is their lack of transparency for users which makes it hard to understand the system's functioning and assess the correctness of the outputs created. The black-box nature of such technologies, particularly those rooted in deep learning, may impede the trust that users place in them. This issue clearly also arises for AI components embedded in a larger application context. In the application use case introduced, users may be unsure why the answer to a certain question asked by the system prioritizes certain item attributes and not others. There is, therefore, a need to explain the relation between statements made in the conversation and the actions taken in the GUI, as well as how the user's GUI actions influence the content and flow of the conversation. The field of Explainable AI (XAI) aims to shed light on the intricate workings of AI models, yet the explanations provided in typical XAI approaches tend to be steeped in technical jargon and algorithmic processes and are often not aligned with users' real needs. For example, Nunes and Jannach [20], in a survey paper on explanations in decision support systems - especially recommendation systems, where the target audience is largely lay users - found that more than half of the proposed explanatory models attempt to describe the inference process. Yet, it becomes increasingly questionable whether users are interested in this kind of information. Often, the very details intended to illuminate the AI's decisions often end up obfuscating them. In the case of conversational components integrated in applications, explanations can only be helpful for users if they can explicate why the system takes a certain action in the context of the application domain. The algorithmic method for producing the actions is likely not the main concern for users. Application-specific explanations, however, may require substantial knowledge not only about the functioning of the application but also, and even more so, about the application context, its background, requirements and constraints in general. In the use case scenario presented, for example, explanations may need to convey general knowledge about technologies and designs used for laptops to understand why certain features are relevant for a task. This requirement goes way beyond the structured data that the application may use but asks for being able to convey more general, yet still domain-specific knowledge. Large foundation models, either domain-specific or fine-tuned to the domain concerned may offer the basis for such broader and more effective explanations but the development of such models and their use in applications integrating AI components is still a largely open question.

From a more general perspective, one of the issues with current XAI explanations is their model-centric focus, producing explanations only within the confines of algorithms and data patterns. This approach neglects the inclusion of external information that may be critical to contextualize decisions. Without broader context, explanations remain narrowly focused, limiting their relevance and meaningfulness.

Another concern with current XAI efforts is their reliance on post hoc rationalizations. Such explanations are produced after the AI has already made a decision, and thus abstract from the actual operational logic, which renders this approach vulnerable to misguided explanations that follow a simplistic or linear narrative that does not accurately represent the often complex, non-linear process behind AI decisions [29]. While such rationalizations may seem more tangible and closer to human explanatory patterns, there is a risk of oversimplification that could create a false sense of understanding in users.

4 Conclusion

The soaring capabilities of current AI technologies have led to a renaissance of conversational interaction techniques, resulting in powerful conversational agents that can afford almost human-like dialogs. They bear the potential to interact with and control applications in a very flexible and user-controlled manner. Yet, the benefits of conventional GUI interfaces is indisputable due to their advantages with respect to efficiency, user guidance, and memory relief. Conversation and GUI represent two interaction paradigms that have complementary benefits and limitations, suggesting that integrating them as alternative, yet tightly coupled methods of interacting with an application may benefit users in many respects.

From an interactive systems engineering perspective, however, there are still many open issues and challenges that need to be solved. These issues range from the architectural design of integrated applications, over the provisioning of shared knowledge as common ground to specific questions of interaction and conversation design and implementation.

In this brief overview of questions arising when integrating conversational agents and GUIs in an application, we have presented the use case of a recommender system to illustrate some of the challenges. Achieving a close, two-way synchronized integration of the interaction components will likely require revised application architectures as well as adapted AI components that drive the conversation. A central concern is the provision of shared data and knowledge as common ground for enabling a deep integration. Large foundation models, such as large language models have already started to provide promising options for engineering applications with hybrid and integrated, interactive components.

Our starting point for elaborating the challenges have been issues arising in the context of recommendation systems. While this may constitute a limitation of our account, we believe the challenges described apply to a wider range of applications. Yet, the set of challenges described is limited, and in the rapidly evolving field of AI, new challenges and solutions will likely arise at a fast pace.

References

1. Abu-Salih, B.: Domain-specific knowledge graphs: a survey. J. Netw. Comput. Appl. **185**, 103076 (2021). https://doi.org/10.1016/j.jnca.2021.103076
2. Aliannejadi, M., Azzopardi, L., Zamani, H., Kanoulas, E., Thomas, P., Craswell, N.: Analysing mixed initiatives and search strategies during conversational search. In: Proceedings of the 30th ACM International Conference on Information & Knowledge Management, pp. 16–26 (2021). https://doi.org/10.1145/3459637.3482231
3. Brabra, H., Baez, M., Benatallah, B., Gaaloul, W., Bouguelia, S., Zamanirad, S.: Dialogue management in conversational systems: a review of approaches, challenges, and opportunities. IEEE Trans. Cogn. Dev. Syst. **14**(3), 783–798 (2022). https://doi.org/10.1109/TCDS.2021.3086565
4. Brie, P., Burny, N., Sluÿters, A., Vanderdonckt, J.; Evaluating a large language model on searching for GUI layouts. Proc. ACM Hum.-Comput. Interact. **7**(EICS), 1–37 (2023). https://doi.org/10.1145/3593230
5. Dash, T., Chitlangia, S., Ahuja, A., Srinivasan, A.: A review of some techniques for inclusion of domain-knowledge into deep neural networks. Sci. Rep. **12**(1), 1040 (2022). https://doi.org/10.1038/s41598-021-04590-0
6. Felfernig, A., Friedrich, G., Jannach, D., Zanker, M.: An integrated environment for the development of knowledge-based recommender applications. Int. J. Electron. Commer. **11**(2), 11–34 (2006). https://doi.org/10.2753/JEC1086-4415110201
7. Hearst, M.A.: Search User Interfaces. Cambridge University Press, USA (2009)
8. Horvitz, E.: Principles of mixed-initiative user interfaces. In: Proceedings of the SIGCHI Conference on Human Factors in Computing Systems, pp. 159–166 (1999). https://doi.org/10.1145/302979.303030
9. Hutchins, E.L., Hollan, J.D., Norman, D.A.: Direct manipulation interfaces. Human-Comput. Interact. **1**(4), 311–338 (1985)
10. Jannach, D., Manzoor, A., Cai, W., Chen, L.: A survey on conversational recommender systems. ACM Comput. Surv. **54**(5) (2021). https://doi.org/10.1145/3453154
11. Kleemann, T., Ziegler, J.: Blending conversational product advisors and faceted filtering in a graph-based approach. In: Abdelnour Nocera, J., Kristín Lárusdóttir, M., Petrie, H., Piccinno, A., Winckler, W., (eds.), Human-Computer Interaction – INTERACT 2023, vol. 14144, pp. 137–159. Springer Nature Switzerland (2023). https://doi.org/10.1007/978-3-031-42286-7_8
12. Koren, J., Zhang, Y., Liu, X.: Personalized interactive faceted search. In: Proceedings of the 17th International Conference on World Wide Web, pp. 477–486. WWW'08, Association for Computing Machinery, New York, NY, USA (2008). https://doi.org/10.1145/1367497.1367562
13. Lewis, P., et al.: Retrieval-augmented generation for knowledge-intensive NLP tasks. Adv. Neural. Inf. Process. Syst. **33**, 9459–9474 (2020)
14. Liu, C., Li, L., Yao, X., Tang, L.: A survey of recommendation algorithms based on knowledge graph embedding. In: 2019 IEEE International Conference on Computer Science and Educational Informatization (CSEI), pp. 168–171 (2019). https://doi.org/10.1109/CSEI47661.2019.8938875
15. Ma, Y., Ziegler, J.: Initiative transfer in conversational recommender systems. In: Proceedings of the 17th ACM Conference on Recommender Systems, pp. 978–984 (2023). https://doi.org/10.1145/3604915.3608858
16. Ma, Y., Ziegler, J.: The effect of proactive cues on the use of decision aids in conversational recommender systems. In: Adjunct Proceedings of the 32nd ACM Conference on User Modeling, Adaptation and Personalization, pp. 305–315 (2024). https://doi.org/10.1145/3631700.3665186

17. Ma, Y., Kleemann, T., Ziegler, J.: Mixed-modality interaction in conversational recommender systems. In: IntRS'21: Joint Workshop on Interfaces and Human Decision Making for Recommender Systems, p. 17 (2021)
18. Musto, C., Basile, P., Semeraro, G.: Hybrid semantics-aware recommendations exploiting knowledge graph embeddings. In M. Alviano, G. Greco, & F. Scarcello (Hrsg.), AI*IA 2019 – Advances in Artificial Intelligence, pp. 87–100 (2019). Springer International Publishing. https://doi.org/10.1007/978-3-030-35166-3_7
19. Nielsen, J.: AI: First New UI Paradigm in 60 Years (2023). https://www.nngroup.com/articles/ai-paradigm/. Accessed May 2024
20. Nunes, I., Jannach, D.: A systematic review and taxonomy of explanations in decision support and recommender systems. User Model. User-Adap. Inter. **27**, 393–444 (2017). https://doi.org/10.1007/s11257-017-9195-0
21. Pasupat, P., Jiang, T.-S., Liu, E., Guu, K., Liang, P.: Mapping natural language commands to web elements. In: Riloff, E., Chiang, D., Hockenmaier, J., Tsujii, J., (eds.), Proceedings of the 2018 Conference on Empirical Methods in Natural Language Processing, pp. 4970–4976. Association for Computational Linguistics (2018). https://doi.org/10.18653/v1/D18-1540
22. Suchmann, L.B., Krämer, N., Ziegler, J.: Branching preferences: visualizing non-linear topic progression in conversational recommender systems. In: Adjunct Proceedings of the 31st ACM Conference on User Modeling, Adaptation and Personalization, pp. 199–205 (2023). https://doi.org/10.1145/3563359.3597380
23. Sui, Y., Zhou, M., Zhou, M., Han, S., Zhang, D.: Table meets LLM: can large language models understand structured table data? a benchmark and empirical study. In: The 17th ACM International Conference on Web Search and Data Mining (WSDM '24) (2024)
24. Sun, L., Chen, X., Chen, L., Dai, T., Zhu, Z., Yu, K.: META-GUI: Towards Multi-modal Conversational Agents on Mobile GUI (arXiv:2205.11029) (2022). arXiv. https://doi.org/10.48550/arXiv.2205.11029
25. Vakulenko, S., Kanoulas, E., De Rijke, M.: A large-scale analysis of mixed initiative in information-seeking dialogues for conversational search. ACM Trans. Inf. Syst. **39**(4), 49:1–49:32 (2021). https://doi.org/10.1145/3466796
26. Van Dam, H.: Synergy of LLM and GUI, Beyond the Chatbot (2023). https://towardsdatascience.com/synergy-of-llm-and-gui-beyond-the-chatbot-c8b0e08c6801. Accessed 03 May 2024
27. Weidele, D.K.I., et al.: Empirical evidence on conversational control of GUI in semantic automation. In: Proceedings of the 29th International Conference on Intelligent User Interfaces, pp. 869–885 (2024). https://doi.org/10.1145/3640543.3645172
28. Zhang, Z., Takanobu, R., Zhu, Q., Huang, M., Zhu, X.: Recent advances and challenges in task-oriented dialog systems. Sci. China Technol. Sci. **63**(10), 2011–2027 (2020). https://doi.org/10.1007/s11431-020-1692-3
29. Ziegler, J., Donkers, T.: From explanations to human-AI co-evolution: charting trajectories towards future user-centric AI. I-Com: J. Interact. Media **23**(2), 263–272 (2024). https://doi.org/10.1515/icom-2024-0020

Experience 2.0 and Beyond – Engineering Cross Devices and Multiple Realities (EXDMR)

A Use Case Study on Fear and System Perception in Haptic VR vs. Physical High-Fidelity Medical Prototype Testing

Jamil Joundi[1](✉), Ine Van der Cruyssen[2], Laetitia De Leersnijder[2], Sam Van de walle[2], Jelle Demanet[1], Klaas Bombeke[1], Koen Beyers[3], Vanessa Vankerckhoven[3], and Jelle Saldien[1]

[1] Department of Industrial Systems Engineering and Product Design, imec-mict-UGent, Ghent, Belgium
{jamil.joundi,jelle.demanet,klaas.bombeke, jelle.saldien}@ugent.be

[2] Hitlab, Howest, Belgium
{ine.van.der.cruyssen,laetitia.de.leersnijder, sam.van.de.walle}@howest.be

[3] IDEVAX/RobID, Antwerp, Belgium
koen.beyers@idevax.be, vanessa.vankerckhoven@idevax.com

Abstract. Full-fledged medical system evaluations of high-fidelity prototypes can be costly. Development, transportation, and breakage of high-fidelity prototypes make considering virtual reality (VR) as a replacement an interesting option. The question rises however if both types of testing (VR and high-fidelity real-life prototype testing) are perceived in the same way by participants. This study compares the perceived user experience (UX) of haptic VR testing with a real-life prototype within the use case of an automated vaccination device. A medical prototype was evaluated in terms of usability (SUS) and hedonic, pragmatic and attractiveness attributes (AttrakDiff). The results show that both prototypes are rated with similar scores in terms of usability, pragmatic and hedonic qualities and attractiveness. The reporting of the participants indicated that in both scenarios the anticipation right before the skin prick was the most frightening. The preliminary results of the physiological data show mixed results between both conditions.

Keywords: Virtual Reality · User Testing · Haptic Feedback · Robot-vaccination · Medical Applications

1 Introduction

In the field of industrial product development, conveying product concepts to end users is traditionally achieved using technical drawings, sketches, and physical prototypes [1]. High fidelity prototypes are useful to evaluate how users experience a procedure before deploying the final system. The main purpose of high-fidelity prototypes is displaying the final functionality and the looks of the system [2]. However, these one-off

L. Zaina et al. (Eds.): EICS 2024, LNCS 15518, pp. 173–188, 2025.
https://doi.org/10.1007/978-3-031-91760-8_12

prototypes are inflexible and expensive [2]. They can be costly to build and maintain. Physical prototypes are also inflexible in modifications and fragile to transport [3]. For these reasons, it might be more beneficial to use a virtual setup which is flexible and visually indestructible [1]. VR shows great potential in the context of medical device development, since it facilitates testing in a specific context [4], reduces the creation of large physical set-ups and can be used for remote testing [5]. Faust [6] highlighted the possibility of VR to evaluate product performance, ergonomics and operation in household appliances, communication devices and automotive parts. Previously, the product performance domain was researched by Soderman [3], Bordegoni [1, 7, 8] and Park [9]. Their most interesting findings revolve around the way participants succeed in the interactions with virtual product prototypes. For this reason, this study compares user interactions in a virtual haptic environment as well as in a physical environment with a real prototype. This study considers VR as a possible tool for evaluating the prototype with final users. The research situates itself within the general domain of physical user testing in VR.

Academic literature lacks comprehensive evaluation of virtual prototypes of medical products. Therefore, this study aims to analyse the user experience in this domain. Within the medical space, Lorenz [10] already analysed an early virtual reality user experience and usability assessment of a surgical shape memory alloy aspiration and irrigation instrument. However, in their study the procedure was experienced through the eyes of the surgeon. In the study of Hinricher [11], the effects of virtual reality and test environment altered the evaluation on user experience, usability, and mental workload. This evaluation was conducted by aspiring doctors, and the VR prototype failed to provide a haptic impression of the tested blood pressure monitor.

We are interested in how patients will perceive the prototypes and whether these VR prototypes can used interchangeably with their real-life counterparts in terms of user experience when haptic feedback *is* provided. This makes the application of VR in the context of this use case less trivial and better suited compared to an experience without haptics. To measure the perception of the prototype, usability is often used as an indicator of the user's perception of the experienced interactions with the system. The system usability scale (SUS) developed by Brooke offers an instrument to measure the usability and consists of a set of 10 questions. [12]. The questions probe if the system was easy to use, if technical support was needed and if it was easy to learn how to use the product amongst others. Next to the aspect of usability, the perception of the prototype plays a role in system UX assessment. The model of Hassenzahl [13] assesses the perception of products by categorizing product qualities into three groups: hedonic qualities, and pragmatic qualities and attractiveness. The hedonic qualities focus on the appeal to a person's desire of pleasure and avoidance of boredom and discomfort. The hedonic qualities are divided in qualities related to identity and stimulation. The hedonic qualities revolving around identity measure whether the system was connecting, professional, presentable or looks expensive. The hedonic qualities regarding stimulation probe if the system was innovative, creative, or fascinating. The pragmatic qualities are oriented towards achieving goals. They indicate whether the system was simple, practical, clear, and controllable. Finally, the attractiveness attributes reflect whether the system was attractive, inviting and pleasant to use. These qualities were included in the

Attrakdiff questionnaire as the result of the study by Hassenzahl in 2006 [13]. If the response regarding usability and attractiveness is similar, it shows that VR prototypes can be used within the development process of medical devices to evaluate usability and attractiveness.

In the context of user experience within the medical field, it is important to understand when medical procedures induce fear. Some medical devices are daunting for patients during use [14]. For example, big CAT scanners are transformed into more child friendly variants to alleviate the fear during scans. In relation to the proposed use case of this paper, fear of needles was already researched by Hako [15].

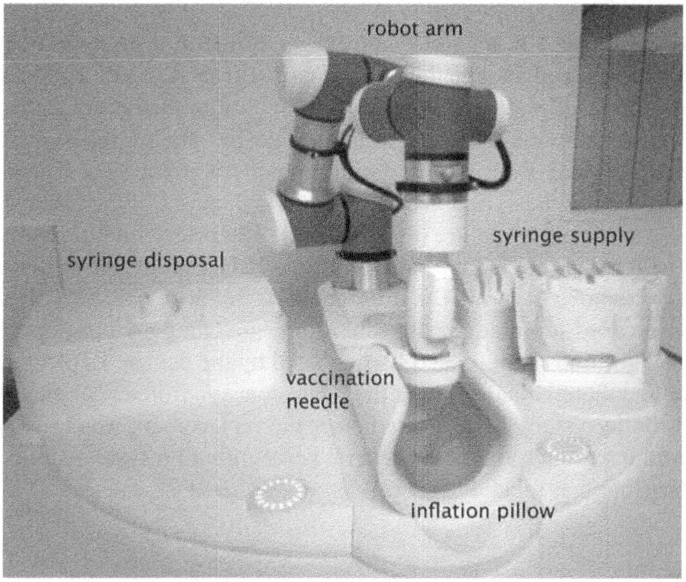

Fig. 1. Schematic of RobID vaccination device

Similarly to the general UX aspects, VR prototypes might induce the same fear response as their physical counterparts. We expect participants to report similar experiences after experiencing VR or real-life (RL) prototypes in relation to fear. Evaluating fear using quantitative and qualitative data is important since previous work on the use case indicated that it is an influential aspect of the resulting user experience. The idea behind this study is to evaluate if the experience offered by VR prototypes is comparable to the experience of high-fidelity prototypes. Testing can be performed in virtual environments to assess whether people find the scenario which they are presented with fear inducing. Given the robotic nature of our use case, the Robot Anxiety Scale (RAS) [16] or Negative Attitudes towards RobotS (NARS) scale [17] measures anxiety towards robots. In addition to questionnaires, physiological measures such as breathing, heart rate and electrodermal activity can provide insights in the fear induced in participants during a medical scenario [18].

EDA is particularly sensitive to emotional arousal, providing an objective measure of the sympathetic nervous system's activation, often linked to anxiety and fear [19]. This makes it a valuable tool in scenarios where participants' physiological reactions to stressors—such as a needle prick—are evaluated. This data, when combined with subjective reports, helps in drawing more comprehensive conclusions about the effectiveness and user perception of VR prototypes in medical device testing.

2 Method

2.1 Use Case: Vaccination Robot

The comparison of the VR scenario with the high-fidelity prototype is based on the use case of an automated vaccination device called Rob-ID [20]. This device aims to vaccinate individuals, eliminating the need for manual administration. In this vaccination device, users place their non-dominant arm in the device. Next, a pillow inflates to fixate the lower arm followed by a prick administered by a robot arm. These actions are preceded by collecting the syringe and followed by disposal of the syringe. The whole vaccination is very short by nature (40 s in total). The prick is administered via a very short needle which does not induce pain sensations [21]. Finally, the pillow deflates, and users are free to remove the arm. The different parts of the device are depicted in Fig. 1. Since the device does not induce pain sensations, the company developing it wants to decrease the needle and robot related fear induced by the device. Replacing the manual administrator and therewith alleviating the white coat syndrome [22] may induce a new fear for the robotic system. To assess whether the replacement was less fear inducing, semi-structured interviews assess the general perception of a system along with system clarity and possible fear related triggers.

2.2 Participants

Twenty-eight participants (17 male; Mage = 25.9; SDage = 4.73) took part in the study. Selection of participants did not require any specifics. Three participants were left-handed and, in that way, suggested a representative left-handed sample. The self-reported needle phobia [15] was rather low ($M = 1.69$ out of 5, $SD = .539$), robo-phobia [16] was moderate ($M = 2.44$ out of 5, $SD = 0.706$). Twenty-four participants were university or PhD students and possessed computer knowledge (all participants reported average or expert levels of computer knowledge). Half of the group reported high levels of gaming experience. Four persons piloted the setup to establish comparable seamless experiences in both conditions. The virtual counterpart was also tested out by the company of the use-case.

2.3 Apparatus

An apparatus similar to the final product was built to validate the VR scenario in comparison to its real-life counterpart. This was made of 3d-printed parts, connected to an air pump (see Fig. 3). In VR, the skin prick was administered by the experimenter at the

Fig. 2. VR scenario (left) and High-fidelity testing (right)

right time in the virtual scenario, when the virtual machine descended towards the arm of the participant. Before the manual administration occurred, a physical pillow inflated synchronously with the virtual scenario.

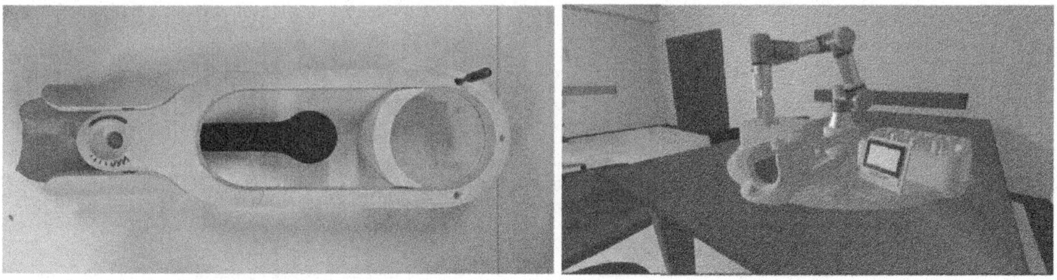

Fig. 3. Physical set-up accompanying the virtual scenario

2.4 Procedure

To assess the differences between VR testing and high-fidelity prototype testing, an A/B testing protocol was used to probe for the similarities and differences between the experience. The experiment applied a within-subjects design where two conditions were counterbalanced between participants. This was done by alternately starting with the virtual or realistic condition for each new participant. Since a between subject design would require a large sample, the choice for a within subject design was driven by the aim to reduce recruitment cost during this early study. The participants agreed to the informed consent of the study. No specific ethical approval was filed, but for the project a general approval for performing VR experiments was granted. Testing was performed with students and colleagues. The testing procedure consisted of a pre-questionnaire where participants reported age, computer experience and fear of needles. After the pre-questionnaire, EDA sensors, heart rate and respiration monitor, were attached to the participant. Next, the participant executed the first scenario followed by a questionnaire and then executed the second scenario followed by another questionnaire. In the last step, the participants removed the sensors.

Seven randomly selected participants were asked to do a semi-structured interview. The questions probed into clarity of the system, triggers of fear, absence of humans in the process and a reflection on using VR for such tests.

The VR condition (Fig. 2 left) utilized the Vive Pro Eye headset [23] in combination with a state-of-the-art gaming computer (using a RTX 2070 graphics card). The VR simulation was built in Unity game engine [24] and linked to a server where the actions happening in the virtual environment were logged. Along with visual experience, a wizard-of-oz prototype of the vaccination device was 3d-printed (see Fig. 4, left). In the right time during the scenario, the vaccination device inflates, and a fake vaccination was administered by one of the experimenters.

The physical condition (see Fig. 2, right) used a high-fidelity prototype for testing the final user experience of the vaccination system (see Fig. 1). In a similar fashion as in the first scenario, the vaccination system inflates. Next, a robotic arm moves to the location of the lower arm to administer a fake vaccination.

2.5 Design

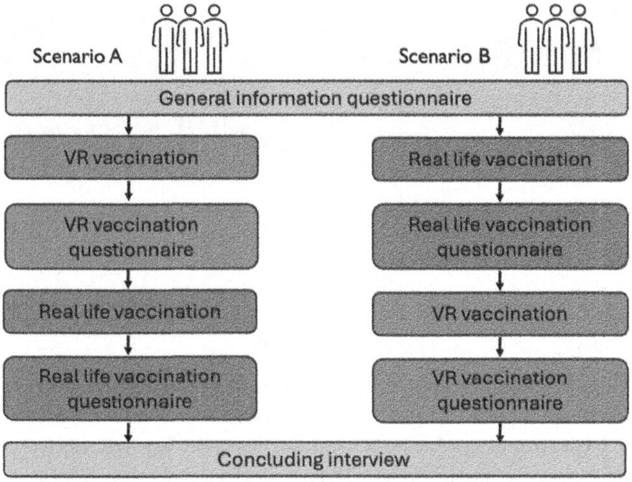

Fig. 4. Experimental design

This study applies a within-subjects design. The independent variable studied in this research is the vaccination method. This variable has to levels Virtual Reality (VR) and real life (RL). The dependent variables studied in this paper are UX aspects, heart rate, breathing rate, skin conductance. The UX aspects studied in this paper were usability (SUS) and hedonic, pragmatic and attractiveness attributes (AttrakDiff). The order of the conditions was counterbalanced, and a concluding semi-structured interview was done with seven participants.

2.6 Measurement Tools and Analysis

This study design offers a solid comparison between high fidelity prototypes and VR prototypes. By performing the assessment right after the actual experience, the participants were able to give accurate survey responses. Heart rate, respiration rate and EDA signals were recorded using the Biopac Nomadix hardware and software [25] in both conditions. After each condition SUS [12] and AttrakDiff [13] questionnaires were administered probing for the usability and attractiveness of the system. The questionnaires and physiological data were analyzed using JASP (a free and open-source program for statistics) [26]. Both the system usability data as the Attrakdiff attributes were analyzed using paired samples t-tests. The subcategory 'hedonic qualities stimulation' and 'hedonic qualities identity' were analyzed using a Wilcoxon signed rank test since the data of this category was not normally distributed. This analysis allowed us to compare the perceived usability and product qualities of both prototype evaluation set-ups. Next the results were checked for order effects, none were found. Finally, the qualitative data was re-evaluated using Bonferroni correction. The physiological data was parted into three sections corresponding to different phases of the vaccination process, namely the anticipation period, which was the phase before administering the needle (eight seconds), the injection period, which was the phase during administration of the needle (four seconds), and lastly the post injection period, which was the phase after administering the needle (nine seconds). The data of all physiological measures was analyzed using a 2 by 3 repeated measures ANOVA, where Greenhouse-Geisser corrections were applied whenever Mauchley's test indicated a violation of the sphericity assumption, in combination with paired samples t-tests when the interaction of the ANOVA was significant.

In addition to the collected physiological data, heart rate variability (HRV), more specifically the root mean square of successive differences between normal heartbeats (RMSSD), was calculated. For the purpose of this calculation outliers were removed, with a cut-off score above 100 ms, resulting in a smaller sample of 20 participants. Specific skin conductance responses (SCR) to events were determined using the onset, meaning only the onset of the anticipation phase, the injection phase and the post injection phase were considered as events. On average, SCR occurs between one and five seconds after onset of an event. To compensate for the possible non-detection of SCR occurring within the longer time periods of eight and nine seconds of the different phases this range of five seconds was extended to seven seconds.

3 Results

The testing protocol was properly executed, and all data collections were registered and usable. Both scenarios resembled each other closely, according to the participants. The participants showed high levels of system understanding and were able to form an opinion on the use of an automated vaccination device in real-life.

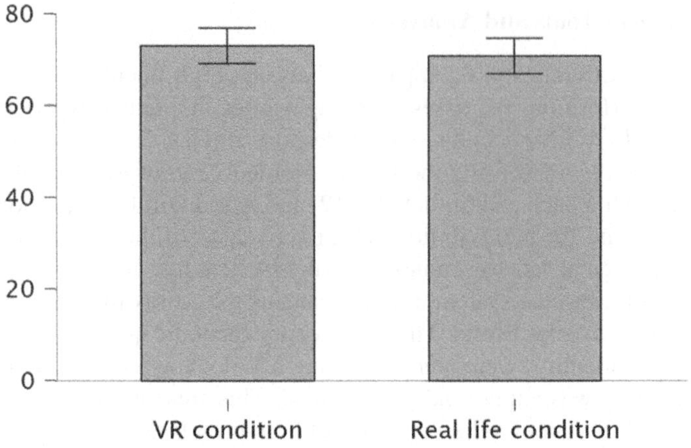

Fig. 5. Comparable usability results between VR scenario and High-fidelity testing

3.1 Questionnaires

The analysis of the SUS questionnaire shows that the participants found the system equally usable in VR compared to the physical prototype. Both scenarios showed close results in terms of system usability. The reported system usability of the VR prototype had a mean score of $M = 73.125$, $SD = 12.088$. The reported system usability of the real-life prototype had a mean score of $M = 70.893$, $SD = 14.389$. A paired samples t-test revealed no significant difference between the evaluated prototypes, $t(27) = 0.839$, $P = .409$. The effect size was also small ($d = .159$). This indicates that the participants did not experience a difference in perceived system usability. The visualization (see Fig. 5) illustrates the small differences in usability between the conditions graphically.

The reported pragmatic qualities of the VR prototype had a mean score of $M = 4.924$, $SD = 0.730$. The reported pragmatic qualities of the real-life prototype were $M = 4.85$, $SD = 0.685$. A paired-samples t-test revealed no significant difference between the two prototypes, $t(27) = 0.608$, $P = .548$. The effect size was small ($d = 0.115$). This means that the participants did not experience a difference in the pragmatic qualities of the two prototypes.

The reported attractiveness of the VR prototype had a mean score of $M = 4.669$, $SD = 0.871$. The reported attractiveness of the real-life prototype had a mean score of $M = 4.724$, $SD = 0.873$. A paired samples t-test revealed no significant difference between the two prototypes, $t(27) = -0.507$, $P = .616$. However, the effect size was small ($d = -0.096$). This means that both prototypes moderately differed in attractiveness.

The reported hedonic qualities for identity of the VR prototype had a median score of $M = 4$, $SD = 0.598$. The reported hedonic qualities regarding Identity of the real-life prototype had a median score of $M = 4$, $SD = 0.643$. A Wilcoxon signed rank test revealed a significant difference between the two prototypes, $W = 74.5$, $P = .018$. The effect size was medium to large ($r = 0.419$). After Bonferroni correction ($\alpha = 0.01$), the result remains no longer significant. This means that both prototypes did not differ in hedonic attributes regarding identity of the product. The reported hedonic qualities for stimulation of the VR prototype had a median score of $M = 4$, $SD = 0.410$. The reported hedonic qualities regarding Identity of the real-life prototype had a median score of $M = 5$, $SD = 0.958$. A Wilcoxon signed rank test revealed a significant difference between the two prototypes, $W = 32.0$, $P = .001$. The effect size was large ($r = 0.702$). After Bonferroni correction ($\alpha = 0.01$), the result remains significant. This means that both prototypes did differ in hedonic attributes regarding stimulation of the product.

3.2 Semi-structures Interviews

After the experiment, most participants' answers steered toward a more informative onboarding before starting the procedure. A participant stated: *"I would give an introduction and show what would happen during the process (to comfort patients)"*. They also stated that a real person in the was still preferred to lower the barrier in comparison to conventional vaccinations. The interviews revealed that the moment right before the prick was the most fear inducing and reported low-to-moderate levels of stress. A participant reported: *"The inflation part was the most unpleasant, I felt stuck"*. A participant stated that the use of a non-interactive arm 3d model in VR induced a disconnect between the body and portrayed visuals. A participant stated: *"my fingers are not moving along, putting my arm in something I can't see is unpleasant"*. Overall, the answer from the interview reflected the findings of the questionnaires in terms of usability and system perception. Generally, participants reported a positive attitude towards the system: *"I would see myself using this after some time"*.

3.3 Physiological Results

3.3.1 Heart Rate

The analysis of the heart rate data revealed no significant effect of the real life versus VR condition, $F(1, 27) = 1.523$, $P = 0.228$, ${\eta_p}^2 = 0.053$. However, a significant effect was found for the different phases of the vaccination process, $F(2, 54) = 5.607$, $P < .05$, ${\eta_p}^2 = 0.172$, as well as a significant interaction between the conditions and phases, $F(2, 54) = 12.986$, $P < .001$, ${\eta_p}^2 = 0.325$. The ANOVA was followed up with a paired samples *t*-test, which showed a significant difference in heart rate between both conditions during the anticipation phase, $t(27) = 2.961$, $P < .05$. This difference was however not found for the injection phase, $t(27) = -0.245$, $P = .809$, nor for the post injection phase, $t(27) = 0.543$, $P = .591$. Overall, these results indicate an increased heart rate during the anticipation phase as opposed to the other phases in the vaccination process, suggesting a higher stress level in expectation of the administration of the needle, rather than during the administration itself. Yet, this increase is only noted with the high-fidelity prototype as opposed to the VR prototype. These results are illustrated in Fig. 6.

3.3.2 Heart Rate Variability

The analysis of heart rate variability (HRV) showed that the condition proved to be significant, $F(1, 19) = 8.009$, $P < .05$, ${\eta_p}^2 = 0.297$, indicating a difference in heart rate variability between the high fidelity prototype and the VR prototype. A post hoc paired samples *t*-test showed an overall lower HRV for the high-fidelity prototype, $M_{\text{difference}}$

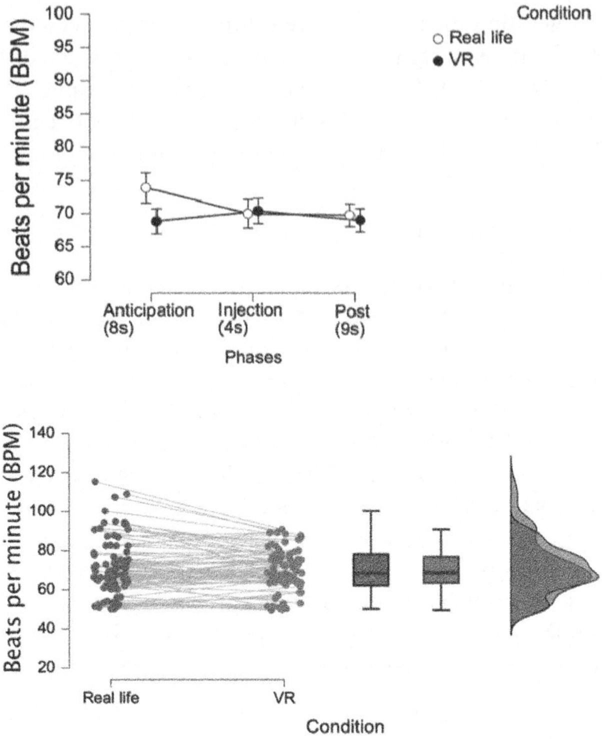

Fig. 6. Average heart rate given the phase (anticipation, injection and post injection; top), raincloud plot of the heart rate depending on condition (real life or VR; bottom)

= –10.976, $d = -0.551$, $P_{Holm} < .05$, suggesting a higher stress level in comparison to the VR prototype. These results are visualized in Fig. 7.

3.3.3 Respiration

The analysis of the respiration data revealed a significant effect of the condition type on breathing rate, $F(1, 27) = 14.061$, $P < .001$, $\eta_p{}^2 = 0.342$, with an overall higher breathing rate during the real life condition compared to the VR condition, $M_{\text{difference}} = 2.705$, $d = 0.517$, $P_{Holm} < .001$, as illustrated in Fig. 8. While neither the type of phase, $F(2, 54) = 1.490$, $P = 0.235$, $\eta_p{}^2 = 0.052$, nor the interaction between the conditions and phases, $F(2, 54) = 0.449$, $P = 0.640$, $\eta_p{}^2 = 0.016$, proved to be significant. These results suggest an overall higher stress level during the interaction with the high-fidelity prototype.

3.3.4 EDA

The analysis of the general skin conductance level (SCL) revealed no significant differences between the high-fidelity prototype and the VR prototype, nor between the three different phases of the vaccination process. Similar results were found in the analysis of

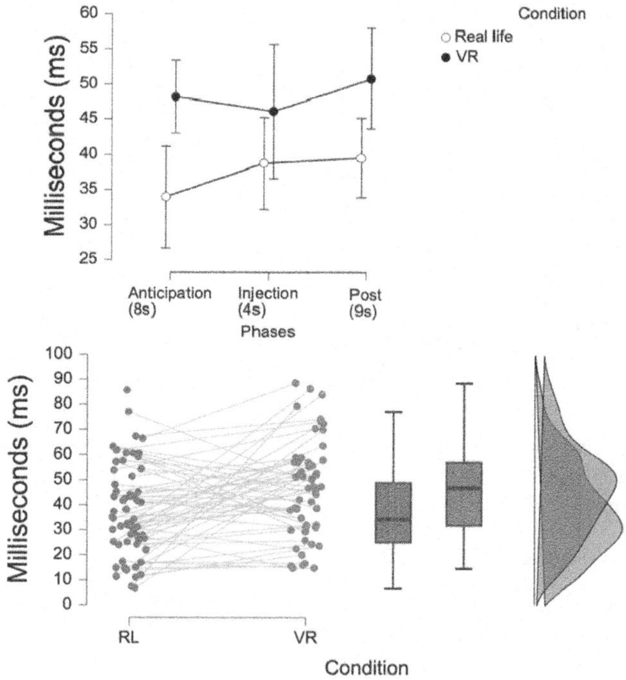

Fig. 7. Average heart rate variability (RMSSD) in milliseconds given the phase (anticipation, injection or post injection; left), raincloud plot of HRV depending on condition (real life or VR; right).

the specific skin conductance responses (SCR) related to the three different phases. Neither the condition type, $F(1, 27) = 0.834$, $P = .369$, $\eta_p{}^2 = 0.030$, nor the type of phase, $F(1, 40) = 1.632$, $P = .211$, $\eta_p{}^2 = 0.057$, significantly influenced the skin conductance responses. No significant interaction effect was found, $F(2, 54) = 1.016$, $P = .369$, $\eta_p{}^2 = 0.036$ (Fig. 9).

4 Discussion and Conclusion

4.1 Summary of the Findings

These results indicate that to participants there is no clear difference between the usability of the system, or the pragmatic qualities investigated. We believe that the virtual test was useful for system evaluations and visual recommendations, given the many remarks of participants and the comparable system usability scores. Albeit, the Attrakdiff questionnaire showing differences in hedonic qualities regarding stimulation, the main goal of this setup was evaluating the moment when the most fear was induced. In both the virtual and physical setup, the participants reported the same moments of anxiety (when the pillow inflates and anticipation anxiety right before the vaccination). This finding might indicate that the more concrete questions lead to similar assessment between both prototypes (moment of fear, usability, pragmatic and attractive qualities). This, compared

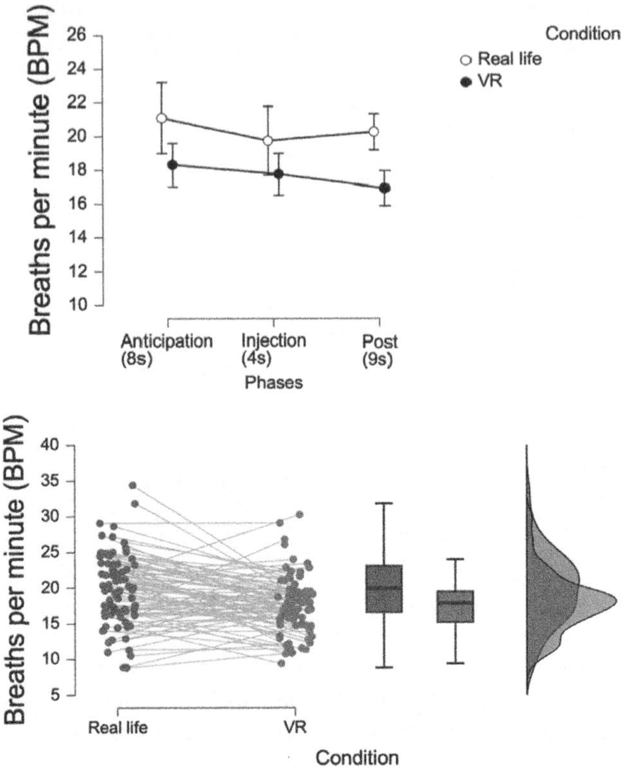

Fig. 8. Average breathing rate (left) given the phase (anticipation, injection and post injection), raincloud plot of respiration rate depending on condition (real life or VR; right).

to more vague questions leading to significantly different scores (hedonic qualities stimulation) or borderline scores (hedonic qualities identity). It might be possible that the two evaluation methods would differ in perceived experience when the VR scenario was rated with a lower usability score. Previous research by Hinricher [11] found more clear-cut differences. This can perhaps be explained by the increased usability and realism in current VR technology.

The finding that the participants indicated the moment right before the vaccination as the most fear inducing is partly confirmed by the physiological data, where we found a higher heart rate in the anticipation phase than in the injection and post injection phase, although this difference was only present in the real-life condition but not in the VR condition. In the other phases (injection and post injection) there was no difference between VR and real life. This could be explained by the scenario which overall did not induce a lot of fear in the participants when observing the absolute value. As a result, the difference becomes harder to detect. Similarly, the skin conductance data analysis also showed no significant difference between VR and real life in general. This differs from the respiration data and the heart rate variability, where breathing rate was overall higher and heart rate variability lower for the real-life condition than for the VR condition. The difference in breathing rate can be attributed to the high variability that occurs with

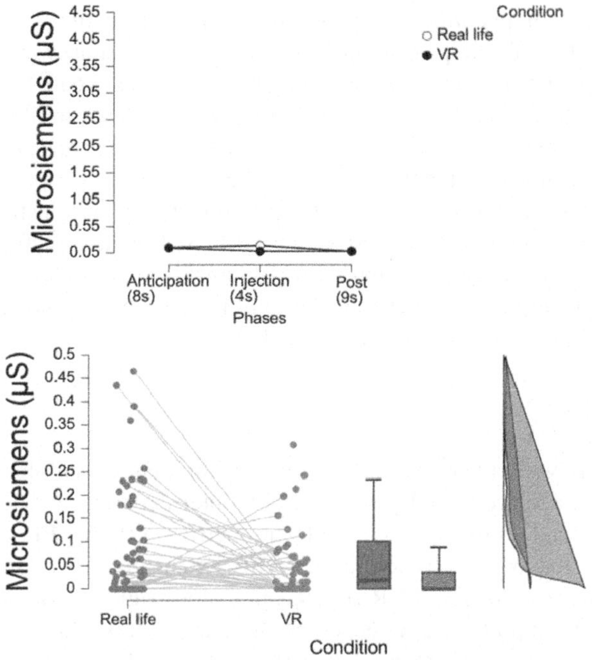

Fig. 9. Average skin conductance response (SCR) given the phase (anticipation, injection and post injection; top), raincloud plot of SCR depending on condition (real life or VR; bottom).

this metric. Nonetheless, delving deeper into the non-significant results might result in a combined robust metric to assess the fear induced by such a system. Further research might also provide much needed nuance and confirmation needed in this type of research.

4.2 Limitations

In order to get a more sensitive measure of the stress levels HRV (RMSSD) was calculated. However, this measure is possibly biased. To calculate HRV as accurately as possible, studies have suggested that a recording period of around five minutes is sufficient, whereas a period of 24 h is considered ideal, yet less practical [27]. The current study, however, does not stick to this recommended minimum duration. Instead, HRV was calculated using the duration of the three phases of the vaccination process (eight, four and nine seconds), resulting in a total recording period of only 21 s. A study by Shaffer et al. (2020) [28] has explored the use of ultra short-term measurements of around 10 s as opposed to 5 min. Results suggested that, while these short periods can provide a short snapshot of the HRV values, they tend to be less reliable and are more prone to artifacts and fast fluctuations. Thus, the results regarding HRV might be distorted and may not represent a reliable outcome, and in its turn a reliable representation of the stress levels.

Specific skin conductance responses (SCR) were calculated based on a time window of seven seconds, which is a broader range than recommended for detecting possible responses to events happening during one of the phases of the vaccination process. Each onset of a phase (anticipation, injection and post injection) was considered as an event, however within the time window of each phase other events took place, such as movements of the robotic arm in both the real life and the VR condition, thus, the time in which a skin conductance response was considered as a response to a specific event was extended. This however resulted in overlap between phases, especially between the injection phase (lasting four seconds) and the post injection phase (lasting nine seconds). This could have resulted in possible errors where an SCR is incorrectly attributed to the injection phase, or incorrectly attributed to the post injection phase. Each SCR was manually checked and latency between the onset of the phase and the response was recalculated to gain greater control of this challenge.

4.3 Future Work

A follow-up study will collect more data points from a larger sample, mostly focusing on diversifying in age group and gaming or computer experience. The continuation of this study will extend on the analysis of physio metric reactions (EDA, respiration and HR) of the participants to both conditions. This extension will focus on the specific physiological metrics, such as SCR peaks, on a more rigid interaction timeline [18] compared with the reported experiences of the participants. Based on this research, fear reducing recommendations can be implemented in the vaccination scenario and iteratively tested.

4.4 Conclusion

This early test indicates that haptic VR prototype testing might alleviate some issues with high-fidelity prototype testing, however the resulting analysis reports mixed results regarding the studied variables. Questions in terms of usability, hedonic qualities and attractiveness of both prototypes revealed that the usability remained the same in both conditions. However, some results of the AttrakDiff questionnaire were on the borderline of indicating a difference, indicating a possible difference in hedonic qualities of both testing systems. The physiological data showed no significant difference between VR and real life in the skin conductance data and the injection and post injection phase of the heart rate data. This differed from the respiration data and the heart rate variability, where breathing rate was overall higher and heart rate variability lower for the real-life condition than for the VR condition.

Acknowledgements. We thank Ward De Muynck from OCTOO to support this research with performing the qualitative user interviews. We also thank Noémie De Vlaminck for the supporting analysis of the physiological data.

Disclosure of Interests Authors have no competing interest to declare.

References

1. Bordegoni, M., Ferrise, F.: Designing interaction with consumer products in a multisensory virtual reality environment. Virt. Phys. Prototype **8**(1), 51–64 (2013). https://doi.org/10.1080/17452759.2012.762612
2. Tiong, E., et al.: The economies and dimensionality of design prototyping: value, time, cost, and fidelity. J. Mech. Des. **141**(3) (2019). https://doi.org/10.1115/1.4042337
3. Söderman, M.: Virtual reality in product evaluations with potential customers: an exploratory study comparing virtual reality with conventional product representations. J. Eng. Des. **16**(3), 311–328 (2005). https://doi.org/10.1080/09544820500128967
4. Maempel, H.-J., Horn, M.: Audiovisual perception of real and virtual rooms. J. Virt. Real. Broadcasting **14**(5), 33–34 (2017). https://doi.org/10.20385/1860-2037/14.2017.5
5. Matthes, C., et al.: The collaborative virtual reality neurorobotics lab. In: 26th IEEE Conference on Virtual Reality and 3D User Interfaces, VR 2019 - Proceedings, pp. 1671–1674 (2019). https://doi.org/10.1109/VR.2019.8798289
6. Faust, F.G., et al.: Mixed prototypes for the evaluation of usability and user experience: simulating an interactive electronic device. Virtual Reality **23**(2), 197–211 (2019). https://doi.org/10.1007/s10055-018-0356-1
7. Ferrise, F., Graziosi, S., Bordegoni, M.: Prototyping strategies for multisensory product experience engineering. J. Intell. Manuf. **28**(7), 1695–1707 (2017). https://doi.org/10.1007/s10845-015-1163-0
8. Bordegoni, M., Ferrise, F., Lizaranzu, J.: Use of interactive Virtual Prototypes to define product design specifications: a pilot study on consumer products. In: ISVRI 2011 - IEEE International Symposium on Virtual Reality Innovations 2011, Proceedings, no. Figure 1, pp. 11–18 (2011). https://doi.org/10.1109/ISVRI.2011.5759592
9. Park, H., Son, J.S., Lee, K.H.: Design evaluation of digital consumer products using virtual reality-based functional behaviour simulation. J. Eng. Des. **19**(4), 359–375 (2008). https://doi.org/10.1080/09544820701474129
10. Lorenz, M., Neupetsch, C., Rotsch, C., Klimant, P., Hammer, N.: Early virtual reality user experience and usability assessment of a surgical shape memory alloy aspiration/irrigation instrument. In: 26th IEEE Conference on Virtual Reality and 3D User Interfaces, VR 2019 - Proceedings, pp. 1056–1057 (2019). https://doi.org/10.1109/VR.2019.8798144
11. Hinricher, N., König, S., Schröer, C., Backhaus, C.: Effects of virtual reality and test environment on user experience, usability, and mental workload in the evaluation of a blood pressure monitor. Front. Virtual Reality **4** (2023). https://doi.org/10.3389/frvir.2023.1151190
12. Brooke, J.: SUS: A 'Quick and Dirty' Usability Scale (1996)
13. Hassenzahl, M.: Hedonic, emotional, and experiential perspectives on product quality. Encyclopedia Hum. Comput. Interact. (2006)
14. Klllç, A., et al.: Using virtual technology for fear of medical procedures: a systematic review of the effectiveness of virtual reality-based interventions. Ann. Behavi. Med. **55**(11). Oxford University Press, pp. 1062–1079 (2021). https://doi.org/10.1093/abm/kaab016
15. Hako, S., Kambara, K., Ogata, A.: The development and validation of the multidimensional fear-of-injection scale. Health Psychol. Behav. Med. **10**(1), 806–817 (2022). https://doi.org/10.1080/21642850.2022.2116328
16. Nomura, T., Suzuki, T., Kanda, T., Kato, K.: Measurement of negative attitudes toward robots (2006)
17. Sverre Syrdal, D., Dautenhahn, K., Lee Koay, K., Walters, M. L.: The Negative Attitudes towards Robots Scale and Reactions to Robot Behaviour in a Live Human-Robot Interaction Study (2009)

18. Jang, E.H., Byun, S., Park, M.S., Sohn, J.H.: Predicting individuals' experienced fear from multimodal physiological responses to a fear-inducing stimulus. Adv. Cogn. Psychol. **16**(4), 291–301 (2020). https://doi.org/10.5709/acp-0303-x
19. Faghih, R.T., Stokes, P.A., Marin, M.F., Zsido, R.G., Zorowitz, S., Rosenbaum, B.L., Barbieri, R.: Characterization of fear conditioning and fear extinction by analysis of electrodermal activity. In: 37th Annual International Conference of the IEEE Engineering in Medicine and Biology Society (EMBC), pp. 7814–7818 (2015). https://doi.org/10.1109/EMBC.2015.7320204
20. Jovanovic, K., et al.: Digital innovation hubs in health-care robotics fighting COVID-19: novel support for patients and health-care workers across Europe. IEEE Robot. Autom. Mag. **28**(1), 40–47 (2021). https://doi.org/10.1109/MRA.2020.3044965
21. Beyers, K.C.L., Rbeihat, M.N.M., Vasconcelos, S.D., Pasmans, D., Verwulgen, S., Vanker-ckhoven, V.V.J.: Preclinical evaluation of performance, safety and usability of VAX-ID®, a novel intradermal injection device. Vaccine **41**(31), 4609–4615 (2023). https://doi.org/10.1016/j.vaccine
22. Pioli, M.R., Ritter, A.M., de Faria, A.P., Modolo, R.: White coat syndrome and its variations: differences and clinical impact. Integrated Blood Pressure Control **11**, 73–79 (2018). https://doi.org/10.2147/IBPC.S152761
23. HTC corporation. https://www.vive.com/sea/product/vive-pro-eye/overview/ HTC vive pro eye
24. Unity game engine. https://unity.com Unity Game Engine
25. BIOPAC. https://www.biopac.com/product-category/research/bionomadix-wireless-physiology/BiopacNomadix
26. JASP Team, https://jasp-stats.org . JASP (Version 0.18.3) [Computer software]
27. Schmitt, L., Regnard, J., Millet, G.P.: Monitoring fatigue status with HRV measures in elite athletes: an avenue beyond RMSSD?. Front. Psychiol. **6**, 1664–042X (2015). https://doi.org/10.3389/fphys.2015.00343. https://www.frontiersin.org/journals/physiology/articles/https://doi.org/10.3389/fphys.2015.00343
28. Shaffer, F., Meehan, Z.M., Zerr, C.L.: A critical review of ultra-short-term heart rate variability norms research. Front. Neurosci. **14**, 1662–453X (2015). https://doi.org/10.3389/fnins.2020.594880. https://www.frontiersin.org/journals/neuroscience/articles/https://doi.org/10.3389/fnins.2020.594880

Towards Realizing Collaborative Systems to Enable Telework in Part Manufacturing

Taimur Khan[1(✉)], Philipp Schworm[1], Margit Pohl[2], Matthias Klar[1], Jan C. Aurich[1], and Achim Ebert[1]

[1] RPTU Kaiserslautern-Landau, 67663 Kaiserslautern, Germany
{taimur.khan,philipp.schworm,matthias.klar,jan.aurich, achim.ebert}@rptu.de

[2] Vienna University of Technology, 1040 Vienna, Austria
margit.pohl@tuwien.ac.at

Abstract. Part manufacturing is an important aspect of industrial production where automation allows a range of manufacturing processes to be completed without the need for manual human activities. Still, human tasks are essential to maintain consistent functioning and part quality. Thus, part production is vulnerable to reduced workforce restrictions (e.g., pandemics). Several technologies, like remote assistance and teleoperation, have the potential to enable new forms of collaboration based on interactive systems. We argue that, given the high complexity of the collaborations, high usability must be the primary priority during design. Research is needed to investigate how Human-Centered Design (HCD) might be used to build and implement collaborative systems that allow telework in complex industrial environments to deal with workforce reductions caused by pandemics or personnel shortages. Ultimately, the target should be a system that uses technology (e.g. Augmented Reality, AR) across devices and user types to counteract productivity and quality problems in reduced workforce situations.

Keywords: Human-Centered Design · Collaborative Systems · Telework · Augmented Reality · Part Manufacturing

1 Problem Statement

Industrial production is typically comprised of the sequential activities of part manufacturing and assembly. While part manufacturing is defined as the production of individual parts for eventual assembly or direct delivery to customers, assembly is the process of putting together a completed product from finished individual parts or partially assembled units [37]. Machining (e.g. milling, turning, and drilling) is a common method of part manufacturing. As of today, machining processes in part manufacture are usually performed automatically on machine tools equipped with computer numerical control (CNC) that execute part-individual computer programs containing all essential manufacturing activities [25]. Additionally, part manufacturing tasks are often performed on machining centers (multi-machine operation for higher productivity), which extend the

L. Zaina et al. (Eds.): EICS 2024, LNCS 15518, pp. 189–209, 2025.
https://doi.org/10.1007/978-3-031-91760-8_13

capabilities of CNC-based machine tools and enable both unattended operation for a significant amount of time [12] and permit one person to operate several machines in parallel. Machining centers can constantly make parts with many machining features using highly automated systems and equipment, eliminating the need for manual processes. This makes machining centers suitable for large series part manufacture, such as in the automotive industry [25].

Despite high degree of automation in part manufacturing, certain recurring human activities are still essential to sustain productivity and ensure the quality of the manufactured parts [12]. For example, to manufacture a part series on a machining center, initial changeover and setup procedures, such as creating and testing CNC programs, calibrating the machine, or measuring and adding tools to the tool changer, must be completed [38]. Setup tasks are required only once each series but might take a large amount of time, hence their execution time has a direct impact on productivity [33]. Following setup, human tasks are mostly focused on monitoring and maintaining the normal operation. This comprises periodic supply and removal of raw and finished components to and from storage systems, as well as routine monitoring duties, such as visual identification of missing or defective tools and auditive detection of anomalies (e.g. chatter) [34]. In addition, operators also ensure the quality of manufactured parts, for example, through routine measurements, as well as problem-specific replies to deviations. This may include, for example, the adjustment of tools or fixtures, which demands cognitive abilities. Furthermore, liquids, lubricants, and consumables must be replenished manually, which also applies to tools that have reached the end of their service life. In addition, the positioning controls must be verified for any offsets that may have occurred over time. According to Weck and Brecher [38], equipment cleaning and chip removal may be required. In the event of a detected disturbance (for example, a crash), steps must be taken to restore the machining center to normal operation. The duties outlined above are infrequent and often vary between executions. Furthermore, they mix cognitive and physical operations and necessitate human skill. These factors, together with the requisite flexibility and adaptability, make tasks that ensure part manufacturing difficult to automate and heavily reliant on the physical presence of human experts.

If the above-mentioned tasks are skipped when experts are not present, productivity and quality issues, as well as machine downtime, are likely to arise. This effect was seen in the COVID-19 crisis. To manage the pandemic in manufacturing facilities, common recommendations included encouraging sick workers to remain home or establish flexible work hours, such as staggered shifts [26]. Some governments even required all workplaces to close temporarily in order to prevent workplace illnesses. According to Accenture [1], difficulties in workforce availability and productivity emerged as a result. The reliance on a limited group of experts has a significant impact on part manufacturing. Even a few absent professionals severely limit the available workforce and the ability to complete the required duties. This applies not only to COVID-19, but also to annual influenza outbreaks and future pandemics, where similar precautions (e.g., social distance and telework) are implemented to prevent spread [3]. Other industries, such as IT, address these difficulties by transferring employees to telework. Applying this principle to part manufacturing, productivity might be maintained even with a smaller on-site workforce. Despite these potentials, manufacturing shows comparably low application of telework, which results from the required physical manipulations on-site [10].

Several concurrent technological developments however provide promising possibilities to overcome these challenges by enabling telework and collaboration in part manufacturing: Modern machining centers offer remote access to control panels including status information and in some circumstances remote control [29]. Furthermore, web-based cameras and technologies like Augmented Reality (AR) enable interactive visualization of respective points of interest. This is important, since the performance of collaborative tasks is increased if the visual context is shared, coordination is improved and a common understanding is established more easily [11]. Communication based on direct verbal and visual synchronous communication technologies further promotes remote collaboration [7]. Regarding physical interactions, advances in collaborative robots (cobots) show potentials in reduced workforce situations: In selected tasks, this might enable a remote expert to perform tasks from home while physical manipulations are done by a cobot on-site. Alternatively, a task that requires two persons might be performed by just one person and a cobot. Finally, fast internet connections that are available to 88% of all households in the European Union [9] promote telework by providing fast and reliable data transfer. The upcoming 5G cellular network standard further enriches possibilities of collaboration, e.g. through reduced latency and increased bandwidth. Integrating these technologies could enable telework in part manufacturing by forming new modes of collaboration in which qualified teleworking experts collaborate with human helpers and cobots on-site to perform the required human tasks (see Fig. 1). Additionally, the reverse where the expert is on-site and the worker is remote is also important and the resulting potentials need to be also assessed.

This article describes research undertaken as part of the *PartRe²Work* project. The goal of this project is to look at how part manufacturing should be structured and how technical appliances should be designed in this context to support more telework in this field. For example, some monitoring or assistance tasks can already be conducted remotely in multi-machine operations across several sites. However, there is possibility to go further by transferring the workforce remotely rather than on-site. From the standpoint of HCD, this is especially difficult because the technical appliances integrated into such manufacturing systems are exceedingly varied and may necessitate distinct approaches of investigation. Nonetheless, these systems must be combined into a cohesive whole. Traditional procedures used by HCD may have limited utility. The *PartRe²Work* project aims to create and assess a framework enabling manufacturers to partially relocate on-site manufacturing tasks to telework during decreased workforce scenarios.

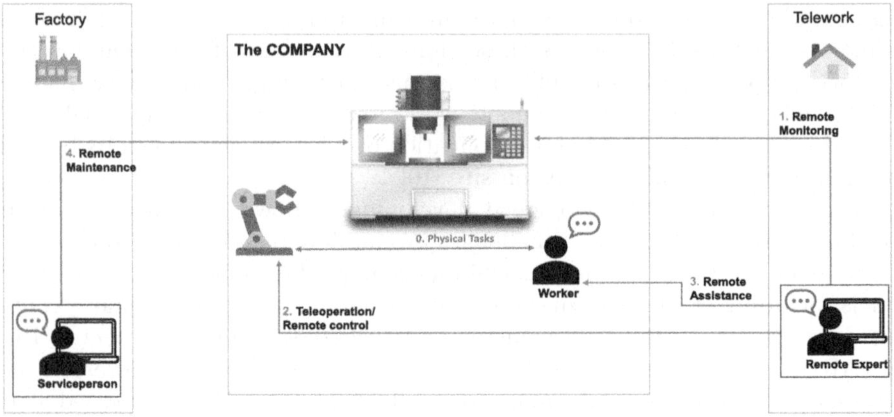

Fig. 1. Example system to enable new collaboration modes to maintain part manufacturing (red are physical tasks, blue are virtual) (Color figure online)

2 State of the Art

Current research in this context can be grouped into four directions (see Fig. 1): Remote assistance studies methods to enable assistance by remotely connecting two persons. Remote maintenance addresses the remote collaboration of an on-site user with an expert for maintenance and service processes. Cobots enable to collaborate with humans within a shared space, or where humans and robots are in close proximity. Lastly, teleoperation of machines focuses on controlling and monitoring machine tools without direct physical access.

Regarding remote assistance, AR is used in a framework for assembly tasks which is validated with user studies [13]. Additional approaches describe requirements for an AR-based framework including local cameras with the goal of assisting on-site personnel regarding problems on a machine where a remote operator accesses the machine's CNC control interface [29]. As handling disturbances is an essential task in part manufacturing, remote maintenance is of relevance for the envisioned approach. Some approaches consider AR as one mean to assist remote monitoring or maintenance (e.g., [23,35]). Here, technicians remotely collaborate with users on-site to assist with maintenance tasks. One approach proposes a method to perform monitoring and maintenance remotely. Maintenance tasks are however limited to accessing digital machine information to prepare visits of service personnel [22]. Alves et al. [5] present an AR-based quality control system capable of generating virtual content to guide operators by overlaying information in a video stream while performing real-time validation. Also cobots show potential for the envisioned collaboration modes, since their productivity would not be affected during a pandemic. Furthermore, they allow scenarios, in which a remote user uses a cobot on-site for physical manipulations (e.g. [19]). However, creating part manufacturing collaboration modes by integrating machines, cobots, information or communication systems and humans inevitably leads to questions, how and in which way adequate task sharing takes place (e.g., [2,6]). Considering new forms of collaboration between humans, machines, information and communication systems, further strategies can be expected with new requirements regarding the design of new teleworking methods and possibilities along the human-technology-organization concept. These requirements should be derived, investigated, and analyzed regarding use cases with the goal of an efficient balance between a productivity and human centered oriented set up. Altogether, symbiotic human-robot work systems provide an auspicious setting for new modes of collaboration under uncertain access conditions, but still need grounded research with special emphasis to the integrated and user-centered design and development of assistance systems. Teleoperation of machine tools potentially enables telework access to machines and is subject of several approaches that e.g. allow a remote user to monitor the absolute and relative motions of all axes as well as to control the spindle speed and feed rate of a machine tool [36]. The implementation of a remote system for the manufacture of turned parts is also described. In this work, continuous visual feedback with cameras is streamed and remotely controlling a CNC machine is allowed. Manual tasks on-site that exceed the scope of the CNC control are not considered [4]. Furthermore, remote monitoring and control of a CNC machine tool are investigated by Oliveira et al. The approach is limited to functions of the control panel (e.g. “Start program”). Tasks that are described above and require manual operations are not considered [27]. Furthermore, Rogowski aims at remotely controlling and programming machine tool features like auxiliary devices or loading CNC programs. In addition, a camera provides visual feedback of the machine state to the teleoperating user. The interaction with the machine is however not suitable for the described tasks in part manufacturing, as an asynchronous approach is chosen, in which specific CNC programs are submitted remotely which are subsequently executed [30]. In the envisioned context, on-demand, synchronous control inputs are required.

Research from the four research directions partly addresses questions that arise when investigating telework modes for part manufacturing. However, none of the approaches in these fields is capable of performing all required activities: Remote assistance methods mainly aim at assisting in physical tasks, mostly from assembly. Assisting in machining operations is rarely considered in implemented approaches. Even though the necessity was pointed out by Rasmussen et al. [29], no approach shows a systematic integration of remote assistance with remote control that would enable the remote expert to directly interact with the machine. Remote maintenance approaches also omit to exploit the potential that lies in remote machine control. While maintenance is a crucial task, remote maintenance approaches aim at customer service, which implies that the remote expert is a qualified service employee, trained in the remote interaction with on-site users. In contrast, the envisioned expert-helper collaboration has to be ramped up in exceptional situations that occur suddenly and are not daily routine for those involved. Hence, the systems and modes of collaborations need to be specifically designed for this purpose including a high usability for intuitive operation and fast ramp-up.

This is not explicitly covered in existing remote maintenance approaches. Additionally, cobots provide beneficial elements to support part manufacturing under reduced personnel constraints. Existing approaches are however limited to physical interactions and do not cover other aspects of part manufacturing. Current approaches therefore only partly address the needs of the described collaboration forms. Integrating cobots in such constellations further raises unsolved questions of human-cobot task distribution. Machine tool teleoperation approaches also encompass single aspects of the envisioned collaboration modes, such as remote monitoring and interaction, as well as video surveillance of the machine's current state. Such approaches are however limited to tasks that can be performed via the machine's control system and exclude all manual tasks on-site. Despite video feedback, the remote expert cannot interact with the machine (e.g. manual adjustment of a fixture).

In addition, no previous approach addresses the problem of reduced workforce in part manufacturing. Even if the foundations from the four research directions can be integrated, the resulting interactions between the humans and the technical systems needs to be specifically designed for this purpose. Further, collaboration can become complex, unpredictable and undetermined as a result of different skills of those involved, the heterogenous character of the tasks and the integration of digital technologies. This leads to a complex solution space, from which the envisioned collaboration modes need to be designed. In this context, research needs to find ways of mastering this complexity and achieving the goal of maintaining part manufacturing operation.

3 The Human Element in Manufacturing

It is becoming increasingly apparent that a high level of usability via HCD is the key to success not only for IT systems, online services, and telecommunications products but also the manufacturing and industrial sectors [28]. There exist some research works that apply HCD in the realms of manufacturing: Semi-structured interviews were conducted with companies about the impact of the application. The research project *AuQuA* applies HCD for the development of assembly support systems [39]. A similar focus is chosen by Römer et al. who also develop an assembly assistance system [31]. Another approach develops production planning and control assistance systems using the HCD framework [24]. In the work of Kluge et al., the design of a fault-finding application for manufacturing is described [18].

An important aspect in the context of HCD in manufacturing is how to design systems supporting human communication and collaboration. The characteristics of human collaboration have to be taken into account to ensure that efficient and effective systems are developed. The field of CSCW (Computer-Supported Cooperative Work) addresses such issues. In this context, two different dimensions play an important role: places and time. Collaboration can take place at the same time or at different times, and at the same place and different places [16]. In many cases, collaboration in part manufacturing will take place at the same time but different places (e.g., when an expert supports on-site personnel in monitoring or maintenance tasks), but other applications are possible. Mayer et al. [21], for example, investigated asynchronous remote collaboration. This kind of collaboration was based on spatial capture and replay of body movements. Former work processes were represented, and workers were able to view movements and interactions of persons showing how to fulfill tasks step-by-step. The researchers showed that there are no differences between synchronous and asynchronous collaboration as far as completion time, cognitive workload and usability were concerned. Rumsey and Dantec [32] point out that the introduction of virtual collaboration tools often requires organizations and work processes to be restructured. When introducing such technologies, appropriate infrastructure has to be provided. Stand-alone solutions are often not successful.

In general, the growing influence of the Industry 4.0 principle in production systems entails an amalgamation of technologies such as virtual environments, unstructured data, and complex simulation models, and all this latest industrial automation must be integrated with human capabilities. This has led to the Human-Centered Manufacturing (HCM) movement, which integrates the strength, efficiency, repetitiveness, and precision of automation with the knowledge, versatility, and ability of human operators resulting in hybrid systems of tremendous potential in terms of manufacturing processes and safety for employees [28]. Despite the potential and importance of HCD and usability, to date only a limited number of approaches apply HCD in manufacturing. No approach focuses on part manufacturing or machine tools in general.

4 Engaging a Human-Centered Design

To take into account the previous mentioned potentials and challenges a framework is developed to apply HCD principles for telecollaboration modes for part manufacturing scenarios. This framework, based on the approach provided in [17], involves several sequential steps. Following the ISO 9241-210 standard for HCD for interactive systems (see Fig. 2), the design and development is to be centered around the iterative steps of specifying the context of use, specifying the user requirements, producing design solutions, and evaluation of the design. Firstly, the user context is identified using HCD methods such as "identification of stakeholders", "context-of-use analysis", and "survey of existing users". Subsequently, requirements specifications are derived, encompassing user-related, organizational, and operational requirements. These requirements are elicited through methods such as "stakeholder analysis", "scenarios-of-use", and "task-function mapping". Following this, design solutions are formulated. This process is divided into conceptualization and prototyping, employing techniques like "storyboarding" and "paper prototyping".

At the point of publication specifying the context of use and "stakeholder analysis" and "scenarios-of-use" under specifying the user requirements has been completed with actual users of the system.

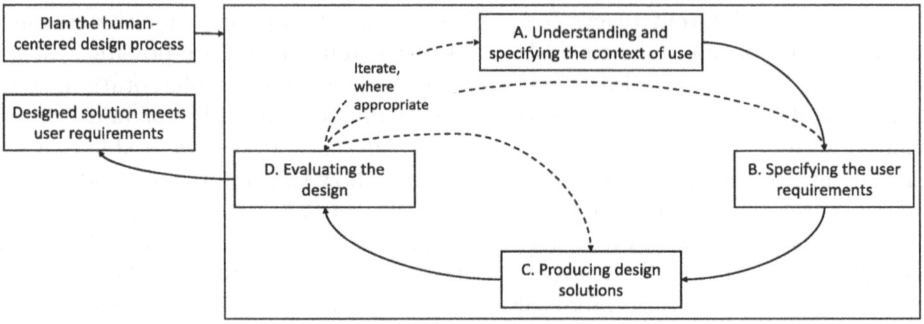

Fig. 2. HCD for interactive systems based on ISO 9241-210 [15]

4.1 Specifying the Context of Use

Prior to the context of use analysis, a stakeholder analysis was conducted to identify the main stakeholders involved in the environment under study. This analysis was carried out through interviews with both industrial and scientific personnel who operate within this specific environment. The identified stakeholders can be categorized into several groups:

- **Machine operators**: Responsible for the smooth operation, setup, and monitoring of machines and parts throughout the manufacturing process. Within this group, a distinction is made between individuals with vocational training or higher degrees (e.g., technicians) and auxiliary workers. Auxiliary workers may not be able to perform all tasks independently and may require support for certain tasks.
- **Shop floor managers**: These stakeholders oversee all machinery and are responsible for task distribution, supervision, and ensuring the smooth operation of the shop floor.
- **Service workers**: This group includes both internal and external personnel responsible for maintaining the machinery. Internal service workers typically handle routine and straightforward maintenance tasks, such as refilling oil, while more complex issues, such as problems with machine control systems, are usually addressed by external service personnel.
- Additionally, individuals responsible for task scheduling, such as process engineers, were identified. In some cases, these responsibilities may also be handled by shop floor managers. Furthermore, executives and other bystanders were identified, although they do not engage directly with the machinery within the typical production environment.

Following this stakeholder analysis, the context of use analysis was initiated using a structured questionnaire (see Appendix A for details). According to Maguire [20], the questionnaire was organized into four key sections: goals, tasks, environment, and user. The user section was placed last to prevent potential demotivation among participants when answering questions that might exceed their perceived qualifications. Most questions provided multiple-choice options, but space was also included for individual responses. The questionnaires were sent to individuals working in both industry and scientific institutes with a manufacturing focus from the previous identified stakeholder groups. To date, five participants have responded. Although the sample size is limited, preliminary commonalities have been identified. In the goals section, respondents were asked only about their primary objective in manufacturing and some related subgoals. As expected, given the well-established nature of production goals in manufacturing, the primary objective identified was to ensure production of high-quality products according to customer requirements with low lead times. The task section of the questionnaire focused on the participants' roles in manufacturing, structured according to the stakeholder analysis. This included tasks related to machine operation, maintenance, supervision, and troubleshooting processes. Additionally, participants were asked to specify the main field in which their tasks are applied, such as machining (e.g., milling, grinding, turning), assembly, joining, casting, or additive manufacturing. Given that machining and assembly are the primary processes in industrial production, participants were selected accordingly. This ensured that only individuals working in relevant manufacturing fields were included in the study. To streamline the questionnaire, the task section was designed so that participants first indicated whether they were involved in a specific task. Only if they confirmed involvement were they required to answer further questions in that direction. This approach ensured that participants only responded to questions relevant to their daily activities, reducing unnecessary burden. Participants were then asked to detail their daily tasks while operating machinery. The primary tasks described included setting up machines, programming CNC codes, and monitoring machines during operation. The most commonly reported challenges and obstacles encountered were programming errors, operator errors, and unknown correlations. Additional issues included the lack of necessary fixturing aids and the physical challenges of working with heavy objects in CNC-controlled machines. For manual-controlled machines, the primary difficulties mentioned were machine vibrations, tool wear, noise, and interference, compounded by the absence of feedback in the form of error codes. Manual clamping and fixturing were also highlighted as significant concerns. The following section of the task analysis focused on activities that involve significant manual effort or are prone to errors. The results predominantly highlighted quality assurance tasks, such as checking tool conditions and measuring both tools and workpieces. Additionally, setup tasks were identified as error-prone, including the measuring and fixturing of workpieces, clamping, calibration tasks, and CNC program verification. Routine service tasks, such as refilling oil, were also noted for their manual effort requirements. Another section of the questionnaire explored troubleshooting processes when an error occurs. The findings revealed that operators typically first attempt to handle the error independently. If they are unable to resolve the issue, support is sought from the shop floor manager or external service personnel. Troubleshooting is usually conducted on-site or remotely, using a camera to provide instructions. However, participants identified several challenges in the troubleshooting process. The requirement for extensive experience was noted as a significant hurdle, along with long waiting times for support, which were frequently mentioned as problematic.

The environment section of the questionnaire aimed to capture the characteristics of the participants' working environments. All participants are employed in the metalworking industry, with some also involved in plastic processing. The work is conducted indoors in noisy environments, necessitating the use of protective equipment such as gloves. Teams typically consist of 10 to 50 people, with individuals responsible for operating multiple machines. In the subsequent part of the environment section, participants were asked about the degree of automation in their workspaces and their satisfaction with it. A low level of automation was reported primarily in the area of machine monitoring and tasks such as loading and unloading workpieces, setup, cleaning, safety detection and troubleshooting processes. Low satisfaction was particularly noted in tasks such as cleanup, setup, loading, troubleshooting of complex single-part manufacturing, and the use of older equipment. Reliability issues were also mentioned concerning the consumable parts of the machines and machine control software, though the overall reliability was generally rated positively. Similar to the work of [5], a participant mentioned AR-based quality control system generating virtual content to guide operators by overlaying information in a video stream. Safety measures in the workplace were also addressed, focusing on repetitive training and supervision. Both approaches are implemented to ensure that machinery is used correctly and to minimize the risk of accidents.

The final section of the questionnaire focused on the users. All participants have at least vocational training, with experience levels ranging from a minimum of 5 years to over 15 years in the field. Most participants are familiar with state-of-the-art manufacturing technology and are proficient in using PCs and touchscreens for machine control. However, with individual exceptions they are less familiar with emerging technologies such as collaborative robotics, HCI technology, remote operation, and automated sensing.

4.2 Specifying the User Requirements

Based on specifying the context of use, the next step involves specifying the user requirements; a key component of which is to develop the scenarios of use. Three use cases have been identified as objects of investigation, each differing in terms of automation degree. These use cases are as follows (see Fig. 3):

1. **EMCO MaxxTurn 45 Machining Center**
2. **Röders RXP601DSH Machining Center**
3. **Deckel FP1 Milling Machine Tool**

Use case	1	2	3
Automation degree	High	Medium	Low
Machine tool and automation elements	**EMCO MaxxTurn 45 Machining Center** CNC Control Cobot-assisted part handling Automated Material Flow Automated Tool Change Remote Control Access	**Röders RXP601DSH Machining Center** CNC Control Manual Part Handling Manual Material Flow Automated Tool Change Remote Control Access	**Deckel FP1 Milling Machine Tool** Line Motion Control Manual part handling Manual Material Flow Manual Tool Change Only local access

Fig. 3. Use cases

The scenarios of use will be directly based on these use cases. These use cases align with the context of use analysis, where it was found that some participants are familiar with collaborative robots and high levels of automation, while others work with manually controlled machines. By considering these three exemplary use cases, the full spectrum of participant experiences and environments can be addressed. The scenarios of use for the three identified use cases are structured to include a regular operation scenario (Scenario 0) and three potential disruption scenarios. The scenarios align with the automation degrees of each use case, ensuring that the range of possible issues, from highly automated to fully manual processes, is considered.

Use case 1: EMCO MaxxTurn 45 Machining Center

- **Scenario 0: Regular operation**
  The machine undergoes standard operations including setup, NC code programming, machining, monitoring, and quality control with cobot-assisted part handling.
- **Scenario 1: Unexpected downtime**
  The machine unexpectedly stops due to an unidentified error. The operator runs diagnostics, identifies the issue, and decides on a course of action, possibly involving external support.

- **Scenario 2: Safety breach**
  The machine detects a foreign object or human in the safety zone, triggering an automatic shutdown. The operator ensures the breach is resolved before resuming operations.
- **Scenario 3: Finished parts not passing quality control**
  A finished part fails quality control. The operator investigates whether the issue is a random error or a systematic problem, halting production if necessary to troubleshoot.

Use case 2: Röders RXP601DSH Machining Center

- **Scenario 0: Regular operation**
  Similar to use case 1, the machine performs standard operations with manual part handling.
- **Scenario 1: Wrong NC code**
  During the initial check, the machine detects a syntax error in the NC code. The operator reviews and corrects the code before proceeding.
- **Scenario 2: Incorrect parameter settings**
  An incorrect feed rate is set, leading to quality issues during machining. The operator stops the machine, adjusts the parameters, and resumes operation.
- **Scenario 3: Finished parts not passing quality control**
  As in use case 1, a part fails quality control, and the operator determines whether the error is isolated or systematic, halting production if necessary.

Use case 3: Deckel FP1 Milling Machine Tool

- **Scenario 0: Regular operation**
  The machine operates manually, including setup, machining, and quality control.
- **Scenario 1: Incorrect parameter settings**
  Similar to use case 2, an incorrect parameter setting leads to quality issues. The operator stops the process, corrects the settings, and resumes machining.
- **Scenario 2: Incorrect tool selection**
  The wrong tool is selected for the operation, leading to a process stop to prevent damage. The operator corrects the tool choice and resumes the task.
- **Scenario 3: Finished parts not passing quality control**
  Identical to use case 1 and use case 2, the operator assesses the failure and determines the necessary steps to resolve the issue before resuming production.

Based on the scenarios of use, the next step involves designing a targeted questionnaire that will capture detailed insights from operators. This questionnaire will focus on the scenarios of use, providing crucial data for deriving specific system requirements. Further, HCD activities such as task-function mapping and personas will seek to complement the scenarios of use and complete the specifying the user requirements phase. These requirements will then guide the development of design solutions tailored to the needs identified in this phase. This process ensures that the system design is grounded in real-world operations, enhancing its applicability and effectiveness in industrial settings.

5 Discussion and Future Work

Once the above framework is completed, the next step is the evaluation of the system. Especially the evaluation of novel systems in manufacturing from a human-centered point of view is one of the main challenges in this process. Büttner & Röcker [8], Rasmussen & Gronbak [29] and Zigart et al. [40] point out that many investigations are conducted in laboratory settings and not with real users. They argue that results obtained from these studies are sometimes difficult to apply in real-life settings because conditions in manufacturing companies are usually much more complex than in a laboratory. Furthermore, laboratory studies often use non-experts as study participants who are not acquainted with work processes and who have no appropriate technical qualification. Büttner & Röcker [8] try to explain why, nonetheless, many studies are conducted in laboratory settings and with non-experts. They assume that there are mainly two reasons why it is difficult to conduct user studies with company employees. First, company employees usually have tight schedules and are, therefore, not available for study purposes. Evaluation methodologies like extensive user studies or more experimental approaches can interfere with work processes. Second, especially during the development stage, usability studies are not possible due to confidentiality problems.

In the literature, several different approaches are suggested. Büttner & Röcker [8] suggest a combination of reviewing existing documentation, observation with limited possibility of asking questions and inspection-based approaches. Rasmussen & Gronbak [29] used semi-structured interviews with only a few experts. Zigart et al. [40] adopted a mixed methods approach comprising a questionnaire-based quantitative survey, a quantitative process-based comparison and qualitative interviews. Interviews seem to be a method that is often used. Nevertheless, for the area of part manufacturing conducting interviews in this context might be difficult. The possibilities to support telework in part manufacturing are quite diverse and heterogeneous. Answers in such interviews, therefore, tend to be very general and contain only very abstract information. This makes it difficult to develop concrete guidelines or recommendations on how to introduce telework in part production.

Researchers from the area of User Experience (UX) suggest using contextual inquiry, a mix of interviews and observation, to identify the requirements for work processes and the advantages of the adoption of novel technologies [14]. They argue that it is not sufficient to conduct interviews because workers are often not consciously aware of requirements and possibilities of novel technologies. Observation can uncover requirements of the work processes not yet identified by stakeholders. In this context, a holistic approach should be adopted [40]. Zigart et al. propose to use multi-criteria evaluation models, encompassing economic, technical, and user related goals. They point out that many evaluation studies concerning technical systems (in their case AR and VR systems) only address very few criteria and often miss criteria relevant for practical decisions. They argue that when research is transferred from the lab to industry, an appropriate mix of different criteria have to be considered to make well-founded decision. Future work should test the practicability of this approach and check whether the information gained in this way is able to provide a foundation for concrete recommendations or guidelines for the implementation of telework in part production and similar industrial environments. In this context, aspects of human communication and collaboration should also be considered. IT-systems not designed appropriately might impede interaction between employees.

Based on the literature review and our experience so far, we would argue for using a "light-weight" approach to evaluating the implementation of collaboration tools in part manufacturing. Especially, when researching the implementation of systems with real users and in the field, this seems to be preferable to more systematic forms of investigations. Due to the high workload of employees in that area, more systematic approaches are often not feasible. A combination of reading documentations, observation, interviews and surveys seems to be indicated. This approach has to be adapted to the concrete situations researchers encounter in the field. Future research will show how this approach can be adapted to evaluation processes concerning the application of virtual collaboration tools in part manufacturing.

Acknowledgments. This work has been partly funded by the German Research Foundation (DFG) under Grant No. 505568854. Additionally, we would like to thank to all other project team members (Bernd Brenter, Taeho Kang, David Kostolani, and Sebastian Schlund) for their valuable comments and insights.

Appendix A Context-of-use questionnaire

PartRe2Work Context of Use Questionnaire

Thank you for participating the survey.

This questionnaire aims to establish the users, the task, the environment and the goals that are involved in the process of manufacturing using robots and machinery.

Our target participants are individuals who are involved in the manufacturing process, particularly those that interact with the machines in some way.

Goals

1. What is the primary objective of your primary part manufacturing processes?

   Mark only one oval.

   ◯ Ensuring high-quality
   ◯ Reduce lead time
   ◯ Reduce waste (task, production, material, etc.)
   ◯ Meeting deadlines
   ◯ Ensure continous production

2. What are specific goals while operation of a CNC/manual controlled machine tool regarding monitoring, trouble shooting, and set up processes?

Tasks

3. What would you say is your primary role in the manufacturing process?

   Mark only one oval.

   ◯ Machine operator
   ◯ Setup technician
   ◯ Maintenance technician
   ◯ Process/product engineer
   ◯ Supervisor
   ◯ Other:

4. What is your primary task regarding manufacturing, operation, monitoring of machines?

   Check all that apply.

   ☐ Milling
   ☐ Turning
   ☐ Grinding
   ☐ Assembly
   ☐ Molding
   ☐ Other:

5. What are some subtasks that you are constantly involved in?

   Check all that apply.

   ☐ Setup of machines
   ☐ Monitoring of machines
   ☐ Troubleshooting
   ☐ Supervision
   ☐ Other:

Tasks

Machine operation

6. Are you responsible for operating the machine?

   Mark only one oval.

   ◯ Yes
   ◯ No *Skip to question 13*

Tasks

Tasks while machine operation

7. Please briefly explain to us how you operate your machines and what you are doing while operation.

8. What do you particularly find inconvenient when you operate the machine (occurs very often, requires a lot of time to resolve, physically demanding, etc..), and how ? Please describe.

Tasks

Challenges while operation

9. What are the most common challenges or obstacles you encounter while operation of a ...

   Check all that apply.

	Noise and interference	Lack of feedback from machine	Material variation	Tool wear and breakage	Programming errors	Machine vibration
operation of a manual controlled machine	☐	☐	☐	☐	☐	☐
operation of a CNC controlled machine	☐	☐	☐	☐	☐	☐

10. *Check all that apply.*

	Operator error	Missing workpiece fixturing aids	Tooling setup process	Alignment issues	Machine calibration	Material selection and preparation
manual controlled machine	☐	☐	☐	☐	☐	☐
CNC controlled machine	☐	☐	☐	☐	☐	☐

11.

Check all that apply.

	Process parameter adjusting	No given procedure	No error codes	Lack of experience	Unknown correlations	Not the necessary authorization
manual controlled machine	☐	☐	☐	☐	☐	☐
CNC controlled machine	☐	☐	☐	☐	☐	☐

12.

Check all that apply.

	Required help is not provided	Unavailability of relevant process parameters	Overload on information	Data collection and analysis	Material clamping and fixturing	Physically work with heavy objects
manual controlled machine	☐	☐	☐	☐	☐	☐
CNC controlled machine	☐	☐	☐	☐	☐	☐

Tasks

Manual effort

13. **Are there any tasks that require significant manual effort or are prone to errors?**

Check all that apply.

	Monitoring chip formation	Quality incspection/assurance	Ensuring proper alignment, fixturing, and clamping	Machine condition monitoring	Emergency situations
Options	☐	☐	☐	☐	☐

14.

Check all that apply.

	Workpiece inspection	Tool inspection	Tool changes	Workpiece and tool measuring	Workpiece clamping
Options	☐	☐	☐	☐	☐

15.

Check all that apply.

	Physical inspection of machine	Program verification	Fluid and lubricant checks	Zero point calibration	Safety checks
Options	☐	☐	☐	☐	☐

Tasks

Troubleshooting

16.

If there are issues with the machine or process, how do you solve it?

Mark only one oval.

- ◯ I call my supervisor *Skip to question 18*
- ◯ I call technical support *Skip to question 18*
- ◯ I perform an initial troubleshooting to see if I can fix it, if not, I call support
- ◯ Other: ____________

Tasks

Tasks while troubleshooting

17. **What troubleshooting measures are you doing?**

____

Tasks

Troubleshooting

18. **When someone else performs the troubleshooting, how is it done?**

Mark only one oval.

- ◯ The troubleshooter is on site, and takes over
- ◯ The Troubleshooter gives instructions or helps via phone call without camera
- ◯ The Troubleshooter person gives instructions or helps via video chat / use of a camera
- ◯ I don't know
- ◯ Other: ____________

19. **What do you particularly find inconvenient while troubleshooting (occurs very often, requires a lot of time to resolve, physically demanding, etc..), and how ? Please describe.**

____

Tasks

20.

Are there any other tasks in your day-to-day work that are not mentioned yet?

____

Environment

21. **Choose all keywords that describe your working environment.**

Check all that apply.

- [ ] Indoor
- [ ] Spacious open space
- [ ] Environmental control (temperature, humidity, ...)
- [ ] Low Temperature (0-)
- [ ] Personal protective equipment required
- [ ] No human in vicinity allowed during operation
- [ ] High noise
- [ ] Low visibility
- [ ] Outdoor
- [ ] High dust
- [ ] High Temperature (30+)
- [ ] Metalworking industry
- [ ] Woodworking industry
- [ ] Plastic processing industry

22. **Within your team, how many people do you work with?**

Mark only one oval.

- ◯ Only me
- ◯ 2-5 people
- ◯ 5-10 people
- ◯ 10-50 people
- ◯ 50+ people

23. **How many machines are you responsible for?**

Mark only one oval.

- ◯ 1
- ◯ 2-5
- ◯ 6-10
- ◯ 10+

24. **On a scale of 1 to 5, how automated would you say the following aspects of your manufacturing process at work are?**

Mark only one oval per row.

	1 - Completely manual	2	3	4	5 - Fully automated
Overall operation of the machine	◯	◯	◯	◯	◯
Product quality monitoring	◯	◯	◯	◯	◯
Troubleshooting	◯	◯	◯	◯	◯
Setup and preparation	◯	◯	◯	◯	◯
Loading of materials and unloading of products	◯	◯	◯	◯	◯
Cleanup	◯	◯	◯	◯	◯
Machine state (parts, tools) monitoring	◯	◯	◯	◯	◯
Safety detection (obstruction, foreign material)	◯	◯	◯	◯	◯

25. **How satisfied are you with the state of how things are automated? Think about how convenient it is for you, specifically relating to automation.**

Mark only one oval per row.

	1 - Not satisfied at all	2	3 - Neutral	4	5 - Completely satisfied
Overall operation of the machine	◯	◯	◯	◯	◯
Product quality monitoring	◯	◯	◯	◯	◯
Troubleshooting	◯	◯	◯	◯	◯
Setup and preparation	◯	◯	◯	◯	◯
Loading of materials and unloading of products	◯	◯	◯	◯	◯
Cleanup	◯	◯	◯	◯	◯
Machine state (parts, tools) monitoring	◯	◯	◯	◯	◯
Safety detection (obstruction, foreign material)	◯	◯	◯	◯	◯

26. **On a scale of 1 to 5, how reliable are the machines and equipment you work with?**
Reliable machines hardly break down, and cause very little disruptions to your work.
Unreliable machines frequently have issues, and unforseen errors happen very often.

Mark only one oval per row.

	1 - Not reliable at all	2	3	4	5 - Very reliable	Can't say, I dont use them
Overall machinery	◯	◯	◯	◯	◯	◯
Tool parts of the machine	◯	◯	◯	◯	◯	◯
Consumable parts of the machine	◯	◯	◯	◯	◯	◯
Machine control software	◯	◯	◯	◯	◯	◯
Automation systems (e.g. assembly robots, automated tool feeder)	◯	◯	◯	◯	◯	◯
Monitoring systems/software	◯	◯	◯	◯	◯	◯
Quality measurement tools	◯	◯	◯	◯	◯	◯
Hardware interaction interfaces	◯	◯	◯	◯	◯	◯
CAD/CAM software for machine set up	◯	◯	◯	◯	◯	◯

27. Choose one of the aspects from the previous question that you are particularly unsatisfied with. What are the main challenges for improving the automation degree?

28. What safety measures are needed in your working environment?

Check all that apply.

- [ ] Standard protective clothing (e.g. Gloves)
- [ ] Specialized protective clothing (e.g. Heat protection suit)
- [ ] Protective equipment (e.g. Protective fence)
- [ ] Repetive trainings
- [ ] Permanent supervision
- [ ] One-time supervision
- [ ] Other:

User

29. What is your age?

Mark only one oval.

- 19 or below
- 20 to 29
- 30 to 39
- 40 to 49
- 50 to 59
- over 60

30. What is the highest level of education you have received?

Mark only one oval.

- School degree
- Vocational training
- Technican
- Bachelor Professional
- Bachelor
- Master Professional
- Master
- Doctorate

31. How much experience do you have in your field?

Mark only one oval.

- Less than one year
- 1 - 5 years
- 6-10 years
- 11-15 years
- 15+ years

32. On a scale of 1 to 5, how familiar are you with the following technology?

Mark only one oval per row.

	1 - Not familiar at all	2 - Vargue aware of the concept	3 - Learned the basics	4 - Learned more thaan the basics	5 - Very familiar
State-of-the-art manufacturing technology of your field	◯	◯	◯	◯	◯
HCI technology like VR, AR, XR	◯	◯	◯	◯	◯
Automated sensing of machines and materials	◯	◯	◯	◯	◯
Collaborative robotics	◯	◯	◯	◯	◯
Intelligent machines	◯	◯	◯	◯	◯
Remote operation of machines	◯	◯	◯	◯	◯

33. How familiar would you say you at using the following devices? On a scale of 1 to 5, with 1 being completely unfamiliar, and 5 being very familiar.

Mark only one oval per row.

	1 - I don't know how to use them	2 - I know somewhat how to use them	3 - I know enough how to use them for common tasks	4 - I know enough to be able to use them for work	5 - I am an advanced user
PC / Laptop (Keyboard and Mouse)	◯	◯	◯	◯	◯
Smartphone and touch screen devices	◯	◯	◯	◯	◯
Virtual reality headsets and glasses	◯	◯	◯	◯	◯

References

1. Accenture: Covid-19: Adapting manufacturing operations to new normal (2020). https://www.accenture.com/ro-en/insights/consulting/coronavirus-supply-chain-manufacturing-operations
2. Adams, J.A.: Multiple robot/single human interaction: effects on perceived workload. Behav. Inf. Technol. **28**(2), 183–198 (2009). https://doi.org/10.1080/01449290701288791
3. Ahmed, F., Zviedrite, N., Uzicanin, A.: Effectiveness of workplace social distancing measures in reducing influenza transmission: a systematic review. BMC Public Health **18**(1), 518 (2018). https://doi.org/10.1186/s12889-018-5446-1
4. Álvares, A.J., Ferreira, J.: WebTurning: teleoperation of a CNC turning center through the internet. J. Mater. Process. Technol. **179**(1–3), 251–259 (2006). https://doi.org/10.1016/j.jmatprotec.2006.03.096
5. Alves, J.B., Marques, B., Dias, P., Santos, B.S.: Using augmented reality for industrial quality assurance: a shop floor user study. Int. J. Adv. Manuf. Technol. **115**, 105–116 (2021). https://doi.org/10.1007/s00170-021-07049-8
6. Bailey, R.W.: Human Performance Engineering: Using Human Factors/ergonomics to Achieve Computer Systems Usability, 2nd edn. Prentice Hall International Paperback Editions, Hoboken (1991)
7. Bottecchia, S., Cieutat, J.M., Merlo, C., Jessel, J.P.: A new AR interaction paradigm for collaborative teleassistance system: the POA. Int. J. Interact. Des. Manuf. (IJIDeM) **3**(1), 35–40 (2009). https://doi.org/10.1007/s12008-008-0051-7
8. Büttner, S., Röcker, C.: Applying human-centered design methods in industry - a field report (2016). https://doi.org/10.24406/publica-fhg-395028, https://publica.fraunhofer.de/handle/publica/395028
9. European Commission: Households with broadband access (15042020). https://ec.europa.eu/eurostat/databrowser/view/tin00073/default/bar
10. European Commission: Telework in the EU before and after the COVID-19: Where we are, where we head to (2020). https://ec.europa.eu/jrc/sites/jrcsh/files/jrc120945_policy_brief_-_covid_and_telework_final.pdf. Accessed 07 Aug 2023
11. Gergle, D., Kraut, R.E., Fussell, S.R.: Using visual information for grounding and awareness in collaborative tasks. Human-Comput. Interact. **28**(1), 1–39 (2013). https://doi.org/10.1080/07370024.2012.678246
12. Groover, M.P.: Automation, Production Systems, and Computer-integrated Manufacturing, 5th edn. New York, Pearson (2018)
13. Gurevich, P., Lanir, J., Cohen, B.: Design and implementation of TeleAdvisor: a projection-based augmented reality system for remote collaboration. Comput. Support. Coop. Work (CSCW) **24**(6), 527–562 (2015). https://doi.org/10.1007/s10606-015-9232-7
14. Hartson, R., Pyla, P.: The UX Book: Process and Guidelines for Ensuring a Quality User Experience, 1st edn. Morgan Kaufmann Publishers Inc., San Francisco (2012)
15. ISO: Ergonomics of human-system interaction - Part 210: Human-centred design for interactive systems. Standard, International Organization for Standardization, July 2019
16. Johansen, R.: Groupware: Leading business teams (1991)
17. Khan, T.K., Schworm, P., Glatt, M.F., Ugoji, C., Ebert, A., Aurich, J.C.: Engaging human-centered design to maintain part manufacturing under reduced workforce restrictions. Prod. Eng. Res. Dev. **18**, 733–750 (2024). https://doi.org/10.1007/s11740-024-01275-1

18. Kluge, A., Termer, A.: Human-centered design (HCD) of a fault-finding application for mobile devices and its impact on the reduction of time in fault diagnosis in the manufacturing industry. Appl. Ergon. **59**(Pt A), 170–181 (2017). https://doi.org/10.1016/j.apergo.2016.08.030
19. Liu, H., Wang, L.: Remote human-robot collaboration: a cyber-physical system application for hazard manufacturing environment. J. Manuf. Syst. **54**, 24–34 (2020). https://doi.org/10.1016/j.jmsy.2019.11.001
20. Maguire, M.: Methods to support human-centred design. Int. J. Hum. Comput. Stud. **55**(4), 587–634 (2001). https://doi.org/10.1006/ijhc.2001.0503, https://www.sciencedirect.com/science/article/pii/S1071581901905038
21. Mayer, A., Combe, T., Chardonnet, J.R., Ovtcharova, J.: Asynchronous manual work in mixed reality remote collaboration. In: De Paolis, L.T., Arpaia, P., Sacco, M. (eds.) Extended Reality, pp. 17–33. Springer Nature Switzerland, Cham (2022). https://doi.org/10.1007/978-3-031-15553-6_2
22. Mori, M., Fujishima, M.: Remote monitoring and maintenance system for CNC machine tools. Procedia CIRP **12**, 7–12 (2013). https://doi.org/10.1016/j.procir.2013.09.003
23. Mourtzis, D., Vlachou, A., Zogopoulos, V.: Cloud-based augmented reality remote maintenance through shop-floor monitoring: a product-service system approach. J. Manuf. Sci. Eng. **139**(6), 061011 (2017). https://doi.org/10.1115/1.4035721
24. Nelles, J., Kuz, S., Mertens, A., Schlick, C.M.: Human-centered design of assistance systems for production planning and control: The role of the human in industry 4.0. In: 2016 IEEE International Conference on Industrial Technology (ICIT), pp. 2099–2104. IEEE (2016). https://doi.org/10.1109/ICIT.2016.7475093
25. Norberto López de Lacalle, L., Campa, F.J., Lamikiz, A.: Milling. In: Davim, J.P. (ed.) Modern Machining Technology, pp. 213–303. Elsevier (2011). https://doi.org/10.1533/9780857094940.213
26. Occupational Safety and Health Administration: Covid-19 guidance for the manufacturing industry workforce (2020). https://www.osha.gov/Publications/OSHA4002.pdf
27. Oliveira, L., Álvares, A.J.: Axiomatic design applied to the development of a system for monitoring and teleoperation of a CNC machine through the internet. Procedia CIRP **53**, 198–205 (2016). https://doi.org/10.1016/j.procir.2016.06.099
28. Oliveira, M., Arica, E., Pinzone, M., Fantini, P., Taisch, M.: Human-centered manufacturing challenges affecting European industry 4.0 enabling technologies. In: Stephanidis, C. (ed.) HCII 2019. LNCS, vol. 11786, pp. 507–517. Springer, Cham (2019). https://doi.org/10.1007/978-3-030-30033-3_39
29. Rasmussen, T.A., Gronbak, K.: Tailorable remote assistance with RemoteAssistKit: a study of and design response to remote assistance in the manufacturing industry. In: Nakanishi, H., Egi, H., Chounta, I.-A., Takada, H., Ichimura, S., Hoppe, U. (eds.) CRIWG+CollabTech 2019. LNCS, vol. 11677, pp. 80–95. Springer, Cham (2019). https://doi.org/10.1007/978-3-030-28011-6_6
30. Rogowski, A.M.: Remote programming and control of the flexible machining cell. Int. J. Comput. Integr. Manuf. **28**(6), 650–663 (2015). https://doi.org/10.1080/0951192X.2014.900862
31. Römer, T., Bruder, R.: User centered design of a cyber-physical support solution for assembly processes. Procedia Manuf. **3**, 456–463 (2015). https://doi.org/10.1016/j.promfg.2015.07.208

32. Rumsey, A., Le Dantec, C.A.: Manufacturing change: the impact of virtual environments on real organizations. In: Proceedings of the 2020 CHI Conference on Human Factors in Computing Systems, pp. 1–12. CHI 2020, Association for Computing Machinery, New York, NY, USA (2020). https://doi.org/10.1145/3313831.3376535
33. Sekine, K., Arai, K., Sekine, K.: Kaizen for Quick Changeover: Going Beyond SMED. Productivity Press, Cambridge [nachdr.] edn. (2011)
34. Stavropoulos, P., Chantzis, D., Doukas, C., Papacharalampopoulos, A., Chryssolouris, G.: Monitoring and control of manufacturing processes: a review. Procedia CIRP **8**, 421–425 (2013). https://doi.org/10.1016/j.procir.2013.06.127
35. Vorraber, W., Gasser, J., Webb, H., Neubacher, D., Url, P.: Assessing augmented reality in production: remote-assisted maintenance with HoloLens. Procedia CIRP **88**, 139–144 (2020). https://doi.org/10.1016/j.procir.2020.05.025
36. Wang, L., Orban, P., Cunningham, A., Lang, S.: Remote real-time CNC machining for web-based manufacturing. Robot. Comput. Integr. Manuf. **20**(6), 563–571 (2004). https://doi.org/10.1016/j.rcim.2004.07.007
37. Warnecke, H.J.: Der Produktionsbetrieb 2: Produktion, Produktionssicherung. Springer-Lehrbuch, Springer Berlin Heidelberg, Berlin, Heidelberg, zweite, völlig neubearbeitete auflage edn. (1993). https://doi.org/10.1007/978-3-642-97446-5
38. Weck, M., Brecher, C.: Werkzeugmaschinen 4: Automatisierung von Maschinen und Anlagen. VDI-Buch, Springer-Verlag Berlin Heidelberg, Berlin, Heidelberg, 6., neu bearbeitete auflage edn. (2006). https://doi.org/10.1007/978-3-540-45366-6
39. WZL: Auqua: Augmented intelligence based quality assurance of assembly tasks in global value networks (2020). http://auqua.wzl.rwth-aachen.de/en/default.html
40. Zigart, T., Kormann-Hainzl, G., Lovasz-Bukvova, H., Hölzl, M., Moser, T., Schlund, S.: From lab to industry: lessons learned from the evaluation of augmented and virtual reality use cases in the Austrian manufacturing industry. Product. Manuf. Res. **11**(1), 2286345 (2023). https://doi.org/10.1080/21693277.2023.2286345

Rendering Realities with XR Technologies - Opportunities and Challenges to Create Experiences

Danzhu Li[1,2](✉) and Gerrit van der Veer[1,3]

[1] Luxun Academy of Fine Arts (LAFA), Liaoning, China
lidanzhu@me.com
[2] University of Twente, Enschede, Netherlands
[3] Vrije Universiteit Amsterdam, Amsterdam, Netherlands

Abstract. This paper explores the integration of visual and auditory perception in real and virtual contexts, emphasizing the need for synchronized soundscapes in artistic experiences. It highlights the advancements in XR technologies (VR, AR, MR) and their impact on sensory experiences, particularly in dynamic visual arts. This study promotes a holistic approach to art, integrating multi-sensory inputs to enhance engagement and inclusivity, and explores the artistic possibilities supported by multimodal XR technologies.

Keywords: Experience · XR (VR · AR · MR...) Technologies · Visual Arts · Human Perception · Interactive Art · Audience Engagement · Perceptual Stimuli · Aesthetic Values · Immersive Audio · Multi-sensory Art

1 Introduction

In recent years, the game industry and film industry are the most active in the development of XR (VR, AR, MR...) technology. The authors use XR or Multi-Modal R technologies to encapsulate the emergence of various Reality-based technologies, including but not limited to Virtual Reality, Augmented Reality, and Mixed Reality. We observe a developing trend in contemporary visual arts towards interactivity, customization, and even integration with emerging technologies. Among many senses, vision and hearing currently are the most common research subjects. The development of technology is gradual, as in XR technology, after the visual development gradually matured, sound began to be valued as an important perception. Then there is we expect a future use of touch, smell, taste and so on. Art is not merely a visual or auditory perception, it encapsulates a broader, holistic experience that engages multiple cognitive and emotional processes. Drawing from cognitive psychology and ergonomics, this paper discusses how human perception, triggered by sensory stimuli and cognitive processes, leads to a state of "experience" that includes understanding, emotion, valuation, and the tendency to act (Sect. 2). When we encounter art, this interaction results in a multi-layered experience where perception drives a deeper cognitive response. The holistic nature of

L. Zaina et al. (Eds.): EICS 2024, LNCS 15518, pp. 210–223, 2025.
https://doi.org/10.1007/978-3-031-91760-8_14

experience, particularly in the context of art, involves a complex interplay of understanding, emotions, values, and actions. Individuals engage with art not just by perceiving it, but by attributing meaning, reacting emotionally, and positioning the artwork within their personal aesthetic, cultural, and social frameworks. This is true across all art-related activities, including creation, exhibition, and interaction (Sect. 3).

Furthermore, the understanding of the world or art is framed within the context of personal experience, shaped by attention to agents and the surrounding environment (referred to as the backcloth). In artistic experiences, agents and props take on dynamic roles, becoming focal points or fading into the background based on their relevance to the viewer's immediate context. Art, by its very nature, seeks to elicit these profound experiences, making it both a sensory and cognitive journey for the observer. As this paper explores, understanding how art triggers and shapes experience is essential for appreciating the depth of human interaction with creative works. In Sect. 4, we explore the experiences and challenges of integrating modern art with multimodal R technologies and multisensory technologies through the examination of several classic cases.

2 Experiencing Art is More Than Perception

2.1 Human Perception Enables Experience – a Holistic Phenomenon

Cognitive Psychology and Cognitive Ergonomics taught us that cognitive mental processes (attention, understanding, feeling, information procession, remembering, intention, decision making) are triggered by perception of stimuli that appear to a human by activating the human senses (vision, hearing, smell, taste, pressure, pain, temperature, etc.) as well as by the results of cognitive processes (memories, expectations, fears, needs, decisions, etc.) [1].

Perception may result in an "active" cognitive state that may have characteristics like being aware of what is perceived, attributing meaning, paying attention, focusing or avoiding, and interacting with (elements in) the outside world.

We label this state: Experience is a holistic phenomenon [2] that consists of 4 aspects of the reaction of an individual in relation to a work of art:

a. Understanding: meaning attributed to the perceived stimulus in the current context and needs, including sensual input (internally seeing, hearing, tasting,... Even if there may not be an actual physical stimulus of the related sense);
b. Emotions: feelings, attributed to the content of piece of art or to encountering it, e.g., active vs. passive; pleasant vs. unpleasant, [3];
c. Values: valuation of the artwork (it content, its makers, its message, all in relation to the individual's esthetical, political, religious, and cultural values) that leads to being more or less attracted vs. appalled;
d. Tendency to Act (e.g., to memorize, focus, avoid, interact,...)

Experience, as we discuss it in this paper, is relevant in art-related situations and relevant for all aspects of a "production" and "consumption "of art (design, construction, buying and selling, performance, participation), if:

- it is perceived (it has an appearance) or is referred to;

- allows reaction (including rejection, observation, appreciation, and/or possible interaction);
- and in some way is understood (a function or meaning is attributed to it).

2.2 The Cognitive Aspect of Experiencing is Understanding the World

Understanding a current stimulus in the world, or art, means in a holistic sense being aware of "what is going on", where we currently choose to point our attention to: the story, the discourse, the perceived state/need/question/challenge, the re-action considered or intended (including focusing/waiting/enjoying/ignoring); and being aware of "the context" – one's personal situation (including relevant needs or the lack of them) and the environment, which includes agents, props, and backcloth. Significant (potentially interacting) agents (e.g., people, vehicles, ICT) receive attention whenever we are interacting, considering interaction, or challenged to interact.

E.g., when walking on the pavement, we may understand a car is slowing down beside us (a sudden change in the movement of the scenery) and making a hooting sound (a sudden change in the soundscape). Or our screen "tells" us (by a sound, or by opening a small text screen) that we have an appointment 15 min from now. Agents (entities that we identify because we notice their activity) are perceived to stand out against the Backcloth, even if in some situations their visibility or audibility is not optimal. A perceived change of their state will trigger action, like moving the head, focusing the eyes, mentally inspecting the triggered sensory memory ("what did I hear just now?"), or actively changing the backcloth or the contrast between agent and backcloth (grasping a binocular or flashlight, changing the sound level of the computer, or closing the curtain), or hitting the OK button.

The backcloth, in understanding the world, is the environment that is available for perception, but currently not the focus of attention:

a. The visual Scenery: The landscape that is visible in front of me during a walk, which changes when I turn my head, including agents when I am not focusing on them. The scenery includes my visual input of the dancing crowd around me when I am attending an open-air concert and focusing on the performance on stage. I am aware of the scenery, but I am not currently paying attention to any details. When I am interacting through my 27-in. screen, the scenery is mainly whatever is rendered there. On the background picture of my choice, many icons are visible showing available objects and apps, and several windows are open where I could choose to read or act. Most of this, however, is currently just scenery when I am editing my text in a selected window, as long as I continue to face my screen. When I am wearing my VR headset, the scenery is supposed to change whenever I move my head, but if I am focusing on a specific object or avatar, the scenery is just there, changing as I could expect in relation to my movements.
b. The Soundscape: sounds that reach my ears at the current position of my head, though I am not focusing my attention to. Like the scenery, the soundscape changes whenever I move my head. This may include the noise of the wind during my walk at the countryside, the sound caused by the sheep and the birds, the ticking of my clock when I am working in my living room, and the soft melodies played by a student of my wife on her clavichord in the next room. I am aware of all of this, but currently I

have chosen to attend to other things. When behind my screen, even the sounds caused by me typing or moving my mouse at the drawing board is part of the soundscape, but when I am currently using a screen reader, the text pronounced is the focus of attention.

Elements of the backcloth may suddenly reach attention and change the experienced world: A ticking clock in my living room is generally part of the soundscape. But when its percussion stops, the sudden change of a rather stable element in my home sound scape calls my attention, and it even may wake me up. E.g., When my clock strikes the hours, it steps forward from the soundscape, and it triggers me to count: "4, 5, 6, 7" – and I will be happy that a visual check confirms my counts: The act of paying attention started the counting at the correct moment, when the soundtrack of the first couple of strikes in the auditory memory started decaying. When the music student next door hits a wrong key and replays the note, I am distracted by the sudden changing number of beats in the bar, though I did not record the incorrect note. When I seem to hear steps at the garden path, I become alert to possible signals from the hallway, expecting, either a signal by the doorbell, or the clatter from the mailbox lid.

2.3 Art Aims at Triggering Experiences

Experience is a main goal of artistic artifacts: products (tangible and intangible pieces of art that one may design, produce, sell, donate, own, or keep) and services (intangible experiences or treatments that one may offer, provide, or enjoy).

Experiencing art includes visual/audible/tactile/smell/taste/etc. aspects of works of art: performances; visits in a gallery or museum; writing or reading a script, music score, or design sketch; etc., as well creating or wearing costumes, make-up, and jewelry. Aiming at experience, a script for a performance may include the explicit design of facial expressions [4], posture [5], movement and gestures [6];

Redirecting attention in the experience of arts may occur by agents (human, or machines) playing their part according to the story, the script, the music score, or improvising. In interactive art, agents may in fact be (part of) the audience.

Props (objects, perceivable information) are part of the backcloth if they do not receive attention as part of an action or interaction but may be considered relevant elements in the current world, or agents, when they trigger attention.

3 Modern Art is a Living Phenomenon

Contemporary visual art is applying a variety of rich technical means to attract the audience, aim at experiences, or even let them co-create [7]. Galleries and museums tend to provide multi-sensory experiences and interactivity. Recent advancements in Cognitive and Computer sciences, along with new technological opportunities, have expanded these experiences from limited auditory and visual communication to dynamic interactive contexts like virtual reality and multimodal realities, incorporating multimedia displays such as sound, touch, smell, and taste.

Traditional painting, sculpting, and film are increasingly unable to satisfy the demands of the contemporary market and are being replaced by a blend of multiple elements. More artists are adopting new technologies and tools, engaging in interdisciplinary collaboration, and aiming to communicate and interact with their stakeholders through their artworks, thereby fostering various new cultural phenomena. The main goal is to enhance the experience. Understanding this shift can help stakeholders in the art world contribute to the future of art ecology [8].

3.1 Experience with Art

Contemporary dynamic audio-visual art includes diverse forms such as film, drama, animation, games, interactive and installation art, and digital art. These art forms share common principles focused on captivating and engaging audiences. In recent years, there have been significant advancements in artistic creation within the visual art domain. Film, in particular, stands out as the most representative medium, with a well-established industrial chain, mature processes, and vibrant performances. [9]. For all traditional art forms, we might state that a distinctive aspect of it is the intention of one human being (e.g., the "artist") to provide an artifact (and frequently a situation to go with it) that solicits some experience in other humans.

Artists are generally aware of the fact that they cannot dictate the aesthetic experience, but they have some aim, and they use their skills and knowledge to reach that aim. The artist elicits specific perceptions by triggering certain sensations or employing metaphors, metonymy, and hints through audio-visual language. The objective is to engage the psychological phenomena of emotions, imagination, and associations in the recipient (the audience or experiencer), influencing their interests and interactive responses. The audience's examination, taste, understanding, and responses to art constitute a holistic experiential process that encompasses sensory, cognitive, emotional, and practical aspects.

3.2 Cultural Diversity and Aesthetic Experience

Appreciating artworks from different cultures requires understanding their unique cultural norms. British cinema excels in drama, influenced by its rich dramatic heritage, while Indian films are known for lengthy narratives and musical sequences. Cultural genes, like genres (the "DNA" in artworks) deeply shape expression across forms like painting, sculpture, architecture, and dynamic visual art. For example, in film and animation production, from inception: storytelling, scriptwriting and storyboarding, cultural elements set the work's foundational tone. Artists blend personal experiences with adaptations, recorded in scripts, sketches, or storyboards, reflecting their perspectives.

The mastery of storyboarding, marked by specific terms and symbols, is essential for key stakeholders such as directors and concept animators. For instance, in the animated film "Legend of the Universe" (Fig. 1), the incorporation of traditional Chinese decorative painting was influenced by both the cultural background of the script (based on ancient Chinese mythology) and the artistic training of the co-creators in decorative painting techniques at art school. This ensured coherence in the film's aesthetic elements such as color palette, rhythm, motion, and soundtrack. However, viewers from different cultural contexts may interpret the film differently, depending on their familiarity with Chinese traditional culture.

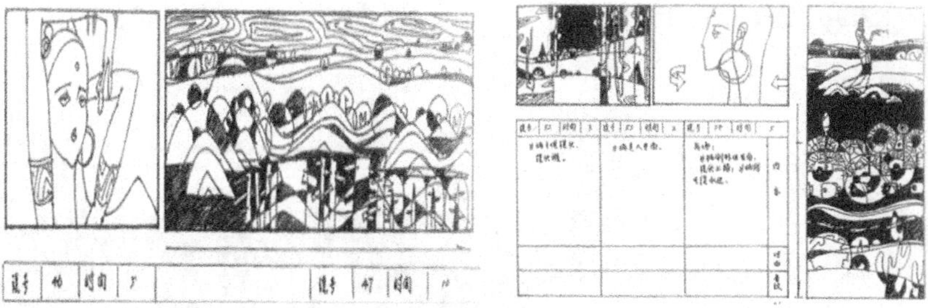

Fig. 1. Storyboard of animated film "Legend of the Universe". Image by courtesy of Luxun Academy of Fine Arts.

Art exhibitions held during specific cultural contexts often require visitors to possess a foundational understanding of artistic traditions to fully appreciate the exhibited works. Alternatively, the exhibition might aim at providing new cultural understanding to "foreign" visitors, by not only showcasing the technical aspects of painting but also aim to convey cultural narratives and aesthetic sensibilities that otherwise only resonate deeply with knowledgeable viewers. This selective approach ensures that the audience's experience is enriched by their cultural background and artistic insights, highlighting the importance of expertise in shaping meaningful encounters with art.

When artists are mindful of cultural constraints, they can create works that reflect and respect cultural diversity, leading to the emergence of innovative styles and languages in art. Figure 2 illustrates a multilingual presentation during a Sichuan opera show, demonstrating an approach: by incorporating multiple languages, the performance seeks to appeal to a broader audience, bridging cultural gaps and enriching the audience's understanding of the opera's narrative and cultural significance. Authors in this paper have the experienced and appreciated local performances in Russia, the Czech Republic, Catalonia, and China, though our language portfolio is Dutch or Chinese, and English. We understood the plot, sometimes just from the performance (choreography, emotional expression, body language, costumes, sound, rhythm and intonation), sometimes enriched by subtitles on auxiliary screens.

This way, theaters may serve a multicultural audience, and local art forms are experienced and recognized across cultures. Increasingly, this approach also appears in movies, TV and video demonstrations nowadays. The new opportunities of interactive environments, including Virtual presence, may allow additional support for a multicultural audience, by providing selective control based on eye tracking or movement tracking and other rich technological means.

3.3 Scenes, Spaces, and Dimensions: Their Impact on the Artistic Experience

In contemporary art, three narrative modes exist: static, dynamic, and interactive narration. Each technique offers diverse expressions, capable of evoking various experiences. Presentations and viewing take place in distinct scenes and spaces, ranging from physical environments to virtual contexts. Artists employ different techniques and tools to convey scenes, spaces, and dimensions, with science and technology providing novel opportunities.

Fig. 2. Screens at both sides of the stage display subtitles in Chinese, English Japanese, Korean. Pictures by the first author.

Static Narration. Static narration in art has a long history of conveying time, space, environment, emotions, and values through various elements such as scenes, props, colors, composition, light and shade, perspective, and expressions. This is evident in art forms like painting, sculpture, architecture, and still photography.

The artist's unique handwriting, brushstrokes, and texture are also essential components of expression. For instance, in Chinese painting, the foreground is depicted using dark and thick ink with heavy brushwork, while light ink and brushwork suggest depth and distance, creating rhythmic changes in spatial intensity (Fig. 3).

The viewing experience also offers a means to experience spatial and scene changes. In traditional Chinese scroll painting, for instance, as the scroll is unfurled, viewers can observe the timeline of the story or spatial clues within the scene. The expanding canvas enables viewers to experience scenery and landscape transformations within the artwork [10].

Fig. 3. Animation Short Film - "Desire" (Computer Graphic simulation of Ink Painting) from the School of Media Animation, Luxun Academy of Fine Arts.

Dynamic Narration. With technological advancements, narrative methods have expanded from text and static picture sequences to dynamic and interactive formats. Art forms like film, drama and animation now utilize dynamic and interactive language to engage the audience [11].

Dynamic narrative encompasses several factors, including cinematographic movements (e.g., zoom, pan, follow), editing techniques (shot assembly, montage language), performances (action, emotion, actor's lines), and the use of subtitles and sound (music, sound effects, voice over). These elements collectively contribute to the engaging and evolving nature of dynamic narration.

Scenes are crucial in dynamic narratives, especially in filmmaking. Scenes contribute to the storyline, artistic style, and cultural context, and serve as symbols or metaphors for character and plot development.

Props depicting character traits or providing crucial plot clues. In static narratives like oil paintings, props can be central, while in dynamic narratives, they serve as ongoing clues, as seen in the French film "The Red Balloon," where the balloon guides the plot.

Computer graphics are increasingly used for scene rendering and prop modeling in movies and games.

Costumes and makeup reflect cultural background, character traits, and emotions, often using metaphors.

Performance is key in dynamic arts, with actors using voice, body, and movement to convey emotion and information.

Sound enhances dynamic narration, contributing to the rendering of the space and dimensions of the scene (echo), signifying props (clock ticking, weather, movement of water and vegetation. Sound effects like music over may contribute to emotional, cultural, and historical awareness, and tone, volume and rhythm of voice are explicit narration forms, intended to affect the audience's understanding and response.

Interactive Narration

Interactive performances and media offer new possibilities for audience engagement, allow the audience (as a temporary group in a theater space or as individuals) to move through scenes or story, to provide feedback, and to make choices. This interactive narrative relies on technology to facilitate audience-story interaction, enabling features such as audience behavior perception, analysis, and information feedback [12].

4 Exploring Multimodal R Technology in Contemporary Visual Art: Unprecedented Experiences, Creativity, and Challenges

This section aims to explore the potential of technology in supporting multimodal interactive art, with a particular focus on the application of XR technology in rendering both reality and augmented reality in the realm of art.

4.1 Revolutionizing Entertainment Experience: Evolution of Theater, Film, and Gaming

The integration of new technologies revolutionized the way we experience theater, film, and gaming. Audiences are no longer passive spectators but active participants in immersive with interactive narratives. This shift in experience has led to changes in **storytelling**, **scriptwriting**, and audience engagement (**tendency to act**) (see Sect. 3).

Theater spaces like "Unique Henan - Land of Drama" offer multidimensional experiences where the audience becomes part of the performance. Participants can choose different paths, make decisions, and engage with the narrative in a personalized way (https://themindcircle.com/unique-henan-land-of-drama/). Similarly, films like "VR Noir-A Day Before the Night" merge cinema, gaming, and virtual reality, allowing audiences to assume **roles** and shape the **story** through their choices (Fig. 4).

Fig. 4. VR Noir-A Day Before the Night. Source: official website [13].

4.2 Integration of Multi-sensory Artistic Creation and Multi-modal R Technology

The MSG Sphere Las Vegas is a spherical immersive experience center (https://www.thespherevegas.com/science). This technological marvel not only enhances the visual aspect but also integrates an advanced acoustic system (**Soundscape**) utilizing "beam-forming technology", and infrasound tactile systems, to envelop the audience with a truly immersive experience. Moreover, the venue incorporates a customized olfactory system, releasing scents that correspond to different themes (**Scenery & Backcloth**), adding yet another dimension to the audience's sensory involvement.

Practitioners in electronic music have always been developing new instrument forms to fully explore the possibilities of their new electronic medium [14]. Michel Waisvisz, a Dutch composer and inventor, created "The Hands," a pioneering electronic musical instrument in the 1980s. The device allowed him to control electronic music through hand gestures, using sensors to manipulate sound in real-time. This innovative instrument blended music with movement, making his performances highly expressive (Fig. 5). "The Hands" had a significant impact on live electronic music, influencing future developments in the field. Figures 6, 7, and 8 show the design of different versions of "The Hands," a device consisting of two handheld controllers strapped to Waisvisz's hands. Equipped with sensors like accelerometers, pressure sensors, and switches, these controllers detect hand movements and convert them into data that controls various sound parameters, such as pitch, volume, and effects. This input is processed in real-time to produce sound output, enabling the performer to dynamically shape the music through an interactive feedback loop. These interactive installations empower artists as well as interacting participants to engage with the (possibly even multimodal) representation of their actions, encouraging them to reconsider their creation in real time.

Fig. 5. A video recording of Michel Waisvisz performing live with the electronic instrument "The Hands." Filmed by the author at the Nieuwe Instituut in Rotterdam, Netherlands.

Fig. 6. The electronic instrument "The Hands." Filmed by the author at the Nieuwe Instituut in Rotterdam, Netherlands.

Another example is the "Synesthesia Machine", where technology merges visual and olfactory experiences (Fig. 9.) By analyzing the audience's expressions and triggering the release of different scents, this experiment exemplifies the evolving possibilities for perceptual interactions in art. Wearable devices supporting olfactory experience have been adopted in artistic creation like the " FeelReal virtual-reality mask "(Fig. 10.).

Fig. 7. Components of "the Hands": ultrasonic receivers, ultrasonic transmitter, pitch keys, pressure sensors and so on. Filmed by the author.

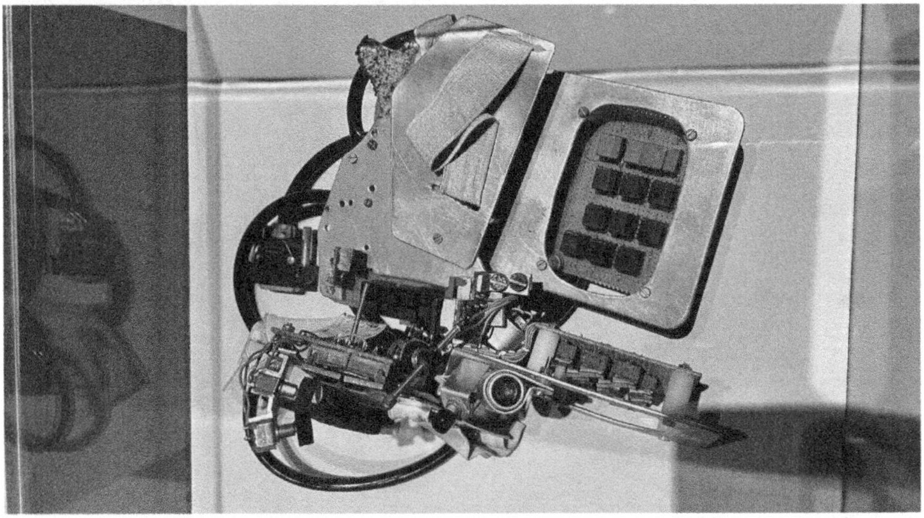

Fig. 8. Components of "The Hands" version 1. Filmed by the author.

FeelReal is worn below the VR visor. It contains an odor generator (Smell-O-Vision!), wind generators, water mist openings and a microphone.

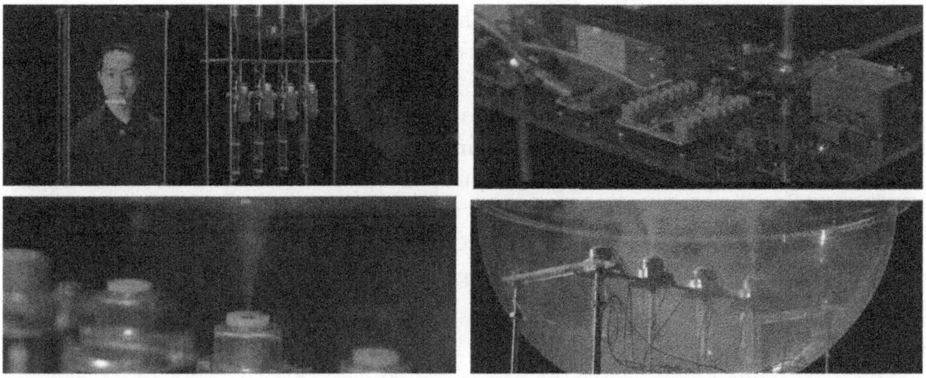

Fig. 9. The "Synesthesia Machine" (2021) consists of two main components: an image capture device on the left and a scent generation device on the right. When an audience member enters the image capture area and stays for 3 s, a camera captures their facial expression, which is then analyzed by an AI program. Based on the facial expression analysis, the scent generation device releases varying proportions of scent liquids (wood, chemical, fruit, and foul) from test tubes into a mixing chamber. The mixed scent is then diffused and blown out by a fan, creating a scent experience based on the viewer's expression. [15].

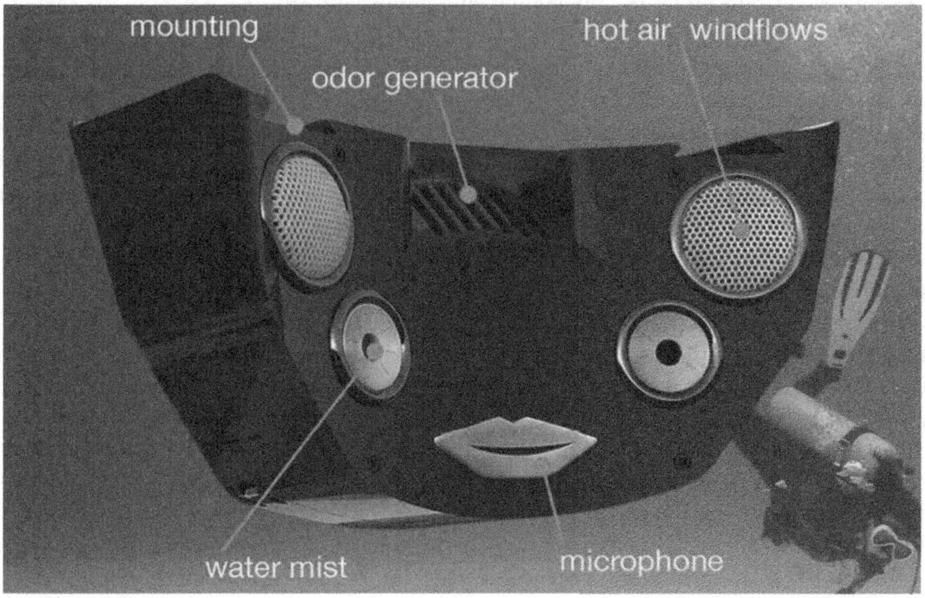

Fig. 10. " FeelReal virtual-reality mask" can help experience smell in virtual scenes. (2015) [16].

4.3 Interactive Art

Based on the aforementioned cases, it is important for stakeholders to recognize that interactive art based on multimodal R technology enhances participant engagement and enjoyment. However, it should be noted that the experiential process of such art forms requires adaptation and learning, and necessitates continuous improvement and updates based on user experiences.

Edmonds delineates four distinct stages of interactivity in his work "The Art of Interaction": adaptation, learning, anticipation and deeper understanding [17]. These stages, derived from his experiential insight, align with our earlier discourse on the holistic nature of experience, comprising four key aspects: Understanding, Emotions, Values, and Tendency to Act. Integrating these theoretical frameworks can assist stakeholders in cultivating their creativity and facilitating immersive experiences.

5 Summary

The development of multimodal R technologies faces substantial challenges, particularly in hardware. AR/VR headsets and head-worn optical devices, such as brain-computer interfaces, require significant efforts to resolve issues related to rendering, chips, materials, sensors, energy consumption, networks, user experience, information security, industrialization, and ethics, etc. As the Metaverse and Digital Twin technologies advance, it becomes clear that headsets alone are insufficient to meet the diverse needs of virtual "Avatars." Future innovations will likely see wearable devices become more compact and integrated into clothing, enhancing interaction and offering richer multi-sensory experiences [18].

The integration of virtual reality with interactive narrative techniques is shifting audience perspectives, with immersive audio [19] playing a crucial role in enhancing the realism of artistic experiences. This emerging field requires further development and broader application in interactive art, addressing technical, user experience, design, and cultural dimensions. The interplay of these elements is vital for advancing the future of interactive and immersive art.

In the arts, we observe a growing trend towards perceptual translation, where artists substitute one sense for another to create novel experiences. Our experimental project, "Ears on My Back," exemplifies this approach by enabling Deaf artists to explore soundscapes through dynamic volume and frequency ranges and synchronize rhythms with visuals [20]. This innovative device highlights the potential of sensory substitution to expand artistic expression and foster deeper connections with diverse audiences.

In summary, as technology and artistry converge, the potential for immersive experiences to transform how we perceive and interact with art is boundless. The continuous evolution of multimodal R technologies promises to unlock new dimensions of creativity and sensory engagement, paving the way for a future where artistic expression is richer, more inclusive, and profoundly impactful.

References

1. Van der Veer, G.C., Bagnara, S., Kempen, G.A.M., (eds.) Cognitive ergonomics: contributions from experimental psychology. Acta Psychologica **78**(1–3) (1992)
2. Vyas, D., van der Veer, G.C.: Experience as Meaning: Some Underlying Concepts and Implications for Design. Proc. of ECCE-13. ACM Press (2006)

3. Cherry, K.: The Everything Psychology Book: Explore the human psyche and understand why we do the things we do. ThriftBooks (2010)
4. Frijda, N.H.: Recognition of emotion. Adv. Exp. Soc. Psychol. **4**, 167–223 (1959)
5. Van Wieringen, P.C.W., Van der Veer, G.C., Van der Meulen, G., Adèr, H.J.: Dimensions of perception of posture in dance. Hum. Mov. Sci. **1**, 73–86 (1982)
6. Fikkert, F.W., van der Vet, P.E., van der Veer, G.C., Nijholt, A.: Gestures for large display control. In: Kopp, S., Wachsmuth, I. (eds.) Gesture in Embodied Communication and Human-Computer Interaction, 8th International Gesture Workshop, GW 2009, pp. 245–256. Springer Verlag, Berlin/Heidelberg (2010)
7. Li, D., van der Veer, G.: From painter to interaction designer: the evolution of visual art things. In: Joshi, A., Balkrishan, D., Dalvi, G., Winckler, M. (eds.) Adjunct Proceedings INTERACT 2017, pp. 139–149. Springer, Mumbai (2017)
8. Li, D., van der Veer, G.: Supporting the experience of stakeholders of multimedia art – towards an ontology', beyond interactions. IFIP Int. Fed. Inf. Process. (2020) '
9. Giannetti, L.: Understanding Movies (14th Edition). Pearson (2017)
10. Li, D., vanderVeer, G.:From painter to interaction designer: the evolution of visual art things. In: Joshi, A., Balkrishan, D., Dalvi, G., Winckler, M. (eds.) Adjunct Proceedings INTERACT 2017, Mumbai, pp. 139–149. Springer (2017)
11. Petrie, D.W., Boggs, J.M.: The Art of Watching Films, 10th edn. McGraw-Hill Education, New York (2017)
12. Yao, Y., Mi, H.: A Design Experience for Interactive Narrative Based on User Behavior. Design Culture(s)/Cumulus Roma 2020. Sapienza University of Rome (2020)
13. VR Noir: A Day Before the Night. Official website (2016). https://www.startbeyond.co/case-studies/vr-noir
14. Bongers, A.J.: Anthropomorphic resonances: on the relationship between computer interfaces and the human form and motion. Oxford University Press (2013)
15. The "Synesthesia Machine" of artist Shuai Hu. Source: MANA New Media Art Station (2021). https://mp.weixin.qq.com/s/pgCVqVqLfx2cNUd1owD08g
16. Kooser, A.: FeelReal virtual-reality mask gives you a whiff of the game, CNET Media, Inc. (2015). https://www.cnet.com/tech/gaming/feelreal-virtual-reality-mask-gives-you-a-whiff-of-the-game/. Accessed 20 Aug 2024
17. Edmonds, E.A.: Edmonds: The Art of Interaction. Conference: Create10 - The interaction design conference (2010). https://doi.org/10.14236/ewic/CREATE2010.2]
18. Ball, M.: The Metaverse: And How It Will Revolutionize Everything. Liveright Publishing Corporation, 179–203 (2022)
19. Sawaguchi, M.: Immersive Audio Music Up and Running. Immersive creation in 5G UHD Era - Avid, Dolby, Genelec, the comprehensive solutions Summit Forum (2019). https://mp.weixin.qq.com/s/rO_edyKXiY8jg_hnt4iMCg
20. Li, D., van der veer G.: Ears on my back - experiencing the soundscape without hearing In: Ardito, C., et al. (eds.): INTERACT 2021, LNCS 13198, pp. 453–473, Springer Nature Switzerland AG (2022). https://doi.org/10.1007/978-3-030-98388-8_41

Mixed Reality-Based Assistive Technology for Enhanced Hand Function in Age-Related Conditions

Xinjun Li[1(✉)] and Zhenhong Lei[2(✉)]

[1] Cornell University, New York, NY 10044, USA
xl863@cornell.edu
[2] Rhode Island School of Design, Providence, RI 02903, USA
brad.zh.lei@gmail.com

Abstract. This study presents an innovative Mixed Reality (MR) assistive device designed to enhance grip stability for individuals with degenerative and age-related hand conditions such as Rheumatoid Arthritis (RA) and Osteoarthritis (OA). By integrating MR overlays with an advanced servo motor locking mechanism, the device provides dynamic grip assistance that adapts to user needs in real-time. The MR system offers interactive visual cues and feedback, supporting users in performing daily tasks with improved hand function and reduced strain. Beyond assistance, the device serves as a rehabilitation tool, guiding users through personalized exercises that promote strength, dexterity, and hand stability. This paper details the design and engineering process, highlights the potential clinical applications, and underscores the device's role in empowering users to maintain autonomy in daily activities despite the challenges posed by RA and OA. The results suggest promising implications for leveraging MR technology in assistive healthcare solutions, particularly in enhancing quality of life for individuals with compromised hand functionality.

Keywords: Augmented Reality · Mixed Reality · Assistive Device · Haptic Feedback · Geriatric Care · XR Healthcare · Hand Dexterity · Ergonomic Hand Motion

1 Introduction

The increasing prevalence of degenerative conditions, including Rheumatoid Arthritis (RA) and Osteoarthritis (OA), combined with age-related declines in muscle strength, underscores a critical need for the development of advanced assistive technologies. These technologies aim to improve hand functionality and thereby enhance the quality of life for affected individuals [1] (Fig. 1).

Osteoarthritis (OA) and Rheumatoid Arthritis (RA) are two of the most prevalent forms of arthritis, significantly impacting individuals' hand functionality, particularly in

X. Li and Z. Lei—Contibuted equally.

L. Zaina et al. (Eds.): EICS 2024, LNCS 15518, pp. 224–234, 2025.
https://doi.org/10.1007/978-3-031-91760-8_15

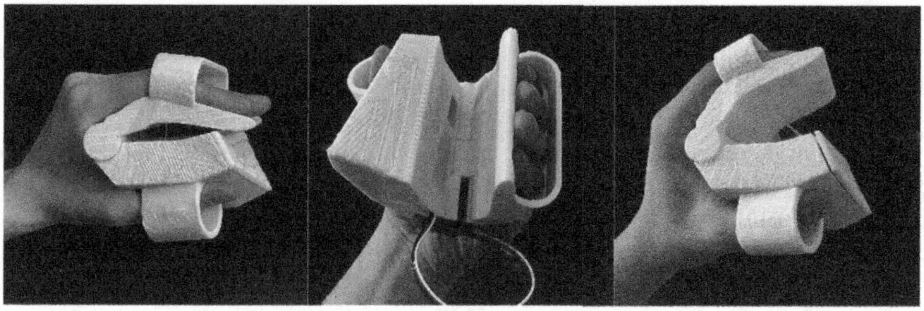

Fig. 1. Design prototype

older adults. OA is a degenerative joint disease characterized by cartilage breakdown, leading to pain, stiffness, and reduced range of motion. Over time, this deterioration results in the formation of bone spurs and can cause considerable discomfort, limiting individuals' ability to perform daily tasks involving gripping, holding, and manipulating objects. In contrast, RA is an autoimmune disorder that primarily affects the joints, causing inflammation in the synovial membrane. This inflammation leads to pain, swelling, and joint deformities, often affecting both hands symmetrically. RA is driven by an immune response that targets joint linings, resulting in the progressive degradation of joint structures. Both conditions profoundly impact individuals' quality of life, creating an increasing need for innovative assistive devices to enhance grip stability and support hand functionality.

These conditions markedly hinder individuals' abilities to carry out daily activities, leading to diminished autonomy and overall well-being; therefore, addressing these challenges is crucial.

This paper presents an innovative assistive device that combines mixed reality (MR) technology with a servo motor locking mechanism to address grip stability and rehabilitation issues. By integrating mechanical support with real-time MR feedback, the device creates a dynamic and interactive environment that adapts to users' needs, enhancing rehabilitation engagement.

Developed through a user-centered design approach in collaboration with healthcare professionals, the device incorporates user feedback at every stage to ensure it meets the specific requirements of individuals with hand impairments. The development process—from initial concept to preliminary evaluation—demonstrates the device's potential to advance assistive technology significantly. By offering an MR-enhanced interface tailored for those with grip-related challenges, this device represents a noteworthy progression in applying mixed reality to healthcare, particularly in rehabilitation.

2 Comparative Analysis

Contemporary approaches to managing hand functionality impairments resulting from RA, OA, and age-related musculoskeletal decline are primarily centered around deploying mechanical assistive devices. These devices, which include customized gloves and grip aids, are specifically designed to support and enhance the user's ability to manipulate objects by compensating for the reduced strength and dexterity that typically accompany these conditions. These mechanical aids play a crucial role in restoring functional independence, enabling users to perform everyday tasks that would otherwise be challenging or impossible.

In parallel, there has been a growing interest in using digital tools that leverage MR technologies. These tools create immersive, interactive environments that are utilized to improve motor skills through structured rehabilitative exercises. The MR environments are designed to engage users in a manner that traditional rehabilitation methods often fail to achieve, providing a more stimulating and potentially more effective rehabilitation experience [2, 3]. The interactive nature of MR can encourage consistent participation in rehabilitative exercises, which is a key factor in achieving long-term functional recovery.

Despite the benefits offered by mechanical assistive devices and MR-based tools, a critical gap still needs to be in integrating these technologies into a cohesive, sustained rehabilitative strategy. Mechanical devices, while effective in providing immediate physical support, often lack the capability to deliver the dynamic, responsive feedback that is essential for continuous rehabilitation. Without this feedback, the user may not be adequately challenged or guided, potentially limiting the effectiveness of the rehabilitation process [4, 5]. Conversely, MR-based rehabilitation tools, although they provide interactive and engaging experiences, typically do not offer the physical stabilization required by individuals with severe impairments. This lack of physical support can hinder the effectiveness of the exercises, particularly for users who require assistance in maintaining grip stability during rehabilitation.

3 Methodology

While both mechanical assistive devices and MR-based tools have shown promise in supporting individuals with RA, OA, and age-related hand impairments, the question remains: How can a mixed reality-enhanced assistive device improve grip stability and rehabilitation outcomes for individuals with these conditions? This study seeks to address this question by exploring the integration of mechanical stabilization with real-time, MR-driven feedback to create a cohesive rehabilitative tool. By combining these elements, we aim to offer a solution that not only provides immediate physical support but also promotes sustained engagement in rehabilitation activities, ultimately enhancing users' functional independence and potential for long-term recovery.

To address these limitations, we have developed an innovative MR-enhanced assistive device that uniquely integrates real-time physical support with interactive digital rehabilitation. This device combines the mechanical stabilization capabilities of traditional assistive devices with the adaptive, responsive features of MR technology, offering a comprehensive solution that meets both the immediate and long-term needs of users. The mechanical component of the device ensures that users have the necessary support to perform tasks safely and effectively, while the MR component provides real-time feedback and adaptive guidance, promoting continuous engagement in rehabilitative exercises.

The integration of these two elements within a single system represents a significant advancement in the field of assistive technology. By providing both immediate physical stabilization and sustained rehabilitative engagement, our device addresses the dual challenges of functional support and long-term recovery. This approach not only stabilizes grip and facilitates object manipulation in the short term but also actively contributes to the improvement of hand mobility and strength over time. By fostering continuous engagement in rehabilitation, the device enhances the user's potential for long-term functional recovery, which is particularly crucial for individuals with progressive degenerative conditions such as RA and OA, as well as those experiencing age-related declines in hand function.

Furthermore, the development of this MR-enhanced device was guided by a rigorous, user-centered design methodology. This methodology involved extensive collaboration with healthcare professionals, ensuring that the device was tailored to the specific needs of individuals with hand impairments. User feedback was incorporated at multiple stages of the development process, from initial concept design to preliminary evaluation, to ensure that the final product met its intended users' practical and therapeutic needs. This iterative design process not only enhanced the device's functionality but also ensured its usability and acceptance among end-users, further contributing to its potential impact on the field.

In conclusion, our MR-enhanced assistive device represents a substantial contribution to the development of more effective and integrated rehabilitation solutions. By bridging the gap between mechanical support and interactive rehabilitation, this device offers a novel approach to managing the complex challenges associated with degenerative and age-related hand impairments, thereby advancing the capabilities of assistive technologies in this domain [6].

3.1 Design Research Procedure Breakdown

Research Phase:
We thoroughly examined existing therapeutic modalities for Rheumatoid Arthritis (RA) and Osteoarthritis (OA). This investigation highlighted significant deficiencies in the effectiveness of current physical aids and virtual rehabilitation methods. Collaborations with clinical experts enabled us to tailor our development trajectory to meet the nuanced requirements of these patient populations.

Conceptualization:
Collaborative brainstorming sessions led to the formulation of a mixed-reality device concept. This innovative idea integrates physical joint support with interactive augmented reality (AR) rehabilitation. Iterative feedback from healthcare professionals and prospective users was instrumental in refining the concept, ensuring its practical applicability and relevance to those affected by hand impairments.

Design and Development:
We focused on enhancing conventional support mechanisms by incorporating adaptive features. These features accommodate various hand sizes and joint conditions, making the device versatile for a wide range of users. Additionally, we developed a robust AR component designed to deliver practical rehabilitation exercises, thereby merging mechanical support with engaging digital therapy.

Evaluation and Testing:
Subjecting the prototype to rigorous evaluations based on established RA and OA treatment protocols, we concentrated on assessing two main aspects: the efficacy of the physical support provided by the device and the engagement level offered by the AR system. This dual focus ensured that both mechanical and interactive elements met therapeutic standards.

Refinement:
We utilized insights from initial evaluations to enhance the device further, allowing it to surpass the capabilities of existing therapeutic solutions. Adjustments were made to improve user comfort, adaptability, and overall effectiveness.

Validation:
Comprehensive trials with a broader spectrum of participants aimed to verify the device's effectiveness and substantiate its benefits as an all-encompassing treatment strategy for RA and OA. Data collected confirmed the device's potential to significantly improve patient outcomes.

From initial concept to full validation, our developmental journey underscores a commitment to creating a customized solution that addresses both the immediate and evolving needs of RA and OA patients. By merging cutting-edge technology with a user-centered design philosophy, we have developed a device that not only provides mechanical support but also enhances patient engagement through interactive rehabilitation. This holistic approach represents a significant advancement in the application of mixed reality to healthcare, particularly in the field of rehabilitation.

4 Prototype Design Procedure

4.1 Design Rationale

In our endeavor to address the challenges associated with Rheumatoid Arthritis (RA) and Osteoarthritis (OA), we developed the design methodology for our assistive device within a multidisciplinary framework that integrates principles from biomechanics, ergonomics, and user-centered design (Fig. 2). This comprehensive approach was crucial for creating a prototype that accurately replicates the natural mechanics of hand movements, with a particular emphasis on the grip patterns necessary for daily tasks. By grounding the design in biomechanical principles, we engineered the device to closely align with the anatomical and functional aspects of hand movement, ensuring it effectively supports the user's ability to interact with objects in an efficient manner.

The engineering focus was on achieving biomechanical precision by designing the device's structure to conform to the natural curvature of the hand in its resting state. This intentional alignment was incorporated to enhance ergonomic comfort and reduce the risk of strain during use. Paying close attention to the hand's natural curvature was critical, as it provides a foundation for a design that minimizes stress on the joints and muscles—an aspect particularly important for users with RA and OA who are prone to discomfort and fatigue. The design aimed to optimize the interaction between the device

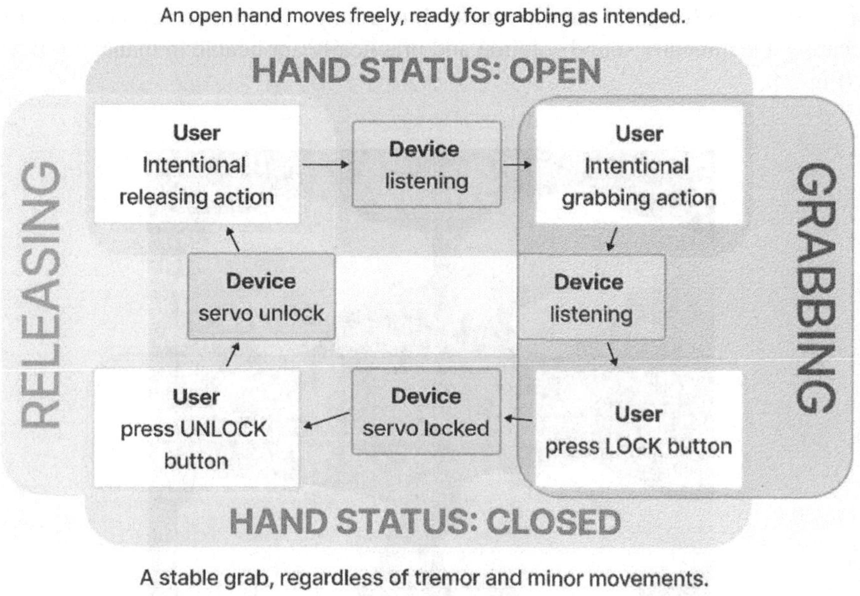

Fig. 2. Functional Diagram

and the user's hand, creating a seamless interface that supports both passive and active hand functions.

The ideation process also integrated insights from ergonomics to ensure that the device could be used over extended periods without contributing to additional strain or injury. Ergonomic studies evaluated how the device interacts with the user's hand anatomy, focusing on factors such as grip force distribution, joint alignment, and pressure points. These studies informed design decisions that enhanced the device's ability to provide adequate support while maintaining high comfort. By aligning the device with the hand's natural resting position, we created a design that not only supports the functional requirements of daily activities but also addresses the ergonomic needs of users with degenerative joint conditions.

We employed a user-centered design approach throughout the ideation phase, incorporating feedback from potential users and healthcare professionals. This iterative process allowed us to refine the device's functionality to meet the needs of individuals with RA and OA better. By engaging with end-users and clinicians, we gathered critical insights that informed the design, ensuring that the device replicates the natural grip mechanics and integrates seamlessly into the user's daily routine. The collaborative nature of this process was key to developing a prototype that is both functionally robust and aligned with the therapeutic goals of managing hand impairments.

The resulting design represents an innovative approach to assistive technology. The intersection of biomechanics, ergonomics, and user-centered design has led to a device that effectively replicates the natural mechanics of hand movements while also addressing the user's comfort and usability needs. Integrating multiple disciplines was crucial in creating a technically sound solution and practically applicable in managing RA and OA (Fig. 3).

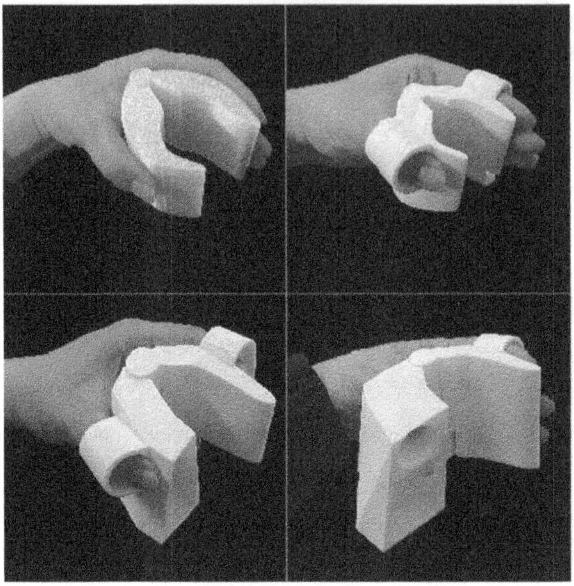

Fig. 3. Device Mock-up and Iteration Process

4.2 Physical Prototype Device Design

To address the challenges faced by individuals with Rheumatoid Arthritis (RA) and Osteoarthritis (OA), whose joint stiffness and pain often diminish grip strength and dexterity, our device incorporates a servo motor to enhance the hand's opening and closing mechanisms. This integration is crucial for tasks that require sustained muscle strength, such as holding a book or securely gripping a handle. By balancing mechanical assistance with natural hand movements, the servo motor significantly increases users' autonomy in daily activities, allowing them to perform tasks more effectively and comfortably (Fig. 4).

To facilitate the transition between the hand's open and closed states, we developed a dual-phase mechanism designed to support both gripping and releasing actions essential for daily tasks. The first phase initiates the "grabbing" action through an accessible trigger mechanism that requires minimal force to engage. This design consideration aligns with the ergonomic and functional needs of our target population, particularly individuals with limited hand strength due to conditions like Rheumatoid Arthritis (RA) and Osteoarthritis (OA).

Fig. 4. The user holding a book with the help of the device

The second phase manages the "releasing" action via an ergonomic command that disengages the servo motor, allowing the hand to return to its natural open position with minimal effort. This ensures that users can easily release objects without undue strain, enhancing overall usability.

The device is constructed as a dual-component system connected by a hinge and incorporates a feedback servo motor strategically placed in the thumb. Positioning the servo motor in the thumb is a deliberate design choice, recognizing the thumb's critical role in grip stability and precision. This configuration enables the device to more accurately replicate natural hand movements, providing essential support for executing gripping and releasing maneuvers with increased stability and reduced strain.

Moreover, the design includes a gearing system that adjusts the stiffness of the servo motor, allowing users to modulate grip strength according to the specific requirements of different tasks. For example, increasing motor stiffness accommodates activities that require a firmer grip, such as holding heavier objects, while decreasing stiffness is suitable for more delicate tasks. This adaptability enhances the device's functionality across a variety of activities, making it a versatile tool for individuals with varying levels of hand impairment.

4.3 AR Prototype Design

The device is systematically integrated with a smartphone using a Unity-based application, which leverages the camera's functionality to provide AR assistance. This integration enables the user to point the camera at specific objects, such as a book, to facilitate interaction with the application. Upon activation of the "Grab Suggestion" feature, the application initiates a detailed analysis of the object by processing a series of successive frames captured by the camera. This computational process includes assessing the object's dimensions, orientation, and other relevant attributes, which are critical for determining the most effective approach to grasping it.

The system utilizes algorithms within the application to generate optimal grasping recommendations based on the captured data. These recommendations guide the user on how to manipulate the object efficiently. As the user attempts to grasp the object, their hand movements are captured in real-time and reflected on the smartphone display. This real-time feedback is made possible by the gyroscope embedded within the device, which records precise movement data and transmits it back to the application.

The integration of this system exemplifies a sophisticated combination of physical interaction and virtual guidance. The gyroscope ensures accurate tracking of hand movements, allowing the application to present a real-time, virtual representation of the user's actions. This process enhances the user's ability to execute tasks with improved precision, utilizing AR-based recommendations to navigate the physical manipulation of objects more effectively (Fig. 5).

Fig. 5. Smartphone AR interface.

4.4 User Testing

To evaluate the device's functionality and enhance user comfort, we conducted preliminary qualitative testing with a focus group of individuals diagnosed with Rheumatoid Arthritis (RA) and Osteoarthritis (OA). The feedback obtained from these participants was instrumental in refining the device's features. Participants reported improvements in their ability to perform daily tasks and experienced reduced discomfort, highlighting the ergonomic design and user-friendliness of the device. Although these insights were based on initial feedback and lacked comprehensive quantitative analysis, the study demonstrated the device's potential and identified areas for further enhancement. The augmented reality (AR) component and telehealth functionalities received particularly positive responses, underscoring the need for more extensive studies to thoroughly assess the device's efficacy and to optimize its design for a broader user population.

5 Discussion

The findings from this study suggest that the MR-enhanced assistive device holds significant potential to improve hand functionality and independence for individuals with RA and OA. By providing real-time feedback, adaptive guidance, and physical support, the device addresses both immediate functional needs and long-term rehabilitative goals. Additionally, the MR technology allows for a highly engaging and interactive experience, encouraging users to participate consistently in rehabilitation activities, which is crucial for sustained improvement.

Beyond the immediate application for RA and OA, the MR interface developed for this device offers promising opportunities for broader use. This technology could be adapted to assist individuals with other hand impairments, such as those recovering from hand injuries, stroke, or neurological conditions affecting hand function. Such expansion could enable a wider range of users to regain hand functionality and maintain their independence in daily activities.

Moreover, enhancing the AR interface to accommodate varying levels of digital experience could further improve the device's accessibility and usability. Customizable settings that adjust the complexity of visuals and instructions would allow novice users to navigate the interface with ease, while still enabling experienced users to utilize advanced features. Simplified controls and guided tutorials could also support users unfamiliar with MR technology, fostering an inclusive and effective rehabilitative experience for diverse populations.

This user-centered approach to interface design will be essential as we explore broader applications, helping ensure that the device can cater to individuals across different skill levels and rehabilitative needs. Further research should focus on refining the MR interface to optimize usability and testing the device across a broader population to assess its efficacy in various rehabilitative contexts. By continuing to adapt and improve the technology, we can maximize the impact of MR in assistive and rehabilitative healthcare.

6 Conclusion

This research explores the integration of Mixed Reality (MR) and Human-Computer Interaction (HCI) in developing therapeutic interventions for RA and OA. The device combines ergonomic hand motion support with augmented reality technology, addressing both physical and perceptual challenges associated with these conditions. Engineered for adaptability, it accommodates various hand sizes and joint mobility constraints, making it accessible to a wider range of users.

Beyond its physical design, the device is designed for different levels of user interaction with the MR system, ensuring it can effectively serve individuals with varying degrees of hand function and familiarity with digital interfaces. Participants reported improvements in motor control and functional independence, suggesting the device's potential to enhance daily activities for those affected by RA and OA.

These observed improvements underscore MR's role in potentially elevating users' quality of life by offering both physical support and addressing cognitive demands essential for the rehabilitation of chronic joint conditions. This study highlights MR's value in therapeutic applications, opening new possibilities for improving patient care and rehabilitation outcomes.

Future research will focus on refining the user interface for greater usability, especially for those less experienced with digital systems. Enhancing MR and HCI integration will be crucial for expanding the device's effectiveness across diverse populations, further exploring MR's potential in inclusive, impactful therapeutic approaches for RA and OA management.

References

1. Pereira, M.F., Prahm, C., Kolbenschlag, J., Oliveira, E., Rodrigues, N.F.: Application of AR and VR in hand rehabilitation: a systematic review. J. Biomed. Inform. **111**, 103584 (2020). https://doi.org/10.1016/j.jbi.2020.103584
2. Mois, G., et al.: Perceptions from people aging with a mobility impairment towards using tele-technology for exercise. Proc. Hum. Factors Ergon. Soc. Ann. Meeting **63**(1), 11–15 (2019). https://doi.org/10.1177/1071181319631040
3. Li, X., Lei, Z.: Ergonomic hand motion assistance and ar rehabilitation: bridging the gap in tremor disorder therapies through mixed reality. In: 2024 IEEE Conference on Virtual Reality and 3D User Interfaces Abstracts and Workshops (VRW), Orlando, FL (2024). https://doi.org/10.1145/3514206
4. Kolsanov, A., Chaplygin, S., Rovnov, S., Ivaschenko, A.: Augmented reality application for hand motor skills rehabilitation. Int. J. Adv. Comput. Sci. Appl. **11**(4) (2020). https://doi.org/10.14569/ijacsa.2020.0110408
5. Gu, Y., et al.: A review of hand function rehabilitation systems based on hand motion recognition devices and artificial intelligence. Brain Sci. **12**(8) (2022). https://doi.org/10.3390/brainsci12081079
6. Gonsher, I., Lei, Z.: Prototype of a force-feedback tool for mixed reality applications. Interactions **29**(2), 23 (2022). https://doi.org/10.1145/3514206

Experience 2.0: Mixed Realities and Beyond

I. Scott MacKenzie(✉)

Department of Electrical Engineering and Computer Science, York University, Toronto, Canada
mack@yorku.ca

Abstract. We examine current mixed reality (MR) environments, looking at what they are, what can and cannot be done, and the challenges and possibilities looking forward. The contribution of Milgram and Kishino's one-dimensional mixed reality model from 1994 is acknowledged with possibilities noted for extending the model to two- and three-dimensions. The challenges and possibilities for MR looking forward are summarized as seven community challenges (CCs) derived from current research and to be examined by MR researchers.

Keywords: Virtual reality · augmented reality · mixed reality · extended reality · multiple realities · heads-up display · see-through display · wall-size display · fogscreen · holographic display · brain-computer interface · sense of smell · olfactory display · tactile feedback · community challenges

1 Introduction

The environments of interest in this paper are virtual reality (VR), augmented reality (AR), and mixed reality (MR). These were explored at the workshop, "Experience 2.0 and Beyond - Engineering Cross Devices and Multiple Realities" on July 25, 2024, as part of *The 16th ACM SIGCHI Symposium on Engineering Interactive Computing Systems, EICS '24*. The goal of the workshop was to look at the "reality" spaces – what they are, where they are, and where they are headed. Of concern is the user experience (UX) and the engineering of realities and devices to enhance such in future contexts.

We focus on mixed modalities that include novel devices triggering multiple human senses and in different contexts. The term "mixed reality" or "MR" is meant to encompass VR, AR, and related environments, and go inside and beyond the common interpretations for each. We also pose research questions with each presented as a community challenge (CC). The questions arise from examples that expose interactions that challenge and push the boundaries of the mixed reality space.

Notably, the EICS workshop marked the 30-year anniversary of the publication of Milgram and Kishino's seminal[1] paper, "A Taxonomy of Mixed Reality Visual Displays." In it, they explored what at the time was the emerging world

[1] More than 9700 citations on Google Scholar (September 2024).

L. Zaina et al. (Eds.): EICS 2024, LNCS 15518, pp. 235–253, 2025.
https://doi.org/10.1007/978-3-031-91760-8_16

of mixed realities. They did so using a descriptive model. See Fig. 1. Descriptive models are visualizations with labels and narratives that deconstruct a problem space into constituent parts [23, Chapter 7]. They are tools for thinking – for identifying the parts, what they are, how they relate to each other, and the possibilities offered. In Fig. 1, we see a world Milgram and Kishino anticipated with the "real" at one end, the "virtual" at the other end, and "augmented" variations within. They use "mixed reality" as an umbrella term to encompass the possibilities.

Fig. 1. Milgram and Kishino's mixed reality continuum [26].

The terms featured in Milgram and Kishino's paper are well-travelled in the HCI literature. Figure 2 shows the results from a search of the number of publications using these terms in the ACM Digital Library. The chart is organized as a timeline beginning in 1980, before HCI emerged as a field of study.

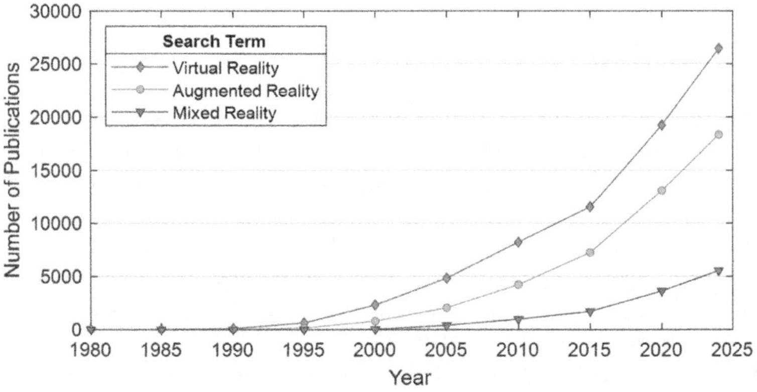

Fig. 2. Cumulative number of publications by year in the ACM Digital Library using the terms "virtual reality," "augmented reality," and "mixed reality."

Milgram and Kishino's model is one dimensional, expressing a single property ("degree of reality") along a continuum. This is the simplest rendering for a descriptive model. See Fig. 3a. If two dimensions are identified for a problem space, then Fig. 3b applies. An example of a model space in two dimensions is the positioning of an artefact along one axis for "form" (design) and a second axis for "function" (engineering) [23, Figure 4.2]. If a problem space is described along three dimensions, then Fig. 3c applies. An example here is Flavián et al.'s "EPI Cube" which characterises MR environments in a three-axis space according to their degree of embodiment, presence, and interactivity [10, Figure 6].

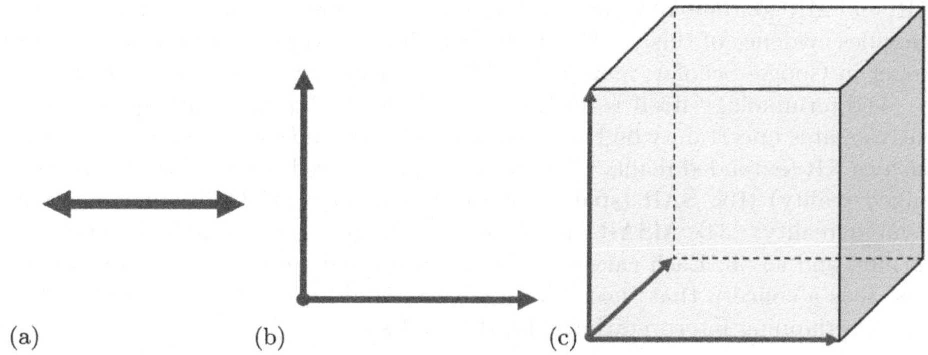

Fig. 3. Visual rendering for descriptive models by dimension. (a) one-dimensional, 1D. (b) two-dimensional, 2D. and (c) three dimensional, 3D. Each axis is a continuum, positioning the problem space along a property of interest.

In Milgram and Kishino's paper, they also propose extending their model along additional dimensions, comprising the following elements:

- World knowledge ⇒ what we know of the world displayed
- Fidelity ⇒ the level of realism in the world displayed
- Presence ⇒ the degree of illusion that the observer experiences

Each was represented visually in their paper as a one-dimensional (1D) rendering as per Fig. 3a. Although not explored by Milgram and Kishino, it might be possible to combine any two of the 1D properties into a 2D model as per Fig. 3b or all three of the 1D properties into a 3D descriptive model as per Fig. 3c. The challenge with a 3D rendering is positioning environments within the space in a manner that is intuitive and revealing. For this, an interactive VR application might help. Research awaits.

2 Position Topics

Below are the topics raised in this position paper. Each includes examples and is followed with a community challenge in the form of a research question. The intent here is not to answer the research questions, but to offer the questions as points of discussion or research for the MR community.

2.1 Terminology

Considering the three terms in Fig. 2, "virtual reality" is the most common (26,469 occurrences), followed by "augmented reality" (18,346 occurrences) and mixed reality (5,546 occurrences). The curves show no sign of flattening as VR, AR, and MR continue to inspire HCI researchers today. A closer look at citations provides evidence of this: Of the 9700+ citations to Milgram and Kishino's 1994 paper in Google Scholar, more than 4700 citations are from 2020 or later.

The terminology itself is an issue, since the overlap in reality spaces inherently creates uncertainty on the boundaries of each and fosters additional terms, such as XR (extended reality) [28,35], UR (unmediated reality) [44], PMR (pure mixed reality) [10], SAR (spatial augmented reality) [3], OAR (olfactory augmented reality) [34], MSAR (multi-sensory augmented reality) [2], metaverse [27,46], and so on. Each carves out a niche in the diverse space of mixed realities. It is a concern that these terms are bantered about in myriad ways, often with overlapping interpretations [40,41]. And so,

CC1. What are the important terms for multiple reality environments? List, define, and organize in a glossary.

We leave this for the MR community to address at a later time.

2.2 The Forgotten Senses

A common refrain for mixed reality is heightening the sense of immersion or presence. This means, among other things, engaging all the human senses. The visual channel is well represented in all setups. This is expected as most people obtain about 80% of their information though the sense of light [1]. There is generally and understandably less attention directed at the auditory and tactile senses (depending on context, of course). The senses of smell and taste are barely represented, if at all.

Mixed reality is an area within HCI that seems particularly suited to applications leveraging the human sensory channel of smell. This is due to the immersion experienced by the user. As an example, Niedenthal et al.'s olfactometer is a graspable olfactory display for virtual environments [30]. See Fig. 4. Their research tested new interaction domains for the human olfactory experience that involve active exploration and directed sniffing of odour blends. The device contains four gas chambers containing scents and attaches to a HTC Vive hand controller. Valves on the device control the flow and blending of scents. They evaluated the device in a user study with a virtual wine cellar game. Results indicate that the device is intuitive to use and stable enough for long-term smell training sessions. In another study [31], they demonstrate that use of an olfactory display has the potential to increase the sense of presence in virtual environments.

Although Niedenthal et al.'s olfactory display is a separate handheld device, one can imagine the display as built-in to a headset and engaging the nasal cavity much like the headset's visual display engages the eyes.

Fig. 4. A handheld olfactory display for use in virtual environments [30].

As another example, Zulkarnain et al. [49] created a mixed reality environment by adding the sense of smell to a VR setup. They created and studied virtual sensory booths where users are presented with an immersive yet controlled environment for assessing smells. See Fig. 5. Users wore head-mounted displays. In a training session, they visited sensory booths with items of food on plates. Later, the participants visited booths with empty plates and experienced smells presented through test tubes containing scented sticks and attempted to identify the food item. Zulkarnain et al. note that their mixed reality lab has the potential for cost savings in consumer research.

Fig. 5. Mixed reality sensory booth for consumer research on food (after [49]).

Smell and taste, along with the other senses and the mind, are the formative pillars in Ericsson's Internet of Senses, a futuristic look at computing [8]. See Fig. 6. The 2019 report was based on an online poll of users from 15 cities worldwide, with at least 500 respondents from each city.

Many scenarios in the Ericsson report assume that smell and taste will be realized through digital means for future interactions. For smell, 60% of respondents predict it will be possible to digitally visit forests or the countryside and

Fig. 6. Formative pillars in Ericsson's Internet of Senses (after [8]).

experience the natural smells of those places. For taste, 40% anticipate a revolution in online shopping, with the ability to digitally taste samples from the comfort of their devices. And so,

CC2. For each mixed reality environment, to what extent are the human senses represented?

The CC above is not a yes-no checklist. Each sense is a multi-dimensional space. So, depicting the presence of a sense in MR needs an appropriately rich presentation. For example, sound or auditory content is common, but is the sound monophonic or stereo? Are there directional cues in the sound and, if so, are the cues omni-directional or limited to, say, a horizontal plane of −180° to +180°? And what type of sounds are present: sounds from people, from nature, or synthetic sounds? Within each of the categories, there are sub-categories. If the environment includes sounds from people, are they voiced or unvoiced, speech or non-speech, computer generated or natural, and so on. This elaboration for the sense of sound applies to the other senses as well – something for the MR community to explore.

We will shortly say more about the sense labelled "Mind" in Fig. 6.

2.3 Mixing Real and Virtual

Although head-mounted displays (HMDs) are inseparable from VR, mixed reality as an extension of VR invites the use of additional novel display technologies that often mix real and virtual content. Examples include see-through displays (aka heads-up displays) [15,45,48], holographic displays [16,36], wall displays [17,19,25], fogscreens [37,47], and so on.[2]

See-Through Displays (Automotive Applications). A popular MR application is automotive interfaces (or cockpits) that are augmented with see-through displays (sometimes smart glasses). See Fig. 7.

As expected, the bulk of the automotive research in MR is in simulated environments. Since the application is driving, the environment is unlikely to include a head-mounted display. And so, the visual channel is mostly real – the road

[2] Although this section's focus is visual displays, the term "display" applies to any computer output channel that engages human senses. This includes, for example, auditory displays and tactile displays.

Fig. 7. Mixed reality with see-through displays in simulated automotive environment (after [5]).

ahead – but is augmented with additional displays, as depicted in the Fig. 7. For this reason, the environment falls closer to the real end of Milgram and Kishino's real-virtual continuum, perhaps at position 2 or 3 in Fig. 8. Whether the position is 2 or 3 might be a matter of other issues, such as whether the environment's audio content is fully real (position 2) or partly synthetic (position 3).

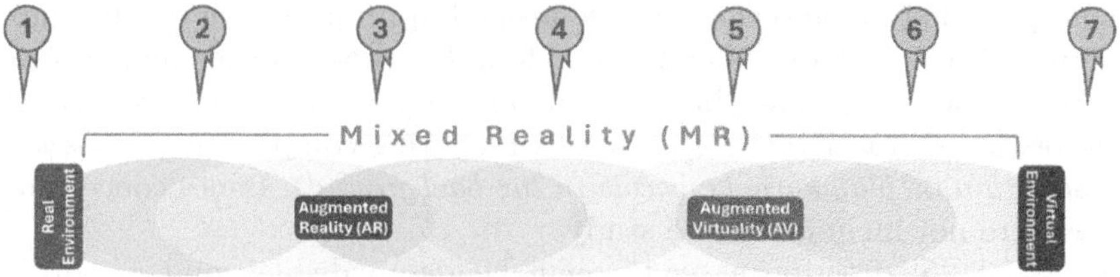

Fig. 8. Placing environments in the MR continuum (after [26]).

And so,

CC3. For each mixed reality environment, what is the environment's position in Milgram and Kishino's mixed reality space?

In some setups, simply pegging the environment at a position in the MR continuum might not be possible. For example, in the setup described by Schmidt and Yigitbas [39], the environment's position in the MR continuum is dynamic. This is enabled since modern VR headsets are equipped with front-facing cameras on the outside of the device cover. In their transitional cross-reality system, a real-virtual control (RVC) appears as a slider to allow the user to set the environment's position in the MR space. See Fig. 9. This is done via a "transition manager" to activate or deactivate environment layers and adjust the internal logic of the application accordingly. The transparency of layers allows other layers below to potentially shine through. However, objects in layers are opaque and block content in adjacent "lower" layers.

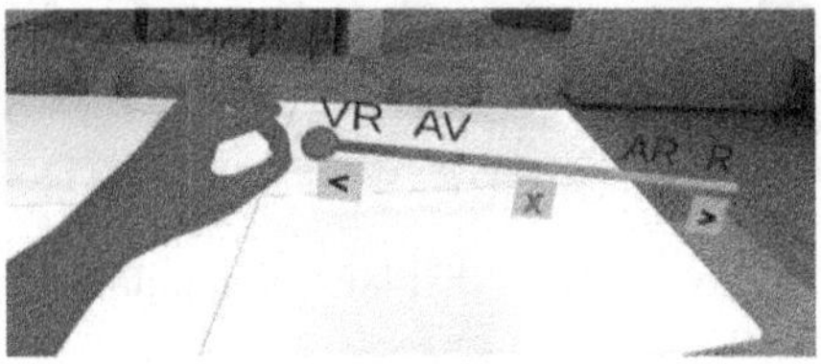

Fig. 9. RVC slider. The user grabs the red sphere of the slider with their thumb and index finger and drags it to set the current position of the environment in the MR continuum (from [39, Figure 6]).

Ch et al. [6] conducted an elicitation study using a mock-up of a heads-up windshield display. See Fig. 10a. The goal was to see if drivers would use gestures or voice commands to interact with an in-vehicle interface. For 24 tasks, participants provided numerous examples deemed appropriate for gesture input or voice input. No significant difference was found between the agreement rates for gestures vs. voice commands, but Ch et al. also found a relatively low acceptance overall for the interaction tasks, some of which were complex (e.g., *bookmark an audio selection* or *play karaoke vocals in the background*). Issues concerning distraction were not included in the study.

Cao et al. [5] describe a see-through heads-up display and gesture input method to allow drivers to interact with and see menu selections and messages without looking away from the road. Their setup used an acrylic board positioned on an angle above an Apple iPad. Information on the iPad was visible on the see-through acrylic board. See Fig. 10b. The motivation was to maintain vehicular safety.

Safety is a concern in mixed reality environments that involve driving, flying, riding a bicycle, walking about, or other potentially hazardous tasks. And so,

CC4. What safety issues emerge in the application of mixed realities?

Holographic Displays. Holographic displays remain mostly a research topic with commercial applications largely on the fringe of HCI. This is expected: Research with an emerging technology tends to initially focus on "what can be done" rather that "how well it can be done." Reviewing the literature reveals that user studies with holographic displays are rare. Usability is largely reported through informal testing or anecdotal narratives. Most research with holographic displays focuses on the implementation details.

(a) 

(b) 

Fig. 10. Heads-up display. (a) Demonstration of heads-up display with in-vehicle tasks controlled by voice prompts and voice commands (after [6]). (b) An acrylic board functions as a see-through display and presents safety information to the driver (after [5]).

An exception is the Hololens product-line from Microsoft, aimed initially at the gaming market, but also for medical AR [12] and for developers with an eye to new possibilities. An impediment to wide-spread consumer adoption, however, is the price tag: $3500 for Hololens 2.[3]

Ihara et al. [16] used holographic displays that allowed remote and local users to co-exist and collaborate in a mixed reality environment. A remote "holographic user" collaborates with a local real user in a shared space for touching, grasping, and manipulating objects. See Fig. 11a. Their HoloBots environment combines a Hololens 2 with an Azure Kinect and Sony Toio mobile robots in creating a broad world-in-miniature telepresence experience. See Fig. 11b.

Sargolzaei et al. [38] use Hololens 2 to reconstruct game sessions for action-adventure games and first-person shooter games. Their GAMR system combines a Unity plugin with the HoloLens 2 MR headset to aid developers in understanding player behaviors within the MR environment. Post-game analyses are based on recorded and reconstructed gameplay sessions, leveraging the capabilities of holographic images from different perspectives.

[3] https://www.theregister.com/2023/04/17/microsoft_hololens_windows_11/.

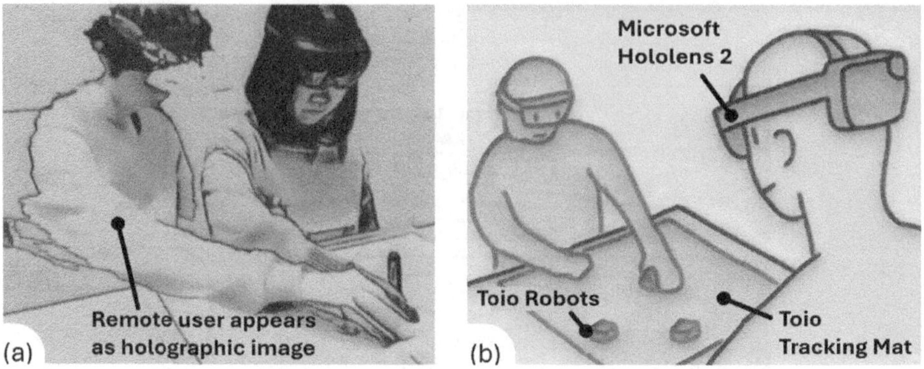

Fig. 11. HoloBots [16]. (a) Local user and holographic rendering of remote user. (b) The remote user is tracked by an Azure Kinect (not shown) and appears as holographic user in the local environment, which includes a Microsoft Hololens 2 and Sony Toio tangible robots.

2.4 Standardized Testing

Ihara et al. [16] present an evaluation of their HoloBots system, comparing hologram-only, robot-only, and hologram+robot conditions. The evaluation used qualitative measures, such as user responses to SUS and NASA-TLX questionnaire items, but no quantitative measures of performance.

In other HCI areas, such as research on target selection or text entry, there are standardized tasks for evaluating user performance with new interaction methods. For target selection, standardized testing typically involves using a Fitts' law task as per ISO 9241-411 [18]. For text entry, standardize testing involves users entering phrases of text selected at random from a standard set [24] while the speed and accuracy of their performance is measured and compared.

One benefit of standardized testing is that across-study comparisons are possible. The same might be possible for mixed reality environments. An example might be a robot-like pick and drop tasks [43] since this involves grasping and manipulation objects as required in Ihara et al.'s [16] HoloBots system. One possible implementation is the disc transfer task or pin transfer task described by Fitts [9]. See Fig. 12. In VR, the task would likely benefit from including a home and final position for the hand and perhaps the same for the user's point of view (POV) or position in the environment.

And so,

CC5. What are the possibilities for representative tasks and quantitative measures for standardized testing of mixed reality environments.

Fogscreens. A fogscreen is another example of a novel display for mixed reality. Fogscreens are immaterial mid-air displays formed from flowing light-scattered

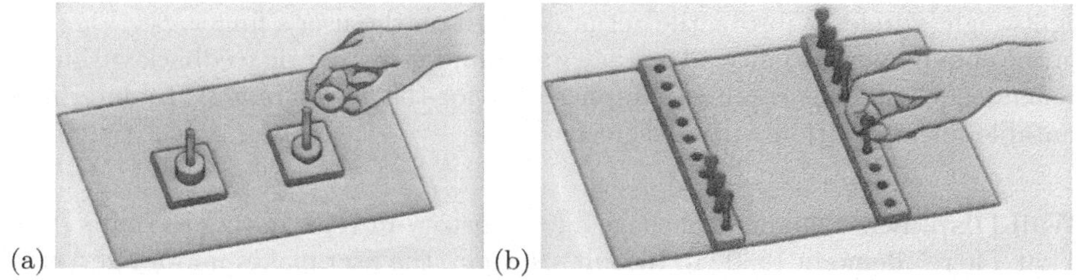

Fig. 12. Possible standardized tasks for evaluating MR setups. (a) Disc transfer task. (a) Pin transfer task (after [9]).

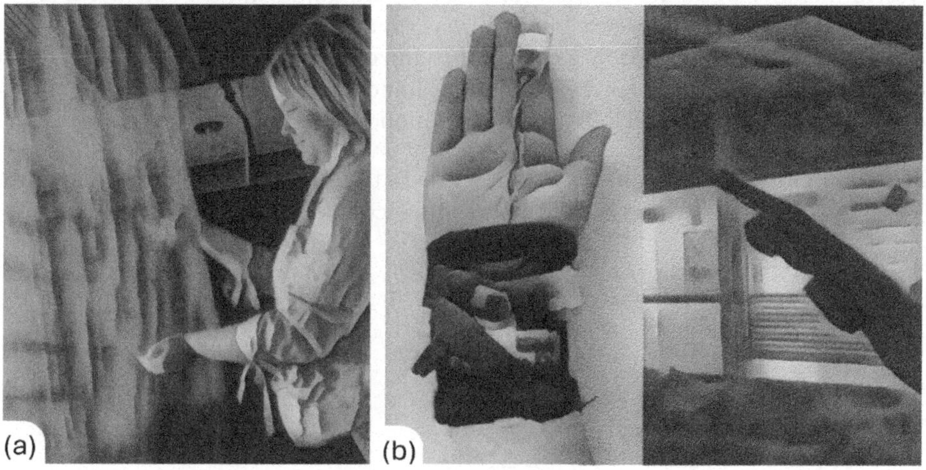

Fig. 13. Fogscreen [37]. (a) Users can reach into, even walk through, a fogscreen. (b) Interaction with tactile feedback.

particles – like fog. They bring new possibilities for displaying information in MR environments. Users can touch, reach into, even walk through a fogscreen. See Fig. 13a. Most commonly, fogscreens are found in settings such as trade shows, theme parks, or museums. Equipped with appropriate sensors, a fogscreen can act as an interactive display [20,32,33].

Remizova et al. [37] researched a fogscreen setup, focusing on interaction. Yes, fogscreens are enticing, even playful, but what are the possibilities for interaction? A critical issue is feedback. Users can reach into a fogscreen and touch or grab objects, but providing a sense of that might have benefits for performance or experience. In Remizova et al.'s setup, the position of the hands in the fogscreen was digitized using a motion-sensing Microsoft Kinect. Their study used a Fitts' law task, a per ISO 9241-411 [18], where participants reached into the fogscreen to acquire and select targets. Two selection methods (tapping, dwelling) and two feedback modes (audio-visual, audio-visual+haptic) were compared in a within-subjects user study with 20 participants. The haptic feedback method used a lightweight wireless vibrotactile actuator worn on the user's finger. See Fig. 13b. In the end, no performance advantage was found using haptic feedback vs. audio-visual feedback. This result has implications for the design of gestural interfaces suitable for interaction with fogscreens.

Wall Displays. Wall displays have a long history in HCI, dating to Bolt's "Put That There" demo in 1980 [4]. In Bolt's system, the user makes mid-air gestures, moving their hand to point to objects or locations on a wall-size display and then issues voice commands.[4] See Fig. 14. Bolt's system was a room with a large projection screen and an instrumented chair with a microphone for the user. The system included voice recognition for simple commands and a Polhemus 6 DOF tracker mounted on the user's hand. It was, perhaps, the first VR "Cave."

A common feature in Bolt's cave and Remizova et al.'s fogscreen is that both systems require on-body hardware (6 DOF hand tracker, haptic finger actuator) and off-body[5] hardware (chair with microphone, motion sensor). And so,

CC6. For each mixed reality environment, what on-body and off-body hardware is present and what is its role for input control or output display?

Fig. 14. Wall-size display in Bolt's "Put That There" demo from 1980 (after [4]).

James et al. [19] used a wall display in a collaborative work setting. See Fig. 15. The wall display was public – viewable to all. Users wore head-mounted displays providing additional virtual surfaces viewable to all team members. Each user also had a personal space viewable only to them. The personal space moved about with the user. Their research included a user study with 24 participants acting in pairs to solve a collaborative task either using the wall display alone or using the wall display augmented with the personal space and virtual surfaces. The design included a standardized questionnaire with items for mental

[4] Viewable on YouTube at https://www.youtube.com/watch?v=4XkUdwdq_-k.

[5] The term "on-environment" is also used [42].

Fig. 15. Wall display, personal space, and shared virtual surfaces for collaborative work (after [19]).

demand, physical demand, ease of use, enjoyment, etc. They also gathered quantitative measures of performance, such as task completion time. The questionnaire responses indicated a significantly better user experience for the wall+AR environment. However, the difference in task completion time between the wall-only and wall+AR conditions was not statistically significant. With this, we revisit a previous research question; see CC5.

2.5 And Beyond

Returning to the Ericsson poll [8], respondents commented on a variety of future scenarios. For one scenario, 59% of respondents believe it will be possible in the future to see map routes on VR glasses by simply thinking of a travel destination. This implies that mixed realities in the future may also include a brain-computer interface (BCI) with interactions driven, at least in part, by a user's thoughts.

Although there is considerable research on brain computer interfaces (e.g., [11,14,21,29]), mainstream applications remain elusive. This is partly due to the need to wear an electroencephalogram (EEG) cap with conductive gel, electrodes, and wires. Furthermore, most BCI systems are expensive and the set-up and calibration are complicated. So there is a technology gap for BCI systems for use by non-experts outside the lab.

In an attempt to address the issues just noted, Hou et al. [13] tested an inexpensive BCI product aimed at the gaming and VR markets. The NextMind,[6] introduced in 2019 and priced at $300, is a wearable sensor module with nine comb-shaped dry electrodes to pick up EEG signals and send them to the computer for processing. See Fig. 16a. De Pace et al. [7] used the NextMind device to

[6] https://ar.snap.com/welcome-nextmind.

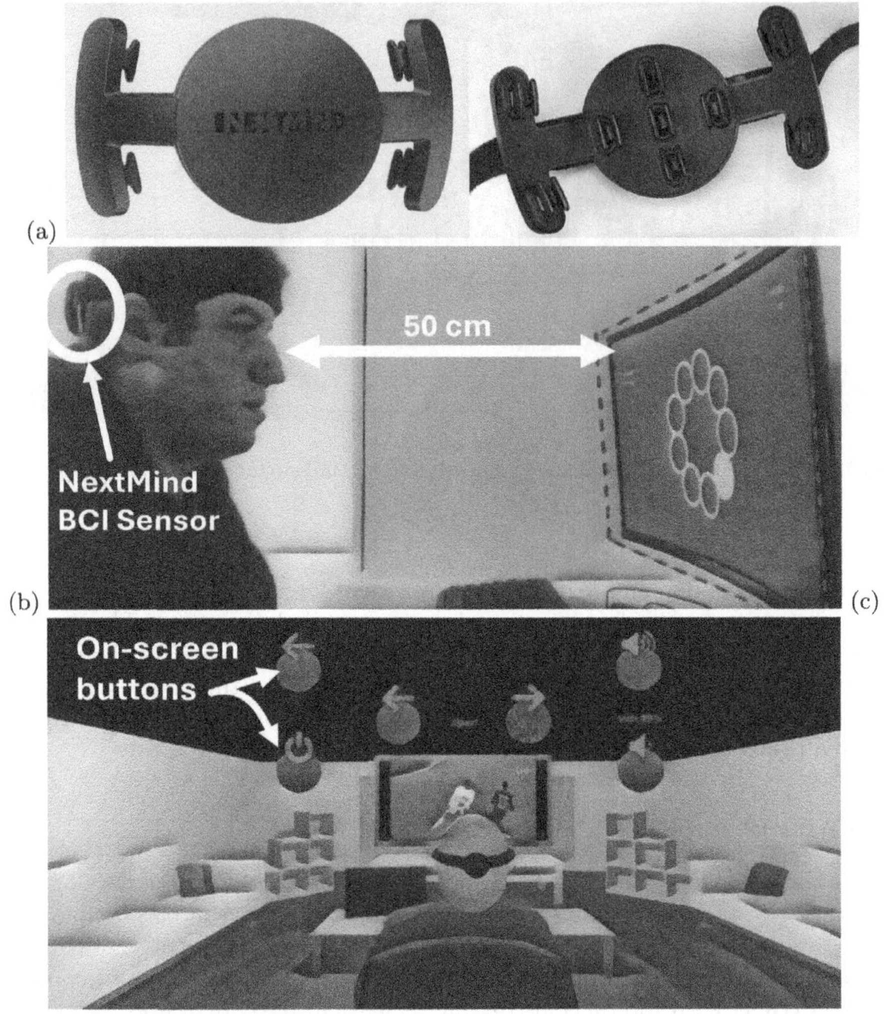

Fig. 16. NextMind brain-computer interface. (a) Device. (b) Experiment setup. (c) Use-case simulation for wheelchair and TV control (after [13]).

control a telerobotic arm in a pick-and-place task. They reported that selecting objects was "easy, fast, and reliable" (p. 1).

NextMind uses steady-state visually evoked potentials (SSVEP) whereby distinguishable brain responses occur when the user looks at an interface with objects flashing at different frequencies. In Hou et al.'s user study [13], six participants selected on-screen targets by looking at the targets. One task involved target selection as per ISO 9241-411 [18]. See Fig. 16b. The mean throughput achieved was 0.82 bits/s. This is quite low, considering that a similar task with touch-based selection yields throughput of ≈7 bits/s [22]. However, this is a notable result given that selection was performed simply by looking at targets and without using a eye tracking apparatus.

A second task was a use-case demonstration where a user selected on-screen buttons to steer and move a virtual wheelchair. See Fig. 16c. Once the wheelchair was in front of a TV, the user selected on-screen buttons to change the channel and control the volume.

Although Hou et al.'s setup used steady-state visually evoked potentials, BCI systems can also work through "motor imagery," whereby the user consciously thinks of certain actions, such as clenching a fist or raising a foot, while the signals emitted by the brain coincident with that action are measured, identified, and acted on in unique ways. However, it is not feasible at the present time for BCI systems to detect and act on open-ended thought patterns, such as a travel destination. And so,

CC7. What is our mixed-reality wish-list – interactions we cannot do today but would enjoy and benefit from should they be possible in the future?

3 Conclusion

In this position paper, we presented a cross-section of mixed reality environments and for each looked at the technology, what can be done, and where challenges lie. The context was the 2024 EICS workshop, "Experience 2.0 and Beyond - Engineering Cross Devices and Multiple Realities." The challenges were collected together in a series of community challenges which were offered as discussion topics for the workshop.

We conclude by again citing the important contribution of Milgram and Kishino's 1994 descriptive model for reality spaces than combine the real with the virtual.

References

1. Asakawa, C., Takagi, H.: Text entry for people with visual impairments. In: MacKenzie, I.S., Tanaka-Ishii, K. (eds.) Text Entry Systems: Mobility, Accessibility, Universality, pp. 305–318. Morgan Kaufmann, San Francisco (2007). https://doi.org/10.1016/B978-012373591-1/50016-4
2. Bilbow, S.: Developing multisensory augmented reality as a medium for computational artists. In: Proceedings of the Fifteenth International Conference on Tangible, Embedded, and Embodied Interaction – TEI 2021, pp. 72.1–72.7. ACM, New York (2021). https://doi.org/10.1145/3430524.3443690
3. Bimber, O., Raskar, R.: Modern approaches to augmented reality. In: Proceedings of SIGGRAPH 2006, p. 1-es. ACM, New York (2006). https://doi.org/10.1145/1185657.1185796
4. Bolt, R.A.: "Put-That-There": voice and gesture at the graphics interface. In: Proceedings of the 7th Annual Conference on Computer Graphics and Interactive Techniques - SIGGRAPH 1980, pp. 262–270. ACM, New York (1980). https://doi.org/10.1145/800250.807503

5. Cao, Y., Li, L., Yuan, J., Jeon, M.: Increasing driving safety and in-vehicle gesture-based menu navigation accuracy with a heads-up display. In: Adjunct Proceedings of the 14th International Conference on Automotive User Interfaces and Interactive Vehicular Applications – AutomotiveUI 2022, pp. 212–214. ACM, New York (2022). https://doi.org/10.1145/3544999.3551502
6. Ch, N.A.N., Tosca, D., Crump, T., Ansah, A., Kun, A., Shaer, O.: Gesture and voice commands to interact with AR windshield display in automated vehicle: a remote elicitation study. In: Proceedings of the 14th International Conference on Automotive User Interfaces and Interactive Vehicular Applications – AutomotiveUI 2022, pp. 171–182. ACM, New York (2022). https://doi.org/10.1145/3543174.3545257
7. De Pace, F., Manuri, F., Bosco, M., Sanna, A., Kaufmann, H.: Supporting human-robot interaction by projected augmented reality and a brain interface. IEEE Trans. Hum.-Mach. Syst. 1–10 (2024). https://doi.org/10.1109/THMS.2024.3414208
8. Ericsson: 10 hot consumer trends 2030: The Internet of senses. Technical report, Ericsson ConsumerLab (2019). https://www.ericsson.com/4ac661/assets/local/reports-papers/consumerlab/reports/2019/10hctreport2030.pdf. Accessed 15 Apr 2024
9. Fitts, P.M.: The information capacity of the human motor system in controlling the amplitude of movement. J. Exp. Psychol. **47**(6), 381–391 (1954). https://doi.org/10.1037/h0055392
10. Flavián, C., Ibáñez-Sánchez, S., Orús, C.: The impact of virtual, augmented and mixed reality technologies on the customer experience. J. Bus. Res. **100**, 547–560 (2019). https://doi.org/10.1016/j.jbusres.2018.10.050
11. Fouad, M.M., Amin, K.M., El-Bendary, N., Hassanien, A.E.: Brain computer interface: a review. In: Hassanien, A.E., Azar, A.T. (eds.) Brain-Computer Interfaces. ISRL, vol. 74, pp. 3–30. Springer, Cham (2015). https://doi.org/10.1007/978-3-319-10978-7_1
12. Gsaxner, C., et al.: The HoloLens in medicine: a systematic review and taxonomy. Med. Image Anal. **85**, 102757 (2023). https://doi.org/10.1016/j.media.2023.102757
13. Hou, B.J., et al.: Feasibility of a device for gaze interaction by visually-evoked brain signals. In: Proceedings of the 2022 Symposium on Eye Tracking Research & Applications – ETRA 2022, pp. 62.1–62.7. ACM, New York (2022). https://doi.org/10.1145/3517031.3529232
14. Hougaard, B.I., et al.: Who willed it? Decreasing frustration by manipulating perceived control through fabricated input for stroke rehabilitation BCI games. Proc. ACM Hum.-Comput. Interact. **5**(CHI PLAY), 235.1–235.19 (2021). https://doi.org/10.1145/3474662
15. Hubenschmid, S., Zagermann, J., Leicht, D., Reiterer, H., Feuchtner, T.: ARound the smartphone: investigating the effects of virtually-extended display size on spatial memory. In: Proceedings of the ACM SIGCHI Conference on Human Factors in Computing Systems – CHI 2023, pp. 527.1–527.15. ACM, New York (2023). https://doi.org/10.1145/3544548.3581438
16. Ihara, K., Faridan, M., Ichikawa, A., Kawaguchi, I., Suzuki, R.: HoloBots: augmenting holographic telepresence with mobile robots for tangible remote collaboration in mixed reality. In: Proceedings of the 36th Annual ACM Symposium on User Interface Software and Technology – UIST 2023, pp. 119.1–119.12. ACM, New York (2023). https://doi.org/10.1145/3586183.3606727

17. Irlitti, A., et al.: Volumetric mixed reality telepresence for real-time cross modality collaboration. In: Proceedings of the ACM SIGCHI Conference on Human Factors in Computing Systems – CHI 2023, pp. 101.1–101.14. ACM, New York (2023). https://doi.org/10.1145/3544548.3581277
18. ISO: Ergonomics of human-system interaction - Part 411: Evaluation methods for the design of physical input devices. Report Number ISO/TS 9241-411:2012, International Organisation for Standardisation, Geneva, Switzerland (2012)
19. James, R., Bezerianos, A., Chapuis, O.: Evaluating the extension of wall displays with AR for collaborative work. In: Proceedings of the ACM SIGCHI Conference on Human Factors in Computing Systems – CHI 2023, pp. 99.1–99.17. ACM, New York (2023). https://doi.org/10.1145/3544548.3580752
20. Jumisko-Pyykkö, S., Weitzel, M., Rakkolainen, I.: Biting, whirling, crawling - children's embodied interaction with walk-through displays. In: Gross, T., et al. (eds.) INTERACT 2009. LNCS, vol. 5726, pp. 123–136. Springer, Heidelberg (2009). https://doi.org/10.1007/978-3-642-03655-2_15
21. Koike, Y., Hiroi, Y., Itoh, Y., Rekimoto, J.: Brain-computer interface using directional auditory perception. In: Proceedings of the Augmented Humans International Conference – AH 2023, pp. 342–345. ACM, New York (2023). https://doi.org/10.1145/3582700.3583713
22. Scott MacKenzie, I.: Fitts' throughput and the remarkable case of touch-based target selection. In: Kurosu, M. (ed.) HCI 2015. LNCS, vol. 9170, pp. 238–249. Springer, Cham (2015). https://doi.org/10.1007/978-3-319-20916-6_23
23. MacKenzie, I.S.: Human-Computer Interaction: An Empirical Research Perspective, 2nd edn. Morgan Kaufmann (an imprint of Elsevier), Cambridge (2024). https://www.yorku.ca/mack/HCIbook2e/
24. MacKenzie, I.S., Soukoreff, R.W.: Phrase sets for evaluating text entry techniques. In: Extended Abstracts of the ACM SIGCHI Conference on Human Factors in Computing Systems – CHI 2003, pp. 754–755. ACM, New York (2003). https://doi.org/10.1145/765891.765971
25. Maquil, V., Anastasiou, D., Afkari, H., Coppens, A., Hermen, J., Schwartz, L.: Establishing awareness through pointing gestures during collaborative decision-making in a wall-display environment. In: Extended Abstracts of the ACM SIGCHI Conference on Human Factors in Computing Systems – CHI 2023, pp. 104.1–104.7. ACM, New York (2023). https://doi.org/10.1145/3544549.3585830
26. Milgram, P., Kishino, F.: A taxonomy of mixed reality visual displays. IEICE Trans. Inf. Syst. **E77-D**(12), 1321–1329 (1994)
27. Mirza-Babaei, P., Robinson, R., Mandryk, R., Pirker, J., Kang, C., Fletcher, A.: Games and the Metaverse. In: Extended Abstracts of the 2022 Annual Symposium on Computer-Human Interaction in Play – CHI PLAY 2023, pp. 318–319. ACM, New York (2022). https://doi.org/10.1145/3505270.3558355
28. Mukhopadhyay, A., Sharma, V.K., Gaikwad, P.T., Sandula, A.K., Biswas, P.: Exploring the use of XR interfaces for driver assistance in take over request. In: Adjunct Proceedings of the 14th International Conference on Automotive User Interfaces and Interactive Vehicular Applications – AutomotiveUI 2022, pp. 58–61. ACM, New York (2022). https://doi.org/10.1145/3544999.3552527
29. Nicolas-Alonso, L.F., Gomez-Gil, J.: Brain computer interfaces, a review. Sensors **12**(2), 1211–1279 (2012). https://doi.org/10.3390/s120201211
30. Niedenthal, S., Fredborg, W., Lundén, P., Ehrndal, M., Olofsson, J.K.: A graspable olfactory display for virtual reality. Int. J. Hum Comput Stud. **169**, 102928 (2023). https://doi.org/10.1016/j.ijhcs.2022.102928

31. Niedenthal, S., Lundén, P., Ehrndal, M., Olofsson, J.K.: A handheld olfactory display for smell-enabled VR games. In: IEEE International Symposium on Olfaction and Electronic Nose – ISOEN 2019, pp. 1–4. IEEE, New York (2019). https://doi.org/10.1109/ISOEN.2019.8823162
32. Palovuori, K., Rakkolainen, I.: Improved virtual reality for mid-air projection screen technology. In: Proceedings of the International Symposium on Communicability, Computer Graphics and Innovative Design for Interactive Systems – CCGIDIS 2013, pp. 25–33. Blue Herons Editions, Bergamo, Italy (2013). 10.978.8896471/227
33. Palovuori, K., Rakkolainen, I.: Improved interaction for mid-air projection screen technology. In: Association, I.R.M. (ed.) Virtual and Augmented Reality: Concepts, Methodologies, Tools, and Applications, pp. 1742–1761. IGI Global, Hershey, PA (2018). https://doi.org/10.4018/978-1-5225-5469-1.ch082
34. Pamparău, C.: Dare we define olfactory augmented reality? In: Proceedings of the 2023 ACM International Conference on Interactive Media Experiences Workshops – IMXw 2023, pp. 52–55. ACM, New York (2023). https://doi.org/10.1145/3604321.3604376
35. Rauschnabel, P.A., Felix, R., Hinsch, C., Shahab, H., Alt, F.: What is XR? Towards a framework for augmented and virtual reality. Comput. Hum. Behav. **133**, 107289 (2022). https://doi.org/10.1016/j.chb.2022.107289
36. Rebol, M., Lake, B., Reinisch, M., Pietroszek, K., Gütl, C.: Holographic sports training. In: Companion Proceedings of the 2023 Conference on Interactive Surfaces and Spaces – ISS 2023, pp. 70–73. ACM, New York (2023). https://doi.org/10.1145/3626485.3626547
37. Remizova, V., et al.: Mid-air gestural interaction with a large fogscreen. Multimodal Technol. Interact. **7**(63), 1–18 (2023). https://doi.org/10.3390/mti7070063
38. Sargolzaei, P., Rastogi, M., Zaman, L.: Advancing mixed reality game development: an evaluation of a visual game analytics tool in action-adventure and FPS genres. In: Proceedings of the ACM on Human-Computer Interaction, vol. 8, No. CHI PLAY, Article 290, 32 p. ACM, New York (2024). https://doi.org/10.1145/3677055
39. Schmidt, L., Yigitbas, E.: Development and usability evaluation of transitional cross-reality interfaces. Proc. ACM Hum.-Comput. Interact. **8**(EICS), 263.1–263.32 (2024). https://doi.org/10.1145/3664637
40. Skarbez, R., Smith, M., Whitton, M.: It is time to let go of 'Virtual Reality'. Commun. ACM **66**(10), 41–43 (2023). https://doi.org/10.1145/3590959
41. Speicher, M., Hall, B.D., Nebeling, M.: What is mixed reality? In: Proceedings of the ACM SIGCHI Conference on Human Factors in Computing Systems – CHI 2019, pp. 1–15. ACM, New York (2019). https://doi.org/10.1145/3290605.3300767
42. Suzuki, R., Karim, A., Xia, T., Hedayati, H., Marquardt, N.: Augmented reality and robotics: a survey and taxonomy for AR-enhanced human-robot interaction and robotic interfaces. In: Proceedings of the ACM SIGCHI Conference on Human Factors in Computing Systems – CHI 2022. ACM, New York (2022). https://doi.org/10.1145/3491102.3517719
43. Vaiani, G., Paternò, F.: End-user development for human-robot interaction: results and trends in an emerging field. Proc. ACM Hum.-Comput. Interact. **8**(EICS), 252.1–252.40 (2024). https://doi.org/10.1145/3661146
44. Wang, X.M., et al.: The geometry of the vergence-accommodation conflict in mixed reality systems. Virtual Reality **28**(95) (2024). https://doi.org/10.1007/s10055-024-00991-4

45. Wigdor, D., Forlines, C., Baudisch, P., Barnwell, J., Shen, C.: LucidTouch: a see-through mobile device. In: Proceedings of the ACM Symposium on User Interface Software and Technology – UIST 2007, pp. 269–278. ACM, New York (2007). https://doi.org/10.1145/1294211.1294259
46. Xu, J., et al.: Metaverse: the vision for the future. In: Extended Abstracts of the ACM SIGCHI Conference on Human Factors in Computing Systems – CHI 2022, pp. 167.1–167.3. ACM, New York (2022). https://doi.org/10.1145/3491101.3516399
47. Yamada, W., Manabe, H., Ikeda, D., Rekimoto, J.: RayGraphy: aerial volumetric graphics rendered using lasers in fog. In: Proceedings of the 2020 ACM Symposium on Spatial User Interaction - SUI 2020, pp. 11.1–11.99. ACM, New York (2020). https://doi.org/10.1145/3385959.3418446
48. Zhao, S., Tan, F., Fennedy, K.: Heads-up computing: moving beyond the device-centered paradigm. Commun. ACM **66**(9), 56–63 (2023). https://doi.org/10.1145/3571722
49. Zulkarnain, A.H.B., Kókai, Z., Gere, A.: Assessment of a virtual sensory laboratory for consumer sensory evaluations. Heliyon **10**(3) (2024). https://doi.org/10.1016/j.heliyon.2024.e25498

Examining Semantic Coupling in Augmented Reality

Nina Rosa(✉)

Wageningen University and Research, Droevendaalsesteeg 3, 6708PB Wageningen, The Netherlands
nina.rosa-dejong@wur.nl

Abstract. Augmented reality (AR) requires the real environment to be part of the experience. Semantic coupling, the degree of connection between the physical and the virtual, has been explored as a way to create more immersive AR experiences. Studies that have investigated semantic coupling have used AR in a very specific way, leading to a possible misinterpretation of when semantic coupling can be used, and how to design for it. In this position paper, I examine the literature on semantic coupling, place and aura, and describe which types of places future AR studies studying or applying semantic coupling should consider, how to create semantic coupling without the need for a complex narrative, and how to ensure and verify a degree of connection in semantic coupling experiments.

Keywords: Augmented Reality · Mixed Reality · Semantic Coupling · Place · Aura · Experience · Immersion

1 Introduction

Augmented reality (AR) research from the 1990s and 2000s saw a large interest in improving technology, and there was less attention for user experience; there were still few guidelines on how to create 'good' AR experiences. Now, there are aspects which are consistently considered important, such as immersion, presence, and engagement, but it is still not agreed upon what a 'good' AR experience is. More recently we are seeing the anticipated research interest in evaluating user experience [1] and designing for certain experiences [6]. Design guidelines for AR applications for specific contexts are also increasingly being developed [11,39].

One interesting factor that AR introduces that may influence user experience is the actual place in which the experience occurs, since the real environment is always part of the of the experience. Some AR applications integrate unique aspects of the real surroundings into the experience, while others do not [38]. In this position paper, I zoom in on this particular concept of semantic coupling.

Semantic coupling can been defined as the degree of connection between the AR application and the physical space in which it is experienced [13,38].

L. Zaina et al. (Eds.): EICS 2024, LNCS 15518, pp. 254–268, 2025.
https://doi.org/10.1007/978-3-031-91760-8_17

This concept reportedly first emerged in 2005 by Reid et al. [31] under the phenomenon "magic moments" in the context of location-based audio AR. One particular type of magic moment would occur when aspects from the physical and virtual worlds would unexpectedly collide [31]. Since then others have studied semantic coupling and similar concepts, but there is no agreed upon terminology, and the phrases 'semantic' and/or 'coupling' only appear sporadically. Moreover, due to the history of AR research, semantic coupling has become locked within location-based research, while it could be equally relevant for the experience of non-mobile applications. Lastly, while there are a number of empirical studies on semantic coupling, there is no predefined method with which one could state that a given physical world is strongly or loosely coupled to a given virtual one.

The purpose of this position paper is to examine the concept of semantic coupling in order to delineate its role and use in future AR research. First, an overview of literature that has discussed or applied the concept of semantic coupling is provided. Second, expressions of the importance of places from Human-Computer Interaction (HCI) and AR literature are discussed. Third, a discussion is presented based on tendencies in past semantic coupling research and shows what potential future research that focuses on designing for immersive experiences could entail. Finally, suggestions for the design of semantic coupling experiments are provided.

In this paper, a broad notion of AR is used: everything can be augmented, and the virtual augments that to which it relates [35]. Similarly, augmentation can occur across modalities [33]. This means that works labeled as location-based, mixed reality (MR), and pervasive games are included. It is also worth noting that Georgiou and Kyza [13] previously provided and overview on semantic coupling studies. While they focused on empirical studies on narrative coupling, here those and more studies are presented in more detail to understand how semantic coupling in general was achieved and how it was experienced.

2 Literature on Semantic Coupling in AR

2.1 Magic Moments

The works by Reid et al. [31] are typically referenced as the first mention of a meaningful connection between real and virtual content. The authors studied situated mediascapes: mobile, location-based narrative experiences. In the analysis of their mediascape *Riot! 1831*, they found that participants experienced what the authors called magic moments: memorable moments that people valued and enjoyed. There were four types of these moments, one in particular being "unexpected connections between physical and virtual worlds" [31, sect. 3.2] such as a hearing a virtual seagull cry and then seeing a real one fly over. The high ratings of enjoyment, immersion, and history coming alive are attributed by the authors to magic moments. Reid et al. [30] also showed that there were positive correlations between these ratings, and they inferred that immersion was a positive determinant for enjoyment and vice versa, and that history coming alive was a special form of immersion.

In a different mediascape, *Scape the Hood*, the authors gave special attention to collecting sounds from the real location, in order to create magic moments [29]. Similar to before, they found high ratings of, amongst others, enjoyment, immersion, and importance of listening to the stories in the exact location. Participants commented that the close connection between what you see and what you hear positively affected the experience.

Reid et al. [28] also published experience design guidelines for situated mediascapes, with one section devoted to "meaningfulness of the place". There, they differentiate between three types of places that can be chosen depending on how important the location is for the mediascape: arbitrary linkage (any place of certain size), physicality (place with certain characteristics that are important but actual geography is not), particular location (actual location and physical artifacts are significant and meaningful to the mediascape) [28].

Lastly, Reid [27] presented a spectrum concerning the relevance of place for location-based games, from neutral (the place is used for solely the spatial properties) to high (place has a strong association in terms of its significance, meaning and integration within the narrative of the game), reflecting the arbitrary linkage and particular location definitions from the previous design guidelines [28].

Interestingly, this collection of works by Reid et al. is not the first mention of connecting real places to virtual narratives. In the context of what pervasive games should look like, Ericsson [10] expressed his opinion that, just like roleplaying games, pervasive games require that the narrative of the game be consistent with the real world. Stories should essentially be set in the modern world, and things like magic can be included but should be hidden or integrated with day-to-day existence. Ericsson uses quotes from other works to reflect how artifacts, actors, and visual and sound effects (i.e. magic moments) are required.

2.2 Levels of Semantic Coupling and Types of Connections

Wetzel et al. [38] also noted the importance of semantic location context, and it became one of three dimensions in the categorization of mobile AR games. The game can be location independent (the location is not relevant for the game), loosely coupled (played with very little relation to enclosing places), or contextual (the game has a strong narrative relation to the location they are played in). Krüger [17, table 3] describes levels of contextuality, not as a scale, but by looking at whether there is thematic relevance between an AR application's context and the physical environment and/or anchors (markers), and whether the environment and/or anchors are fully visible despite virtual elements.

A different interpretation of coupling is given by Schraffenberger and Van der Heide [35]. There, the authors investigate what is real and what is augmented in AR, and state that the virtual content augments that to which it relates, which can concern a spatial relation and/or a content-based relation. Similarly, Ellenburg et al. [9, sect. 3.2] present a two-dimensional design space for overall perceived unity in a mixed reality environment. The dimensions are spatial coupling and semantic coupling, of which the latter they define as "a contextual connection and relation of virtual content items with [...] real world objects."

They highlight that a binary definition (i.e. something is or is not coupled) is insufficient to differentiate contextual connections in detail.

2.3 Empirical Studies

The works by Reid et al. [28,30,31] use an empirical approach, and other studies have followed the same approach. Paay et al. [24] argue that humans are drawn to fiction when it interweaves historical fact and real places with which we may be familiar. The location-based fiction *Who killed Hanna Holmgaard?* was developed, where factual and fictitious events in the city of Aalborg take place. The designers combine digital components with real locations and objects such as the use of digitally altered photographs in order to create fuzzy boundaries between story and environment. Audio was appreciated by participants as something that created an atmosphere that blended with the real city and made the story come to life, and participants who were residents claimed that they had learned new things about their city.

In a series of studies, the location-aware AR game *TimeWarp* was developed where participants travel to different time periods in the same city [21,38]. In the first version, the main element of semantic coupling is the story being based on the historic tale of elves in Cologne. Participants could see the elves and virtual elements visually overlaid on portable see-through displays. The evaluation found peaks and drops in immersion, and the potential solution provided for the drops is to integrate real people and objects into the game, e.g. to make real use of street ambiance, coinciding with Reid et al.'s [29] description on how to create magic moments. In *TimeWarp 2.0*, the elves were traded in for robot-elves to better match the time travelling theme, and virtual elements were planned to more carefully match the content of the real world, such as a virtual wedding by a real church [38]. Based on the evaluations of both versions, mobile AR game design guidelines are provided, such as adding atmospheric scenery objects, sounds and smells to help the player immerse themselves into a narrative place.

Rossitto et al. [34] analyzed the location-based audio theater drama, *Maryam*, designed around loose coupling. They found that immersion in the narrative contributed to the particular sense of place "being at the theater", and also the wandering contributed to their imagination of being transported somewhere else, in the time and place where the main character lived. Participants mentioned wanting more connections, i.e. wanting more magic moments, yet they also described enjoying using their imagination to create the associations to make sense of the ambiguity. Associations could be physical or activity-based, and being familiar with the neighborhood played a role in how the connections were made. The authors argue that loosely coupled designs can offer enjoyable, engaging and immersive experiences.

Raeburn et al. [26] created the location-based AR story experience *MapStory* that can be experienced anywhere. The story uses buildings and places of meaning, such as a school and a church, that are usually present in cities, and when they do not exist, a visual overlay is created on a smartphone screen in an open space. Virtual clues were added to the scenes that players needed to interact with. The evaluation showed, amongst others, that when comparing real sites to AR sites participants experienced less match between the visited site and the one described, and found it harder to imagine the story events playing out at the site. Comments showed that being familiar with the area made it harder to think about it in terms of a new story, and that AR could have given more chances to immerse. Comments also suggested deeper immersion only happened when aspects of the story temporarily paralleled something in the real world environment, i.e. during magic moments.

Similarly, Li et al. [19] designed a method to automatically adapt stories to real-world locations based on contextual compatibility using an optimization-based approach. In one of the user studies, the authors evaluated the player experience regarding the compatibility between event and location, by comparing a condition where the optimization used compatibility, walking distance, and equal distribution of walking as costs, and a condition where only the latter two were costs. Location compatibility was rated significantly higher in the compatibility condition than in the no compatibility condition, and all users agreed that the compatibility condition led to a more reasonable storytelling.

While these experiences and games were evaluated by the general public, some experiences are specifically catered to tourists. Ballagas et al. [2] created a game *REXplorer* with a dramatic narrative and some historical facts, not as a replacement for tour guides, but to help tourists become interested in the history of Regensburg. By "casting spells" (using a device as a wand) the system provided the players with fictitious stories based on the true events. The system would save recordings and images that were later blogged for the users to share with friends. Some users became very immersed, as illustrated by neglect of safety precautions. Participants had a hard time remembering facts, but they did build important connections to history, which combined with the personalized webblog could result in new knowledge.

Lastly, Weerasinghe et al. [37] studied whether learning vocabulary in context could be enhanced by means of AR. Their application, *VocabulARy*, visually annotates objects in AR with corresponding first and second language words (written and audio), a keyword (mnemonic) and its visualisation. The authors compared AR with keywords, AR with keywords and visualisation, non-AR with keywords, and non-AR with keywords and associations. In the non-AR case users saw a virtual kitchen or office scene with matching virtual objects via a tablet while seated in an empty real room, while in the AR case users were seated in a kitchen or office with real objects. Results showed that AR scored better than non-AR in terms of mental effort and task-completion time, and visualization scored better than just keywords in terms of immediate and delayed recall, learning efficiency, mental effort and task-completion time. This indicated that showing keywords and visualisations in context of immediate surroundings (i.e. AR with semantic coupling) resulted in better learning than showing them in a virtual scene (i.e. non-AR).

2.4 Systematic Studies

There are a few studies that have investigated semantic coupling systematically. Karapanos et al. [16] performed an experiment with tourists using a location-aware narrative in Funchal, *iLand*, where participants would stand at a specific (stationary) location in the city, and watch a video that either took place in that original location, a location with the same atmosphere, or an arbitrary location, following the distinction by Reid et al. [28]. Results showed that experiencing a narrative in the original location led to increased immersion and heightened imagery compared to the control condition. In the same atmosphere location, there was also heightened immersion but not heightened imagery, i.e. no experienced magic moments, possibly due to confusion and disengagement arising when searching for connections in the same atmosphere location but not finding them.

In a series of studies, Georgiou and Kyza [12,13,18] investigated the relation between immersion and learning, by creating two educational location-based AR games, *Mystery at the lake* on eutrophication and bioaccumulation [12,18], and *Mysterious disease* on microbes and pathogens [13]. An evaluation of the first game showed there were improvements to be made in interface, content, locality and context. With respect to locality, students reported that investigating an environmental case where it had unfolded positively contributed to their sense of immersion; yet, they still needed greater coupling [12,18]. Therefore in the redesign they also let students engage with both the real and virtual worlds, e.g. test real water from the lake. Especially props in the second iteration enhanced immersion since it created connections, i.e. students experienced magic moments. Regarding learning, the second iteration (with other improvements besides locality) led to more engagement with the activity and more engagement in obtaining information.

For the second game, semantic coupling was specifically of interest [13]. The authors expected that with stronger semantic coupling, there would be greater immersion and better learning outcomes. The game was set in a university building where a disease outbreak had taken place, and the authors compared a strong coupling condition (QR codes in related rooms, and props) to a loose coupling condition (QR codes in unrelated rooms, no props). Children in the strong coupling condition reported more immersion and achieved better learning scores than children in the loose coupling condition. Moreover, there were numerous positive correlations between the immersion and learning measures for the strong coupling condition, which were mostly absent in the loose coupling condition. According to the interviews, reasons for the differences in experienced realism included the purposeful placement of the QR codes and the props.

Wu et al. [40] performed an experiment where participants were shown a virtual butterfly on top of their real hand using a smartphone. The authors examined three forms of relations between real and virtual on, amongst other measures, realism and presence [40]. The relations were contextual (e.g. location related to butterflies, following Wetzel et al. [38]), physical (e.g. gravity), and interactive (e.g. natural). Note the absence of narrative in this application.

For the contextual relation specifically, they found increased realism, but not increased presence, possibly due to the novelty factor of AR, yet the general conclusion was to always include contextual relationships in AR experiences, so the user's focus is not only on the virtual content.

Lastly, Cheng et al. [7] present their application, *SemanticAdapt*, which creates MR layouts of offices such that object placement takes semantic connections between objects (real and/or virtual) into account, for example by preferring when elements and objects which share semantic associations are placed in close proximity. This application was tested against a control application without semantic requirements, and it was found that *SemanticAdapt* resulted in a reduction of required adjustments by the user after seeing the initial layout, and a reduction of misplaced items, both by approximately 35%. The authors suggested that future studies also take into account depth of semantic associations; for example, a PDF could be associated with 'reading' and 'article', or more deeply by the topic of its content. This is similar to the case made by Ellenburg et al. [9].

While these studies are primarily based on a system having 'built-in' relations, there are also applications that let the user decide whether to create relations or not. One highlighted here is the study by McGookin et al. [22], where participants created digital location-based graffiti that others could view, as a form of social network . The authors expected participants to create primarily place-related tags, but only 60–80% of tags were intended to relate to the place they were created, and only 20–60% of tags were interpreted as having a relationship with the environment. The authors explain that the relationships were of two types: physical and semantic, which echoes the spatial and content-based relationships defined by Schraffenberger and Van der Heide [35].

2.5 Overarching Themes

Looking at the discussed studies, there are two notable overarching themes. Firstly, most studies are on mobile location-based applications, where large spaces serve as locations that people have to traverse, likely a product of the technological abilities of the 1990s and 2000s. These spaces are generally parts of cities that are already considered meaningful because they contain history. Secondly, the coupling typically happens through narrative, i.e. the story concerns the location in which the experience takes place. Again, it can be seen seen that stories are developed around characters that live in or wander the city. In the next section, we discuss the importance of place in different types of experiences.

3 Space, Place and Aura

Discussions on what makes a certain place meaningful have been ongoing for decades. Here, one of the most influential notions of place is highlighted before discussing notions specific to HCI and AR. In his book, Relph [32] takes a phenomenological approach to describe how we experience spaces. Very generally speaking, a space is of geographical nature, while a place has some added meaning from an experiential perspective. The identity of a place is defined by the setting, the activities that happen there, and meaning, and lies in large part in the experience of an "inside" that is distinctive from an "outside", reflecting familiarity with and belonging to a place. Then, authentic place-making occurs when there is sensitivity to the significance of place in everyday life. Placelessness occurs when meanings and identities of places are ignored or lacking.

Within HCI, Harrison and Dourish [15] discuss the differences between space and place in the context of collaborative (office) systems. They argue that designers are seeking a sense of place rather than space: appropriate behavioral framing rooted in cultural understandings about behavior and action. Places are spaces that are valued, and the sense of place must be forged by the users over time. Collaborative systems need to be designed to support the duality of space and place [15].

While these concepts have provided significant guidance for research, they do not explain why different places create different responses from users. This problem was noticed by MacIntyre et al. [20]. To measure the user's sense of emotional engagement, rather than relying on presence (in terms of "being there"), they propose the concept of aura. This concept is derived from Benjamin's [3] notion of aura in the humanities, where aura is the "unique phenomenon of a distance, no matter how near." MacIntyre et al. [20, sect. 2] define aura of an object or place as "the combination of its cultural and personal significance for a user or group of users". Places of cultural significance have placeness, or a sense of place following Harrison and Dourish, but these places can also have other special personal significance, creating aura. Technology can leverage aura to improve the experience by bringing the place/object "closer" to the user, and technology can enhance aura by increasing the connection between the place/object and user. The authors argue that aura also bears an important relationship to space and place, where embodiment is a key aspect. They state that "just as place was developed to supplement the concept of space, [...] place now needs to be supplemented with the concept of aura" [20, sect. 5]. There is a strange relationship between VR's presence (in the sense of non-mediation) and aura, which is further examined in later works [4,5]. In these works, they also explain why aura enhancement occurs in MR. Where a VR reproduction of a place or object may diminish aura, or only give a "memory of aura", in MR the experience is both immediate and mediated [4,5]. The physical presence should enhance aura, and the medium could further enhance aura by building a sense of distance-through-proximity [4,5].

Note that these works were published around the same time as the collection of works by Reid et al. [27,29–31]. Since then the majority of works have referenced magic moments or semantic coupling; the concept of place is not frequently mentioned (from the above works only in [21,22,27,34]), let alone the concept of aura. One recent study that successfully brought these related, yet until now quite isolated, concepts together was Sharma et al. [36]. The authors performed a systematic literature review to find the salient variables that MR play designers need to consider when selecting space, and how these variables impact the experiences. A brief description is provided on related concepts, including MR, AR, space, place, and aura. The result was a framework for selecting space based on two dimensions: continuity (individual, isolated, continuous, ubiquitous spaces) and specificity requirements (open, templated, place). Here, place is a templated space with added aura. Note that the specificity categories coincide with the levels defined by Reid et al. [28]. One of the main conclusions is that the continuity of space drives the need for virtual data that is linked to a physical world location [36].

Lastly, in a recent work Pitman [25] explores how motion-sensitive but not locative technologies can help create aura in common places, for generating environmental affect. The case game *Sin Sol* is a green art game on ecological collapse. It shows plants overlaid on the camera feed of a smartphone, and in order to interact with visible but far away plants, the user must walk up to them. This requires players to play the game outside in large open spaces such as parks, which in turn may allow the user to compare their own positionality and surroundings with that of the avatar and the collapse the avatar describes. This comparison helps players be aware of signs of climate breakdown, and appreciate the natural world more deeply. Playing the game in an already auratic area such as the Ilkley Moor showed virtual forests that were absent in real life, as vegetation is kept to a minimum for raising and shooting grouse, creating a very provacative scene. The author explains that the avatar offers the player a way of reading the environment that imbues it with aura, and the game contrives to restore the aura of the environment [25].

4 Discussion

Based on the works discussed in Sects. 2 and 3, the gathered insights are combined, and a number of questions are posed. These are based on the two overarching themes: large culturally relevant locations being used, and semantic coupling occurring through narrative.

4.1 Large Locations and Aura

Looking at works categorized by Sharma et al. [36] as "in place" (i.e. the locations have aura), it is clear that mostly parts of cities have been explored, but also cemeteries and archeological sites. There are undoubtedly many more types of large spaces that are culturally and personally significant. One question that arises is whether semantic coupling can only happen in large spaces, since so far this has been the setting for the majority of studies. Sharma et al. explicitly state that although they found no combination of "individual" "place-based" AR game systems, they noted that there is no reason these systems should not exist. In Sect. 2, there were few non-mobile "individual" cases, i.e. where the user was not required to walk [7,9,16,37,40]; these found that semantic coupling contributed positively to immersion, presence, perceived unity, layout or learning. Looking at magic moments of type "unexpected connections between real and virtual" specifically, they do not require walking or large areas; multiple magic moments can happen in a single location. While the magic moment design checklist [27] was intended for mediascapes in large spaces, many of the aspects are easily translatable to small meaningful spaces.

Another question that arises is whether there needs to be a specific balance between cultural and personal significance of places in order for them to have aura and consequently enhance the AR experience. Section 2 showed that familiarity generally creates deeper immersion [24,31,34], except when it clashes with your understanding of a place [26]. Would these moments of immersion have been stronger if the familiar places had been even more personally significant, such as one's own workplace, school, or home, or weaker because it clashes with the role of that place in your own life? On the other hand, it is imaginable that AR experiences that are semantically coupled to any of these more personal locations could be more emotionally engaging. For example, one could argue that for the average person the most personally significant place is home. Although at first glance an individual's home does not have cultural significance, Relph [32] argues that homes are not just the foundation of our own identity as individuals, but also of our identity as members of a community. Moreover, there are examples of experiences that are transformed through AR simply by bringing them into homes, such as *Mario Kart Live: Home Circuit* [23]. Although I do not propose aura as a requirement for AR, it may help researchers understand the types of significance that matter.

4.2 Narrative

In the discussed studies, there were different types of relations and connections between real and virtual content. Schraffenberger and Van der Heide [35] defined real and virtual having spatial or content-based relationships, which is reflected in the location independent AR games described by Wetzel et al. [38]: each game only focuses on spatial relationships, and they lack content-based relationships. Even though these games had narratives, the narratives occurred only on the virtual side of the games. On the other hand, one could argue that the narrative used for semantic coupling is an example of the content-based relationships. In most of the works described in Sect. 2, the intended connection between virtual and real is through narrative, yet intended or desired magic moments concern a blending of content-based and spatial relations. That is, generally, objects or events are mentioned in the narrative, but are not the core of the narrative, and are designed to create ambiance and coincidences, such as seagulls [31], stairs [34], and weddings [38]. Similarly, for loose coupling, Rossitto et al. [34] found only two types of associations: physical or activity-based, both of which help the setting, but not the main story, as designed.

Narrative has been the go-to way to create semantic coupling in AR. Narrative-based learning specifically has been shown to be effective in enhancing and holding interest in topics [14], thus for such a context using a narrative is logical. Karapanos et al. [16] explains how narrative alone could arguably be immersive by itself, as demonstrated by the "book problem", by tapping into psychological immersion as opposed to perceptual immersion. But even this does not mean that complex narratives are necessary for semantic coupling or even immersive experiences in general. What if the main focus of the application is not necessarily to learn, but just to experience or feel or think about (non-)fiction? This was demonstrated by Wu et al. [40] and Weerasinghe et al. [37], who use a more abstract (or arguably, more basic) type of semantics: placing virtual content in an environment that makes sense. Reusing the home example from earlier, one could imagine food-related AR experiences to be most immersive in the kitchen, and plant-related AR experiences to be most immersive in the garden. The experience could revolve around play, learning, or just becoming emotionally engaged with a topic, like food-waste or biodiversity.

5 Designing Experiments with Semantic Coupling

Now that considerations for future research on semantic coupling have been provided, how to study and apply the concept in an experiment is briefly addressed. In Sect. 2.4, studies that systematically investigate semantic coupling were described. While it is indisputable that the used conditions differ in relevance for each experience, it is still interesting to consider what alternatives could have been used, or how the specific choices were made; how does one go about choosing the locations? For example, while Reid et al. [28] explain that three types of places could be used depending on if place is an integral element of the experience, how would one know beforehand whether a place is indeed significant or meaningful?

One way to approach ensuring the conditions are chosen well is to run a pilot study and ask potential participants what they would consider spaces that are and are not related or connected to a narrative or abstract concept. This was attempted in a recent thesis project on using AR to teach about waste separation rules, where potential participants were asked early in the design phase which locations they associated with waste separation, within the boundaries of a university [8, p. 12]. Then, to check whether the condition was experienced with the intended level op coupling, manipulation check questions were asked: "I often throw away waste in this type of space", "I associate this type of space with waste separation", "The physical space of the activity is connected to the waste separation theme of the activity". Despite only finding small differences in presence, the results of the manipulation check showed that the locations were well chosen [8, p. 14]. For a similar result, Karapanos et al. [16] asked participants whether they noticed any elements from the physical environment that surrounded them in the audio-visual narrative, and if they did, to point them out. The most specific elements were reported in the strongly coupled condition, general atmosphere elements were reported in the loosely coupled condition, and none were reported in the control condition.

Georgiou and Kyza [13] used both location aspects and props to create the largest difference between conditions, but arguably this would not have made sense in the study by Wu et al. [40]. While the use of props is facilitated by the narrative component, note it is still possible to include props in a scenario without narrative. Taking the kitchen example from before, one could make use of props that are typically found in kitchens, such as cutlery, pots, a refrigerator and a waste bin. This was also seen in the work by Weerasinghe et al. [37], where the office space contained objects like scissors, an envelope, and sticky notes.

Lastly, it is important to understand where semantic coupling should be placed in the greater context of AR experiences. Generally, AR applications serve a certain purpose, with learning outcomes being one of the most common desirable outcomes. Such outcomes are generally influenced by mediators such as immersion [13] or presence. In turn, these mediators are influenced by factors, which are for example used to design the conditions of experiments (e.g. low-immersion and high-immersion conditions). I argue that semantic coupling should be considered as such a factor. Therefore, achieving semantic coupling, and an experienced coincidence of real and virtual, is something for which should be designed. Reid et al. [28] have published a work on exactly this for mediascapes.

6 Conclusion

In this position paper existing literature on semantic coupling and on the concepts of space, place and aura was investigated. There are a few main takeaways from the insights gathered from these studies. Firstly, aura has made apparent that AR with semantic coupling does not necessarily need large locations, just locations that are meaningful. The locations are meaningful when they are culturally and/or personally significant, but not necessarily both. Semantic coupling can therefore also be applied in small meaningful places. Future AR studies that aim to create immersive experiences that are emotionally engaging should consider the location in which the experience occurs. With the rise of AR head-mounted displays, which are still often tethered to a computer, it is possible a large portion of these future immersive experiences will be designed for small spaces. Secondly, narrative has been used to enable semantic coupling, but scenarios were described that demonstrate that narrative is not essential to semantic coupling. This is particularly interesting for experiences that for example do not have learning as a focus, but just the experience of (non-)fiction. Future AR studies could consider experiences that do not rely on narrative, by choosing spaces that are already relevant to the topic at hand. Lastly, suggestions were provided on how future AR studies could approach designing an experiment using semantic coupling, specifically, by estimating meaningfulness beforehand based on conversations with potential participants, and performing manipulation checks afterwards. Props can help amplify the difference between low and high coupling conditions, and ways to incorporate props in small meaningful locations without narrative were described. This position paper has illustrated in which ways semantic coupling can enhance AR experiences, and future researchers should consider semantic coupling when designing AR experiences and research.

Disclosure of Interests. The author has no competing interests to declare that are relevant to the content of this article.

References

1. Arifin, Y., Sastria, T.G., Barlian, E.: User experience metric for augmented reality application: a review. Procedia Comput. Sci. **135**, 648–656 (2018). https://doi.org/10.1016/j.procs.2018.08.221
2. Ballagas, R., Kuntze, A., Walz, S.P.: Gaming tourism: lessons from evaluating REXplorer, a pervasive game for tourists. In: Indulska, J., Patterson, D.J., Rodden, T., Ott, M. (eds.) Pervasive 2008. LNCS, vol. 5013, pp. 244–261. Springer, Heidelberg (2008). https://doi.org/10.1007/978-3-540-79576-6_15
3. Benjamin, W.: Art in the age of mechanical reproduction. In: Illuminations: Essays and Reflections, pp. 217–252 (1968)
4. Bolter, J.D., MacIntyre, B., Gandy, M., Schweitzer, P.: Benjamin's crisis of aura and digital media. Cinéma & Cie. Film Media Stud. J. **6**(8) (2006)
5. Bolter, J.D., MacIntyre, B., Gandy, M., Schweitzer, P.: New media and the permanent crisis of aura. Convergence **12**(1), 21–39 (2006). https://doi.org/10.1177/1354856506061550
6. Buljat Raymond, B.: The potential of augmented reality for tackling environmental sustainability challenges: an approach combining design science and behavioral science. Dissertation, Université Côte d'Azur (2023). https://theses.hal.science/tel-04167165
7. Cheng, Y., Yan, Y., Yi, X., Shi, Y., Lindlbauer, D.: Semanticadapt: optimization-based adaptation of mixed reality layouts leveraging virtual-physical semantic connections. In: The 34th Annual ACM Symposium on User Interface Software and Technology, UIST '21, pp. 282–297. Association for Computing Machinery, New York (2021). https://doi.org/10.1145/3472749.3474750
8. De Vos, K.: Presence and learning in the context of household recycling. Master's thesis, Utrecht University (2024). https://studenttheses.uu.nl/handle/20.500.12932/46133
9. Ellenberg, M.O., Satkowski, M., Luo, W., Dachselt, R.: Spatiality and semantics - towards understanding content placement in mixed reality. In: Extended Abstracts of the 2023 CHI Conference on Human Factors in Computing Systems. CHI EA '23. Association for Computing Machinery, New York (2023). https://doi.org/10.1145/3544549.3585853
10. Ericsson, M.: Enchanting reality: a vision of big experiences on small platforms. In: DiGRA Conference (2003)
11. Gavish, N., Gutierrez, T., Webel, S., Rodriguez, J., Tecchia, F.: Design guidelines for the development of virtual reality and augmented reality training systems for maintenance and assembly tasks. In: BIO Web of Conferences, The International Conference SKILLS 2011, vol. 1, p. 00029. EDP Sciences, EDP Sciences, France (2011). https://doi.org/10.1051/bioconf/20110100029
12. Georgiou, Y., Kyza, E.A.: A design-based approach to augmented reality location-based activities: investigating immersion in relation to student learning. In: Proceedings of the 16th World Conference on Mobile and Contextual Learning. mLearn 2017. Association for Computing Machinery, New York (2017). https://doi.org/10.1145/3136907.3136926

13. Georgiou, Y., Kyza, E.A.: Bridging narrative and locality in mobile-based augmented reality educational activities: effects of semantic coupling on students' immersion and learning gains. Int. J. Hum Comput Stud. **145**, 102546 (2021). https://doi.org/10.1016/j.ijhcs.2020.102546
14. Glaser, M., Garsoffky, B., Schwan, S.: Narrative-based learning: possible benefits and problems. Communications **34**(4), 429–447 (2009). https://doi.org/10.1515/COMM.2009.026
15. Harrison, S., Dourish, P.: Re-place-ing space: the roles of place and space in collaborative systems. In: Proceedings of the 1996 ACM Conference on Computer Supported Cooperative Work, CSCW '96, pp. 67–76. Association for Computing Machinery, New York (1996). https://doi.org/10.1145/240080.240193
16. Karapanos, E., Barreto, M., Nisi, V., Niforatos, E.: Does locality make a difference? Assessing the effectiveness of location-aware narratives. Interact. Comput. **24**(4), 273–279 (2013). https://doi.org/10.1016/j.intcom.2012.03.005
17. Krüger, J.M.: Augmented reality for learning: the role of contextuality, interactivity, and spatiality for AR-based learning experiences. Ph.D. thesis, Duisberg Ession University (2023). https://doi.org/10.17185/duepublico/78994
18. Kyza, E.A., Georgiou, Y.: The impact of materiality on the design of mobile, augmented reality learning environments in non-formal, outdoors settings. In: Ceratto Pargman, T., Jahnke, I. (eds.) Emergent Practices and Material Conditions in Learning and Teaching with Technologies, pp. 183–197. Springer, Cham (2019). https://doi.org/10.1007/978-3-030-10764-2_11
19. Li, W., Li, C., Kim, M., Huang, H., Yu, L.F.: Location-aware adaptation of augmented reality narratives. In: Proceedings of the 2023 CHI Conference on Human Factors in Computing Systems. CHI '23. Association for Computing Machinery, New York (2023). https://doi.org/10.1145/3544548.3580978
20. MacIntyre, B., Bolter, J.D., Gandy, M.: Presence and the aura of meaningful places. Pres. Teleoper. Virtual Environ. **6**(2), 197–206 (2004)
21. McCall, R., Wetzel, R., Löschner, J., Braun, A.K.: Using presence to evaluate an augmented reality location aware game. Pers. Ubiq. Comput. **15**, 25–35 (2011). https://doi.org/10.1007/s00779-010-0306-8
22. McGookin, D.K., Brewster, S.A., Christov, G.: Studying digital graffiti as a location-based social network. In: Proceedings of the SIGCHI Conference on Human Factors in Computing Systems, CHI '14, pp. 3269–3278. Association for Computing Machinery, New York (2014). https://doi.org/10.1145/2556288.2557266
23. Nintendo: Mario Kart Live: Home Circuit (2020)
24. Paay, J., et al.: Location-based storytelling in the urban environment. In: Proceedings of the 20th Australasian Conference on Computer-Human Interaction: Designing for Habitus and Habitat, OZCHI '08, p. 122–129. Association for Computing Machinery, New York (2008). https://doi.org/10.1145/1517744.1517786
25. Pitman, T.: 'Go Outside and Play It!': a scenographic approach to finding aura in sci-fi, cli-fi, augmented reality art game, Sin Sol/No Sun. Romance Stud. **41**(1), 65–85 (2023). https://doi.org/10.1080/02639904.2023.2180943
26. Raeburn, G., Tokarchuk, L., Welton, M.: Creating immersive play anywhere location-based storytelling using mobile AR. In: De Paolis, L.T., Arpaia, P., Bourdot, P. (eds.) AVR 2021. LNCS, vol. 12980, pp. 209–226. Springer, Cham (2021). https://doi.org/10.1007/978-3-030-87595-4_16

27. Reid, J.: Design for coincidence: incorporating real world artifacts in location based games. In: Proceedings of the 3rd International Conference on Digital Interactive Media in Entertainment and Arts, DIMEA '08, pp. 18–25. Association for Computing Machinery, New York (2008). https://doi.org/10.1145/1413634.1413643
28. Reid, J., Cater, K., Fleuriot, C., Hull, R.: Experience design guidelines for creating situated mediascapes. Mobile and Media Systems Laboratory, HP Laboratories Bristol (2005)D
29. Reid, J., Clayton, B., Melamed, T., Hull, R.: Scape the hood: a design case study of a location-based digital story mediascape. In: Proceedings of the First International Conference on Digital Interactive Media Entertainment and Arts (2006)
30. Reid, J., Geelhoed, E., Hull, R., Cater, K., Clayton, B.: Parallel worlds: immersion in location-based experiences. In: CHI '05 Extended Abstracts on Human Factors in Computing Systems, CHI EA '05, pp. 1733–1736. Association for Computing Machinery, New York (2005). https://doi.org/10.1145/1056808.1057009
31. Reid, J., Hull, R., Cater, K., Fleuriot, C.: Magic moments in situated mediascapes. In: Proceedings of the 2005 ACM SIGCHI International Conference on Advances in Computer Entertainment Technology, ACE '05, pp. 290–293. Association for Computing Machinery, New York (2005). https://doi.org/10.1145/1178477.1178529
32. Relph, E.: Place and placelessness. Pion London (1976)
33. Rosa, N., Werkhoven, P., Hürst, W.: (Re-)examination of multimodal augmented reality. In: Proceedings of the 2016 Workshop on Multimodal Virtual and Augmented Reality. MVAR '16. Association for Computing Machinery, New York (2016). https://doi.org/10.1145/3001959.3001961
34. Rossitto, C., Barkhuus, L., Engström, A.: Interweaving place and story in a location-based audio drama. Pers. Ubiq. Comput. **20**(2), 245–260 (2016). https://doi.org/10.1007/s00779-016-0908-x
35. Schraffenberger, H., Van der Heide, E.: Everything augmented: on the real in augmented reality. J. Sci. Technol. Arts **6**(1), 17–29 (2014). https://doi.org/10.7559/citarj.v6i1.125
36. Sharma, H.N., Alharthi, S.A., Dolgov, I., Toups Dugas, P.O.: A framework supporting selecting space to make place in spatial mixed reality play. In: Proceedings of the Annual Symposium on Computer-Human Interaction in Play, CHI PLAY '17, pp. 83–100. Association for Computing Machinery, New York (2017). https://doi.org/10.1145/3116595.3116612
37. Weerasinghe, M., et al.: Vocabulary: learning vocabulary in ar supported by keyword visualisations. IEEE Trans. Visualizat. Comput. Graph. **28**(11), 3748–3758 (2022). https://doi.org/10.1109/TVCG.2022.3203116
38. Wetzel, R., Blum, L., Broll, W., Oppermann, L.: Designing mobile augmented reality games, pp. 513–539. Springer, New York (2011). https://doi.org/10.1007/978-1-4614-0064-6_25
39. Wetzel, R., McCall, R., Braun, A.K., Broll, W.: Guidelines for designing augmented reality games. In: Proceedings of the 2008 Conference on Future Play: Research, Play, Share, Future Play '08, pp. 173–180. Association for Computing Machinery, New York (2008). https://doi.org/10.1145/1496984.1497013
40. Wu, Q., Li, Y., She, Y., Liu, F., Luo, Y., Yang, X.: Bridging virtual and reality in mobile augmented reality applications to promote immersive experience. In: Proceedings of the 2022 International Conference on Advanced Visual Interfaces. AVI 2022. Association for Computing Machinery, New York (2022). https://doi.org/10.1145/3531073.3531122

A Cross-Device Interaction with the Smartphone and HMD for Vocabulary Learning

Maheshya Weerasinghe[1(✉)], Matjaž Kljun[1,3], and Klen Čopič Pucihar[1,2,3]

[1] University of Primorska, 6000 Koper, Slovenia
{maheshya.weerasinghe,matjaz.kljun,klen.copic}@famnit.upr.si
[2] Faculty of Information Studies, Novo Mesto, Slovenia
[3] Stellenbosch University, Stellenbosch, South Africa

Abstract. Cross-reality (XR) systems facilitate interaction between devices with differing levels of virtual content. By engaging with a variety of such devices, XR systems offer the flexibility to choose the most suitable modality for specific task or context. This capability enables rich applications in training and education, including vocabulary learning. Vocabulary acquisition is a vital part of language learning, employing techniques such as words rehearsing, flashcards, labelling environments with post-it notes, and mnemonic strategies such as the keyword method. Traditional mnemonics typically rely on visual stimuli or mental visualisations. Recent research highlights that AR can enhance vocabulary learning by combining real objects with augmented stimuli such as in labelling environments. Additionally,advancements in generative AI now enable high-quality, synthetically generated images from text descriptions, facilitating externalisation of personalised visual stimuli of mental visualisations. However, creating interfaces for effective real-world augmentation remains challenging, particularly given the limited text input capabilities of Head-Mounted Displays (HMDs). This work presents an XR system that combines smartphones and HMDs by leveraging Augmented Reality (AR) for contextually relevant information and a smartphone for efficient text input. The system enables users to visually annotate objects with personalised images of keyword associations generated with DALL-E 2. To evaluate the system, we conducted a user study with 16 university graduate students, assessing both usability and overall user experience.

Keywords: Cross-reality interaction · Mixed reality · Smartphones · Head-mounted Displays · Keyword method · Text-to-image synthesis · Context-based vocabulary learning · Augmented reality

1 Introduction

While the distinction between Augmented Reality (AR) and Virtual Reality (VR) systems is expected to blur over time [44], it is still informative to place

L. Zaina et al. (Eds.): EICS 2024, LNCS 15518, pp. 269–282, 2025.
https://doi.org/10.1007/978-3-031-91760-8_18

them on the Paul Milgram's reality-virtuality continuum [23] based on the degree of virtual content used. This placement can facilitate the discussions on transitions between different environments on the continuum [4], interactions across the continuum [27], and mixed-reality collaboration [19]. This is called cross-reality (XR) interaction [43], which offers the flexibility of modality selection and transition between systems based on current needs. We are presenting such a system that supports vocabulary learning.

Learning vocabulary is an important part of learning a foreign language and several techniques to aid learning exist. These techniques include, among others, formal learning (reading and rehearsing the words), flashcards (cards with words in the foreign language on one side and their translation/image on the other), physically labelling objects with foreign words in the environment (placing post-it notes on objects), and use of different mnemonics such as the keyword method. Each technique employs distinctive strategies for easing memorisation. For instance, formal learning relies on repetition, while flashcards rely on creating a mental link between what is on the front and back side of the card through card flipping. In the case of physically labelling words in the environment, learners rely on the environmental context to provide experiences that will help in memorising new words [29]. Most of these techniques rely on either using images/objects as the visual stimulus (e.g. flash cards or physically labelled objects), or mentally creating visualisations inside one's head. The latter is used in the keyword method, which requires the learner to mentally visualise an association between the object for the foreign word being learnt and a phonetically similar sounding word(s) (called keyword) to the one being learnt [1,35]. When recalling a foreign word, one tries to remember this association, which in turn helps recalling the word. This method has been shown to be very effective for vocabulary learning [2].

Encountering foreign words in their natural context, such as physically labelling objects in our immediate surroundings, has also been shown to enhance vocabulary learning [29]. Newer systems have used AR to combine real world objects with augmented visual stimulus, which acted as an important catalyst for vocabulary learning [17,40]. Other systems combined AR capabilities to digitally label objects in physical surrounding and the keyword technique [47–49]. However, these systems incorporate pre-defined keyword/association visualisations in the physical environment. These pre-defined keywords/associations are limited to predetermined set of physical objects, restricting the expansion of the vocabulary learning as new objects are introduced. Addressing this limitation could involve incorporating the option for users to create their own visualisations of keywords/associations. However, generating such personalised visualisations was, until recently, very difficult or close to impossible.

This has changed with recent advances in synthetically generated images with text-to-image generators that merge together unrelated concepts with semantic coherence (such as "two plants wresting together"). These text-to-image generators take a natural language description as an input and produce an image that matches that description. Current state-of-the-art text-to-image generators such as OpenAI DALL-E 2[1] [33] or Stability-AI Stable Diffusion[2] [38] are capable of producing high-quality realistic images that can be used for generating personalised user-defined keyword and association visualisations.

Developing an interface that allows users to effectively appropriate real world environment with digital elements, such as personalised keywords and visualisations derived from text descriptions, remains a challenge. This involves identifying, tagging and augmenting physical objects, a process complicated by the limited text input capabilities of head-mounted displays (HMDs), which makes them less suitable for such tasks.

In this paper, we designed and developed an XR system that combines (i) the use of a smartphone to create personalised keyword/association pairs for vocabulary learning, leveraging smartphones' fast and efficient text input capabilities, and (ii) the use of HMD to present information in a coherent and meaningful way within the real-world context, which has proven effective in various learning scenarios [47,48]. Thus, our system allows users to visually annotate objects in AR with personalised keyword/association visualisations generated by DALL-E 2 text-to-image generator, using a smartphone.

2 Research Background

2.1 Mnemonics and the Keyword Method

Research on memory and learning has demonstrated that comprehension and recall can be influenced by instructional methods and techniques [9]. One such instructional technique are mnemonics [31]. Mnemonics connect what needs to be learnt to prior knowledge through the use of visual and/or acoustic cues, thus encoding new information with something more accessible or meaningful to the user. Various mnemonic techniques exist, including phonetic systems, keywords, rhyming words, and acronyms [31]. The "keyword method" for vocabulary learning requires learners to create a mental visualisation of a memorable link between the familiarly-sounding word to a phonetic pronunciation of a foreign word and the object it represents [2]. For instance, the Spanish word for a letter is "carta", which in English sounds like "cart", and the visual link between the two can be imagined as "a letter in a shopping cart".

The keyword method has proven effective in the memorisation of vocabulary [28] and provides a powerful tool for learning words that have a high degree of "imageability" (e.g. moon vs. truth) [37], or for word pairs (the object a foreign word represents and the familiarly-sounding word) between which the learner can form a mental visualisation of some kind of semantic link or association [11]. Forming a mental visualisation of the association with the keyword method, and then externalising it into a visual stimulus could provide additional cue that can be encoded during the memorisation process. In the past it was not easy to find pictures of mental visualisations such as "a letter in a shopping

[1] https://openai.com/dall-e-2/.
[2] https://stability.ai/.

cart". However, novel AI text-to-image generators can be used to externalise such visualisation by generating photo-realistic synthetic images [3].

2.2 Text-to-Image Synthesis

Automatically creating images that semantically match a user-provided text description is a challenging problem, which has proved elusive until the emergence of deep generative models. In the last five years, different deep generative models have been devised to synthesise images from text, including Generative Adversarial Networks (GANs) [36], Variational Auto-Encoders (VAEs) [15], flow-based models [50], autoregressive models [12], and more recently diffusion models [38]. Nowadays they are considered state-of-the-art approaches to text-to-image generation.

DALL-E [34] is a transformer architecture to autoregressively model the text and image tokens as a single stream of data. To reduce the context size of the transformer (up to a factor of 192) without a large degradation in visual quality, the researchers used a discrete VAE to compress 256×256 RGB images into a 32×32 grid of image tokens. DALL-E 2 [25] uses a diffusion decoder to invert a CLIP image encoder [32]. Since the inverter is non-deterministic, DALL-E 2 can produce multiple images corresponding to a given CLIP embedding. However, DALL-E is just one of the approaches that can produce photo-realistic images that could be good enough to be used to externalise mental visual links of the keyword method. Other solutions include Imagen [39], Midjourney[3], and Stable Difussion [38].

2.3 Context-Based Vocabulary Learning

Besides using a variety of techniques to ease vocabulary learning [22,31], encountering words in context can also enhance memory retention [28]. It has been shown that people are more motivated to learn, when they perceive the relevance of the content within a given situation or find the subject matter intriguing [26]. For example, being in a foreign country's café setting is likely to spark interest in acquiring the necessary vocabulary and phrases to describe the environment and order coffee. Additionally, contextual cues enable the formation of associations that aid in later recall in similar circumstances and settings [51]. In other words, new words relevant to the learning context are more likely to be recalled than unrelated words [10].

Augmented reality (AR) has the ability to provide context-specific information in an interactive manner and a considerable body of research showed that AR can be an ideal technology to support learning in real-world contexts, including learning vocabulary. For instance, some systems provided labels of new words corresponding to real-world objects [8,40], while others created imaginary settings to describe and enhance the physical properties of everyday objects [16,45]. Studies have also reported that AR improved learning achievements and boosted

[3] https://www.midjourney.com.

motivation, engagement and collaboration among learners [14]. While Fujimoto et al. [13] have shown that users can memorise AR information better if it is shown within the location of a target object compared to dislocated information.

Several studies presented applications for learning vocabulary using handheld AR devices. Hautasaari et al. [14] developed the VocaBura smartphone application for learning vocabulary during dead time. The application tracks users' GPS locations and presents vocabulary related to the current location via audio. A study comparing this approach to an audio-only method showed that 7 days after the study, participants in AR condition could recall significantly more words. Santos et al. [40] presented a handheld AR system that displays text, images, animation and sound next to corresponding real-world objects to learn Filipino or German. They compared this system to a non-AR tablet application using a flash card method. Their results indicate that in the immediate recall after the experiment non-AR users performed better, yet this difference was not detected for long-term retention. Contrary, a recent study has shown a better recall of words in AR context-based vocabulary learning in the real world compared to context-based vocabulary learning on the tablet [47].

Studies have also shown that AR technology for language learning can contribute to increased motivation and enjoyment [7,20]; however, these can dwindle over time. Other researchers caution about technical limitations of using AR for language learning such as educators' limited proficiency with the relatively new technology [18] or the trade-off between connecting the experience to the context of the current location and providing a flexible and portable experience [49].

Systems for learning vocabulary with AR HMDs initially used some sort of marker to align virtual content with physical objects. Vazquez et al. [46] presented a platform (WordSense) that detects objects in the physical environment and augments them with additional content for language learning including words, sentences, definitions, videos and audio. However, no formal user study was conducted to evaluate the system. Another AR HMD system for language learning is ARbis Pictus [17], which labels objects in the user environment with the corresponding vocabulary in the target language. The researchers compared this system to a conventional flashcard-based system and found that AR was more effective and enjoyable and participants could remember words better both shortly after the experiment and four days later. However, the significance of these findings is limited, because the flashcard and AR systems were inherently different. For example, with flashcards the word was shown on the opposite side to the image depicting word meaning thus the image and word were never shown together. This was not the case in the AR condition where word annotations were always visible for all objects in the scene. Therefore it is not clear if AR accounted for the improved performance or the different learning approach.

Recent studies have also shown that combining the keyword method with context-based learning in AR offers many advantages for language and vocabulary learning [47,48]. For instance, Weerasinghe et al. [47] reported that vocabulary learning in AR supported by pre-defined keyword visualisations improved learning performance (recall and efficiency), and boosted motivation, engagement and user experience compared to screen based (tablet) learning. However, the system used pre-defined keywords and associations with visualisations, rather than allowing users to come up with their own personalised keywords and associations (i.e., USER-DEFINED).

2.4 Smartphones as an Input Devices for HMD AR Displays

Many AR HMD systems rely on specialised controllers or hand-tracking with mid-air inputs, which can be combersome for textual inputs. Extended use of external controllers or reliance on hand-tracking can also lead to user fatigue, impacting the long-term use. Smartphones present a compelling alternative as text input devices for AR HMDs, addressing the aforementioned challenges with their built-in touchscreens and familiar interface. Typing with smartphones is cognitively less demanding and increases input accuracy compared to mid-air gestures. This is particularly beneficial for tasks that require frequent or prolonged text entry, such as typing descriptions, note-taking, messaging or entering text commands in AR environments [24]. The portability of smartphones makes them an ideal companion for AR HMD devices, particularly in mobile or on-the-go scenarios. Unlike bulkier controllers or keyboards, smartphones are lightweight, easily accessible, and often already owned by users. This reduces the hardware burden and allows for seamless transitions between different AR experiences without the need for carrying additional devices.

In collaborative AR environments, smartphones can facilitate shared interactions. For example, users can use their smartphones to control shared virtual objects, annotate AR scenes, or communicate via text with others in the same augmented space. This enhances the collaborative potential of AR HMD systems and contributes to a more immersive and engaging experience overall [6]. Thus, smartphones as input devices for AR HMDs offer a practical solution to the limitations of traditional controllers and hand-tracking methods. By providing a familiar, efficient, and portable interface, smartphones can enhance the usability and accessibility of AR HMD systems.

3 AR Vocabulary Learning System

The system was developed as an AR HMD application on the Microsoft HoloLens 2[4]. We used the Unity3D game development environment[5] and the MRTK Mixed Reality Toolkit[6] for user interface design and input integration. We selected DALL-E 2 as the text-to-image generator for its state-of-the-art capabilities at the time of the development.

The system allows users to observe their physical environment, where certain objects are labelled with a AR buttons indicating available translations. Upon clicking a button, the English and Slovenian words (target language in this example) appear, along with a button for audio pronunciation of the word in a target language (see Fig. 2: Left).

[4] https://www.microsoft.com/en-us/hololens.

[5] https://unity.com/.

[6] https://docs.microsoft.com/en-us/windows/mixed-reality/mrtk-unity.

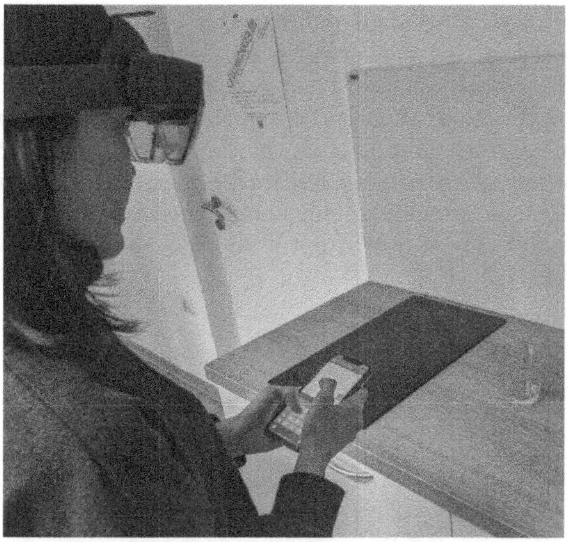

Fig. 1. Vocabulary learning user wearing the Hololense HMD and holding the input mobile device.

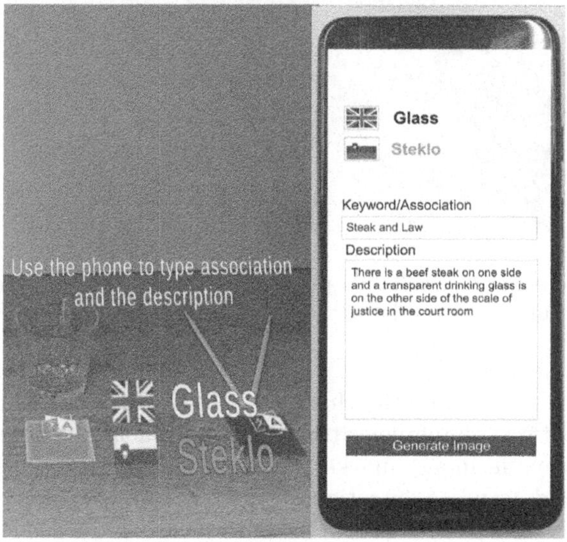

Fig. 2. Right: Initial AR annotations with the English word (Glass) and the Slovenian word (Steklo). Left: Smartphone application for users to enter the personalised keyword and description of the association for a given word.

Upon clicking the AR button again, a notification prompts users to enter a keyword (a familiar-sounding word to the pronunciation of a foreign word in a target language) and an association (a description of the visual link between the keyword and the object) on a smartphone (see Fig. 2: Right). The smartphone (we used Google Pixel 3) thus serves as the text input device. After entering the keyword and association, users generate images by clicking the "Generate Image" button on the smartphone. The association serves as a prompt for image generation. A menu with four images then appears on the HMD AR display (see Fig. 3), allowing users to select the image that best represents their mental visualisation of a memorable link. This image, the keyword, and the association, along with the previously shown English and Slovenian words, then appear by the object (see Fig. 4).

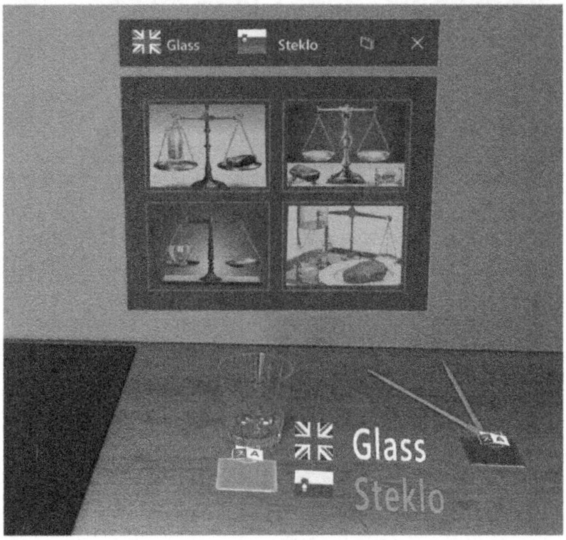

Fig. 3. AR view of the selection menu presenting four different images generated using DALL-E 2 text-to-image synthesis with the description of the association as a prompt.

For camera pose tracking, the HoloLens inbuilt tracking system was used. To initialise the positions of augmentations in our application, we used Vuforia [30] and our custom-made image markers. We opted for markers in order to support a reliable and accurate detection of physical objects that correspond to the set of vocabulary. These markers were removed from the scene after initialisation. While object recognition techniques could support arbitrary environments without prior preparation, our focus was on developing a robust system with predefined objects to explore the personalised keyword method vocabulary learning system using AR and text-to-image synthesis.

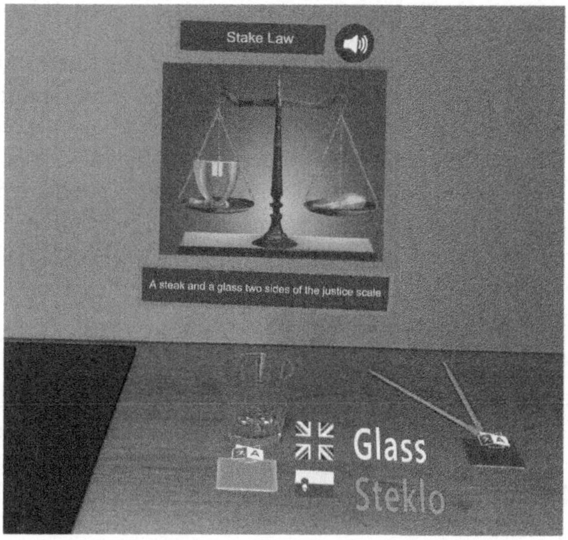

Fig. 4. AR view showing the selected image from the menu in Fig. 3, the keyword and the description of the association.

Also, a careful consideration was given to the selection of annotations and image size. Previous research showed the size of images affects our ability to remember image content during naturalistic exploration [21]. However, in such exploration individuals are first asked to freely explore an image without any instructions and are then asked about the details observed. As such there is no guarantee that the visual attention is equally distributed across the observed image, and as the image gets smaller so does the key information, which makes it easier to miss it.

To prevent participants from missing key information, we designed our application to effectively guide visual attention. The application shows visualisation of only one word at a time, which avoids cluttering the scene and overloading participants with too much information. Furthermore, we specifically chose to place AR buttons on the physical surface at close proximity to objects of which words were being learnt. This led users to the appropriate physical location from which AR visualisations are clearly visible as the corresponding annotation and image sizes were appropriated for such viewing.

4 User Study and Results

A user study was conducted to evaluate the usability and user experience of the developed prototype system. Participants were presented with ten physical objects related to a kitchen environment and asked to use the system to learn the corresponding Slovenian words for each object (see Fig. 1).

4.1 Participants

Participants were 16 university graduate students (Masters' and Doctoral) who volunteered and consented to the study. None of the participants had any prior knowledge of the Slovenian language (identified via a short competency test questionnaire). All participants had advanced proficiency in English (selected based on the TOEIC scores > 785, working proficiency plus able to communicate effectively in any situation[7], $\overline{x} = 889$ and $SD = 70.8$). The sample included two (2) female participants (12.5%). Participants were aged between 23 to 32 ($\overline{x} = 26.6$ and $SD = 2.9$).

4.2 Procedure

Participants first signed a consent form. After a brief explanation of the learning task, they were given the opportunity to ask any questions about the study and were informed they could withdraw at any time. Before the main task, participants completed a five-minute training session using a demo application to familiarise themselves with the system's interface and interaction. They were then instructed to complete the language learning task, which involved learning 10 words.

After completing the task, participants filled out two standard questionnaires: the System Usability Scale (SUS) [5] and the short version of the User Experience Questionnaire (UEQ) [41,42], both reliable and standardised tools. Additionally, they completed a mental effort assessment (NASA-TLX) and a recall questionnaire, which evaluated their immediate ability to remember the words they had just learned.

4.3 Results

Although data on mental effort and recall performance were collected, this paper focuses only on reporting the system's usability and user experience results.

In SUS questionnaire participants rated our AR vocabulary learning system with a strong score of, 75, which is close the high usability benchmark of 80 and above the good usability threshold of 68. This positive result suggests that usability issues are unlikely to negatively affect user learning performance, providing a solid foundation for future system enhancements.

The short version of the UEQ-S uses eight items/questions, reported on a 7-point Likert scale. The first four represent pragmatic qualities (perspicuity, efficiency and dependability) and the last four hedonic qualities (stimulation and novelty) [41]. The UEQ-S questionnaire provides a benchmark to compare user experience of different systems. The mean value for hedonic quality was rated as good ($\overline{x} = 1.36$), while overall user experience was rated above average ($\overline{x} = 1.19$), compared to benchmark scores ranging from 1.02 to 1.39. However, the pragmatic quality was perceived as below average ($\overline{x} = 1.02$), with benchmarks ranging from 0.73 to 1.14. This variation may be due to some participants experiencing difficulties in generating their own keywords and associations.

[7] https://toeic-testpro.com/blog/.

5 Conclusion

The integration of smartphones and head-mounted AR displays presents a promising cross-device interaction approach to vocabulary learning. By leveraging the "keyword method", which traditionally relies on mental visualisations to ease memorising new words in a foreign language, our system externalises these visualisations via generative AI and visualises them using augmented reality. Specifically, the system annotates real-world objects with translations, pronunciations and using the keyword method also personalised keywords, associations, and visualisations generated by the DALL-E 2 text-to-image generator. Our findings suggest that such cross-device approach does not pose issues for users since users in our study transitioned between the smartphone interface and AR interface with ease, even if users rated the system as novel to them. This cross-device interaction between smartphones and AR HMDs offers a novel and engaging method for language acquisition, showing great potential for further educational applications.

Acknowledgments. We would like to acknowledge support from Slovenian Research Agency, grant number P1-0383, P5-0433 and J5-1796 and support from research program CogniCom (0013103) at the University of Primorska.

References

1. Anonthanasap, O., He, C., Takashima, K., Leelanupab, T., Kitamura, Y.: Mnemonic-based interactive interface for second-language vocabulary learning. In: Proceedings of the Human Interface Society, HIS, vol. 14 (2014). https://api.semanticscholar.org/CorpusID:233489373
2. Atkinson, R.C.: Mnemotechnics in second-language learning. Am. Psychol. **30**(8), 821 (1975). https://doi.org/10.1037/h0077029
3. Attygalle, N.T., et al.: Text-to-image generation for vocabulary learning using the keyword method. In: To appear in the Proceedings of the 28th International Conference on Intelligent User Interfaces. IUI '25. Association for Computing Machinery, New York (2025)
4. Billinghurst, M., Kato, H., Poupyrev, I.: The magicbook - moving seamlessly between reality and virtuality. IEEE Comput. Graphics Appl. **21**(3), 6–8 (2001). https://doi.org/10.1109/38.920621
5. Brooke, J., et al.: Sus-a quick and dirty usability scale. Usabil. Eval. Ind. **189**(194), 4–7 (1996). https://api.semanticscholar.org/CorpusID:107686571
6. Chatzopoulos, D., Bermejo, C., Huang, Z., Hui, P.: Mobile augmented reality survey: from where we are to where we go. IEEE Access **5**, 6917–6950 (2017). https://doi.org/10.1109/ACCESS.2017.2698164
7. Dalim, C., Sunar, M.S., Dey, A., Billinghurst, M.: Using augmented reality with speech input for non-native children's language learning. Int. J. Hum. Comput. Stud. **134**, 44–64 (2020). https://doi.org/10.1016/j.ijhcs.2019.10.002
8. Draxler, F., Labrie, A., Schmidt, A., Chuang, L.L.: Augmented reality to enable users in learning case grammar from their real-world interactions. In: Proceedings of the 2020 CHI Conference on Human Factors in Computing Systems, pp. 1–12 (2020). https://doi.org/10.1145/3313831.3376537

9. Dunlosky, J., Rawson, K.A., Marsh, E.J., Nathan, M.J., Willingham, D.T.: Improving students' learning with effective learning techniques: promising directions from cognitive and educational psychology. Psychol. Sci. Public interest **14**(1), 4–58 (2013). https://doi.org/10.1177/1529100612453266
10. Edge, D., Searle, E., Chiu, K., Zhao, J., Landay, J.A.: Micromandarin: mobile language learning in context. In: Proceedings of the SIGCHI Conference on Human Factors in Computing Systems, pp. 3169–3178. Association for Computing Machinery (2011). https://doi.org/10.1145/1978942.1979413
11. Ellis, N.C.: The psychology of foreign language vocabulary acquisition: implications for call. Comput. Assist. Lang. Learn. **8**(2–3), 103–128 (1995). https://doi.org/10.1080/0958822940080202
12. Esser, P., Rombach, R., Blattmann, A., Ommer, B.: Imagebart: bidirectional context with multinomial diffusion for autoregressive image synthesis. Adv. Neural Inf. Process. Syst. **34**, 3518–3532 (2021). https://api.semanticscholar.org/CorpusID:237213665
13. Fujimoto, Y., Yamamoto, G., Kato, H., Miyazaki, J.: Relation between location of information displayed by augmented reality and user's memorization. In: Proceedings of the 3rd Augmented Human International Conference, pp. 1–8. Association for Computing Machinery (2012). https://doi.org/10.1145/2160125.2160132
14. Hautasaari, A., Hamada, T., Ishiyama, K., Fukushima, S.: Vocabura: a method for supporting second language vocabulary learning while walking. Proc. ACM Interact. Mob. Wearable Ubiquitous Technol. **3**(4) (2020). https://doi.org/10.1145/3369824
15. Huang, H., Li, Z., He, R., Sun, Z., Tan, T.: Introvae: introspective variational autoencoders for photographic image synthesis. In: Proceedings of the 32nd International Conference on Neural Information Processing Systems, pp. 52–63. Curran Associates Inc. (2018). https://doi.org/10.48550/arxiv.1807.06358
16. Ibáñez, M.B., Di Serio, Á., Villarán, D., Kloos, C.D.: Experimenting with electromagnetism using augmented reality: Impact on flow student experience and educational effectiveness. Comput. Educ. **71**, 1–13 (2014). https://doi.org/10.1016/j.compedu.2013.09.004
17. Ibrahim, A., Huynh, B., Downey, J., Höllerer, T., Chun, D., O'donovan, J.: Arbis pictus: a study of vocabulary learning with augmented reality. IEEE Trans. Visualizat. Comput. Graph. **24**(11), 2867–2874 (2018). https://doi.org/10.1109/TVCG.2018.2868568
18. Khoshnevisan, B., Park, S.: Affordances and pedagogical implications of augmented reality (ar)-integrated language learning. In: Designing, Deploying, and Evaluating Virtual and Augmented Reality in Education, pp. 242–261. IGI Global (2021). https://doi.org/10.4018/978-1-7998-5043-4.ch012
19. Kosmalla, F., Zenner, A., Speicher, M., Daiber, F., Herbig, N., Krüger, A.: Exploring rock climbing in mixed reality environments. In: Proceedings of the 2017 CHI Conference Extended Abstracts on Human Factors in Computing Systems, CHI EA '17, pp. 1787–1793. Association for Computing Machinery (2017). https://doi.org/10.1145/3027063.3053110
20. Li, S., Chen, Y., Whittinghill, D.M., Vorvoreanu, M.: A pilot study exploring augmented reality to increase motivation of Chinese college students learning English. In: 2014 ASEE Annual Conference & Exposition, pp. 24–85 (2014). https://doi.org/10.18260/1-2–19977
21. Masarwa, S., Kreichman, O., Gilaie-Dotan, S.: Larger images are better remembered during naturalistic encoding. Proc. Natl. Acad. Sci. **119**(4), e2119614119 (2022). https://doi.org/10.1073/pnas.2119614119

22. Mastropieri, M.A., Scruggs, T.E.: Enhancing school success with mnemonic strategies. Interv. Sch. Clin. **33**(4), 201–208 (1998). https://doi.org/10.1177/105345129803300402
23. Milgram, P., Kishino, F.: A taxonomy of mixed reality visual displays. IEICE Trans. Inf. Syst. **77**, 1321–1329 (1994). https://api.semanticscholar.org/CorpusID:17783728
24. Pan, Z., Pan, Z., Luo, T., Zhang, M.: Exploring the use of smartphones as input devices for the mixed reality environment. In: Proceedings of the 18th ACM SIGGRAPH International Conference on Virtual-Reality Continuum and its Applications in Industry, pp. 1–7 (2022). https://doi.org/10.1145/3574131.3574451
25. Pan, Z., Zhou, X., Tian, H.: Arbitrary style guidance for enhanced diffusion-based text-to-image generation. In: Proceedings of the IEEE/CVF Winter Conference on Applications of Computer Vision, pp. 4461–4471 (2023). https://doi.org/10.1109/WACV56688.2023.00444
26. Pintrich, P.R.: A motivational science perspective on the role of student motivation in learning and teaching contexts. J. Educ. Psychol. **95**(4), 667–686 (2003). https://doi.org/10.1037/0022-0663.95.4.667
27. Piumsomboon, T., Lee, Y., Lee, G., Billinghurst, M.: Covar: A collaborative virtual and augmented reality system for remote collaboration. In: SIGGRAPH Asia 2017 Emerging Technologies. SA '17. Association for Computing Machinery (2017). https://doi.org/10.1145/3132818.3132822
28. Pressley, M., Levin, J.R., Delaney, H.D.: The mnemonic keyword method. Rev. Educ. Res. **52**(1), 61–91 (1982). https://doi.org/10.3102/00346543052001061
29. Pressley, M., Levin, J.R., Kuiper, N.A., Bryant, S.L., Michener, S.: Mnemonic versus nonmnemonic vocabulary-learning strategies: additional comparisons. J. Educ. Psychol. **74**(5), 693–707 (1982). https://doi.org/10.1037/0022-0663.74.5.693
30. PTC: Vuforia developer portal. https://developer.vuforia.com/. Accessed 27 July 2022
31. Putnam, A.L.: Mnemonics in education: current research and applications. Transl. Issues Psychol. Sci. **1**(2), 130–139 (2015). https://doi.org/10.1037/tps0000023
32. Radford, A., et al.: Learning transferable visual models from natural language supervision. In: International Conference on Machine Learning, pp. 8748–8763. PMLR (2021). https://doi.org/10.48550/arXiv.2103.00020
33. Ramesh, A., Dhariwal, P., Nichol, A., Chu, C., Chen, M.: Hierarchical text-conditional image generation with clip latents, **1**(2), 3 (2022). arXiv preprint arXiv:2204.06125. https://doi.org/10.48550/arXiv.2204.06125
34. Ramesh, A., et al.: Zero-shot text-to-image generation. In: International Conference on Machine Learning, pp. 8821–8831 (2021). https://doi.org/10.48550/arXiv.2102.12092
35. Raugh, M.R., Atkinson, R.C.: A mnemonic method for learning a second-language vocabulary. J. Educ. Psychol. **67**(1), 1–16 (1975). https://doi.org/10.1037/h0078665
36. Reed, S., Akata, Z., Yan, X., Logeswaran, L., Schiele, B., Lee, H.: Generative adversarial text to image synthesis. In: Proceedings of The 33rd International Conference on Machine Learning. Proceedings of Machine Learning Research, vol. 48, pp. 1060–1069. PMLR (2016). https://api.semanticscholar.org/CorpusID:1563370
37. Richardson, J.T., Jones, A.: Mental imagery and human memory. Am. J. Psychol. **94**(3), 550–552 (1980). https://doi.org/10.2307/1422269

38. Rombach, R., Blattmann, A., Lorenz, D., Esser, P., Ommer, B.: High-resolution image synthesis with latent diffusion models. In: 2022 IEEE/CVF Conference on Computer Vision and Pattern Recognition (CVPR), pp. 10674–10685. IEEE Computer Society (2022). https://doi.org/10.1109/CVPR52688.2022.01042
39. Saharia, C., et al.: Photorealistic text-to-image diffusion models with deep language understanding. Adv. Neural Inf. Process. Syst. **35**, 36479–36494 (2022). https://doi.org/10.48550/arXiv.2205.11487
40. Santos, M.E.C., et al.: Augmented reality as multimedia: the case for situated vocabulary learning. Res. Pract. Technol. Enhan. Learn. **11**(1), 1–23 (2016). https://doi.org/10.1186/s41039-016-0028-2
41. Schrepp, M.: Ueq-user experience questionnaire (2019). https://www.ueq-online.org/
42. Schrepp, M., Hinderks, A., Thomaschewski, J.: Design and evaluation of a short version of the user experience questionnaire (ueq-s). Int. J. Interact. Multimedia Artif. Intell. **4**(6), 103–108 (2017). https://doi.org/10.9781/ijimai.2017.09.001
43. Simeone, A.L., et al.: International workshop on cross-reality (xr) interaction. In: Companion Proceedings of the 2020 Conference on Interactive Surfaces and Spaces, ISS '20, pp. 111–114. Association for Computing Machinery (2020). https://doi.org/10.1145/3380867.3424551
44. Speicher, M., Hall, B.D., Nebeling, M.: What is mixed reality? In: Proceedings of the 2019 CHI Conference on Human Factors in Computing Systems, CHI '19, pp. 1–15. Association for Computing Machinery (2019). https://doi.org/10.1145/3290605.3300767
45. Strzys, M.P., et al.: Physics holo.lab learning experience: using smartglasses for augmented reality labwork to foster the concepts of heat conduction. Eur. J. Phys. **39** (2017). https://doi.org/10.1088/1361-6404/aaa8fb
46. Vazquez, C.D., Nyati, A.A., Luh, A., Fu, M., Aikawa, T., Maes, P.: Serendipitous language learning in mixed reality. In: Proceedings of the 2017 CHI Conference Extended Abstracts on Human Factors in Computing Systems, pp. 2172-2179. Association for Computing Machinery (2017). https://doi.org/10.1145/3027063.3053098
47. Weerasinghe, M., et al.: Vocabulary: learning vocabulary in ar supported by keyword visualisations. IEEE Trans. Visual Comput. Graphics **28**(11), 3748–3758 (2022). https://doi.org/10.1109/TVCG.2022.3203116
48. Weerasinghe, M., Quigley, A., Čopič Pucihar, K., Toniolo, A., Miguel, A., Kljun, M.: Arigatō: effects of adaptive guidance on engagement and performance in augmented reality learning environments. IEEE Trans. Visual Comput. Graph. **28**(11), 3737–3747 (2022). https://doi.org/10.1109/TVCG.2022.3203088
49. Wu, H.K., Lee, S., Chang, H.Y., Liang, J.C.: Current status, opportunities and challenges of augmented reality in education. Comput. Educ. **62**, 41–49 (2013). https://doi.org/10.1016/j.compedu.2012.10.024
50. Yang, K., et al.: Mol2image: improved conditional flow models for molecule to image synthesis. In: 2021 IEEE/CVF Conference on Computer Vision and Pattern Recognition (CVPR), pp. 6684–6694 (2021). https://doi.org/10.1109/CVPR46437.2021.00662
51. Yang, S., Mei, B.: Understanding learners' use of augmented reality in language learning: insights from a case study. J. Educ. Teach. **44**(4), 511–513 (2018). https://doi.org/10.1080/02607476.2018.1450937

Author Index

L. Zaina et al. (Eds.): EICS 2024, LNCS 15518, pp. 283–284, 2025.
https://doi.org/10.1007/978-3-031-91760-8

The manufacturer's authorised representative in the EU is Springer Nature Customer Service Centre GmbH, Europaplatz 3, 69115 Heidelberg, Germany. If you have any concerns regarding our products, please contact ProductSafety@springernature.com

Printed and bound by CPI Group (UK) Ltd, Croydon, CR0 4YY
30/09/2026
02225566-0012